Christopher Sandford has reviewed and written about rock music for over twenty years. A regular contributor to titles on both sides of the Atlantic, he has written acclaimed biographies of Mick Jagger, Eric Clapton and Kurt Cobain. His last book, a well-received biography of David Bowie, was praised by the *Daily Telegraph* for being 'perceptively written [and] excellent . . . refreshingly short on fanzine eulogy and tabloid censure'.

Sting

demolition man

christopher sandford

WARNER BOOKS

A *Warner* Book

First published in Great Britain in 1998
by Little, Brown and Company
This edition published in 1999 by Warner Books

Copyright © 1998 by S. E. Sandford

The moral right of the author has been asserted.

A CIP catalogue record for this book
is available from the British Library.

ISBN: 0 7515 2654 1

Typeset by Solidus (Bristol) Ltd
Printed and bound in Great Britain
by Clays Ltd, St Ives plc

Warner Books
A Division of
Little, Brown and Company (UK)
Brettenham House
Lancaster Place
London WC2E 7EN

To Pete Barnes

Contents

Acknowledgements

First, Sting, who understands the importance of primary sourcing. He declined to give me a formal interview. But he was generous with his reasons why. He has never asked to read the manuscript. I hope he'll see this as a fair bid by an author to report on an artist and his starring role in the drama of his time.

For recollections, input and advice, I'm grateful to: Larry Adler, Ann Allsop, Richard Branson, Alan Brown, Jack Bruce, the late William Burroughs, Chris Charlesworth, Noel Chelberg, Elvis Costello, John Cottrell-Dormer, the late Miles Davis, Patrick Deuchar, Elliot Dixon, Suzanne Duvel, Hazel Dye, Alan English, Len Forin, Derek Green, David Greider, Chuck Grice, Jeff Griffin, John Guest, Helen Hall, Steve Harvey, John Hedley, Den Hegarty, Mick Jagger, Dick Jordan, Saskia Kitchen, Chuck Leavell, Cormac Loane, Edward Lovell, Rose Macnab, Branford Marsalis, George Martin, Sister Agnes Miller, Keith Moore, Daniel Morgan, Mike Noble, Robin Parish, Andy Partridge, Peter Perchard, Reg Presley, Neil Rand, Tim Rice, Keith Richards, the late Mick Ronson, Caroline Ryan, Cat Sinclair, Jane Spalding, John Spinks, Lynn Vaughn, Diana Villar, Rik Walton, Dave Wood, John Wynn, W. Wynn and, not least, David Yao.

On an institutional note, source material on Sting, his music and his money was provided by: A&M Records, *Billboard*, Bombay House, the Brazilian Embassy, Brazilian–American Cultural Institute, the British Library, British Newspaper Library,

Companies House, General Register Office, Helter Skelter, IRS, *Melody Maker, Newcastle Evening Chronicle, New Musical Express*, North Tyneside Council, Northumbria Police, Outlandos D'Amour, Performing Rights Society, *Q*, Rainforest Foundation, *Rolling Stone*, St Columba's Presbytery, St Cuthbert's High School, Seattle Public Library, *Seattle Times*, Surrey Sound, University of Washington, Virgin Management and Wallsend Library.

I also interviewed a number of people who prefer not be named. Where sources asked for anonymity – usually citing intense like or dislike of Sting – every effort was made to persuade them to go on the record. Where this was not possible, I've used the words 'a friend' or 'a musician', as usual. Again, I apologize for the frequency with which I've had to resort to this formula.

Finally, personally, my thanks to: American Speedy, A. J. Anderson, Sam Banner, Pete Barnes, the Camlin Hotel, Reverend John Engstrom, Kat and Morgan Evans, Hank Fields, Focus Fine Arts, Lisa Godsicle, Andrew Gordon, the late Myron Graesser, 'Dr' Colleen Graffey, Harborview Medical Center, Tim Holman, Kinetic Kollections, Kinko's, Joan Lambert, Barbara Levy, Emma Lynch, Ken Maples, Jim Meyersahm, The Music Exchange, Lucinda Parish, Chris Pickrell, John and Nancy Prins, Amanda Ripley, Cynthia 'Thrills' Rose, Alan Samson, my father Sefton Sandford, Pippa Sands, Peter Scaramanga, Sue Sims-Hilditch, Fred and Cindy Smith, Katie Spalding, Surrey Cameras, Jim and Jessica Thomas, Ti-fa, Tower 801, Victoria Willis Fleming, and the Zimmermans. A low bow to: Monty Dennison, Malcolm Galfe, Jo Jacobius, Bill Johnson, Terry Lambert, Belinda Lawson, Borghild Lee, Al Meyersahm, Sheila Mohn, David Morgan, Jonathan Morgan, John Prins, and all who were there while I chewed on the bitterest pill of all. Special thanks to Karen Dowdall.

C.S.
1999

List of Illustrations

'I live in the crowd of jollity, not so much to enjoy company as to shun myself'

Samuel Johnson

'. . . you could be my greatest fan,
But I'm nobody's friend, I'm a demolition man'

Sting

1

Outlando

BACK THEN ROCK WAS DEAD, the looks were old hat, and most of the bands were stale and unrewarded. The new decade seemed just like the old one. There was the same pose, the fantasies played out in lewd abandon and brief spasms of wild creativity, the songs, the drugs. On the surface, everything appeared to be normal. The old taboos still hung there, Cliff Richard was in the chart, and everyone over thirty breathed out again.

Then the music changed. The scene shifted. Up came a trio of rare talent and popularity. Originally led by the baroque, polo-playing drummer, the group was hijacked by a morose but famously alert afterthought, who fought with the others about credits and royalties, his own star rising as their self-confidence waned. At any given moment, a minimum of one band member was at war with the rest. Rock groups are notoriously hard things to be in. Not just for the sheer ennui of touring – the repetition, night after night, of identical sets, proving that even improvisation can be boring – the progression through the cold backstage rooms of football stadia, the drugs and other inducements, the marital hazards of random sex, but because of the leader's need to move on, always a nose ahead of his own obsolescence.

So, after a few years, it went. Amid the usual wrangling and the hysteria of the fans, the frontman dissolved the corporate entity (though keeping the Colonel Parker-like manager), disowning that previously held sacrosanct and recycling himself in

1

the guise of a family entertainer. While the back-line musicians drifted off into dubious solo work, TV, film scores and drum-heavy tribal jazz, the star moved one pound's width to the main-stream with every pound earned, taking up residency in the Albert Hall. For years mere mention of the ex-group was high on the list of all three's pet hates. No reunion ever took place, but the band's management were far from idle. A slew of box-sets, doodlings and studio out-takes, T-shirts, videos and nostalgic reissues of past glories all contributed to a royalty flow as healthy residually as in the group's pomp. Finally, not without protest, the three men climbed on to a makeshift stage at the singer's country-house wedding party. They played their most famous number – the old stresses returning again in that cosy vibe – the manager muttering that, even now, ten years on, it was 'too soon' for them to be friends.

The group was Cream, but it was an ominous sketch of The Police if ever there was one. There are strange and telling links between the two bands. Some, of course, are mere coincidence, like the polo; but in other ways – the ways they both became icons and nearly went mad in the process – there are real ties to be made. Above all, it seems that the pressure of life in a trio wove a personally similar spell. In Sting, an artist emerged who mirrored the habits, moods, vanity, drive, talent and endurance of Eric Clapton.

The story of his early life is stark: the Newcastle-born boy who grows up in deprivation. He shares a tiny brick home with a family of six, with whom he fights. Sting would later say of The Police, 'It was brutal, vicious . . . we were just like brothers.' There were those who fondly believed the band, flaunting their matching blond hairdos, to be related; first cousins, even. The acutely aggressive nature of their friendship, if it could be so called, certainly contained all the acid, bitter rivalry of kinship.

At twenty-seven, in pop terms nearly middle-aged, 'Roxanne' turned Sting from modestly successful singer into someone whose smirk loomed out from TV and cameos in films like *Quadrophenia*. He liked to say that he'd lived, and it showed in his face. The strong jaw and X-ray stare gave him a knocked-about look. He seemed much more grown-up than most of pop's new crop of pretty-boys. It helped that fame hadn't suddenly come calling after one demo tape; he had to ring the bell, pound on the door and finally smash on through. One result of Sting's long musical apprenticeship was an unusually wide repertoire and a willingness to experiment. Another was that seven or eight years' graft gave him extra reason to protect his gains.

In time, the tough-man image became proverbial, accepted. Sting's professional reputation was the stuff of myth: the loner from the provinces whose obscure, even shady, origins he's at pains not to clarify: equipped with intelligence, ambition, pride and poverty, he starts on a campaign to set the pop world alight. To reach these goals he takes real risks with his life. Eventually, his sudden success leaves him uncertain of his true identity, and to mask this insecurity he throws up a protective wall of reserve and mystery, topped off by a razor-wire strand of real malice. But behind his formidable cool, he could be a generous and loyal friend. For all his rock-star swagger, he was a man of genuine intellectual humility and thirst for new ideas. Aware that solutions to big problems involve personal commitment and constant adjustment and refinement, he was unafraid of radical views, and gave his time unstintingly to good causes. This proved a strength and a weakness. It enlarged his understanding of major issues – Sting 'grew but never swelled', as one admirer says – but it also opened him to the reproach that he was, as he quite accurately put it, 'a pretentious git'.

Professionally, too, he shunned the pigeonhole. Sting is responsible for some of the most dramatic sounds to emerge from rock's first forty years, and some of the most vivid lyrics. He's also written some of the worst rhymes ever to be etched on to vinyl:

> It's no use, he sees her,
> He starts to shake and cough,
> Just like the old man in
> That book by Nabokov.

> Hey mighty brontosaurus,
> Don't you have a lesson for us?

> Where is the fisherman, where is the goat
> Where is the keeper in his carrion coat?

> If you love somebody set them free.

Musically, too, Sting may have contributed nothing new, instead falling back on the old pop virtues of craftsmanship and an ear for a hook. His stocks-in-trade were well-worn rock-reggae idioms, with jazz undertones. But the familiar formulae were made fresh again by the heart-grabbing poignancy of his slow tunes, the joyful release of his belters, and the raw intensity of his vocals. In short, he enlivened a boring pop scene. Add his flinty good looks, burgeoning film career and flair for the epigram, and it's easy to see why Sting's group were the biggest draw since the Beatles.

What does this popularity say about ourselves? Obviously, that success in the lively arts is still apt to be a function of mystique; that a mix of talent and public relations will win through. The fans can tolerate anything except a failure of image.

There was, first and foremost, the man himself. Sting looked like a rock star. To the paparazzi, he was pure gold – a front-page shot of him, whether tight-lipped and scowling or smirking archly, was usually worth thousands of extra copies. His waspish, barbed interviews were famous, as was the nickname which seemed to fit so perfectly. His mannerisms complemented his good looks. Whether at stage doors or in hotel lobbies, Sting was endlessly accommodating. He signed as many autographs as time and energy allowed. He posed for amateur snaps, discussed his shows, his albums, his hopes and plans, his eyes riveted on his questioner. It was a perfect expression of a responsibility he felt deeply, and it won over scores of fans. So too did his habit of addressing the packed crowds at concerts, whether haranguing a rogue bouncer, or becoming a music teacher leading his huge class in a singalong. His bonhomie in public was matched by a personality that, in private, was more introspective and uncertain than intrinsically stable, and that struck even grizzled rock-business types as warped.

But there was more to his success than a fetching smile and his appeal to pop psychologists in the press. Sting's ambition extended far beyond himself. He used the media to sell The Police, and did all he could to make the group work, including writing a clutch of classic, if evanescent, three-minute hits. When the band self-destructed in 1985–86, Sting took the decision to de-emphasize rock-star values and develop his singing and song-writing, an intelligent, inevitable choice, whatever one thinks of the music that followed. He grew with his audience. His concerns mirrored, and to some extent helped set, the post-Live Aid social agenda: world hunger, the environment, amnesty, Aids, South Africa. Over the next ten years, he upstaged nearly every other musician in the relevance department. From raw misfit to world crusader and father of six, it's tempting to see his progress as that of a young turk into a pillar of the Establishment. Viewed in this light, Sting is one of the great dramatic figures of his age. He was born in the same year as the transistor radio; entered his teens the month the Conservatives were swept from power by Harold Wilson, who promptly awarded the Beatles MBEs; took to music just as faintly tedious models like Weather Report and the Mahavishnu Orchestra made a career in jazz-rock seem viable; moved to London at the height of the media obsession with punk and reggae, which, in his magpie fashion, he used for his own sound; became a visual image of the eighties: a fey power-exercise instructor, exhorting his crowds into fist-pumping frenzy; later, when introspection called, a torch singer and balladeer; a more sober, yet gregarious soul; a family man; a socialist. One reason so many people like Sting is that, by and large, the more they hear from and about him, the more they relate to him.

Demolition Man will give a review of every album Sting has made. It will even tell you the dates he was married, the ages and names of his children, the way he looks and where he lives. A chronology will be provided. If you're interested in how someone becomes a rock star, and what that says about all of us, you should read this book.

A character like Sting needs explanation. What he needs more is *illumination*, a glimpse of the man whose central characteristic is his elusiveness. To cynics, the views he held, the things he said (particularly about the rainforest) sounded like a put-on; surely, they felt, he must be joking. But Sting carried on much the same way at home, among friends. Elsewhere, of course, ironies can be made to surface, a disparity seen between his private life and his public utterances. He'd come to London an idealist, his politics a potpourri of Marxist–Utopian mumblings; within two years, his reputation for self-love had spread so deeply as to become lore. Jazz tradition, which Sting had worn as a kind of chastity belt, was abandoned for the less vagarious world of *Top of the Pops*, marked by his creeping transition from punk to rock. His home life carried on down the same wavy line.

Sting, therefore, wasn't always one to make a virtue of consistency. At least one critic has skewered him as no more than a blank slate, a blue screen on which was scrolled the latest look *du jour* before it, too, joined the long list of torn-up images. Others have praised him precisely for his versatility: ideologically, Sting travelled light. Running as a throughline has been one of the most arresting personalities in British art. Few others can hold a candle to Sting's striking affirmation of individuality. He conferred on rock its sharpest intellectual edge, raising its profile beyond the denim roar of the 1970s and the screwed-up nihilism of today's gods. In brief, Sting was far more than another pop star exciting the soggy hopes of his female fans and the envy of the males. He was, and is, a maturely dedicated artist with fixed views, a Renaissance Man and a virtual symbol of his times. In technical terms, Sting's life is a gloomy intro, an upward bridge, a quirky-but-danceable chorus and a therapeutic last verse, while other rockers are rarely more than a loud honk. He's dabbled passionately in politics, and just as warmly gives his time and money to human-rights groups, often anonymously. Throughout it all he's stuck to the job at hand, determined to write intelligent, semi-joyous songs.

The contradictions not only give Sting's life a certain personal poignancy; they've also combined to keep him in the glare of the public spotlight, first switched on with such voltage in 1979 when 'Roxanne' hit the chart. In a few short years, he became one of the most polarizing figures in pop: in one paper's view, 'St Francis of Wallsend'; in another's, 'a narcissist . . . full of bilious sincerity . . . fascist . . . a wanker'. Sting himself is well aware of his special niche in the rock firmament. He regularly includes coded barbs in his lyrics, like the one about music critics in 'Saint Augustine In Hell'. He's also been at pains to hide the real Gordon Sumner behind the fictive Sting. Play-acting, in the arts, is nothing new, but in his case it begins to look like reincarnation. For years he was a dogged censor of his past, his name, his family. Other yarns were distorted, so that Sting's education, though grim enough, was warped into *Tom Brown's Schooldays*. As recently as 1993, unauthorized biographers were warned: 'Search my house with a fine-tooth comb / Turn over everything 'cause I won't be home / Set up your microscope, and tell me what you see / But you'll still know nothin' 'bout me.'

Sure enough, the extraordinary saga has its blind spots. Sting's life has some of the makeshift quality and histrionics which in music he's so loath to adopt. All this has fed a critical slapstick which has been less than his genius deserves. Sting could have gone along with the myth-making and hagiographies. He might even have chuckled about them. He is, though, too shrewd to believe in his own press; 'Truth,' he famously sang, 'hits everybody.' Sting may not exactly relish the encroaching biographer. But, quite possibly, he can appreciate the irony.

2

The Jazz Singer

NEWCASTLE, THE MOST NORTHERLY ENGLISH CITY, is three hours by rail from London; the same time it takes Sting nowadays to cross the Atlantic.

Around the turn of the century, steam liners built on the river Tyne regularly ploughed the route to New York, and Newcastle-built French- and Italian-owned craft sailed from Mediterranean ports on African, Australian and South American runs. The city was famous, too, even proverbial, for its mining. The nation's engineering giants all had plants there. Coal and steel were exported from Newcastle to every part of the world. The mills blasted night and day; the clang of iron plates made a thought-annihilating thunder. All around lay miles of drab, quarried hills, slag-heaps and allotments. The Tyneside wharves sent up a smell of heaped coke, lumber and stacks of vegetables, hauled south to finance the town's growing commerce and construction. This was the place, full of noise, stench and the sulphurous glare of the shipyard, that fixed itself in the young boy's imagination.

From the far side of fame, Sting had mixed views about Newcastle. On one level, he clearly hated it, running down his family to *Rolling Stone* as 'losers . . . I lived in Newcastle, which would be like Pittsburgh, and the whole thing for me was escape'. On the other hand, it was precisely in his bleak upbringing that Sting felt himself to be remarkable, and in that light that he interpreted his early success. A decade on, he informed a journalist, 'I'm fiercely proud of coming from there. All the same, I still say it wasn't a great place to grow up. Basically it's a love–hate relationship I have.' In private, Sting allowed himself the quip, 'It's a good enough place to grow your food in.'

By mid-century, Newcastle had moved to a semi-rural economy, the suburbs squeezed by rising new construction and link roads just as people and resources fled south. The 1951 census put the population at 291,723, only Britain's eleventh largest city. The major liners were still plying the Atlantic, though not in their previous number; for Cunard, things were never quite the same once the Comet took off commercially from London to New York. The collieries had begun to fold. The dismantling of cooling-towers, the boarding-up of warehouses and shops, the NO WORK TODAY signs nailed on the shipyard gates: all these became depressingly visible symbols of nuclear power and the jet. Meanwhile, much of old Newcastle was bulldozed in a doomed bid to refurbish it as the 'Venice of the North'. What survived was that weird mix of ancient and modern. With its granite churches and dark, flinty offices, the town was solid, gothic, fussily Victorian. The later buildings were all concrete lozenges; acres of dead tramway lines and bridges marking the city centre, where the sole new projects were bewildering roundabouts, one-way systems and mortuaries. Everyone kept miners' hours, up at dawn, in bed by eight or nine. The streets were dead after dark.

Most easterly of the inner suburbs is Wallsend, a zone of light and heavy engineering works, co-ops, bookies, bingo halls and the uncompromising bulk of the Swan Hunter yard, home of the *Mauretania* and scores of other liners before shrinking to solely naval work. (Hadrian's Wall, stretching from the Solway to the Tyne, terminated within the borough, hence the name.) Wallsend, too, was much reduced from the days when a dozen pits, designated by the letters A to L, were excavated under the market square; a town where, in 1951, tradesmen still worked with horses and 'runners' took messages from door to door, before finally bowing to technology; where the great yard owned endless double rows of redbrick houses, leased for a few pounds a week, the terraces winding drunkenly up from the dry docks where hulls would soar over the street so that none of them could see the far bank. According to a shipwright, Len Forin, 'In the fifties, it was still virtually a company town. You either worked for

Hunter's, or someone in your family did ... Hundreds of men cycling downhill to the yard. And pushing their bikes uphill again at night. Up and down, up and down, like a tide. Somehow everything in Wallsend reminded you of the sea.'

Two pictures – one of the *Mauretania*, the other of the King in naval uniform – stared down from the dark-blue wall of the maternity ward where Gordon Matthew Sumner was born on 2 October 1951. His father Ernest and mother Audrey were local people. The family lived in Station Road, an extension of the A186, though then scarcely more than an access route to the docks. Number eighty was an undistinguished three-storey building, four tiny windows and a spyglass looking out into the cobbled street. Facing it, the parish church of St Luke and the Masonic Hall towered above the slate roofs of houses that hadn't changed in seventy years, giving Station Road a dark, claustrophobic feel. Behind lay a maze of dark alleys and backstreets, hardly better than furrows between the slums, with only graffiti or the occasional clothes-line as proof of life. Downhill lay the station itself, where the coke wagons shed their loads in grimy clumps, a post office, the Roman fort and Swan Hunter's gates. On summer nights the few windows were wide open, and the familiar Wallsend smell of oil, coal, gas, horse dung and the metallic reek of ships came up from the river. In winter, conditions in most homes were almost as cold and cheerless as they were outside.

In later years, the older tenants of Station Road and nearby Gerald Street recalled Audrey Sumner as 'a proper lady'. But that was after her son had made it, and in fact, two more ambiguous words could hardly be used to describe her. A physically striking woman, barely out of her teens, Audrey still turned heads when she pushed her baby in his silver pram up the high street. But she sharply rebuffed attempts to get to know her better, and the Marilyn Monroe looks offended as well as attracted. While other mothers passed the time of day in their aprons and curlers, Audrey won fame as the first woman in Wallsend to wear a black Chanel dress. As a result, a certain element of resentment built up against her, and this may well have been the source of the lurid invective periodically daubed on the Sumners' front door. In those archaic times, Audrey was considered something of a sexual pioneer: a glamorous, if cool career woman, vividly unconventional, and a constant enigma to her husband, whom she finally divorced.

Ernie Sumner was a milkman. It was, as his son said, a respectable occupation; but the boredom was total. All his life, Sting's father wanted to work in a wider setting than Wallsend, or even Newcastle. After several years, he did finally buy his own small dairy and move his family to a housing estate in Tynemouth. It was as close as he ever came to realizing his dream of running away to sea. Years later, both his sons emphasized his steadiness, his self-denial and his strong conviction of right and wrong. As adults, they even managed to remember with a certain fondness the beatings that had so terrorized them as children, and they insisted that the punishment was both deserved and beneficial. They respected Ernie as a hard worker, an unwavering Catholic and, within the vast province of the word, a 'good' husband and father. But they feared him as a disciplinarian, harsh and unresponsive – a frustrated man, an angry man. He fought frequently with his wife about money, somehow never quite reconciled with her pay as a hairdresser. Ernie went 'fucking nearly nuts', according to a friend, when Audrey ordered a new Ford Zephyr, with extras, then the last word in consumer luxury. The car attracted curious glances in Station Road for weeks afterwards.

On the morning Gordon Sumner was born the weather broke in a shawl of rain. It was a typical autumn day in Wallsend, foggy and dripping, the mist seeping down like fluid, the surface of the river acting as a filter. The news that Tuesday was of the Middle East, where in Egypt and Iran trade disputes with Britain threatened the peace of the whole region; of Korea, where, with the question of truce negotiations still unclear, five US Eighth Army divisions, including British units, opened a new front; of Vietnam, where the French announced on 2 October that their garrison had withdrawn from Binhlu, near the Chinese border, in the face of attacks by rebel troops; of London, where the King was ill and the Labour Chancellor, Hugh Gaitskell (during an election campaign his party would lose), revealed that Britain had incurred a gold and dollar deficit of $638 million; and of Wallsend itself, where the talk was of an Electrical Trades Union strike, pickets and power cuts.

This was a world still agonizing from the 1930s and '40s, where wounds hadn't yet healed from the war. On 19 October 1951 a treaty was signed formally ending hostilities between the Allies and Germany. The Japanese Diet ratified a similar peace a week later. The cumulative blows of the last twelve years had left Britain on the brink of bankruptcy. On 31 October President Truman signed a Foreign Aid Bill, guaranteeing the UK $7,329 million in loans and credit, though even then the new government would find it hard to hold their country together. Just as the meat ration crept from 1s. 10d.-worth weekly to two shillings, both the butter and cheese quotas were cut. The Fuel Order meant that shopkeepers and most private homes kept their lights doused even in the evening. Women still wore bargain Utility dresses – the rare exception, like Audrey Sumner, hinting of loose living rather than style, self-confidence or a subsequent fashion simply for better clothes. Socially, in the pub or the Companions' Club, sartorial tastes weren't elevated, and nobody bothered with a tie. Professionally, both sexes wore overalls or demob suits; as to baths, most people in Wallsend tended not to overdo them. At times fresh water was rationed to a pump in the town centre. The apparatus was ornate and the water itself a faded cherry colour. Queues were long.

It was a new world he grew up in in the 1950s, unique to the north, peculiar to the time: after the boom of the war economy, work had dwindled in the pits and the docks; the bill for the past was due, and an uncertain future loomed. On the very day Gordon was born, the Labour Party conference heard Nye Bevan speak of Russia's 'distortion' into a military tyranny – the second Soviet A-bomb test took place that night. The arms race began. This reality, closely followed by local rallies against the British nuclear deterrent, drew a sharp line across Gordon's childhood. While the protestor at the time of the Gulf could hardly have been foreseen in the five-year-old at the time of Suez, the threat of global war came to dominate his adolescence and, later, many of his songs. In the 1960s Vietnam suggested, by implication, that a policy of foreign intervention was wrong, and his parents' deep-held pacifism was right. Moreover, it sharpened and deepened Gordon's feelings about authority as a whole, so that from his teens he'd find it less easy to look on 'our so-called superiors' – governments, mainly – with anything but the wry wit of his best songs. A childhood friend speaks of Gordon 'mouthing off about the Pentagon when he was only eleven or twelve. Even then, he had a kind of addiction to causes.' It was doubtless this condition that led him to lend his name to nuclear disarmament groups in the 1980s.

It's easy, and tempting, to see misery in Gordon's family background. Ernie was a classic northern father, a stickler, tough, stern, and with a quick, brute temper. Audrey had a streak of true eccentricity. The times were hard, especially for a sensitive boy concerned about the future. If a child's greatest anxiety – the original fear – is that he'll be deserted by his parents, then he had good reason to be nervous. All the Sumners' neighbours recalled the rows between husband and wife, who, in Forin's words, 'were always on the point of splitting'. There were few luxuries in the house on Station Road. A shilling ticket to the cinema once a week was hard to come by, and the news, at home and abroad, bristled with conflicts. It was enough to make Gordon worried, and it did.

The 1950s were also, on another level, an era of slowly rising expectations. Under the first post-war government, social reform had changed the working man's status for ever. The radical legislation of 1945–51 helped fix the political agenda for the next fifty years, particularly in extending basic rights to the state's weakest citizens. Thus the workhouse and the Poor Law were replaced by a National Insurance scheme; pensions were doubled; education reformed; the NHS opened to every man, woman and child. Freshly nationalized industries like electricity and oil provided 500,000 new jobs. All this, without being seen as such at the time, was the dawn of a revolution in British life. In cold terms, the economic machinery of the nation started up again. By the early 1950s, it was possible to own foreign gadgets and goods, to enjoy art and books unthinkable a decade before. Within a generation, an era of individualism, growth and opportunity would lead to an election being fought (and won) on the slogan 'You've never had it so good'. A glimmer of American consumerism reached even the Newcastle *Journal*, where impressionistic sketches of Frigidaires, Hoovers and Ford Zephyrs jostled with ads for Beecham's Powder, Mendaco Asthma Syrup and other remedies for the northern winter. Immediately following the 1953 Coronation, national television ownership rose by 800,000. In London, the South Bank, home of the Festival of Britain, showed 3-D 'Telecinema' films: *The African Queen, An American in Paris, High Noon. The Archers* began. This combination, as motley as the various ructions after the Great War, never exactly constituted a mood of national optimism, but the world of 1939–45 had been remade. For the first twenty years of

Gordon's life, both the economy and popular culture took off in a way of which his parents could only have dreamt.

He shared a birthday with Mahatma Gandhi and Groucho Marx. A cross between *darshan* and drollery – Sting in a nutshell. As a Libra, he was reckoned to be co-operative; artistic; refined; romantic; strongly opinionated; and terrified of being alone: constantly seeking the perfect balance in life. He gave heavy weight to astrology, and to the etymology of his family name. (Sting's 1993 *Ten Summoner's Tales* was a deliberate pun.) The word refers to the old occupation of sumpter, a driver of pack animals, and to the sumn'r, a petty officer who warned parties to appear in court. Gordon, or 'spacious fort', was chosen by Audrey, who liked the implied Scottish roots. Matthew was Ernie Sumner's second name.

He was a bright, curious boy, spoilt within the limit of the family budget, whom some took to be Audrey's younger brother. Alan English knew the Sumners a few years later, when Ernie had bought out Close's Dairy. 'Everyone was envious of Gordon. Unlike us, he was quite a posh kid. His mum dolled him up, and he always seemed to have his nose in a book.' In a town where a fifth of the population were illiterate, most people travelled by bus and only the women loitering in tight skirts on Buddle Street bothered with their hair, it was inevitable that gossip would accumulate around the bouffant blonde with her fast car and precocious son.

It did accumulate. Even Gordon's pram, a Silver Cross model recalled by one woman as 'like a throne', raised eyebrows along Station Road. Exotic and unknowable to the neighbours, Audrey was, nonetheless, a loving mother to her eldest boy. 'She was by far the greatest personal influence,' a cousin remembers. She supervised Gordon's life, made his meals, bought and mended his clothes, read to him, praised his accomplishments, and lightened the mood in that Dickensian home. He was never in the tradition of temperamental, artistically bent sons, pampered by their mothers and instinctively feared by other children – most of history's mass killers fit the bill – but he undoubtedly drew a powerful charge from Audrey's love. Gordon's father was on one level a model parent, always or usually shrewd, disciplined, in control of himself, but if anyone relied on Ernie for emotional support, they made a mistake.

In later years, Sting would speak movingly about both sides of his family. He reconciled with his father before Ernie died in 1987. Distance, of course, helped to make the relationships better, as they couldn't meddle in Sting's life. But he was still rationalizing his feelings about his parents well into his own middle age. In 1991, he told *Woman's Own* about having helped his father on his 5 a.m. milk-round. 'Dad had a couple of other kids working with him, too, and I always felt they were his favourites. I was just the son, I had to fight for acceptance . . . I wasn't aware of what was going on at the time, of course, but I'm sure my ambition was to get noticed by my father. I remember going home with the county 100-yard trophy – you know, "Look what I've won!" – and he said, "Yeah?" and looked out the window.' Even in his forties, Sting continued to compensate aggressively for the anxieties seared into him as a boy. The rich, famous, fulfilled man the world saw still thought himself a suitable case for therapy. It's a plausible and adequate explanation of his psychiatric recycling that, as he said, 'I wanted to achieve something, to make Dad say, "I'm proud of you." And he never did.' On this reading, Ernie Sumner's treatment of his son resulted in his growing up emotionally stunted.

There were eventually four children: Gordon, Philip, Angela and Anita. By the late 1950s, the house on Station Road was a place of constant ferment. It was a cheerless spot. The front door, up three blood-red stone steps, led to a dark hallway and a parlour, warmed in winter by nothing more than a lacy Victorian fire that gave as much heat as a forty-watt bulb. Back to back were a boxy, bluish television and a pub piano, on which Audrey plunked show-tunes. From upstairs, meanwhile, came the noise of Gordon brawling with his younger brother. The two shared an attic room. Childhood proved a stormy period for both boys, though their defiance took quite different forms. Gordon was high-strung, bumptious, able, lied when it was as easy to tell the truth, frequently sought approval and affirmation, over-reacted to problems and had a temper. Phil kept his feelings to himself – until he too erupted, which was often. The Sumners always said that Gordon took after his mother and Phil after his father. In a large family and a tiny home, competition was the natural order of things. Daily, brother pitted himself against brother. Ernie and Audrey encouraged the rivalry, at least encouraged what they called a 'hands-on' approach to life. Most of all, the siblings wanted to get their hands on one another, and visitors to Station Road recall the hoarse cries from the loft, where, English says, 'the rows followed down one of two lines – violent or life-threatening'.

A man named John Wynn, later friendly with the Sumners, remembers the home as 'packed with junk' and Audrey's surreal touches, like stars hand-painted on the ceiling. A second friend calls it 'a house of horrors', dark, dingy and none too well kept. While the brothers' later accounts both tended to throw light among the shadows, the recollections of the family feuds are infinitely more dramatic than the nostalgic anecdotes meant to stress the Sumners' virtues. The children squabbled; the parents should probably never have married. The only guaranteed lull in the day was dinner time. Years later, all Sting's friends would learn to ignore him during meals, when he said nothing, merely hoovered up the fare at wild speed. Along with the fighting, this early appreciation of food-as-fuel was one of the legacies of Station Road.

Alan English believes the only deep boyhood feelings Gordon developed were with his mother and grandparents. His father was a 'hard man, who worked all hours' and reflected some of the stark views of his faith. As the years passed the children saw relatively little of their mother; the girls withdrew; the boys fought, though even that underestimates a bent that often crossed the line to bloodshed. A woman recalls once coming across the younger son lying semi-conscious in the street, his arms spread 'as if he were being crucified – as he really was'. The reference is to the Sumners' religion. Audrey herself was a member of the Catholic Women's League, and the church came to play a part in all four children's lives. The volatile atmosphere in the house never meant abandoning their beliefs. The family always paid at least lip-service to worship. Every day, morning and night, the Sumners took turns to read from the Bible. At age seven, Gordon sang and served at St Columba's Presbytery and could recite the Latin Mass. Nearly forty years later, he told an interviewer, 'I'm actually rather grateful for a Catholic upbringing – I think it's a great source of symbolism and imagery, of guilt, blood, death and eternal damnation.' He made no bones of his abhorrence of some of the ritual, but called the effect 'great for writing'. For a period in his early teens, he briefly considered the priesthood.

Gordon was skilled at softening hard memories with happy stories. His description of helping on Ernie's rounds, each plump finger snug in the neck of a bottle, follows the admission,

'My dad died angry. And I was angry with him.' Gordon's boyhood may not quite have been of the satiric-northern school,
where want has sometimes become lore. But it was bad enough.
In 1994 he told a TV interviewer, 'As a child I found everything
difficult.' Not all the early stories were spit-shone to a nostalgic
gleam. 'Most of my life has been spent in a state of anxiety,' he
said. 'I'd worry that the house would burn down ... that the
whole family would go out and never come back, or they'd move
and not tell me.' Luckily, his troubled character would also be
the primary source of his inspiration. Many of his best songs
dabble in the old-fashioned realms of bruised ego and failed,
dysfunctional relationships. In the 1970s, Sting's paranoia and
fear of rejection were vented in albums like *Outlandos d'Amour*.
Then materialism and all its problems, together with all Sting's
problems, were anatomized, summarized and brilliantly distorted in *Ghost in the Machine* and *Synchronicity*. As a rock god, he
channelled his demons into some of his best work, writing
endlessly varied lyrics on the central theme of isolation, of life
closing down. As a seven-year-old, his phobia had a more specific
root. 'Who the fuck would I go with if my mother ran off? Stay
with my dad? Nah. And who would take the television? I was very
concerned about that.'

All his life, he was in conflict about his roots. Unlike certain
peers, he never resorted to a raised-by-wolves legend of his youth,
and he publicly apologized the one time he slated his family in
print. Sting both confronted and romanticized his time in Wallsend. By the standards of most stars, he was unusually frank, except
when (as he briefly did) denying his past altogether. At their best,
his lyrics were proof of the continuity of a life he believed had
uniquely qualified him to tackle big themes. The long years in
Station Road dogged all the children long after they left home.
They seem to have affected Gordon more than the rest, and his
talent, he often said, flowed mainly from misery. Behind this boast
lay a broad streak of self-pity, but it directed his sympathy on to
those he saw as fellow martyrs. With suffering came a constituency.

In 1958 Gordon entered St Columba's Infants School, a short
walk across Station Road. Little more than a workman's hut with
rickety chairs and a play-yard, it seemed like a 'fresh hell' to the
new boy. The curriculum emphasized rote learning. 'The gloom

of the two rooms and the constant drone of Latin grammar' is one contemporary memory of the place. Gordon came to life in English classes. Spelling tests aroused both his competitive edge and his hatred of sloppy mistakes. He was an avid reader and wolfed down *Ivanhoe* and *Treasure Island* with the same zeal as his food. The adventures stuck with him and became both a fantasy and escape route from his family. In particular, when it came to a role model, nobody had Gordon's ear quite like Robert Louis Stevenson. Certainly not his parents.

A year later, at St Cuthbert's Junior School, he came under the benign eye of Miss Connell, who, along with his paternal grandmother, emerges as one of two bibliophiles to win his respect, and even a small measure of thanks. By local standards, he was considered freakish: brawny yet bookish, and the butt of more than one schoolyard jape. At St Cuthbert's he expanded his reading to include satirical titles like *Punch,* Orwell's novels, and eventually both social and political history. At home, when he wasn't throttling his brother or out pram-pushing with Audrey, he was usually in his room, reading or writing his diary. John Boyd, Gordon's occasional fellow smoker in the goods yard that lay between their homes, remembers 'he *loved* books. He related to them the way other kids did to football.' A second friend notes that 'literacy, in those days, wasn't necessarily an asset' – and tongues wagged about the milkman's son who preferred the library to the cinema. Both the jokes and Ernie's muttered asides had the exact opposite of the desired effect. The brightest and most focused boy in his class, qualities welded to dazzling vanity and put in the service of a manic ambition, Gordon relished his self-image as a loner. An eventual collision with Wallsend was all but ordained, and it finally came: after that, it took him ten years before he could talk about the place without losing his temper.

Twice a week, Gordon walked past the war memorial on Frank Street to the Catholic presbytery. Once a tin chapel, St Columba's had been furbished up into a redbrick tower with a green cupola, the school itself remodelled as a church hall. Between the two buildings was a courtyard and a curved stone bench where the children played tiddlywinks. Gordon was an altar boy. He's remembered as aloof, unresponsive, with an adequate though not startling voice, and vividly bright. By all accounts, he was one of the sharpest eight-year-olds in church – perhaps the sharpest –

and by most accounts, he knew it. It wasn't just that Gordon was quick and well-read; he was also unusually shrewd from an early age, inquisitive and unintimidated by his religion. There was nothing Gadarene about him. 'He questioned things more than we did,' says Boyd. 'Whatever else you say about him, he had guts.'

The other thing that Gordon had was ego. Bearing in mind that he was tense and frequently paranoid, he showed outstanding skill in converting his problems into a morale-boosting sense of self-value. At home, he'd learned how to set himself apart from everyone else. At school, he went a step further: he discovered how to turn the spotlight on him and him alone. He was, as a classmate puts it, 'a weird mix of ego and insecurity. He knew he was different, and he made sure we did, too.' A personality that 'could spit icicles in July' was matched by his striking looks. Gordon was tall, broad-beamed, with his father's fleshy hands; the tight, long-lipped mouth and permanently narrowed eyes gave him the air of being angry, even when he wasn't. His cropped sandy hair accentuated the hardness of his face. Although the beauty spot and the pointed, almost delicate, unmarked nose could have belonged to a girl, there was nothing effeminate about him. In the back streets of Wallsend, Boyd found out what scores of critics, drummers, publishers and accountants learnt later: 'You didn't fuck with Gordon.'

As well as tutoring with his grandmother, he learnt to write fluently at junior school. From age ten he began spinning stories, written in sloping and spidery gothic script, in which he embellished yarns from his favourite books; friends would help him act out the plots, which chronicled the exploits of Uncle Ebenezer, Riach and Captain Sang. His letters, sometimes stamped and posted to his own mother, laid out his life on paper in a way he'd never have done in person. Almost all were well written; many bore the imprint of a true author: they were rich, uninhibited and crisply phrased, with sudden and surprising jolts of insight. Passionate about English, Gordon could also speak snatches of French and Latin – the last thanks to the Catholic Mass and the preponderance of Roman names around Wallsend. When the family moved from Station Road first into Gerald Street and then a raw new home on a close, he felt, if possible, even more apart.

Like Ernie, his new neighbours lived unquestioning lives, and they taught their sons to do the same. They stressed accomplishment, rather than intellectual hand-wringing or contemplation. The counterpoint to their socialist politics was a closed mind to anything new. Similarly, the counterpoint to Gordon's curiosity was his quietness. The only time he raised his voice was to threaten his brother with a kicking.

As a child, Gordon had watched the skeletons of ships rising over the streets, gradually taking shape before falling into the river and sailing away. Now his bedroom view was of a miniature paved terrace and a garden gnome. The Sumners' new home was on such a drab, featureless estate as grew up close to any large town in the 1950s. It was a notable feat of upward assimilation, but it happened just as Britain came down to earth again with a bump. After Suez, the illusion of 'empire' was shattered for ever. At home, the wounds of national humiliation cut deep. The era of Macmillan, Douglas-Home and Wilson concentrated on prosperity and security. British patriotism was embodied less in military muscle than in sport, science or music. The iconoclastic culture of the 1960s was a direct reaction to the tragi-comic humbling of the Establishment by Nasser. Just as the old, triumphalist Britain wilted, the first stirrings of 'beat' music from America supplied a soundtrack for those, like Gordon, in conscious – sometimes self-conscious – mutiny against their parents' world.

What kind of world? Ernie, in particular, had no spark of novelty or genuine creativity, nor did he encourage them in his family. The dairy business was his life. Interior musing was submerged in a dogged, bloody-minded realism. According to Gordon, 'he hated what he did. His brain was underused.' In short, it was a fate of mute, suffocating despair, which Ernie took as he found it. In his mode of existence, initiative, self-reliance and fear of God were sovereign. Social mobility was limited to mortgaging a home with a small garden. Everyone knew their place. As Gordon later said, 'My parents were very smart. In another era they could have gone to university, done well. But when I'd see things on television as a kid – like people skiing, flying, the good life – I'd ask them about it and they'd say it was for posh people. We were the wrong class.' Even Audrey, who still drew wolf-whistles as she sashayed into her thirties, was a stickler for form. She was always either curtsying or being curtsied to by someone else. It's perhaps difficult today to recall how Britain was rent by the old taboos. Society wasn't just divided, it was vivisected. The codes, *mores* and diffident manners of 1960 seem like some extinct monster out of a Jurassic social order. It was no quirk that the Sumners tugged forelocks to their betters, because someone somewhere, in turn, bent knee to them. Deference was all. Living on Tyneside in the 1960s, whether in Station Road or the Marden Farm Estate, neither parent could have foreseen that their eldest son would one day enjoy a full set of pop-star accessories: a mansion in Wiltshire, a penthouse in Manhattan and a warm rapport with royalty.

If a key exists to Sting's success, it lies in post-war British conformity. Everything he did from 1976 onward was part of a near-religious crusade to slip the privations of his youth. No martyr to the Cross was ever surer in his vision. 'My drive . . . is an attempt to transcend my background,' he said. 'I've rejected it as something I don't want to be like. I grew up with a pretty piss-poor life . . . and the whole thing for me was escape.' Now, in the late 1950s, motive met with opportunity. Whether alone in his room with the radio or, later, chicken-strutting in the ballrooms and bars of Newcastle, Gordon responded to rock with the zeal of a convert. The means by which his own natural gift flowed was an uncle's discarded guitar. By his tenth birthday, Gordon could coax noises from the instrument, playing along to Motown hits and *Melody Maker*'s Top Ten, his eye already on the mainstream horizon. Ernie met his son's interest with indulgence. 'I sent him to a well-known music teacher called Mr Bianti. I think it cost ten bob an hour – a lot at the time.' The lessons ended abruptly in a clash of wills between Gordon and his tutor. But the guitar helped catapult the moody-yet-pliant choirboy into leering adolescence. In 1959 the instrument was still a hobby. Within three years, it was a virtual extension of his nervous system. From then on Gordon Sumner was busy either as a rebel or a pop-based pluralist.

As a rock star, Sting embodied 'the Hamlet complex – schizo-phrenia', as one friend puts it, and numerous people over the years felt he gave the impression of a man everybody and nobody knew, combining a fierce intellect with a solitary soul. He thought so himself. The character he played in the 1982 film *Brimstone & Treacle* intrigued him for just that reason. 'He's a kind of nice boy,'

Sting explained, 'well mannered, but also quite nasty. One minute you're laughing, the next you're squirming.' He was speaking of his alter ego, but it was a telling self-sketch. The complexities and contradictions were traceable both to his roots in the economically and socially stark north-east, and a caste system which ranged from the frighteningly duty-bound to the laughably snobbish. Down the years, he exhibited the classic rock-business traits of vanity and paranoia. Paradoxically, he was also shy and introspective. The combination of a stern father and a pliable, permissive mother produced in the son a character that was volatile, contradictory and wildly driven. It was certain that Gordon would quit his parents' world for a different, more complex one; he 'burnt for it', he once wrote. That left the question of timing. Here, as throughout his career, he enjoyed good luck. In 1959, the year he discovered the guitar, the seductive twelve-bar hits from Detroit and Memphis, if not ringing bells in the far universe, at least gave a sense of kinship to adolescents: as Keith Richards says, 'like finding Man Friday's footsteps'. By 1963, when Gordon entered grammar school, the Beatles had persuaded teenagers everywhere of the professional potential of rock. He seized the commercial prospects materializing on every side as his exit from Newcastle. In London, he succeeded in tying together left-of-the-dial fads – notably reggae and punk – at the exact moment Bob Marley and the Sex Pistols had pumped blood into their respective markets. In a very real sense, he was both the godfather and child of his times.

A month short of his twelfth birthday, he began life at St Cuthbert's Grammar School, riding the diesel train west, along the route of the Roman wall, past the General Hospital, into a belt of mock-Tudor villas and faded Edwardiana, where the immediate neighbours weren't navvies and thugs but a cricket ground and the teacher-training centre. The Sumners' relative poverty dramatized Gordon's achievement. It was another step up the ladder. He'd worked hard, devoting himself especially to English and maths; he had no particular gift for religious studies, though he did well enough to pass the exam into a Catholic direct-grant school. Gordon's precocious, intensely practical intelligence would serve him well at St Cuthbert's. But his personal Zeppelins of arrogance and bombast would still prove a tempting, if constantly moving target. Even passing the eleven-plus put clear water between him and his junior-school friends, most of whom were condemned to the local secondary modern. Gordon's reputation, says Alan English, was 'somewhat la-di-da' as a result. While other eleven-year-olds could look forward to a swift, unqualified graduation at fifteen, he now spoke chirpily of a career in 'the professions'. Audrey had every reason to be proud of her boy in the crested jacket, grey flannel trousers and tie.

In Wallsend, and later Tynemouth, he managed to compose a group of poems that spoke to his personal neuroses, especially those related to loneliness. He also wrote an unusual series of stories about running away to sea, bleak renderings that, a friend says, 'weren't the stuff of most kids'. At other times he turned to TV to make the household reality vanish. Some of the wilder stories of Gordon's youth are in the realm of myth, but the general Newcastle view is that he was both hair-triggered and oddly contained, someone even at the age of eleven whose type was cast.

At St Cuthbert's, an austere, all-male world of secular clergy in gowns, prefects and beatings, Gordon's mix of conceit and introversion placed him squarely in the problem-child tradition. Although the fiction claims he was rebellious from the off, promiscuously gambling and smoking the instant he slouched through the gates, he appears to have been a submissive and attentive pupil during his first year. His report card speaks of 'excellent' application in English and history, and a love of sport. John Wynn remembers Gordon as rapidly winning promotion to the 'fast stream', from where he took O Levels a year early. It was true he was caned a record number of times, and enjoyed something of the prestige of a hard nut. Thanks to his height and prematurely deep voice, he was the first in his class to explore the local pubs. He took liberties with the school uniform, once wedging himself into winklepickers instead of the regulation black lace-ups, provoking his mother, herself no alien to style, to write him a sharp note urging him to 'fit in more'. Whatever its already slim chance of acceptance, Audrey's advice was soon poisoned by the plague called rock and roll. In the meantime, Gordon hovered between the two worlds, famous for his biting sarcasm and invective – he had a Vesuvian temper – rather than for anything he did. (According to an old foe, his one physical show of rage was to 'throw a mug of tea at me. A Coronation mug.') Edward Lovell, the school's head, insists Gordon was never the rabble-rouser he was made out to be, or would later become. 'Our records and personal recollections show that he worked hard and, contrary to popular mythology, was well behaved.' John Wynn remembers his friend as 'not exactly a conformist, hard, brittle and often uptight'. Gordon cultivated the image. Another student recalls the strange progression of his nicknames – from Noddy to Lurch and, then, Killer – the last of which was used in a variety of forms, all threatening, until buried under the weight of the final pseudonym. It was another small bid for respect.

He endured St Cuthbert's for seven years. At the end of the fifth he passed O Levels in English language and literature, geography, maths and art, went on to the sixth form (where he was punished for an impressive array of offences, including failure to shave) and took three A Levels. By then he was spending his evenings in the pub or the Club À Go Go, where most of Newcastle's youth went to smoke, swallow pills and applaud the groups, as under-rehearsed as they were over-amplified, who sweated out a repertoire of Top Twenty covers and post-Hendrix pyrotechnics.

Part of his love of rock was a genuine ecstasy at the words and music. Part relied on a repression that, in a Catholic school, would naturally focus on sex. 'It was, quite literally, anathemic,' says John Wynn. Others learned quickly that Gordon, who often leered at *Playboy*, relished anything taboo. 'He used to drool over these models,' says one classmate. 'The first time I saw a full-frontal bird was on some smutty playing-cards he had. Believe me, that was a novelty for the time and place.' Founded in 1881, St Cuthbert's was as steeped in Victorian morals as any ancient public school. Apart from chapel and work, life existed only in violently competitive sport, cold showers and dire lectures, frequently embellished by slides, on personal hygiene. Sting's later career, and the subject matter of his best songs, could have come about only in response to a warped adolescence. It was, as he said, 'great for writing'.

Steve Harvey, uniquely qualified on discipline at St Cuthbert's, where he was head boy, remembers Gordon as a 'steady lad' with a reputation as a games-player and athlete, and a serial seducer of local girls. 'He was a better-than-average kid' in his first years, with a falling-off later. By his sixteenth birthday, Gordon was an enthusiastic smoker of pot and dabbler in soft drugs. A perfectly credible story is told of him scrambling up the

Outfall at Whitley Bay, leaping between the rocks with his long, runner's legs, a rugby ball in his hand and a reefer clamped in his mouth. It was an image that constitutes the basic theme of Gordon's youth. For every night spent at the Club À Go Go, there was an afternoon of pounding the school playing-fields. For every snide joke behind the clerics' backs there was a neat, well-honed essay. As a rock icon, Sting would speak of having 'hated' his time at St Cuthbert's. His agreeing to present the Duke of Edinburgh Awards to the sixth form there hardly supports this claim, though, as Gordon Sumner, he certainly found a way to rile most of his masters.

Conflict was always there for Gordon, living half in one world, half in the other, and trying to do justice to both. His inconsistency – charm one instant, spleen the next – kept even his family off-balance and strained relations with most of them. What struck him most was the self-supporting use that could be made of words. Day after day he kept up his steady flow of letters, screeds, poems and notes. He'd loved books as a child. As a teenager, he seems to have stumbled, in turn, on writing as a form of therapy. A schoolfriend remembers him saying, 'I keep a diary so I don't go nuts.' Many of his own stories were satires on St Cuthbert's, specifically his form master Father Walsh. The same friend saw some of the doodles, 'quite bizarre for a fifteen-year-old', he drew to decorate his work. There were sketches full of phallic and anal imagery, an arrow piercing a bull's-eye, a nun's habit hitched over her bottom. In one a sword was disembowelling Father Walsh. Such lurid symbols suggest anger, even fury, in Gordon's sex life. He was determinedly graphic in his stories: he'd induced a girlfriend's period, then drunk her blood; he'd 'caught a dose' after bedding another girl, if bedding could be used to describe a mutual ruckus against a brick wall. Anecdote was a place where Gordon felt very much at home. By his mid-teens he was more voluble than before – particularly on the 'guilt, blood, death and eternal damnation' he saw as the key text of his schooldays.

One tip-off to Gordon's anxieties was his deep-seated suspicion. 'He had a lot of cronies, but no mates,' says a St Cuthbert's graduate who would know. Those who met Gordon in the rock cellars of Newcastle or on the Marden estate came away with wildly mixed impressions. He showed his vulnerability through his evasiveness and talent for role-playing. Thus Steve Harvey recalls

Gordon 'always lugging his guitar around' and amusing the school by mugging through the Kinks' 'Sunny Afternoon'; John Wynn, his Wallsend friend who knew him for twelve years, 'never once heard him mention music'. A young relative of the Sumners blundered into the tripwires for Gordon's defences. 'One day at tea I asked him if he knew where I could get a certain LP. Gordon happened to be sitting there next to his dad, and he gave me that squinty, butch look of his, staring me down. "Ask my sisters," he said. Obviously he felt threatened because of Ernie.'

Gordon's need to meet his father's expectations was touching. 'I used to dream about being a milkman,' he once said, 'running around and making them buy *his* milk.' Ernie himself never encouraged the fantasy. He had other hopes for his eldest child, chiefly the nautical life he might have been born for. The two still showed the intuitive awkwardness of an artisan relating to his studiously arty son, but both Sumners found their home life one of growing warmth. By that critical token, Gordon's teenage relationship with his father fits poorly into the 1960s stereotype. Though neither doting nor loving, their rapport was close, if not exactly deep. By the time their relative saw them 'at the mutual starting-line', they were already exhausted from their long uphill trek to the off. With maturity, though, Gordon thought better of his family. In turn, Ernie's hostility to 'beat' music softened, and one or two of its exponents broke through his crust. He even muttered along while Gordon churned Kinks hits from the guitar – a marked reversal for one previously heard to rail at the 'jungle jive' rumbling from the back bedroom.

The ambition that boiled inside the sixteen-year-old, that had already made him a crux to the adult world – 'They all seemed to see something unusual in him,' says English – was creating its pressure to be fed. After mastering the acoustic guitar, Gordon progressed, via an electric bass sold by a schoolfriend, to crude songwriting of his own. By listening to the radio, he grasped what the phenomenon consisted of: he composed four bars at a time, sticking closely to the Motown playbook, reproduced with brilliant mimicry. By that method, he quickly learnt the raw facts of pop craftsmanship. From then on, experience was busy filling out his boyish exuberance as fast as he could get it.

The role models came to him, as they did to millions, under the covers, shivering and belted at the station, or hunched in a deserted classroom in morning break. Radio Luxembourg, above all, was the medium. The Stax/Volt records came through, static-ridden yet somehow intact in all their joyous derangement. As Sting put it, 'the soundscape of my adolescence . . . the music I lost my virginity to, drove my first car to, was soul music . . . Sam and Dave, Al Green, Percy Sledge, Stax, Atlantic. That was burnt into my brain at fifteen or sixteen, and it's always been there.' He paid court to Dylan and the Beatles, slavishly aped the Kinks and in Eric Burdon found a recognizable local hero. By 1966 the catholicism of his taste was already observable. As well as the pop licks echoing thinly from the radio, Gordon also began a self-improvement course in the bebop strains of Thelonious Monk and Charlie Mingus. The first band he saw live was the jazz-blues mongrel of Graham Bond, featuring his early bass idol Jack Bruce. After that Gordon watched every kind of gig, some good, some not so riveting. Rock bottom was touched by Zoot Money's Big Roll Band, where a guitarist then posing as Andy Somers added trippy wah-wah effects to the overweening bilge of the lyrics. The shining climax came on 10 March 1967, when Gordon saw Hendrix at the Club À Go Go. The guitarist's first words on stage were enigmatic. 'Anyone here play?' he asked. 'Get your chops down, and I'll stake my life you'll dig it.' It was a personal challenge, and the response was personal. 'Call me Jimi! Call me Jimi Hendrix!' Gordon told a startled fifth-former at St Cuthbert's.

Gordon's affair with music often included significant elements of disguise. For most of the 1960s he lurched from one fad to another, later dramatizing the process in interviews. 'I always hated rock in my teens. From about fifteen to twenty-five I stopped listening to it because of jazz.' Yet Steve Harvey and others remember a matching love of the soft-focus ballads of Carole King and James Taylor. Later in the decade Gordon talked up Simon and Garfunkel as an antidote to the bombast of Led Zeppelin and their heavy-metal clones: 'They all had long hair and flared trousers, looked horrible and sounded worse.' Perversely, he loved both Hendrix and Cream. Gordon's diary in the early 1970s excitedly charted the progress of acts as far-flung as Donovan and the New York Dolls.

The boyish fickleness became an effective means of hitting his mark and launching an adult career. In 1969 Gordon and a Newcastle friend named Elliot Dixon formed a short-lived acoustic group. The two existed on the loosest basis, playing at birthdays and the occasional dance, before meeting the universal fate of all jazz-inflected teen duos. 'He had these songs,' says Dixon, 'and the first thing that struck me was his imagination. Gordon wasn't happy just churning out Top Forty covers. He had a lot more breadth than me, and more drive. Even then he saw music as a real job.'

Gordon's single-minded pursuit of his goals was characteristic of the teenager already determined to find fame on a wider stage. When he did, both his parents were proud that 'our kid had made it' and 'gotten out of the *Brookside*' of Tynemouth. They never missed his press cuttings and appearances on TV. But they followed them as though Gordon had a permanent starring role in a school play. Even as he travelled around the world, having hit albums and generally being a global icon, they urged him to slow down and 'save something for a rainy day'. It was good advice, and it had the added advantage of being true. But their words, though fair enough, reflected in miniature the basic conflict of Gordon's youth. Even as a boy, he appeared, at best, only half in touch with reality, torn between warring parents, and a fugitive in his own fantasy world. His destiny to be the outsider was blazed early on. Stardom, at this stage, was still improbable; but escape, once Gordon got his hands on a guitar, was inevitable.

Apart from music, his only other long-term relationships were with sex and drugs. He lost his virginity at fifteen. There were the usual fumblings in the dark alleys behind the clubs or under the trees in Marden Park. If the season were summer, the situation might not exclude a night on the beach at Whitley Bay. By 1968 and '69, the world of bottle parties provided Gordon with a different sort of sophistication. During one he met a married woman, recalled only as Ann, who captured his upwardly mobile fancy. 'She was classy, blonde, dolled up like Audrey,' remembers a friend, 'and she was crazy about Gordon. But she wouldn't leave her husband.' The mutual attraction seems credible. Gordon certainly had the magnetism. But he was still only an ogling schoolboy.

Gordon continued his worldly education in the pubs along Newgate Street and Eldon Square in Newcastle, at the Club À Go Go, and in the mysterious new 'yank' and 'chinky' takeaways jostling the carved façades on the promenade. On Saturdays he varied his routine by trawling the town-centre salons and boutiques, as barbers and tailors had now become. Gordon responded to late adolescence with a spree of Mod-induced garb. Dressed in his impeccable uniform of tab collar, Levi's and a parka, he practised on his guitar and pounded the piano. He experimented by playing his cherished singles too fast, or backwards, to dissect the bass lines. He sang. Rather to his credit, he still found time to read. Gordon's floor-to-ceiling shelves held a collection more like a professor's than a student's. The books ran as a throughline in the continuing war with his brother. Philip's own half of the shared bedroom was crammed with football kit. Although Gordon himself could be seen careening wildly around the playing-field for his house XI, his main sports were solitary: climbing, riding, running. He briefly won fame as the Northern Counties 100-yards champion. At eighteen he had a reputation as 'a terrific talker, but a complete loner too; if you asked him a question he didn't like, he just looked through you and went on with what he was saying'. His friends thought of him as narrowly self-centred. He was, in fact, shy.

The oddity was that he had a fully adult susceptibility to loneliness and paranoia as a boy. As early as eleven, Gordon had made a vice of his virtue in passing the exam to St Cuthbert's. 'Immediately,' he said, 'all your friends and contemporaries were shoved away. Your friends considered you an outsider because you went into the town to a grammar school . . . They didn't want to know . . . I was totally bewildered, caught on this treadmill . . . I wished I was at a technical school – somewhere where they taught you something practical.' He revealed his vulnerability through play-acting and bluster. In 1993, he enlightened Q with the view that 'being on stage is a fucking war. That's not confidence you see, that's armour. It's not real.' Much the same protective aegis was in place quarter of a century earlier. Gordon ended one teenage affair by writing a letter to the girl in what she now calls 'sewer' tones. He ordered her not to contact him, never to discuss him with friends, and threatened to spread sexual gossip behind her back. The note was signed with the sobriquet 'Killer'.

The most charitable explanation of Gordon's outburst is that it was a shock tactic and actually concealed a deep fear of the jilt. (The woman claims that it was she, in fact, who broke up.) As a response to the jail he built for himself from his own insecurity, he had a chronic need to act out roles in every relationship. Seen in this morbid light, Gordon's taunts were his clutching at the very bars of his soul. As his ex says today: 'I always felt he was a

chameleon, taking his lead from whoever he was with ... It was
something Gordon always did, and he usually knew what he was
doing.' In particular, he knew the value of dramatic hammer
blows. He was theatrically determined to abuse the girl, and, if
possible, recoup his self-respect. He carped, chided and bullied.
The veiled threats were an unusually confrontational display for
someone noted for his sang-froid in sex. But both the fire and
the ice were equal parts of his burgeoning actor's make-up. The
chivalrous reputation of Gordon Sumner stood low.

For him, man's fate was to be born alone. Throughout his
childhood, Gordon struggled with a nagging sense of being lost,
of having important things to say and no stage from which to say
them. 'I have the kind of ego and the kind of imagination that
practised a lot,' he said. 'As a child, as a teenager, I almost
rehearsed for fame in a way ... I always felt I had to travel, that I
had places to go.' From his vantage as a rock star, he recalled the
giant keels hulking above Station Road before being launched
into the Tyne, never to return. (He was speaking symbolically,
though Ernie still lobbied for his son quite literally to push off to
sea.) Eventually, as a result of muscular pressure from his father,
Gordon obtained, though never used, a merchant seaman's card.

For all his other-worldliness, he still possessed what a relative
calls 'millions of volts of charm'. For some it obscured an
appreciation of his frequent kindness. 'He was an operator,' says
John Boyd. 'He could talk the birds out of the trees. I used to
think Gordon was all flash. But I found out he was actually a
good guy' – particularly to those he saw as fellow-travellers. He
went out of his way to encourage Elliot Dixon's stabs at songwriting. He showered other musicians with praise. He was
generous with his time and help on technical matters of recording. Dixon found him 'about ten years more mature than me',
but was flattered by the attention. 'As far as I'm concerned,' he
says, 'all the stories about Sting-the-shit are a joke. When we went
into the studio he was always punctual, disciplined and friendly.
If you were a musician, he was the nicest guy in the world.'

The final chapter of Gordon's formal education began in 1970
when he passed A Levels in English, geography and economics.
He spent the summer practising and listening to music, sweep-
ing floors and running errands in Ernie's dairy. When that brew

proved insufficiently potent, he found a job as a bus conductor. Every night for four months, he lumbered down suburban vist as, from North Shields to the Ridges estate, dressed in his blue corporation mac and peaked cap. Even in this funereal garb, he seemed to be in a race with life – virtually every trip was a chance to perform. 'You're standing up and they're sitting down,' he later said. 'It's a captive audience.'

After a brief, doomed foray to Warwick University (which he found to be 'school in a different uniform'), Gordon drifted between building work, the dole and jazz-rock for a year. The following spring he exchanged his jeans for a wide-lapelled brown suit and joined the Inland Revenue. 'None of the family could believe it,' says a cousin; nor could his friends. As predicted, Gordon lasted only a few weeks, failing to return one Monday because of 'exhaustion'. The job was too much. According to one of his fellow ciphers, Gordon was employed to do detailed research with a computer, a task demanding in-depth accountancy skill and patience, but this is to give him credit for more technical dash than he possessed. The official archives list him as a file clerk.

Suddenly, Ernie's seeming indifference ended. Though closer than before to his elder son, he was still continually carping at the 'fancy pants' who enjoyed a bedroom and unlimited access to the larder. Gordon, who strove for his father's approval, rebelled when he failed to get it, and grew increasingly tetchy at Ernie's values and ideas. All the guitar duets and mutual outbreaks of goodwill only intensified the violence of their rows. Ernie 'went ballistic', says one relative, when he heard that Gordon's resignation had, in fact, coincided with the Revenue's equally firm hint that his presence would be more sparingly required. The clash was one of many in the summer and autumn of 1971. After his Mod infatuation, Gordon had progressed to a wardrobe of suede jackets and two-tone shoes, his hair long, with a love for pills and a mumbled desire to 'see the world'. Not surprisingly, Ernie was awkward around this moody, younger version of himself. According to his cousin, 'He could barely put up with his kids, he was going through such shit.'* As a result of

*Chiefly, his alienation and eventual divorce from Audrey; and, less grim though no less galling to one of his sensitive nature, the taint-by-association of Benny Hill's 1971 novelty hit, 'Ernie, The Fastest Milkman In The West'.

the pressures steadily building on him from both parents, Gordon applied for a course at the Northern Counties Teacher Training College that September. True to taste, he took a certificate in English and music.

College was the signal for a more determined career policy. At Northern Counties Gordon fell in with an aspirant jazz pianist named Gerry Richardson; they evolved, via the approximate pop-guitar hooks of Elliot Dixon and rehearsals in the Wheatsheaf pub in Newcastle, into Earthrise. Of the group's quality it's perhaps kindest to be silent. Even compared to other pub bands, they were neither startling nor original. Gordon was, nonetheless, a working musician, eking out Top Forty hits and free-form jazz noodlings to a crowd sometimes as big as twenty. Within weeks, he was invited to guest in a local sextet, the Phoenix Jazzmen, boasting an eclectic diet of Chicago blues, Eubie Blake rags and Acker Bilk covers.

He did so looking every inch the part, stepping to and fro in his Jazzmen's black uniform and rendering his briskly melodramatic version of 'The Never-Ending Story Of Love' with nimble-fingered flair. John Hedley, the guitarist, remembers his bassist as the star of a band cruelly hamstrung by the realization that 'all trad jazz fits into one of six chord structures'. Gordon's life in the Jazzmen lasted, in turn, just six months. He achieved little – far less than he claimed to the girls he took on to the beach at Whitley Bay – but far more than his enemies were to claim for him. For the first time, his status-seeking had met an audience. He'd doubled his repertoire, won a nickname, and learned how to engage a single face in the crowd without excluding the rest: no small feat. He wasn't classically handsome, never had been, but teenage girls, in Angela Sumner's words, 'began to drool' over him. Gordon arrived.

In the incestuous way of pub groups, his next move was to join a Phoenix offshoot, the twenty-piece Newcastle Big Band, a sprawling hybrid which gleefully pillaged sounds and liberated them from their original context. Apart from their strange roll-call of jazz, funk and raunchy R&B roots, the Band were known for their Sunday residency in the foyer of the University Theatre (a date mentioned in *Melody Maker*); and their impromptu performance in the nearby car park, powered by the battery from Gordon's puny Citroën Dyane, before being unplugged by the police.

It truly was happening. What took the breath away wasn't so much the speed of Gordon's apprenticeship, but the breadth that constitutes the basic theme of his career. Thanks to Stax, Motown and the other American imports, he was already an aggressively exploratory fan of pop, blues, jazz and gospel-tinged soul. Like everyone, he never quite forgot the music he heard at college: whether the glam-rock ravings of T. Rex and David Bowie or the ambling balladry of the Carpenters. He said later he could remember 'every number-one hit from that era' – and sing a verse of it. As vocal role models he took divas like Cleo Laine and Flora Purim (though never quite scaling the technical ladder to their range). He adopted the bass largely because of his stubby fingers and his early love of Jack Bruce. As the Big Band's Andy Hudson said, 'Gordon's genius came from endless hours of thinking, listening and creating sounds'; and from learning to read music. Some of this alchemy was at work by 1972. Elliot Dixon remembers his friend's first, tentative reggae effusions that year. Gordon impressed a second colleague by playing a thumping disco line he claimed to have written spontaneously 'in five minutes'. Both in Earthrise and the Jazzmen he never played a song the same way twice, and moonlighted voraciously. By his twenty-third birthday, Gordon had dabbled in cabaret and semi-operatic excursions with Andy Hudson. He'd backed strippers in pubs and played in the pit of a local production of *Joseph and His Amazing Technicolor Dreamcoat,* an ordeal he recalled years later to the show's lyricist, Tim Rice. He was cultivating a niche on Newcastle's club and cinema circuit, and, in his rutting crotch-thrusts, bends and squats – somewhere between sex and a gym class – had the makings of a stage act.

What he lacked was a voice. Given the Dixieland traditions at the core of his early bands, Gordon showed rare skill in improvising a range of styles. He was less successful in imbuing his vocals with power, let alone personality. He later spoke of 'not [yet] having a full range'. But even that bleak assessment was charitable. Elliot Dixon says that 'people actually booed when Gordon sang'. A local friend and musician named Dave Wood confirms that 'he didn't have a great voice. But neither did the guy from Lindisfarne. Neither did Dylan. As Gordon got more confident, he caught on.' Whatever the later achievement, in 1973 his singing had a lazy, almost drunken quality, and even on the slower numbers he seemed to be a half-phrase behind the beat, while the delivery that would be simultaneously lacerating, lush, and shrill with reggae overtones was nowhere to be heard.

For most of his teens, Gordon had 'run around with melodies in my head'. He had little difficulty with writing basic tunes. His problem lay not in composing but in self-editing. Sonically, the music covered the gamut from Beatlesque ballads to extended funk-rock workouts. The self-centred lyrics wallowed in Gordon's own life. Even without the pop-melodic discipline that followed, and assuming the world would be as eager as he was to avenge itself on his ex-lovers, the songs were neat, fully fledged and already showed an all-round grasp of rock's roots. By 1976 he'd written 'So Lonely', 'O My God', 'I Burn For You', 'Bring On The Night', 'Don't Stand So Close To Me' and 'Every Little Thing She Does Is Magic': the polished edits sold millions.

From the Big Band Gordon and Gerry Richardson defected to Last Exit, yet another jazz-rock crossover, with tastes running to Chick Corea and Stanley Clarke. With a regular Wednesday set in the Gosforth Hotel and a growing name among a small but intense elite of fans (whose loyalty they repaid with a new song weekly), the band was neither a collection of soloists, nor a lab for Gordon's writings. It was a true unit. Its graduates remember it for its amicability. 'There were no ego trips,' says the sax player, Cormac Loane. 'Gordon was more focused than us. But you'd never have pegged him for a rock star. It was only after he made it he got dynamic.' Yet John Hedley saw that 'Gordon was the driven one . . . Years later I asked him, "What did *you* think of your voice?" "I thought it was fucking great," he said. He meant it.'

As Hedley says, Last Exit's few recordings were often buried in echo and other effects to prop the singer. A local entrepreneur, Alan Brown, strongly taken by the band, duly sent a tape of their set to London, where it eventually reached the BBC magnifico John Peel. Peel rejected it. Brown reluctantly joined the consensus about the shortcomings of Gordon's voice. 'I suggested, in so many words, we should do another demo as an instrumental. "Drop dead," he said. There was no telling him, but the sad truth is he was singing flat.' (Even Audrey Sumner, on first hearing her son with Last Exit, found him 'embarrassing . . . he sounded so gawky'.) When Dave Wood innocently tried to retrieve the tape years later, he came under a storm of threatened writs from Virgin Music. By then the seemingly hopeless case had become a rich, famous and revered rock star, and whole fortunes had been made on his voice.

In the working men's clubs, Last Exit were effective, particularly with their swinging, big-band knees-ups, and their brassy wallop and high hook quotient won local raves. But what worked in Newcastle sadly flopped on the road, especially freighted with Spinal Tap-like travel arrangements. In July 1975 Last Exit accepted an offer to play at the San Sebastian Jazz Festival. Right away, as the group set off by ferry and bus, there was evidence of tension: it centred on their bassist, already known, a colleague says, as 'something of a git' in terms of self-image, who made separate plans to fly to Bilbao. The next two weeks were a riot of drink and of rising enthusiasm, Last Exit for Spain, Spain for Last Exit. Even then, Gordon managed to strike a lone note. 'The rest of us were basically beer-swilling Geordies,' says Cormac Loane. 'He wasn't. Gordon seemed to take it more seriously than we did.' Further stress came just hours before the group's first bill-footing performance. 'Gordon sidled up to me and said he'd had a row with the two roadies,' says John Hedley. 'They'd fucked off home with the van. He wasn't exactly flavour of the month as a result.' It was a forgettable tour for Last Exit, but all of them recalled how it began: stranded, broke, in a foreign country, with 'about three tons of gear' strapped to the now sagging roof of a two-door rental car. After throwing themselves on the mercy of the tourist office, the group ended up playing a six-week series of dates up and down the Spanish coast. John Hedley remembers returning to Newcastle in early September clutching his net profit for the summer, £5.

Gordon, meanwhile, had graduated from Northern Counties with his diploma in English and music. From there he moved, via stints at ditch-digging and bottle-washing, to a job at St Paul's First School in Dudley Lane, Cramlington, six miles north of Newcastle. He always referred to the next year nostalgically. In a romantic sketch of his early career, *Melody Maker* insisted 'his boss encouraged him to take his guitar into school and fool around with that instead of boring them with dusty rhetoric. He got his young wards to tell him what they wanted to talk about, instead of vice-versa ... Many of the kids later came to his early gigs.' Sting himself would say, 'I never gave a fuck about them learning maths or logarithms. I just wanted them to enjoy themselves while they still had time.'

The notion of the hip Mr Chips-figure has proved attractive, and been seized on in Sting's press kits. It was true that his take on education was personal. He found most of the timetable, and all the elaborate school protocol, stale and routine. 'I never gave a fuck' may be dramatic hyperbole, but there was no denying his individuality as a teacher. Gordon loved the chance to entertain, and played several favourites among his eight-year-old pupils. Walking through the school corridors, he surprised many of them by using their nicknames and insisting that he, in turn, be called Sting. He was conscientious about reading to them and acting out well-known plays in class. He could, as he said, 'create a mood'. According to a St Paul's graduate, Gordon had at least one of the qualities of a good tutor. 'He might only give you five minutes of his time, but during those five minutes you thought that nothing else in the world mattered to him.' The head teacher, Sister Agnes Miller, thought he was 'very likeable, in a distant and hazy sort of way. Gordon was always the last to arrive in the morning and left the second the bell rang in the evening. On the other hand, he had terrific charm and a shyness the other staff – all female – found flattering. We probably spoilt him.'

When Gordon was with jazzers he was the epitome of jazz, just as when he was teaching English he was the picture of liberal education. He took his identity from the company he kept, many of whom saw only the image they projected on to him and he bounced back to them. The Sister's memory is striking because it shows a man of fluid, half-formed character. Too much in earnest to be an easy companion or colleague, Gordon nonetheless had a powerful need for affection. A deep sense of isolation and a cramped capacity for self-composure gave him an edge he never lost. The torn jeans and battered Citroën (often seen broken down on the road to Cramlington) both hinted at a man, whatever his merits as an educator, who found it hard to make ends meet. When Sister Agnes once enquired if he needed a loan, Gordon's reply was to snap: 'Thanks, I'm living in a luxury flat in Gosforth.' She never asked again.

As a Catholic school, St Paul's also brought to the surface all

Gordon's conflicts about religion. While he still attended Mass, he came to reject much of the dogma, not just on spiritual grounds but because it jarred with his own junior-school mumblings about Marx and 'the opiate of the masses'. In a twist on the classic phrase, Gordon would later call 'the only religious experience I ever had in my life' one he went through on drugs. Unsurprisingly, Agnes Miller recalls him as 'no great churchgoer'. He did, though, participate in the Christmas service of Reconciliation for the school and local parish, where he chose the story of 'The Woman Taken in Adultery' as his scriptural reading. Those sitting at the front of the church could detect a thin smile on his lips. 'It was just about the most controversial thing he could have done,' according to a parishioner. 'Several people left.'

In 1973, Gordon had moved out of the Sumners' home on the council estate into a shared, cold-water flat in east Newcastle. A year later, he took digs in Jesmond's Eskdale Mansions – the 'luxury' accommodation touted to Agnes Miller, though actually no more than a room in a house owned by the actor Newton Wills. That move was revolution superbly controlled. Where once there had been Ernie and the milk-run, now there was a stew of drugs and girls, and an intoxicating whiff of advance, if not yet, action. In a few short months in late 1974, Gordon had a new address, a new job and a new stage name; and he fell in love. Her name was Frances Tomelty, and when he met her she was playing the part of the Virgin Mary in a Christmas revue called *Rock Nativity*. Not only was she a working actress and thus a perfect target for his eagle eye, but her blunt views on Ulster (where she was born) chimed with his own overheated politics. Within days he was talking up Frances as 'bright, worldly, well heeled, witty, knew the ways of the world' – and yes, he said, 'a great lay'. Hazel Dye, who cleaned the flat at Eskdale Mansions, remembers Gordon's room as 'a war zone, guitars and clothes, mainly sweaters, thrown about, a Scalextric set on the floor and a crucifix on the wall'. Somehow, even in this chaos, few visitors ever forgot the bedside photo of the dark-haired woman, whose brown, intensely wide eyes gave off a hypnotic gaze. 'Frances was stunning,' says Dye. She was also shrewd, highly opinionated and deeply ambitious, for others as well as herself. When, in a bathetic moment, Gordon slated himself as 'a Geordie arsehole', her two-word reply was: 'Leave town.'

The Phoenix Jazzmen's trombonist–frontman Gordon Soloman, recalled by John Hedley as 'something of a lad', had
fancifully imagined the ragbag of journeymen, labourers and
Catholic schoolteachers who filled out his band to be, in reality,
a hard-eyed mob of gangsters and thugs, each with his own
Chicago-type persona. Thus an actuary from South Shields
became Bruiser, and the sax player, dressed in a pinstripe suit
and fedora, answered to Fang. Appraising his bassist's hawkish
nose and Queen Mary-basilisk stare, Soloman came up with the
diminutive Sting. According to Hedley, 'Whenever there was any
aggro from the crowd, Soloman would push him forward with
the words, "Kill, Sting." ' The sobriquet stuck. It combined
brevity with a threat and, as Hedley says, 'summed up exactly
how people thought of him'.

It was a heady moment. But Gordon Sumner only gradually
took on his new ego. Several weeks passed before, in a revolt
against the Jazzmen's dress code, he appeared in a gold and black
striped jersey. (Contrary to legend, the clothes illustrated the
name, not vice-versa.) From then on he dabbled in increasingly
lurid bouts of self-mythologizing. 'Call me Sting,' he kept repeating, in the manner of a schoolboy trying to popularize a self-
coined nickname. 'You must be Sting,' said one fan, supportively.
'Sting, right?' piped up someone else – before, emboldened by
the progress the jazz world seemed to be making, he tried an
unwise and premature stab at converting his family. It took some
time for the laughter to die down. Yet within five years both
Ernie and Audrey would loyally refer to their elder son as 'Sting',
in private as well as in public. Except in Companies House and
his forays to Coutts and Lloyds banks, Gordon Sumner ceased to
exist. Unlike other makeovers in pop folklore – Bowie's stint as
Ziggy Stardust, for instance – he never crossed the chasm into
clinical schizophrenia. He did, though, increasingly come to act
out a part suggested by his waspish epithet. Adopted almost
wholly for romantic reasons, the role would be subject to a downward spiral of unforeseen possession and distortions, so that by
the early 1980s the sharp but shy milkman's son had been twisted
into a monster of rock-star vanity; and, in a conscious scaling-
down of image, broke up his band and sought out people who
would relate to him as 'our Gordon'.

So capable of restraint and Spartan self-control later, Sting made clumsy boasts to his friends. 'I only want to be the best. I'm an egotist,' he said. 'I think it would be false for me to be modest. I know I'm a great singer and a great songwriter.' Even by 1975 his grave and threateningly muscular look seemed to draw attention. The small, pockmarked boy had bulked into a six-footer, unencumbered by even an inch of adult fat. He was especially popular with women, not least for his gravelly, quiet voice – what one lover remembers as his 'velvet fog', and another calls 'a perfect ten' in seduction power. Sting's face was a similar case of taking the rough with the smooth. He looked like a crude sketch for one of Rodin's mournful hulks – rough-hewn and finely chiselled in equal measure. At 150 pounds he was built like a welterweight boxer; his wasp-waist and legs bore the sinewy mark of his days as a runner. After his Mod and beatnik infatuations (more a performance than a case of real acting: he never once owned a Vespa), Sting favoured a wardrobe of T-shirts, vests and every conceivable kind of sweater. As well as the famous prototype, there were pullovers, jerseys, jumpers, cardigans and crew-necks, sweats and slips, and a particularly vivid item in blue check with red vertebral plates, triangular in shape, like a dinosaur's. Because of the clothes, it was still easy to sell him short. 'Sting was like a jazz-playing jerk,' says an ex-friend. 'Which, of course, he was. Guys tended to laugh a bit behind his back. Chicks loved him.'

Here he came: striding through the school hall at St Paul's, late, dressed in jeans and a garish tank-top, his eyes razor-slits and his tight lips set in an equivocal half-smile. His shaggy hair, cropped short at the crown, would wag at the back like a duck's tail; for a period in 1974, he toyed with a beard. Glib and quick-witted, he'd become hardened by his childhood beatings. Instead of hitting back, Sting helped himself to a brutal protective armour of indifference and scorn. A friendly 'hello' could be met with a dazzling show of synthetic charm, his eyes widening and his lower lip curling sideways to make way for some flip aside. Or equally it might be the signal for one of those sudden bursts of truculence that formed the basic pattern of his twenties. Friends would later say exactly what Agnes Miller says: that he was really two people, one convivial, the other cold and tensely vigilant against the world. Even his speaking voice had no fixed centre. By the early 1970s, Sting had realized that 'the bloke reading the news on telly wasn't a Geordie'. He began to sand down his own accent, masking his ambition – and underlying insecurities – by telling people he was tired of being stigmatized as a 'jazz-playing yobbo'.

One of Sting's fantasies in San Sebastian had been that General Franco would die and be replaced by a left-wing regime. He still held an innocent and unshakeable faith in Marxist bounty. He clung to his core beliefs, saw America's hand behind most international crises, voted Labour at every election and enjoyed the prestige of being pictured on the front page of *Red Weekly*.

Of all the myths which Sting swore by, none was dearer to him personally than the notion that Ulster was tyrannized by the British. Some in Newcastle attributed his fanaticism to a faulty reading of Irish history, or to the 'chip on the shoulder' widely diagnosed by Last Exit. Sting was so steeped in the villainous practices of fascism that he fancied governments themselves as mere sadists. Others considered him to be a tool of his Irish-born lover, who was blamed by drinking friends for his conversion to militant causes. Tomelty, already in her late twenties and with a long history of political activism, certainly helped transform the private conservative into a public radical. At least one musician believes that 'he picked up extremism for the same reason he took the nickname – a career move'. What all the theories share in common is a basic underestimation of Sting. His probing mind and shifting politics were the cause and effect of a hard, self-protective core that contained both a gyroscope for maintaining balance and a compass pointing steadily leftward.

Sting certainly became more arty in 1975 after he began seeing Tomelty, whom he married in 1976. She opened his eyes to a world of avant-garde theatre, film and punk 'happenings' on their weekend trawls of London. Both in sophistication and as a physical type, his fiancée inhabited a different world to the bouffant-haired girls who filled out his nights on Whitley Bay. As a rule, Sting's partners had tended to be blonde, amenable and chosen for their charm more than their brains. They were rambunctiously trivial, vacuous, histrionic nags pickled in cultural poverty. Until 1975, his ideal woman conformed firmly to Audrey's model. Even as an adult, Sting was unambiguous about his mother. He credited her for wisdom and courage and especially for imparting to her brood a will to live. Even when, after a violent household row, Audrey smashed her son's guitar against a wall, that shattering blow was no more than a milestone down the road to becoming a musician. Sting later rationalized that, in being balked by his friends, by every teacher and now by his mother, there was only one conclusion to be drawn: 'I *had* to make it.'

Audrey's outburst was exceptional. By and large, Sting's young life and adolescence were centred on her. He was his mother's pride, her clone in looks and character, both equally apt at self-transformation and at transforming their grim environment. Well into the mid-1970s, the two still walked arm-in-arm up the street (once leading Sting to punch a tactless heckler), he in his jazz regalia, she in a mini-skirt or French heels. If not, in the Freudian sense, 'his mother's undisputed darling', Sting was something very close: coddled, cossetted and spoilt, with a dominant female role model. Audrey's feminism seems to have impressed her son, who based his own egalitarian views on it. And her looks also left a mark: almost every lover before Tomelty took after the prototype.

Whether he was a shy, provincial schoolteacher or (as a member of Last Exit says) 'a wannabe thug who claimed he slept with a gun', Sting was well armed with imagination, charisma, and a cobra's tongue where his own turf was at risk. He wasn't passive in such moments. Nor, at this stage, was he fully warped by ego. For all the self-mythologizing, he was still recognizable as Gordon Sumner. Steve Harvey, the St Cuthbert's head boy, saw Sting in 1976 leaving the Playhouse with Last Exit. 'He stopped and chatted. I'll say this much – he had fantastic charm and a knack for seeing life in a funny, wry way.' Alan Brown, who last met him the same year, was also struck how 'he had faith in his own future and in the future of the band'. A fan called Neil Rand speaks of a spark in Last Exit which was absent whenever Sting was. Sometimes his truculence was jam for even his forgiving female colleagues at St Paul's. At other times he was self-effacing and affable, with few close friends but generally popular as a 'steady lad'.

Above all, Sting was the man of unflagging belief in his own destiny. His ambition was an engine that never idled. Sometimes he showed his pathological restlessness in full view, as when, keeping a promise to Tomelty, he moved from the room in Jesmond to a flat in Heaton Hall Road, between Newcastle and Wallsend. More often, his mind worked in response to the stirrings from London. It was the coup taking place in music in 1976, with a reaction to stadia rockers and the need for the middle-class young, anaesthetized by the likes of the Bay City Rollers and Abba, to bolt to the surrealist-anarchic rantings of Johnny Rotten that led Sting back to the world of foam-flecked rock and roll. As with his discovery of Stax and Motown, he responded to punk with missionary zeal. In mid-1976 he began a long and doomed effort to marry Last Exit's jazz-rock fusion with the breakneck sounds emanating from the Roxy in Covent Garden. By then he was a being apart from the other band members, semi-professional rather than semi-amateur, and at breaking point with St Paul's. Sting would later say of this era, 'I had a fantasy to make a living out of being a musician . . . I could see myself in twenty years, a little greyer, as the deputy head in the school . . . I wanted to take a risk with my life.' For years, Gordon Sumner had itched to leave Newcastle. His restiveness had only rarely found expression in more than a few faltering day-trips. Now, in Frances Tomelty, he had a flesh-and-blood escape route. He seized the day.

The wedding took place on 1 May 1976 in St Oswin's Chapel in Tynemouth. Sting agreed to a formal Catholic ceremony. The couple's son, Joe, was born that November.

When Last Exit made an unlikely summer cruise as shipboard entertainment on the SS *Orianna*, the other members saw how marriage had changed Sting. Several people remarked on his composure and spirits, and liked being around him. When a friend asked him for a drink, he was 'a mucker' who managed to be simultaneously autistic and one of the boys.* But people also saw that he kept his emotional distance, as always thinking primarily of his future; the band was secondary. Some of his escapist fantasies now became fact. Sting told one musician that Tomelty had driven to London that week to find the family

---

*'The ship's purser,' Sting said later, 'came up and told me that I wasn't to sing because I was upsetting the lady passengers . . . They were eyeing up the cute little bass player.'

'somewhere to crash'. He quit his day job. John Hedley believes 'Frances was a vital force in kicking Sting up the arse': with her acting contacts in the capital 'a whole oasis sprang up for him' that a year earlier had been a desert. 'He owed her everything.'

As a result of Sting's punk-based songs, full of frenzy and velveteen melody, and his wife's friendly press-agentry, the first talent scouts began to call at the Heaton flat. The BBC's Annie Nightingale was an early fan. A disc jockey from Germany's *Music für Junge Leute* expressed interest in flying Sting to Berlin. Finally, in October 1976, a woman named Carol Wilson signed him to a publishing contract with Virgin Music. The arrangement, quite separate from a recording deal, was for a 50–50 split, rising to 60–40 in Sting's favour after two years – generous terms for a writer whose current jewel was a ditty called '3 O'Clock Shot'. Virgin's chairman Richard Branson still recalls the impact of the crude demo tapes Wilson brought him in London. 'Buried under all the weird arrangements, and the lousy mix, great three-minute rock songs were waving wildly to be let out. I knew he had something, and so did Sting.' The two men's friendship flourished in response both to the material cut at Pathway Studios, and to robust give-and-take. When Sting ingratiated himself with people – talking up Branson as 'a saint' – he was far too shrewd to limit himself to mere flattery. A modicum of bullying was a pleasure both to himself and his patrons. He was thrilled when a small item mentioning Branson and him appeared in the Newcastle *Journal*. The couple's next joint press coverage, six years later, would all be headlines, dirt and mutual abuse.

Nineteen seventy-six, as he says, was 'the crucial year: I decided to have this kid, live with this girl, quit my job, move to London. It was all a big trauma. And then I saw the Sex Pistols, had my hair cut, dyed it; it was like an acid trip . . . It completely turned me around.' Such was Sting's lot as he started south in the Citroën with his wife, baby son, armchair and dog. Overnight, it seemed, the English teacher and part-time jazzer had been converted into a happy family man and a merry prankster. And yet the next two years were often not happy, and the atmosphere was rarely merry. It was an uncertain future Sting was heading to, as well as a sorry past he was fleeing that Christmas.

3

Vision of the Night

IN LATER YEARS OTHER MEMBERS of Last Exit would sometimes look back on that strange winter and wonder at Sting's ambition. The original plan had been for the group to mutually uproot to London. After a safari of record labels, in which they rehearsed and played under Virgin's baton but otherwise barely troubled the capital's A&R men, they skulked home, profoundly disillusioned. 'The whole thing was crazy,' says John Hedley. 'Punk was rampant by then, and no one gave a toss about a bunch of hairy Geordies doing Chick Corea covers. I remember we did one gig at Dingwalls where we actually had to pay to play. Around then it dawned on us we weren't going to move to London.'

And yet the professional man, with his wife and young son, did so. Whether Carol Wilson deserves credit for thinking of it, Sting seized the idea. Not only did he quit St Paul's and leave the flat in Heaton; he severed his moorings from his family, firing off an angry letter to Marden Farm promising to 'show them', to prove himself not just to the Sumners, but to 'everyone who doubted.' Sting's nerve was the greater in view of the fact that he had no real job and nowhere to live. For the first weeks of the new year, home was an actress friend's cold floor. In the classic image of small-town exiles with direction but no destination, Sting went on the dole and scoured the West End looking for work, scrounging a slim living as a model. Perhaps realizing the enormity of his ordeal he sent a second letter, this one to the defecting musicians. 'I'm totally committed to Last Exit, but I'm committed to the Last Exit who said they wanted to make it, who said they were coming to London. Come down or the group's finished.' A more direct note from Sting to an ex-lover read: 'God knows if I'll cop out – I may have to.' The words could have been written by thousands of provincial fugitives who eventually vanished into sales jobs or minor positions with the civil service. More than once that winter, it must have seemed he too would 'cop out' or beat an undignified retreat to Newcastle. That Sting persisted was due, in roughly equal parts, to Tomelty's connections and unshakeable faith in his prospects, and an underlying self-confidence in the fact that he wasn't only in the right place, but there at the right time.

By late 1976, first pub rock and then reggae and punk had become the most talked-about fads in town. The spate of new bands, fanzines, DIY labels and street activity all swung to a zenith in the two years after Sting headed south. It was, if not exactly a revolution, a cyclical shock to the way pop looked and sounded. New groups thrived in reaction against the 'old farts' epitomized by Pink Floyd, Yes and Genesis, while Rock Against Racism put new-wave and reggae on the same bill for the first time. Bob Marley's two riotous shows at the Lyceum, released as the best-selling *Live!*, led to an upsurge in Jamaican music and herbally scented speciality shops. Nothing better illustrated how the ancient rites of rock had dissolved under pressure both from without and within. Suddenly, in the space of a few months, there was a coming together of black and white sounds (the Specials and Madness were only the sunny dawn of punk-reggae fusion, later hammered into the chart by the likes of the Clash), a booming market for off-kilter tunes with minimalist lyrics and, crucially, a hurried modification of ballrooms, derelict cinemas and back rooms of pubs into the manger in which the craze was born.

Sting, whose rapid conversion into a darker, introspective soul found expression not only in his diary and letters, but in the first song he wrote after hitting London,* was among those in the long queues, frequently cleared by the police, forming outside clubs

*'Visions Of The Night'.

like the Roxy, the Nashville, the Hope & Anchor and the Kensington. He studied new wave like an anthropologist. Punk itself, in which musicality was reduced to an option, was never going to claim the Stax fan with a liking for Cleo Laine. For all the 'acid trip' wallop of the Sex Pistols, their impact was strictly a visual and romantic one; Sting approved of the group in principle, and in practice not at all. (In later years Johnny Rotten repaid the compliment by ranting at Sting as 'white trash'.) The quixotic but sensually deft melodies of a band like XTC were a better bet. Sting later told the group's leader Andy Partridge that 'he'd stood at the front of our early gigs with his mouth open'. He was particularly taken with XTC's improvisational dubs, all organ, bass and drums, in which mainstream rockers were saddled with a reggae beat. The same stylistic pile-up, couched in whiplash choruses and teen-angst vocals, became Sting's own sound.

In spring 1977, buoyed by his £16-a-week dole and random modelling fees, he moved his family to a tiny basement flat at 28A Leinster Square in Bayswater. It was an inspired choice. Since the war, the area's indigenous population, mop-wielding land-ladies, Irish lodgers and whores, had slowly given way to students and teenagers, and stucco blocks already shabby had been further degraded into squats and bedsits. The neighbourhood looked anything but flourishing. Leaving Queensway, the place became a zone of tall, crumbling mansions flanked by laund-rettes, pubs and the massive gloom of the Benefits Agency. Number 28 had no pretension to elegance. An iron gate gave on to twelve concrete steps, the stone worn to the thinness of paper, leading to the basement. The dead plant outside the peeling black door chimed with the grim décor of the flat. There were only a few sticks of furniture, a table, Tomelty's theatrical ward-robe, a crib. Light came from the very dim bulb overhead and two candles screwed into empty Portuguese wine bottles. It was damp and leaky and when it rained, which it did constantly that winter, water seeped through the brickwork. Sting wrote some of his best songs there.

In those days, Bayswater and its neighbour Notting Hill were edgy places, haunted by aristocrats and drug-dealers – never mutually bigoted against the thug life – and depressingly familiar with police vans, wailing sirens and riot squads. More pertinently, they were home to a large Caribbean community. By 1976 the local slums were squeezed by the Jamaican grocer and the Dar Al Dawa bookshop, and the drinking clubs around Westbourne Grove were among the first to house ska and reggae. West London generally was a hive of punk. Notting Hill swarmed with all-ages venues and new labels, like Stiff, catering to the whim for breakneck pop, spiky hairdos and bondage. Sting was already listening to the Sex Pistols, the Wailers and the rest every time he turned on *Today* or took the tube to the Roxy. Now he was hearing them blared from a dozen Leinster Square tenements. New wave was literally being taken to the streets. Johnny Rotten and Bob Marley emerged as global stars, providing cultural and musical ambience with an endless panoply of chirps and bleats.

Sting's energy and determination were astonishing enough, but he had an added gift for brilliant mimicry and improvisation. All this noise – from the melodic precision of Stax to the hysterical squall of Stiff – began to congeal in his mind, setting up what one colleague calls 'an encyclopaedic grasp of pop, from Ray Charles to the Clash'. According to John Hedley, he was 'always a canny lad' when it came to songwriting. To Malcolm McLaren, it was 'inconceivable Sting wouldn't have known' that a crossbreed of punk and reggae would appeal to a vast mainstream audience. He certainly knew. But he also knew when to stop, when to re-state first principles. All Sting's early songs in London managed the rare feat of combining melody and fury in equal parts. Lyrical, unfeasibly catchy and set to barnstorming guitars, 'Visions Of The Night' announced the arrival of a major talent.

Just as Last Exit went on hold that winter, a very different band also self-destructed. Three hit albums along with non-stop touring had brought the art-school group Curved Air a cult following but no real fiscal success. By Christmas 1976 they were reduced to wallpapering the Newcastle Polytechnic annual party. According to John Guest, one of 200 students sluggishly bobbing to Curved Air's dentist's-drill violin filigree, always played at ringing volume, the sole point of note was the drummer: an etiolated six-foot-two American whose heavy left hand kept a beat 'like a telegraph pole bashing a dustbin'. His name was Stewart Copeland.

He was then twenty-four, and had been playing drums for twelve years. Sting's own youthful rebellion had been in the head; Copeland's was acted out on the back streets of Cairo and war-torn Beirut. His family might have come from a Fellini script. They were wildly exotic. Copeland's mother was an archaeologist. His father wasn't only a jazz trumpeter but an army intelligence officer – in the first wave to liberate Paris in 1944 – a field agent of the CIA and, later, a freelance spy in the Middle East. After hurriedly leaving Lebanon, the family settled in England. Stewart attended Millfield, then famously billed as 'the most expensive school in Britain', before studying music, public policy and mass communications at the University of California. From there he fell in with his older brother's record label, road-managed Joan Armatrading across America and joined Curved Air when their previous drummer, the strikingly named Florian Pilkington-Miksa, quit. Much the same fate seemed to face Copeland that Christmas in Newcastle. After leaving the polytechnic, he, his girlfriend and a local journalist named Phil Sutcliffe walked down Newgate Street to another college, where Last Exit were playing their final show before straggling south. After two extended jazz workouts, the bass player stepped forward to sing his own 'Fool In Love'. It ended to polite applause.

Back at the bar the beer slopped from Copeland's mug. As he says, 'It was a terrible gig and the numbers were all seven minutes long and very intense. But they went down a storm just because of Sting . . . Because of his raps. Because of his singing. Because of his presence. Sting had then what he has now.' Sutcliffe's introduction led to an exchange of numbers, meetings in Leinster Square and Copeland's Mayfair squat, and, ultimately, rehearsals and recording. In later years, there were mutterings that some of this activity might ideally have involved Last Exit. At least one band member believes 'Sting basically took the Virgin deal and the songs and buggered off. We were in agonies about breaking up, whereas he could see . . . zoom, the bucks. It wasn't very edifying.' Nor was it Sting's problem, however. As he saw it, he'd soft-pedalled his swing away from the collective. 'I'd left my steady job and there they were – the professional musicians – scared to follow.' He was a free agent. Moving rapidly in his smoky glasses and sneakers, Copeland next recruited a guitarist, a Corsican called Henri Padovani, and lobbied his brother for a deal with his low-budget Faulty Records. He even had a name for the new group, a homage to the Copelands' father: The Police.

When, in future, Sting became an eco-logician, yoga-honed pin-up and demigod, certain critics got tetchy, making it a point of honour to show their independence by finding fault. Some had it that The Police's success was no more than a kind of listless fluke. Others (the drummer among them) swore the whole idea of the band was Copeland's, that without him Sting would have hoisted a white flag and slunk home to Newcastle. For the first six months of 1977 The Police existed on the most ad-lib basis. Copeland arranged rehearsals; threw a party at which the mewling, puking Sex Pistols convinced Sting the punk life was for him; paid to record their first single, a two-minute thrash called 'Fall Out'; and wangled a job backing Cherry Vanilla, a female, American version of Johnny Rotten, only more so. (LICK ME read the studs on Vanilla's T-shirt, a slogan she illustrated with her wet, labial leer.) Copeland would say that his chief difficulty with Sting was simply maintaining his morale. 'I had to get a fiver a night, just to keep him. He would have left . . . 'cos he's a real breadhead. And he goes for the money.' Sting's own verdict on the Cherry Vanilla tour cut to the bone: 'It was dire and I was appalled.'

A combination of Copeland, Tomelty and Carol Wilson made him a professional musician. In 1977 Sting paid his due to the union, and the next year joined the Performing Rights Society. But for months he dallied between worlds, toying with a return to Newcastle even while protesting his loyalty to London, considering a dubious job with the pop/R&B crooner Billy Ocean and an even unlikelier berth in the ad-hoc Strontium 90 (unconsciously echoing the nuclear theme of 'Fall Out'), latest in a series of quirky reunions of the rock, jazz and hippy-mythology cult, Gong. Sting played a single show with them on 28 May. The guitarist for the night was Andy Summers.

Somers – as he then was – had already grazed Gordon Sumner's life a decade earlier in the risible Big Roll Band. Years later, the word 'karma' would be used to describe the two men's meetings, even the assonance of their names. That was stretching it, but they certainly enjoyed a recurrent relationship, one that continued through Somers' stints in the New Animals and in a live performance of *Tubular Bells* at Newcastle City Hall – with Last Exit as warm-up. By July 1977, after ferocious suing of the Copelands, he became a semi-detached member of The Police.

They lasted two nights as a quartet. In early August Padovani quit, citing the usual 'musical differences' in public; sacrificed, it was murmured elsewhere, on the altar of his singer's ego. His in-house replacement was the journeyman, hybridized guitarist and affable soul who would never challenge Sting's self-image. Summers was then thirty-four.

The trio never suffered from that overwhelming faith in their 'own bag' that one encounters in art bands, style plates and tenants of the Distressed Musicians' Home. They lacked the maniacal unity of vision of the true pioneer. Yet they had a cold-eyed view of the market, a flexible strategy, and the technical flair to pull it off. Sting believed in punk's and reggae's subversive potential as a pragmatic opportunist, not a disciple. Jeff Griffin, a BBC producer who met him in 1977, believes 'he quite deliberately, and brilliantly, married short, sharp lyrics with a meaty Jamaican groove'. As with all genius moves, only in retrospect did Sting's alchemy seem inevitable, the missing link between mismatched but potent gurus, Rotten and Marley. Nor did the crossover come about in a vacuum. It closely followed 'Watching The Detectives' and narrowly preceded the Clash and Joe Jackson. But where Elvis Costello and a host of chancers moved on, Sting himself became obsessed with the style he satirized as 'reggatta de blanc'. He returned to it repeatedly in his first three albums and refined it later, notably in the adrenalin-packed stomps and funky languor of his solo work.

Sting knew everything it was possible to know about stardom without ever having been a star. To him, fame was an occupation, a *raison d'être*, a vocation, a job in itself, on the same level as music, and his entire life was to be torn between the two. As a result, idiomatically he packed light. Rarely in the long history of rock has expediency been raised to such an art. The Police's winning formula sounded much like Sting's monster in *The Bride* would look, all clanking parts, nuts and bolts, yet with a brute life of its own. Into the mix went a canny, forward-looking medley of pop hooks, exotic rhythms and blond ambition: as Nigel Gray, the group's first engineer and producer says, 'Even before the first chord of the first song, they *looked* like a band.' Speaking from the hindsight of 1987, Sting would admit: 'It was just a clever way of welding different things together.' For at least three years, he was neither mystic, prophet nor revolutionary, neither chaotic nor profound. His universe was rational, his lyrics human, his aspirations short. He was the authentic voice of his times.

The whole new-wave kaleidoscope – from fashion, through film, music and graphic design – was an attempt to make low art 'dangerous' again. At its punkish edges, revolution became less an event than a way of life. Sting, on the other hand, softened his crusade into a marketing opportunity. He was as precise as a slide-rule on the strategy of fame. Above all, he was shrewd enough to realize he could just as easily use punk's tactics as use punk.

He did use them. Even with their accent on songwriting and sleek, congenial appeal over pierced-navel-gazing, The Police would still doff hats to the Sex Pistols. The two had more than just the totemic gobbing and some fast-and-furious riffs in common. They were both nerved to action by the numbing tedium of arena rock and a mutual loathing of heavy metal. Sting later praised Johnny Rotten's evangelical work in tearing down the dinosaurs of pop and, above all, in keeping it simple. 'I personally owe a lot to him ... I don't suppose he gives a fuck whether I say that or not, but I do feel that without any of that initial push we'd still have Gary Glitter.' There were some specific reference points, Sting to punk, punk to Sting. The Jam's 'Eton Rifles' and 'Smithers-Jones' mined the same fiery bass riff and baroque strings as, respectively, The Police's 'Nothing Achieving' and 'Be My Girl – Sally'; Sting's 'It's Alright For You' lurched within a chord of 'Anarchy In The UK'; and so the influences kept coming, swarming and mingling into a throaty snarl over the fat clang of a rhythm guitar.

As a man with a doctrine, Sting took care to measure the distance between himself and the 'arseholes – total thugs', as he stigmatized most punks. The personal edge was real, and it was mutual. On tour with The Police, bands like Chelsea and Brian James & The Brains would rage at the 'little Hitler', whose personal fad for punctuality, professionalism and crowd-pleasing displays of bouncy energy would become the musical house-style of the 1980s. Elvis Costello exploded at Sting in the press. At various times, members of the Clash, the Stranglers and Subway Sect, elements of the Slits and the Buzzcocks and the drummer from the Damned all joined the consensus. Other fringe characters, critics and the like, moaned at his co-opting Mick

Jagger's tricks to moisturize his audience. 'I don't suppose he gives a fuck' was to woefully understate Johnny Rotten's reaction to Sting: he loathed him. They were always implausible punks, the ex-schoolmaster, the middle-aged guitarist and the American art-rocker. All three cordially returned the gall of the bands who mobbed the clubs and junior common rooms in 1977. The feelings were intense, but the intensity was all on one side. While Sting chafed against his detractors, he knew by their bile that he'd made it. As a close friend says, 'It dawned on him they hated his guts because he was together, hard-working, a shit, and, even worse, musical. And he loved it.' Sting's deadpan aside only hinted at how little peer-approval meant to him: 'I wasn't going to be crushed if Dave Vanian refused to speak to me one night at the Roxy.'

What did crush him was lost time. For at least his first year in London, Sting worked at wild pace, as if compensating for the 'interminable dump' of Newcastle. What struck Vanian and the rest wasn't so much the depth of his music as the abyss of his ambition. Sting would later recall 'pushing my four-month-old son across Battersea Bridge ... We walked along Chelsea Embankment and I looked up at all those luxury apartments and said, Joe, one day we'll own a big house like that.' He knew that personal aspirations weren't the only means by which his career flowed. For months, all the group slogged on the college and club circuit. Despite acute discomfort, the fate of playing second or third on the bill and several moments when the very survival of the band seemed in doubt, the trek through England and the continent brought out Sting's awkward genius. Every town and city and hamlet, every nook and cranny eventually became accessible to the pop trio with their faux-jazz singer, flying under the banner and appeal of punk rock. As Copeland's brother says, 'We were very ambitious. Ten per cent more rabid than the other bands ... We'd get these calls saying, "The Snivelling Bathrooms can't make it tonight, can you get up here by eight o'clock?" And we always did.' 'Work defines you,' says Sting. 'Work is your self-esteem. It's you. Find that work and you'll be happy.'

Paradoxically, for someone famously awake at the wheel, he was bored by details. Later in 1977 The Police met at Moore Sloane, a London accountancy firm frequently tapped for free advice by the Copelands. According to Keith Moore, 'I always judged clients, particularly those in the music business, on a "meeting tolerance" scale. My recollection of Sting is that his "meeting tolerance" level was near nil. He was easily bored and was quite content to leave the business side of things to Stewart and Andy. He was quiet and reserved but recognized by all, even at this early stage, as the latent talent.' Some of this apparent lassitude would taint Sting's later dealings with Moore, who in 1995 was jailed for fraud in a dispute over the 'general principles' of an investment strategy.

On 18 August 1977 the trio made their début together at Rebecca's, Birmingham. It happened to be the day news of Elvis Presley's death broke in Britain. Buttonholed by a local reporter at the stage door, Sting was far from sombre. He was, as the man gaseously said, 'a new pretender to the rock throne', and now the king was dead. Onstage that night Sting was that regal mix of high spirits and hauteur by which his claim progressed. He stood with his foot on the monitor, his crotch pumping, bawling the lowbrow lyrics over the pneumatic beat and school-disco PA required to convey the true spirit of punk. The sweet-and-sour song cycle managed to be both abrasive and seductive at once. Even at this early phase, The Police had it all. Their sound was unmistakable from the show's first barn-burning riff. The liberties they took with rhythms were more like sly rearrangements than the lewd blurtings of so many reggae-struck bands, and always in the service of the tune.

A month later they hired a manager. Lawrence Impey, a schoolfriend of Copeland's, whose promises to 'get it together' somehow never extended beyond the daubing of a few crude slogans around Goldhawk Road, lasted till Christmas. By then they had working capital of £200, their first royalties from 'Fall Out'. They also had no record deal, few gigs and fewer reviews. Sting made a virtue even of this gloomy scene. 'It was just journalists who didn't like us . . . In a way it was good for us to be marginalized, good for our resilience.' His gruelling rehearsal regimen began instantly, and brought untold misery to both Sting and his band. When, as a schoolboy, Gordon Sumner had trained for a race, he was, a rival says, 'about as fun to be around as a rhino with a hangover'. It was the same in The Police's rented room in Finchley. Sting knew only one way to practise, and that was hard and without heed for himself or others. It was all the worse because he missed his wife and son, struggled to motivate himself, and, in truth, loathed working without an audience.

They did, through the hit-hungry patronage of a German composer, Eberhard Schoener, play dates in Munich and a single night at the Nashville, in Paris. The set there ended with Sting yelling, *'Vive la France! Vive les flics!'* and whipping the crowd into a cappuccino of Gallic fervour. He encored by walking down the street into the red-light zone and writing the first lyrics of 'Roxanne'.

As a song, it had all the virtues: a clipped tango/reggae beat erupting into a rock chorus. This potent one-two punch translated, eighteen months later, into his first Top Twenty hit. When critics first heard the number, much was made of the gap between The Police's old lyrics, about dead-end jobs and landlords, and the new ones, about faded love and prostitution. It became, therefore, a document: not only expertly put together, but touching on real life. Sting was a master of the bleak paean to the brokenhearted, and a virtuoso at liberating the words with snappy tunes and the whiny, bluesy growl of the vocals.

Before 'Roxanne', the songs were recycled garage riffs of Copeland's and parting rants at Newcastle: from late 1977, words and melody met on equal terms. Both the ballads and the belters were more than just tirades or a collection of greeting-card pleas for peace. They were about passage through pain. 'Next To You', 'So Lonely' (retooled from Last Exit), 'Hole In My Life' and 'Can't Stand Losing You' all deftly tapped love's melodramatic vein; 'Message In A Bottle' touched on despair and alienation and finding solace for the void. Social comment, at this stage, was so tedious that Sting never made much more than a few brief stabs at it. He was a dab hand at analysing his own lot ('Born In The '50s'), and a genius at writing autobiographically in a way that struck sparks. Even his most wretched tunes resounded with the lust to live, and a healthy dose of *amour propre*, as Sting proclaimed in 'Visions Of The Night': 'They say the meek shall inherit the earth / How long will you keep it?'

With 'Roxanne' the band's democracy came apart, as Sting made an elegant move to corner the songwriting. It was of a piece with his bid for stardom. Although he later came to see his

daydream as touchingly puerile, self-inflating in the style of Mr
Toad – a sort of baby's neurotic cry – the guilty internal mono-
logues only came later. For now, fame was still fun; and vindi-
cation. Sting's ambition was unappeasable. By 1978 Copeland
and Summers were reduced to the occasional LP filler and
novelties like the music-hall whimsy of 'Be My Girl – Sally'.
Eventually, in the interests of band unity, Sting signed away a
portion of his royalties to the hapless sidemen. One result was
that Copeland and Summers became his servants as well as his
friends. Another was a creeping resentment against Sting – the
least-known musician of the three – an upstart, who, as he says,
'fought tooth and nail to get things done my way'. In 1977–78
there was a truce, despite moans at the hijacking, as if by some
godlike force, of the group's creative function. Within a year or
two war broke out. By the early 1980s Copeland's strong-though-
silent message to his singer was tattooed across four tom-toms
(FUCK-OFF-YOU-CUNT), a threat he once illustrated by cracking
Sting's rib in the dressing-room.

The sound The Police were chasing turned out to be an
alluring mix of new wave and reggae, with touches of Lou Reed
('White Light/White Heat' informed at least half the early
riffs), Dylan (in the shouted delivery of 'It's Alright For You')
and even Bo Diddley, whose hambone beat was shamelessly
filched in 'Deathwish'. The pumped-up drums and dense,
quavery guitar displayed taste, reach and a versatility the band
would revel in.

Sting's voice was the glue that held together the sprawling concept. By 1978 it was the group's star instrument, hoarse, husky
and yet fully adaptable into the scratchy tenor that serviced
'Roxanne'. The passionate vocal performance and the easy
precision of the band conformed perfectly to the rock-meets-
reggae potpourri of the early singles. Gone was the minimal
warbling and Dean Martin slur of Sting's outings with Last Exit.
Two years of constant practice and exercise – as well as his own
towering self-confidence – had wrought one of rock's once-in-
a-generation voices. His intonation was exquisitely fluid, and he
commanded the subtlest shadings of pitch and texture, the
trickiest reggae vibrato. Sting's newly steeled larynx meant that
even the band's worst material survived quirks like warmed-over
riffs and the pantomime-horse's gallop of the drums. The shiver

with which he rendered the best songs about love and loss lifted them into classics.

Even at this stage he bulldozed the band, organizing endless rehearsals – 'Roxanne' evolved through weeks of practice and torn-up arrangements – once slagging Summers in an acidly worded review. However true his remarks, the note was both arch and tactlessly patronizing of a colleague. It was an example of Sting's lapses of band protocol, along with his impatience when he chafed against mates. It was always thus. As he did with every band he ever led, Sting conducted rehearsals with a bizarre, intrusive, proprietary zeal. Both in Finchley and later, he issued a series of tart, vitrolic asides and strict directives meant to 'tighten' the trio. Their implicit theme was that Copeland and Summers weren't doing their job. Sting's acerbic critiques graced whatever irked him, with little concern for the likely consequences. Even the genial Summers was once driven to tears.

All that winter they endured the leaky cellar in north London, eventually transferring to the studio – via a cash infusion from Copeland's brother – in January 1978. The first sessions at Surrey Sound in Leatherhead gave little clue of the multi-platinum triumph that would come. Between a redbrick dairy and a cab firm, the studio was an unlovely place, furnished in brown pile and crudely divided by slabs of pegboard. Luxury never played a determining role in most punks' lives, but even so the peeling wet walls and sloping ceilings struck Sting as 'a toilet'. Over the next year he spent long hours there, wedged in the narrow control room, brewing coffee in the kitchen and passing convivial nights on the black 'shag sofa' in the foyer.*

He existed on the tiny trickle of money from Eberhard Schoener, the minuscule royalties from 'Fall Out', and modelling assignments scavenged by Tomelty. In early 1978 Sting appeared in commercials for Triumph bras ('I had to grope Joanna Lumley's tits'), Brutus jeans (more 'tits') and, on 22 February, his favourite of favourites, Wrigley's gum. The script for this last flummery called on Sting and two sidekicks to have blond hair and play punk rockers. Overnight, The Police were transformed from slavering indifference into dyed, moptop uniformity. Those with long memories would make the connection

---

*Surrey Sound had been much polished, and upgraded, by 1999.

to other identikit bands in rock folklore, among them the Beatles
and the Monkees. Some of those groups' rabble-rousing potential
was already at work that spring. In March the trio began a British
tour supporting Spirit, the psychedelic band touting a strange
collage of sci-fi and hallucinogenic ballads. The third night was
in Bristol. At first, the crowd behaved like acid-rock fans, merely
standing open-jawed watching The Police in the red and blue
strobe. Then, as Sting cued in the rootsy chords of 'Roxanne', the
Locarno was rudely awakened by impromptu dancing, yells, whoops
and fists shaken aloft. It was an authentic mob orgy, and did
much to announce the advent of a volatile yet inherently tuneful
band millions could identify with. Boundaries of individuality
broke down, and The Police, in their own way, swiftly became
public domain. As the group's manager says: 'That was the first
time the band actually began to gel. That gig . . . the Locarno was
the one where it was just beginning to click in our heads.'

As his fame grew, Sting's double life as a punk agitator and
happy family man took on new complexity. When not busy
drilling The Police, recording or performing, he still returned to
the flat in Leinster Square and became 'Gordo' again. Tomelty
herself played the orthodox wifely role, in the time-honoured
tradition of rockers and their loyal women, doing literally everything for Sting it wasn't vital he do himself. Within a year she was
acting as his *de facto* agent, driver, nurse, cook and housekeeper
to stray musicians. She turned a blind eye to the steady stream of
groupies who filled out her husband's time on the road, and
referred cynics to the mutual vows taken in the stone chapel in
Tynemouth. 'I remember one day chatting to Frances about
fidelity,' said Last Exit's Andy Hudson. 'She pointed out she was
a staunch Catholic and that she was sure Sting would never sleep
with other women.'

Whether lobbying for work or sitting home with his wife and
son, Sting spent most of his time making plans. He pragmatically
believed that 'you need practice as well as principle'. Sting's
detractors would say that his actions were principally designed to
boost his own ego; all part of his plan to exploit the two grunts
and seduce the tabloid groundlings. But there was no denying
the effort. As a friend says, 'He was the kind of guy who made a
list of "things to do today" and steadily crossed them off as he
went.' When the last item was duly ticked, Sting might give that

barely perceptible twitch which, with him, passed for a smile. His methodology seeped down into his leadership of The Police. When a colleague, irked by his steady flow of notes and memos, many of them critical of the band, asked why Sting took 'such an instant dislike to everyone', the quick-witted reply was unanswerable. 'It saves time.'

In April 1978 'Roxanne' was released to rave reviews and indifferent sales, the BBC refusing to vent a lyric 'glamorizing' prostitution. (Four months later, Sting trumped it with a catchy song about suicide.) The ban and word-of-mouth gave The Police a style of voguish rebellion, and their fame cut deeper with each commercial radio play. 'Roxanne' was written up warmly in *Goldmine* and without insult in *Sounds*. It was said to be Mick Jagger's favourite record. According to one critic, 'The Police began to receive phone calls from the Rod Stewart and Rolling Stones offices from people wanting to go to gigs.' By 3 May Sting felt sufficiently confident to join the Performing Rights Society (no. F12531), majestically billing himself as an 'international recording artist and performer'. That summer, he beat Johnny Rotten to the part of Ace Face in Franc Roddam's film of vanished Mod innocence, *Quadrophenia*. Sting charmed the director by talking literature with him. ('We sat around discussing Hermann Hesse ... suddenly he said, "You're perfect. You look perfect." I got the job that day.') Much the same mix of plausibility, ambition and telegenic good looks won him a role in a second, lower-budget feature, *Radio On*.

Meanwhile, work continued to cut The Police's first album. With the unimpeachable authority of his long years in the studio, Sting would slate Surrey Sound as 'a cruddy, funky place with egg cartons on the walls' and, in a fit of wishful thinking, agitate for a move to the Caribbean. By midwinter the small, bare room in Leatherhead had already witnessed the major part of the record. It was a piece in itself, it already existed independently of Sting; it was already his masterpiece. Seven tracks out of ten, and all the backing parts, were ready for production. As a whole, *Outlandos d'Amour* would cement The Police's niche between the great older bands of the fading present – Slade and T. Rex – and those who'd fill their shoes, thrash merchants like Rotten and Strummer. More focused and personal than anything Sting had done before, with lyrics reading as though they'd come straight from his diary, *Outlandos* showed a singer-songwriter who had evolved from a bratty, wide-eyed Mod into a mature artist at the first peak of his genre-busting power.

Much as Sting's craftsmanship was an achievement in itself, at least part of his coup belonged to others. Almost all The Police's songs were built of a collaboration. Copeland and Summers embellished the basic tunes on *Outlandos*. The guitar and drums invariably knitted themselves into a team. Considering the low-rent amenities at Leatherhead, Nigel Gray showed rare skill in forging a blade-sharp sound, at once dense and yet ingeniously full of space for each player, that became the band's hallmark. The studio itself, though unlovely, was a welcome refuge from the frills and gadgetry of other facilities, and gave unique scope to the music. The sloping roof, in particular, allowed for different drum sounds according to where Copeland positioned his kit under the ceiling. The cramped layout of the place afforded distinct acoustic characteristics in a small area, as well as inviting – almost a physical imperative – random interplay between the group. Thus the first bars of 'Roxanne' were ushered in by a plunked piano note and laughter, not the result of a studio experiment involving tape-loops and special effects, but of Sting falling headlong into the keyboard.

While he recorded some of the most enduring songs of the late 1970s, Sting was still barely grubbing an existence. He owed cash to tradesmen, to his landlord, his bank, the taxman, the milkman, the boutique where Tomelty did her shopping, and to most of his friends. He wrote in his diary, 'Money, or lack of it, has raised its ugly head again – Joe is so innocent and vulnerable – God please help us.' The funds from Virgin, along with his commissions and modelling fees, were barely enough to cover expenses and, like all The Police, he existed on a few pounds a week. There was no record-company income. Even when the label's purse-strings loosened, the product predominated over the group. While the rough tapes of *Outlandos* were collected at the studio door and conveyed to London by taxi, Sting, Copeland and Summers travelled in, second class, on the train.

There was always this pathos of slumming. The stage was set for disenchantment and mutual wrangling, an undignified break-up still the band's likeliest fate. But Sting was lucky. He'd married well, and lived in a favourable time and congenial

surroundings. He was even luckier in stumbling across first
Copeland and then his elder brother Miles, a famously alert
hustler who steered Sting through the shark-infested waters of
the punk scene. By 1978 Miles had managed acts as motley as the
Climax Blues Band, Renaissance and Caravan. His major success
had been Wishbone Ash's quasi-mystical hit *Argus*; his failures
weren't to be numbered. According to Miles's partner Dick
Jordan, 'Whatever you say about him, he had incredible flair –
Miles was still driving a Jag while the shoes were falling off his
feet – and fantastic ears. He never saw a bandwagon without a
pathological need to jump on it.' Reinventing himself as a punk
guru in the mould of Malcolm McLaren, Miles took rooms in
Dryden Chambers, Oxford Street – immediately below the Sex
Pistols – as well as an interest in the Roxy Club and the house
organ, *Sniffin' Glue*. He gave moral support and grovelling
coverage to 'Fall Out' (which enigmatically made his magazine's
Top Ten), lent The Police money and offered himself as the
band's saviour, as Jordan says, 'taking the risk that all this might
help his career'. His first negotiating coup was to talk Nigel Gray
into accepting £1,500 to record *Outlandos*, with a second instal-
ment hazily promised after (long after) delivery. In 1978 the
bespectacled Miles was in his early thirties. He favoured wide
lapels and profit margins that narrowed his suppliers' takes. His
heroes were Colonel Parker and Margaret Thatcher. Despite his
authoritarian ambitions, he was a sane, limited, blunt and conscientious soul. Miles set an example of strict morality: long
hours, no drugs or groupies and an unshakeable faith in market
economics. This was the man who would manage Sting for the
next twenty years, and on whom his fate rested.

Although most in his court stressed the differences between
himself and hoary industry types like Allen Klein, Miles actually
belonged to an earlier, vanished world of rock management. The
instant he signed The Police they came under a blitz of memos,
notes, recording schedules and agendas – the same military
regime as Sting's, though now propped by an organization,
offices, a reporting structure and the like. No one who experienced Miles's brand of salesmanship ever forgot it. If there was a
single, defining theme in his pitch, it was to repeat – again and
again – how to 'package' the goods. He understood, as few did,
that tough, precision marketing combined with catchy tunes and

photogenic poses spelled the difference between success and failure. Immense effort went into the way The Police looked and behaved. Miles endorsed the blond cockades at a time when the group were still met by muffled sniggers, or worse. He incorporated the distinctive Police logo used on all their records from 1978. With a dictator's native feel for 'the people', he grasped that the public craved a leader of each group, and that usually that meant the singer (who in this case also played the bass and wrote the songs). Miles was thus the agent who, quite pitilessly, pressed Sting's claims over his brother's. ('Fuck off and play the drums' is one friend's memory of Copeland's terse fiat to his sibling.) The band's all-for-one ethic imploded with 'Roxanne', though no one said so at the time. Sting found himself in the same position as a Cromwell, who insisted he wanted consent, if only he could get it. It took clout, and gall, to promote the late, raw recruit into the chief of Police. Miles's turning to Sting was integral to the group's breakthrough, as was his polishing of the singer's every quip to the band's image as canny, eminently quotable operators. Miles wasn't the first man to groom a group, some would sniff jealously. (As the Sex Pistols' Glen Matlock says, 'he kept trying to pinch ideas from McLaren'.) But he was, nonetheless, stunningly successful in converting The Police's warring members into a potent musical marriage.

With money borrowed from Dick Jordan, the Copelands had pressed 2,000 copies of 'Fall Out' and set up their own home label, Illegal. Six months later, on 22 November 1977, Miles registered a new management company, Firstars. Within five years he was a director of fourteen British-based firms and others whose precise home was hard to fix. Miles owed Keith Moore the book-keeping of his interests, as well as the investment strategy that made The Police rich. Into the empire, meanwhile, came Kim Turner, the group's sound and tour manager, and a third Copeland brother, Ian, their American agent. By mid-1978 Illegal's core structure was in place. Within, Miles loomed over a team whose emphasis on discipline and cost-cutting was as far as one could get from the lax world of rock and roll. Without, punks, rockers, Rastas, hucksters and foreign adventurers, to name some, all jostled together in spin-drier fashion, rising and falling, forming fragile 'scenes', starting new fads which died as quickly as others took their place. In such a world the man of granite had a unique chance to crash through and make a killing.

Miles was a gambler, too, and he rode his luck. Early in 1978, on one of his periodic calls at Surrey Sound, he heard the song Sting described as 'more or less a throwaway', replete with its botched intro. Miles knew instantly that 'Roxanne' would be a hit. He also knew that Illegal had neither the capital nor the resources to sell it. Next day he took a step that showed his new confidence and a first touch of entrepreneurial ambition. Reviving an old contact, he arranged – demanded – a meeting with Derek Green, then head of A&M Records: 'Miles waltzed in, slapped me on my back and said, "I want you to do something you've never done before. Sign a band you've never heard of." He put on "Roxanne". Next minute he said, "I'll make it easy for you: you put out the single and pay us a royalty – nothing up front. I'll pick up the tab for an American tour." Within half an hour we had a deal. After we shook Miles relaxed enough to tell me his brother was the drummer.'

Green and his colleague Mike Noble then saw The Police play a set at London's Roundhouse. According to Noble, of the twenty or so fans present 'half fell asleep and the other half made for the car park'. Despite this ominous start, most of the band's unique sales points were already present: musical sophistication, novelty and energy, as Noble says, 'along with the incredible tension between Sting and Stewart. They loathed each other.' After a second, sweatily incarnated show at the Nashville, terms were duly agreed on 22 March 1978.

Twelve months earlier, A&M had famously signed (and dropped) the Sex Pistols, presenting themselves as new, punk-friendly tycoons who never forgot they were in business to, as they put it, 'bring the music'. It said much for the label's sang-froid, as well as Copeland's nerve, that the two conspired to hire a band which, Green says, 'were sold as pure punks . . . There was no queue behind us.' Over the next year A&M were given ample opportunity to rue their investment. After 'Roxanne' was released, and flopped, The Police took up residency with Eberhard Schoener in Munich. The group used the summer to make their own solo stabs at fame: Copeland in a bizarre outing under his alias Klark Kent, Sting via six weeks' rehearsal and filming of *Quadrophenia*. That August the band unleashed their second A&M single, and second dud. 'Can't Stand Losing You', a shotgun wedding of Bob Marley and the Beatles, summarized Sting's chipper response to failed love: suttee. It, too, earnt a BBC ban. In a later cameo on *The Old Grey Whistle Test*, an explosive burst of aerosol backstage blinded Sting for hours. It was the first of what would be a career of mishaps that might have killed unluckier or less well-conditioned men. Not only was Sting accident-prone, but his lust for life frequently led to macho expressions of his personality, as when he crashed motorbikes or nearly drowned in South Atlantic breakers.

All this activity preceded the release of the first album in November 1978.

The Police, at this early stage, were never just Sting and two hired hands, nor a lab for edgy interactions between the singer's literacy and the drummer's art-rock pedigree and punk persona. They were a fighting unit. Specifically, they fought each other every day in the studio, sometimes physically, more often with below-the-belt quips and traps for their rivals' vanity. After failing to master the one-note riff of 'Hole In My Life', Summers tetchily suggested Sting take over, thereby revealing that he aspired to the guitar. Sting had the sense to refuse, while Copeland was keen to propose himself, an offer which Gray vetoed. A combination of brooding anger, dark hints from A&M and the relentless ticking of the studio clock all brought a zap of high-voltage energy that unkind critics would dismiss as exhibitionism. But the end-product was fluid, imaginative, and nearly as extravagant as Sting's songs. For once, the music didn't do battle with the words. At their very best, both were heart-stopping jolts of emotion.

*Outlandos d'Amour** took the musical vocabulary of reggae to a mainstream audience. The slogging rhythm and neat, chirpily sung tunes made for the sort of stylistic maze that gave 'cross-over' a good name. Yet more critics blamed Sting because the ragged souls who had originally moved him were still struggling, still skint, while their white mimics reaped unheard-of rewards. He made the point himself. 'It's like the Stones in the sixties were just as valid as John Lee Hooker . . . I mean, there is a sense of guilt, that sense of duty to the black man, and whenever we

*At Miles Copeland's insistence, the name was Frenchified from *Outlaws of Love*.

meet black musicians we're interested in what they think of us.'
Unlikely friendships would be forged. Chuck Berry, for one,
became a paid-up member of Sting's fan club, such was his love
of the 'shit-kicking' singles. An enduring bond formed between
The Police and Bob Marley. Muddy Waters admired the 'A to Z
thing' of *Outlandos*. Among the album's roll-call of influences
were nods to calypso, jazz, vaudeville and slick, dead-ahead rock.
It was hard to identify much trace of punk.

Outlandos began at a breathless pogo-pop pace with 'Next To
You' before shifting down into 'So Lonely' – 'No Woman No
Cry' grafted to a headbanging chorus, and, incongruously,
Michael Tippett's favourite rock song. The evolution of 'Truth
Hits Everybody' reversed the stock formula. The tune was
rearranged from a chugging reggae groove into a careening, Who-
style raver. Yet again, the subtle tempo changes, the bold mixing
of musical genres for effect, and the use of offbeat noises yoked
the basic riff to a rich blend of melody and fury. 'Born In The
'50s' was a premature, and sadly underweight, brother of Bruce
Springsteen's 1984 smash, played with no great conviction on the
guitar (possibly because Summers was born in 1942). Real farce
befell 'Be My Girl', power pop padded with an ill-advised cabaret
turn. 'Masoko Tanga' was the show-saving finale: deceptively
simple beats, restrained but serviceable effects, and Sting's
enthralling scat singing. With the knockout punch of 'Roxanne',
Outlandos more than fulfilled its promise.

Reviews testified to the album's twin assets of promiscuous
borrowing and original, bold talent. What excited sociologists
was its ability to trap the present, to 'be here now'. Other critics
were swayed by the vocals and the production that gave
Outlandos' furiously played songs leaping, dynamic arrangements. Thanks to its superior hit rate, with three Top Twenty
singles, the album made millions; but Sting was struck even
more, if possible, by the effect the record had on the industry
and, ultimately, his own long-term finances. *Outlandos d'Amour*
galvanized the post-punk market and spent ninety-six weeks in
the British chart.

On the morning of 20 October 1978, The Police stood,
surrounded by their guitars and cine-cameras and shrouded in
their army-surplus coats, at the chaotic Laker Skytrain desk at
Gatwick Airport. It was exactly a year since Sting had strolled

down a Parisian boulevard and written the first words of 'Roxanne'. Then, the band had been canon-fodder for Wayne County and his sub-punk wailings. Now, for four weeks, they barnstormed north-eastern America: not because their modest record sales warranted a tour, but because Miles Copeland swore by the regional breakout, whereby rave reviews in one city would, said he, set up a coast-to-coast mania for the group. Precedent hardly supported his claim. For one reason or another, most of the other fauna of British punk, the Pistols and Elvis Costello and the Clash, had barely made the Atlantic crossing. A&M themselves had warned the band off the trip. Yet Miles, who possessed the gift of being infinitely plausible as a strategist, had watched other, half-failed tours as a fakir watches a snake. He knew, rightly, that demand would build until The Police would automatically be able to corner part of the booming New York punk market without alienating the heartland – what he called the great average. As he says today, 'We benefited from being one of the first bands of this new generation to come into the States . . . People wanted us to succeed beyond whether they liked the group or not.' It was his greatest risk, and his greatest coup, to campaign successfully across America without a record to run on.

The Laker jet arrived in New York four hours late. Like members of the Monkees, The Police and Kim Turner ran through the terminal, clutching their stage gear, and were driven at wild speed to CBGB's club in the Bowery. After the frantic forty-minute set Miles watched as his brother and Sting debated the proper tempos for their songs, and ended up rolling around in the dressing-room, discussing the matter. It was a suitably vivid omen for the month that followed, The Police ploughing the eastern seaboard, playing bars and gyms and assembly rooms for $200 a night. Sting had gibed at their opening-night venue as 'incredible – like Hades'. Compared to clubs like Grendel's Lair, Philadelphia, and The Rat in Boston, CBGB's enjoyed almost imperial status. Although the national breakthrough came later, Sting's rabid energy and ambition never once flagged on the road. After each show he was apt to sit in a local bar, wearing a Police T-shirt, quoting from various Latin and Greek poets, holding forth on art, capitalism, technology, the riches of the human heart, jazz, Vietnam and America; a poster or concert tickets would change hands. He might then stand up, belch, and in a loud voice sing one of Bessie Smith's blues.

Sting's ad-libbed promotion paid off. At the Firebarn, in Syracuse, there were exactly three paying customers in the house – and a fourth man revealed as a local DJ and programmer. The next morning radio stations from Niagara Falls to Manhattan started playing 'Roxanne'. In a chain reaction, a friend then sent the single to a record-store owner in Austin, Texas, who began to tongue-lash his suppliers into buying it. While the hoped-for rollout failed to follow, The Police had the beginnings of a name.

Sting unwound on the road with bouts of drinking and soft drugs. He formed a close phone rapport with a chat-line friend known only as 'girl three'. They never actually met – that would have been too normal – but spoke for hours from motel rooms and clubs. Sting always asked for her by number. The two 'burnt up the wire', says the woman, with their masturbatory fantasies. Sting, she reports, 'definitely' achieved satisfaction from these long-distance couplings; the girl never did.

A woman he did meet adds merely that he was 'up and down all the time. He was either telling me what a great singer he was, or crying in my arms saying he wanted to quit and be an actor. Napoleonic. Totally schizophrenic.'

On a creative level, at least, the tour achieved its modest aims. While travelling round in a crowded van and staying in slums, the band shared an authentically punk experience. Part of the idea of the trip – booked before *Outlandos* was released – was to give them the chance to bond as a group. Despite the occasional *faux pas* backstage (as when Sting 'went fucking bonkers' at Copeland's provocative query, 'Hi, how are you?'), The Police began to gel: the liberties they took with their best tunes were more like disciplined rewrites than the free-form rags of other bands. Then, somewhere between the first and twentieth nights, an epiphany. 'As we progressed, the two styles [reggae and rock] merged,' says Sting. 'There was none of the stop–start thing. The songs refined themselves.'

Financially, their first contact with America came as something of a shock. The twenty-four dates in twenty-seven days grossed just $6,000. Of that the band existed on $20 a day apiece. By careful budgeting Sting was able to buy a new Fender Precision bass at Manny's in New York. But that and the phone were his only extravagances on the road. By early November he was reduced to nagging his manager for pocket money and drunkenly submitting a personal ad to a New York fanzine. It read:

> POET, 27, married, dreamer, singer,
> songwriter, would like to continue
> living & working if possible.

But even irony got him nothing. Sting flew back to Gatwick on 17 November, hitched a lift to Leinster Square, put a crumpled ten-dollar bill in his wife's hand and said, 'That's it.' As Christmas loomed, he again began berating Miles and Keith Moore for his being 'totally skint' and struck a friend by the 'slow-motion crawl of his hand toward the bill' after a long lunch. As usual when he was under stress, Sting came down with something and took to his bed. Only the need to start a British tour as support to a comedy act roused him, and he spent twelve hours the day before rehearsing.

The show at the Electric Ballroom, London, gave notice of a band who would leapfrog the entire pop field within a year. At a second gig, says Summers, 'the place erupted. Girls throwing their knickers on stage. That's when we knew something was happening . . . A total riot.' Night after night, whether headlining or refusing to meet the bleak fate of warm-ups, The Police staked out a claim bordered by punk's manic desolation and reggae's feelgood languour. Though the group now had company on that turf, they drew more from it than most.

The star of the shows, as much for his presence as his actual playing, was Sting. Two years after turning professional he was a stage pro. The eye turned to him wherever he went. He was one of the most casually virtuosic showmen in a world not short of pumped-up egos, capable of spicing dark, moody lyrics with yarns that were unseasonably sunny, more than holding his own among the lubricious fans. When The Police emerged, following Miles's shouted introduction, the moshers roared; clearly Sting was the man they'd come to see. Whether pogo-ing up and down or tossing off quips which were at once tart and flip, he was the consummate crowd-teaser. Juxtaposed against the bazooka blast of the drums and Summers' jittery guitar, Sting's songs neatly trod the line between the eternal joys of electric rock and bluesy

introspection. The group's collective charisma drove a performance that skilfully stretched a repertoire of only a dozen tunes.
Every 'next big thing' should be this accessible and this
deserving of the title.

On the debit side, The Police seldom allowed themselves the
luxury of letting go. The playing was perfectly competent, but it
rarely summoned the true sense of abandon. Admittedly, loss of
control was never on Sting's agenda; he was happiest burnishing
the songs to a gloss (though, even then, The Police's harmonies
seemed strangely ropy). Shorn of the visuals, and Nigel Gray's
alchemy, the band could sound hollow and retrograde. Jeff
Griffin, who recorded their first-ever radio date (delayed for
months by a BBC technicians' strike), recalls them as 'nothing
great'. Other critics chided their reliance on stagecraft and
jamming, a formula *Sounds* slated as 'the temptation to vamp
through and use the rock edge for insurance, hype up the boogie
section and toss in a certain amount of rifferama . . . Apart from
some ritual tightening and slacking, not much is added.'

Sting brought into rock and roll not just a native habit of graft,
but also a quality that, in Wallsend in the 1950s, came a notch
below life itself: machismo. He not only sang, played and worked
the crowd, but came across as an infinitely keen, if grouchy,
games master, forever running, jumping, strutting, shuffling and
scowling like the hard-nut Geordie he once was. The first song at
the Electric Ballroom, which Sting ended by wading into the
drums, gave evidence that this was something other than
all-round family entertainment. On the other hand, the fact that
he strove so hard for punk muscle is the best proof that,
genetically, he had none. By late 1978 he was the Renaissance
Man of rock, capable of snarling invective one moment,
ingratiating wit the next, and the fans' lust for leadership had
found expression in the green-eyed singer, concave at the waist
and artfully bulging above, still with his back-combed Beatle
mop.

On 13 February 1979 The Police regrouped in Leatherhead to
begin their second album. Among the first numbers Sting
hummed, whistled and noodled on the piano was a tune called
'Message In A Bottle'. The bass and drums held down the fort
for the swirling, hypnotic guitar. It had bottle, the message as
well as the title, a theme that cut right to the dark heart of Sting's

pet theme of solitude; a vocal soaring into something higher than the lyric. A week later the band played the (still unrecorded) song on BBC2's *Rock Goes to College*. This was the signal for one of Sting's Newcastle friends to ring him with the information, 'I saw you on telly. You were crap.'

By the time The Police returned to America in March, steady sales of *Outlandos* had brought a gesture toward luxury. Where their first tour had been a cut-price saga of junk food and cheap rooms, four months later they travelled as a small army. Sting began his pursuit of fame by officially unveiling his new songs, largely concentrating on the problems and pressure of being Sting, and reworking the old ones, about Roxanne, Sally and inflatable dolls. He still wrote open and flexible tunes, accommodating his improvisational ear. Thus 'Message' was regularly worked into a mini-epic of repetition and elaboration, Sting scatting like Louis Armstrong, rolling the 'yo's' around his mouth and reminding the over-thirties of the 'Twist And Shout' school of rock vocals. By the time The Police flew home in April, they felt able to take self-congratulatory ads in the trade titles, insisting simply that they were 'Big in America'. From then on realization met with hope as the pillar of Sting's world. Manager and label outdid each other in wringing hype from the mere accountancy of record sales. The re-released 'Roxanne' hit the UK and US Top Forties, lugging *Outlandos* with it. 'Can't Stand Losing You' was a British number two, while in September 'Message In A Bottle' confirmed that Sting had arrived as the face of 1979.

In the man himself, no matter how much he shunned the 'cocaine and bullshit' glut of his peers, there was a matching transformation in the few months between American tours.

His sort of upbringing – in which, as a relative says, 'a kick in the nuts from Gordon counted as a friendly hello' – could go either way. In the event, Sting grew up self-centred, quick on the draw and exceptionally fast with a put-down. His brother was wary and withdrawn. By 1979, in the first flush of fame, the older Sumner had adapted his childhood problems into viable ways to make it, a well-rounded and swelling ego under a façade designed to convey the reverse. The world knew him mainly as that rare thing, the articulate pop star. When the barbs and the quips, the self-will and the staggering chutzpah were forgotten, people remembered him because he looked, acted and sounded clever. Dick Jordan recalls him as 'the first punk ever to read the *Guardian*'. He was celebrated as the most 'together' star in the rock galaxy: brisk, vigilant, so opinionated, so sharp, so centred (his own favourite word for himself) that most fans and almost all interviewers were hooked. Sting's charm sometimes curdled with self-consciousness – he knew how charming he was – but his intelligence and 'normality' were very real. Even when fame struck he liked to travel on the bus, browse in bookshops and meet old cronies in pubs. Sting never lost touch with the sources of observation for his songs, and only later let the 'cocaine and bullshit' catch at his heels. It seemed to friends that he was shy in private, and in public not at all.

When it came to work, he was cocksure, aloof, haughty, and dotted his lyrics with highbrow clues wherever he could. 'There are a lot of literary references in my songs,' he informed the press. 'I just drop names and that's enough to get somebody interested. A lot of people read *Lolita* because of "Don't Stand So Close To Me".' From the priceless use of the words 'a lot' to the glib superiority ('I just drop names'), to the schoolmasterly bilge, his wasn't run-of-the-mill autism, it was the highly distilled sort. Sting teetered between a modesty polished against his man-of-the-people affectations, and overweening ego.

His colleagues found him exuberantly efficient and strong-willed. 'You should have seen him in the studio,' says a staffer at Surrey Sound. 'He was intense, keyed-up and dictatorial. If he thought something wasn't right, he'd say, "That's bullshit." ' He was a more siren, less blithe spirit than on *Outlandos*. Some of his raw edge came to bear on his fellow musicians. Reg Presley remembers a night when a row brewed about which of the two groups, The Police or the Troggs, would close a show. Sting, says Presley, 'made it clear that, even though we were the bigger name, he never – *never* – wanted to be someone's support'. It was the same jockeying for status that led to a scene when Sting quite literally bumped into Elvis Costello walking down Kensington High Street. 'He looked up, tried to scowl at me, and I just shrugged. And he fucking went off.'

Friendship was already sundered with Stewart Copeland. From 1979, Sting and his drummer fought like ferrets in a sack. Their simmering rivalry, frequently boiling into brawls, took the same basic line as the Sumner brothers' skirmishes, though under greater stress. Sting would do or say something thoughtless that hurt Copeland; Copeland's hurt would put him in an ugly mood; his moodiness annoyed Sting. The first cause of the ill-will, and its throughline for seven years, was a bitter tussle for control and a struggle to the death over songwriting. Its effect was a hot-making and rowdy atmosphere, squabbles on the road and punch-ups in the studio. ('Was Sting a scumbag?' Copeland asks today. 'No. Did I think he was a scumbag? Yes.') In time, events led Copeland to physically build his drums as a Maginot Line against his singer (already forewarned by the FUCK-OFF-YOU-CUNT daubed on the skins). Violence, never far from the surface with The Police, broke out openly during sessions for their second album. In one failed negotiation about vocals, Sting thrust a mike into Copeland's hands and 'gave [him] some medical advice', according to a witness, 'which wasn't too practical'. But drummer outweighed singer by ten pounds and had learnt his fighting on the streets of Beirut; though still sitting at his kit, he managed to lash out and hit Sting, knocking him down and splitting his lip. Both parties later tended to disown such scenes, Copeland restricting himself to the time-worn rubric about 'creative differences'. The truth, Mike Noble says, cut deeper. 'The Police were basically Stewart's band. Obviously he was chuffed to get a bassist who was also a great singer and writer . . . only I don't think he wanted one *that* great.' A second friend is blunter: 'With Sting it was just a matter of time before he made his move. Within six months, he locked up the group.'

Although, during the next five years, critics like *Melody Maker* judged him, and his looks, as affected and deliberately posed, he was in fact natural and merely self-conscious. Once the angora sweaters were gone, Sting, with his plucked eyebrows and delicate, woman's mouth, often looked seductive, always attractive, and yet never wholly welcoming. Two years earlier, he'd succumbed to the indignity of modelling work as 'the only way I could keep from starving'. With the days of peroxide and punk quiffs long gone, his sandy hair reverted to a floppy bouffant, still short at the crown but flicking his cheeks, in the style of David Cassidy. He favoured a closet of T-shirts, outsize jackets and military garb, including a striking, zippered shell-suit that he successively removed on stage. Sting's army regalia and deadpan, equivocal stare were a benchmark of cool. 'He wasn't deliberately setting out to be an enigma,' says Virgin's Richard Branson. He simply realized that the way he dressed and looked was, like his music, out of the ordinary run of the punk mill. At photo-shoots he could strike as many hollow-cheeked poses as Cassidy himself to woo the teenyboppers, but by and large his clothes and looks were an honest form of self-expression. With several notable exceptions, public and press reaction was overwhelming. 'Gorgeous', 'rugged', 'chiselled' and 'hunky' came round like stops on the Circle Line.

Sting wasn't the first rocker to trade in the old-fashioned realms of movie-star glamour. But he was no dewy-eyed tyro, preening on *Top of the Pops* in the hope of exciting the molten dreams of his girl fans and the envy of the boys. Self-confidence, in the core, Thatcherite sense, was the key element. From his drop-dead name onwards, Sting was out to goad, shock and ultimately lure his audience with various lewd versions of himself. Self-projection was a place he fitted well in. Whether on stage, or backstage, he could hold forth for hours in his dry, raspy voice, with only the occasional nod to his Geordie roots (as in his pronunciation of 'Newcastle'). Except for professional engagements, he never returned to the north.

Between April 1979 and February 1980, A&M conjured four failed singles into four re-released hits. More than because they said anything new, the second comings of 'Roxanne', 'Can't Stand Losing You', 'Fall Out' and 'So Lonely' were notable because Miles Copeland reaffirmed Colonel Parker's policy of flinging 'product' at the market, along with dogged hype and a mad schedule. In June the band began their first UK tour as headliners, wove a meander through America, and gave shows in France and Germany, before returning home, where they played two London dates, at separate venues, the same night. 'Message In A Bottle' and 'Walking On The Moon' glossed their year with two number-one singles. Between times, Sting guested on *Roundtable* and *Juke Box Jury*, appeared in *Quadrophenia* and *Radio On*, gave dozens of interviews and generally became a global icon. The solo fame rebounded back to the band. It was a mixed blessing. Both he and, by association, The Police, were fully alive to the lunacy that inevitably attends rock's answered prayers. Celebrity was occasionally fun but also a burden, a daily and deadly bore. Their 'loneliness at the top' was very real, and led them to lose touch with the people who put them there in the first place. Mobs followed them about, and Sting, who as late as 1979 was known to share a pint in the beer tent with fans, learned to skulk out the stage doors of theatres and hockey arenas and run to safety through side streets and roped-off alleys. In December 1978 The Police were a struggling band with four flopped singles. In what seemed like an instant, and was only seven months, they were headlining the Reading Festival. As Sting said, it was unheard of. He'd made 'people talk' about him. It was all paying off.

The Police saved the opening day at Reading. After lacklustre turns by Motorhead, Doll By Doll and the Tourists (latterly Eurythmics), the band invested the bleak, rain-spattered backdrop with rum-warmed reggae and austere yet nasty rockers. Sting, as *Melody Maker* quite accurately said, 'manipulated the people beautifully', a rebel without a pause who bumped and ground his way through the set. What's more, for once the new songs compared well with the old. As 'Roxanne' was followed in turn by 'So Lonely', which gave way to 'Walking On The Moon', the 30,000 crowd could literally see their singles collections come alive. Whipped up by a steady stream of *Yeahhhs* and *Aaawrites* from the stage, the mob's shaken fists stretched back to the far reaches of the site. It wouldn't have been impossible to have persuaded them to chair Sting off like Bobby Moore. The votaries' mood wasn't just euphoric, it was ecstatic. For over an hour, Sting's touch-of-punk act – evident in both his bouncing house style and his raw-throated vocals – was the signal for audience-participatory screams, shouts and yelps, percussive crashes of tin and glass, and choruses swollen into mass singalongs. With the approach to the park awash in Police T-shirts, posters, banners and badges, all inscribed with the stark hieroglyphics of the band logo, and 'Can't Stand Losing You' at number two in the chart, it was hard to deny that fans had got their money's worth, or that the headline in the morning paper, A STAR IS BORN, said it all.

Hyper-promotion and classy melodies notwithstanding, The Police had to work hard for their fame. Jeff Griffin recorded the band for the BBC's *In Concert* in June 1979. 'It was riff rock,' he says; but they 'didn't exactly shine'; unlike the growing collection of gold discs on Miles's wall. Den Hegarty, presenter of Tyne-Tees'

Alright Now, credits the 'huge sound' – the trio accompanying each other with fraternal glee – for the vinyl smashes. Sting himself liked to dwell on the jazzy interplay of the group, how they braved cracking up, but instead clung together. 'The way we work is that I bring a song to them . . . they tear it apart and it ends up arranged by the band as a whole. We fight a lot over the way we do things, but I think that's healthy, because we're all disciplined enough to recognize when someone's being an arsehole and when someone's making a sound musical suggestion.' Nothing better illustrated Sting's appreciation of the rough edge and intimate vibe of old friends (and sometimes enemies) pooling ideas in their rehearsal room. He wanted competent, proven collaborators, men he could turn to for advice and with whom he could share both ups and downs, if not royalties. Democracy was the rope which he clutched in order to keep from drowning.

Sting was shrewd, certainly shrewd enough to know that today's durable groove can become tomorrow's endless rut. Musically, he wanted bustle, activity, trial and error, anything that would transcend the empty roar of arena rock. He was well aware of the diminishing creative returns of slavishly aping a formula. 'There's very few groups with more than three albums. Listen to their first three, fresh and new. Then listen to numbers four to ten and you can tell they're just going through the motions of being rock stars.' He was talking about Mick Jagger, but he was defining a vice, complacency, that he meant to avoid himself. 'The pop-star myth pleases me at the moment, but I don't believe in it and I'm sure I'll tire of it eventually.'

Collectivism may have been the band's motto, but there was no denying who was Police chief. At the very core of their act was the classic rock relationship between singer and talented-but-passive sidemen. 'In Stewart and Andy, I have the best musicians possible to interpret my work,' Sting told a reporter, in a rare lapse of public image. It was the same in the practice den, the studio or on stage. Everything flowed on Sting's word. From the first day of recording *Outlandos*, when he angrily tore up Copeland's and Summers' lyrics to 'Next To You', they knew it was going to be a hard slog. If Sting made life hell for the others, they repaid him in full. 'It wasn't as easy as [Copeland and Summers] just standing aside . . . I had to fight them every step of the way.' And just in case the drummer tried anything funny,

Sting decided to keep a flick-knife in his boot.

One of the ways The Police isolated themselves from punk convention was by showmanship of the sharpest and slickest order. As well as their live sets, TV and radio spots, personal appearances, signings, promotions and interviews, their industry-shaking videos were exactly the right look at the right time for the literal and figurative fifteen-year-olds about to embrace MTV. Copeland's and Summers' histrionics, even when miming the latest hit, rarely scaled the dramatic ladder to hamming. That was one reason why the films were never a life-shaking experience. But they made art out of bad drama. Shot by the married team of Derek and Kate Burbidge, 'Roxanne', 'Can't Stand Losing You', 'Message In A Bottle', 'Walking On The Moon' and 'So Lonely' were bold, funny and fully alive. Exotic locales (including the Kennedy Space Center) brought a raw, visceral energy and warmth missing in most studios. Sting was equally riveting as the gamut-running star, simmering or strutting, wearing a dozen eye-bashing suits, ranging from pinstripes to polka-dots, that were louder than he was. *He* understood amateur theatrics. As a whole, the five promos were pioneers in the art of bringing big-budget production values to the small screen, and a precursor of Sting's roguish cinema roles. Thanks to his potent acting and the Burbidges' novel lenswork, the videos never looked like guerrilla operations done on a shoestring. They bristled with wild inventiveness and humour that shamed other directors and marked Sting as a Hollywood contender.

Depressingly often, a brilliant début album is a cul-de-sac, not a road to greater things: in the industry quip, 'You've got a lifetime to make your first hit and six weeks to cut your second.' *Reggatta de Blanc* wasn't one of those records. *Outlandos* had been a stunning breakthrough. But whereas an Elvis Costello spat out lyrics which seemed to have a full life of their own beyond the tunes, too many of Sting's images meekly returned to their box the second the music stopped. He placed himself between the words and the audience. 'Message In A Bottle' and *Reggatta* suggested that their author was rapidly passing from the role of puppet-master to that of true creator. The songs easily satisfied the definitive pop criteria: they meant something, and you could dance to them.

Sting admitted to nerves about *Reggatta*'s reception. 'I was worried sick . . . I couldn't sleep,' he told *Sounds*. 'I kept asking Nigel Gray whether he really thought we had a record. I couldn't hear it or feel it.' The producer's account of the band 'instantly knowing that "Message" would be number one' hardly supports this claim, though Sting certainly took pains with the album. Derek Green remembers 'him ringing, wanting to play all *Reggatta*'s demos', an offer Green refused with the winning self-snub, 'I'm just a marketing guy' (typical of a relationship between band and label that, though warm, was never close). Sting then called Green's deputy Mike Noble, who made the trek to Leatherhead. All the group, he says, were 'up and bouncing around' at the songs, an enthusiasm A&M fully shared. The press generally concurred: Sting could take pleasure in knowing that his critics for the most part 'got' his lyrics, while agreeing that his songs were sounding better and better.

Reggatta de Blanc was an astonishingly bold leap into superstar-dom. More than just an infectious follow-up to *Outlandos*, the record tapped into Sting's deepest potential and made good on his wildest brags. Essentially, this meant injecting reggae grooves with a rock-and-roll tension that gave the wry, evocative words a joyous snap. The best songs on the album branched off into uncharted territory – intelligent power pop, at least two chords and twenty IQ points removed from their Roxy club roots. It was all over for The Police and punk credibility the first moment they dyed their hair.

With his down-payment for *Outlandos*, Nigel Gray had revamped Surrey Sound to twenty-four tracks and given up com-piling low-fi classics. He was the perfect moderator for The Police's corrosive spats, humorous, patient, a practising doctor and aspiring psychologist who knew enough not to play one man off against another. Professionally, he managed something simi-lar, helping to coin the studio 'space concept', de-emphasizing effects and gimmickry in order to record the band exactly as it sounded live.* *Outlandos* had seemed under-produced, but here Gray struck the perfect balance between subtlety and the trio's

---

*Despite his epic work on *Reggatta*, Nigel Gray never fully reconciled to Miles Copeland's singular brand of accountancy, which withheld payment until the last possible second and went on from there to get nasty. After The Police's third album, a letter was sent to Leatherhead reminding the producer that, 'Without us, you'd still be nobody.' Gray never worked with the group again.

natural punch. The result was cutting-edge rock, and a feast of guitar, rhythm and vocals that seemed to convey far more than three men in an attic room. Its ingredients were Sting's ringing voice, Summers' innovative chorus-technique on the Fender and Copeland's fast-and-furious drums, with a frisky hi-hat. The last stretched out on several fiery workouts, covering the field from Art Blakey to John Bonham, while never descending into tub-thumping. Unfortunately, *Reggatta* also proved that Copeland was no songwriter.

The album opened with 'Message In A Bottle', the percussive bass and twangy guitar quickly working their way into the subconscious and setting up a neat foil for the yarn: in some views, an uplifting tale of human bonding, in others, an angry anthem to Sting's own angst (as in Lennon's 'Help!'). *Reggatta's* title track soared off McCartney-like bass, vocals and sheer inanity (lyric: 'Rio Rio Rioo / Rio Rio Rioo / Rio Riay Riayo'), while the grid-reference for 'It's Alright For You' was Costello via Bob Dylan. In 'Bring On The Night' and 'Walking On The Moon', turbulence gave way to Gray's less-is-more production: the one with its swirling double-tracked voice, oddly reminiscent of Leo Sayer; the other a spare, almost-too-concise vehicle for Summers' guitar chord (later filched by Brian May on Queen's 'Don't Try Suicide'), and a thematic return to the world of 'Space Oddity' and 'Rocket Man'. On 'Moon', Sting crossed a lean groove with a clipped yet upbeat vocal. Never had his singing sounded better or his writing more assured. This was most critics' favourite Police track, and Sting himself joined the consensus.

Democracy capsized the second half of the album. After a clutch of throat-grabbing, three-minute classics, Copeland went for the jocular with the witless 'On Any Other Day'. The drummer's two other tracks were leaden nadirs. Sting's salvage operation included 'The Bed's Too Big Without You' (also in Leo Sayer register) and 'Deathwish' (an almost actionable Bo Diddley lift) before sprinting to the finish with 'No Time This Time', a *Batman* steal and back-to-the-roots rave-up redolent of torn T-shirts, spiky hairdos and gobbing in the Roxy.

From its sassy logo to its landmark blue-and-silver cover, *Reggatta* was an elegantly packaged collection of lively, colliding ideas centred around Sting's voice, which reigned supreme on nine of the eleven cuts. Copeland's misfires served as ironic proof of his rival's genius. With its rich blend of rock and reggae vibes, emotional crescendos and digital-sharp production, *Reggatta* was a fully fledged global hit, making the American Top Thirty and number one in Britain. The most startling image of the year was the sight of Sting signing hundreds of copies of the album surrounded by an adoring mob in Newcastle. Several teenage girls fainted. As he told his family, all the 'blood and sweat' was worth it for this titanic coup alone.

Sting's handling of the business, no less than the actual records, was a *tour de force*, one of the great triumphs of his career. The key to his success was his deliberate ambiguity and deception. As Derek Green says, 'He was totally in charge of himself ... Bright ... Mature ... Sting liked a warm relationship, but always at a distance. He didn't want to be your best mate.' He cheerily risked becoming an object of fear and loathing. Most 'rock suits', he noted, tended to shrink from multilingual swots and know-alls. For others, the intelligent punk was but a *Guardian* leader away from the musician-who-preached. To them, Sting's self-confidence had long since crossed the frontier of bumptiousness to a less attractive conceit, the superiority complex. His cachexy on his career – what an ex-lover calls 'the "fuck-you" belief he was right' – was no shock. Sting's mother spoilt him. His father had all the motivating properties of a bomb. Whatever education this future pop god received, it equipped him with neither a flair for self-effacement, nor any idea of needing one. Sting, Nigel Gray would say, 'beat on' the other Police. Even Summers came to regard him with misgiving; Copeland with real malice. Magnanimously, he'd tried to accommodate himself to the band in the studio, even joining them for a smoke after work. But Sting soon grew tired of trying to befriend people he considered his creative inferiors. 'I'm a great singer and I know it,' he told *Melody Maker*. 'I'm a great songwriter and I know it. Largely because the competition just isn't there.' That he was great had become apparent when fans and copy-hungry hacks began to quiz him not on music but about foreign policy and strikes and Ronald Reagan. His breezy monologues became a rallying point for those who saw an epidemic among rock stars of thinking that being famous for one thing qualified them on anything else. Even in his moments of modesty and self-denial, Sting showed a healthy grasp of his potential. 'If you're in a position of great power, especially with kids, you've got to be aware of the effects of your action, positive or negative.'

Here was a new phenomenon in the punk business: a man at home in the boardrooms and corridors of power, articulate, well-read, headstrong, yet with an internal compass that kept him from drifting too far down the road to self-parody. (Sting showed marginally better sense than most peers in refusing to appear in Paula Yates's book *Rock Stars in Their Underpants*.) It was his peculiar faculty, the faculty of a brilliant but never abstract mind, to gaze at the stars and to see what was under his nose, to uncannily forecast future trends yet stay rooted in the present. His strength was to shift with the great human, moral issues of his times. Sting became one of the chief rock-music spokesmen for the radical left in the early 1980s, before age, wealth and compassion-fatigue narrowed his commitment to one or two causes. He paid a certain price for his change of heart. Having embraced Thatcherite *laissez-faire*, he came in his thirties to an absolute faith in the market, and often locked horns with those less convinced by the work ethic. Accosted backstage by a man in fatigues and Marxist insignia, brandishing a petition (signed by other luminaries, like Bob Geldof) insisting that 'a new order must be established, in which economic rivalry and private profit are barred ... and where competition will be lifted from the animal plane of acquisition to the human plane of cultural creation', Sting's reply was blunt:

'Bollocks.'

Despite the humanizing contradictions, Sting was in show-business for the same reason as anyone else – to win friends and make money. He later spoke of the thrill of 'lying in bed in a hotel in the north of England and [hearing] a window-cleaner whistle "Roxanne" ... When I realized he was singing a tune I'd written, I almost wept.' That was in June 1979. Six weeks later, surveying the upturned faces at Reading, he admitted, 'I felt like God, and I loved it.' By late August, Sting and his son were watching the Who at Wembley from seats in the royal box. Even off-duty, his day was a kind of whistlestop tour of interviews, autographs and posed photos with Joe. Not that Sting was

complaining. Unlike some of his contemporaries, he was excited
by his success: 'I asked for this.'

The very qualities of enthusiasm and ersatz charm were what
kick-started the next forward jump of his career. Having landed a
part in *Quadrophenia*, just two years after The Police's début,
Sting found a mass market with Pete Townshend's tale of
alienated seaside youth. The film quickly won cult status, and the
critics outdid themselves at the Cannes festival. Sting was singled
out for his role as the mohair-clad Mod, cutting a slick dash in
the dance-hall routines and derisively curling a lip at the
Brighton beaks. Though the climax smacked of melodramatic
contrivance, Sting and a young cast – with Phil Daniels to the
fore – gave *Quadrophenia* a gritty verisimilitude in its saga of
rock's lost innocence.

Though basically a cameo, Sting's role had several subtleties.
Was he, as he said, 'the local wide-boy'? Or was he in fact a
menial bellhop, slumming for a taste of low-life? The script,
though at times apparently run up in haste by an unholy mix of
Roddam and Graham Greene, was teasingly ambiguous. There
were real-life parallels in the schizoid Ace: Sting as the Jekyll/
Hyde figure who was more weekend warrior than pill-popping
spiv. The character veered away from the spotty, dysfunctional-
berk stereotype. Sting cascaded from great and chilly heights to
offer a memorably smug performance. Though modest about his
dramatic skills ('Looking good on screen is just a matter of
intelligence . . . I was lucky in [*Quadrophenia*] because I was in it
just long enough to create an impression, and not long enough
to blow it'), he earnt several points for deadpan cool. With his
bottle-blond hair and signature scowl, he was the pin-up of a film
that, though not causing a riot at the box office, became a staple
in art houses and video stores. In 1997 *Quadrophenia* was
re-released amidst bickering about its '15' certificate (down from
'X'), though, as usual when big budgets and egos hang in the
balance, things worked out in the end. Sting had the attention of
a new generation of fans, and they too raved about his icy
menace.

Sting followed it by appearing in Chris Petit's *Radio On*, a
visual backdrop to the music of Ian Dury, Kraftwerk and
Wreckless Eric (and, as Sting said, 'no *Ben Hur*'. It was hard not
to burst out yawning). More notable were the parts he rejected.

In the course of a few weeks he met, and turned down, Francis Ford Coppola and John Boorman, said no to the new Bond film, and snubbed *Rock Follies*. And so the refusals went on, proof of his swelling self-confidence, until the tardy release of a punk classic. In 1978, desperate for money, Sting had been cast in the Sex Pistols' *The Great Rock 'n' Roll Swindle*, playing a rapist who indulges in a deep osculation of his male victim. At the time he met *Swindle*'s director Julien Temple, he had £20 in his pocket and no acting experience whatever. To put bread on the table, Sting agreed to a script that, though flawed, didn't shy from the ugly or grotesque aspects that made the Pistols good copy. He admitted to relief when his part, including the kiss, was left putrifying on Temple's floor. Pirated outtakes from the film enjoyed wide circulation for years afterwards.

What remained, chiefly in *Quadrophenia*, was that unique mix of ice and fire. Sting's frosty charisma was rooted as much in real life as on celluloid. Nothing better shows the native grit than his exemplary behaviour under pressure. When, in 1979, skinheads disrupted a Police show and stormed the stage, Sting held his ground, raising his arms in a welcoming gesture and inviting them to sing along. They immediately fell silent. Despite being a poor flier, he was 'the one man not to freak' when the jet carrying The Police hit turbulence on a flight into New York that year. Nor, as happened in some cases, did the physical and personal strains of life on the road cause him to go to pieces. Sting was organized, alert and took a keen interest in whatever new town he happened to visit. Whether strolling through the native *souks* of Cairo or trawling the streets of Berlin, he was rarely without his camera and notebook, recording his revelatory glimpses into the 'irrational, ineradicable nature of the human soul' – insights that would fill out his lyrics. As he swung away from church-going Christianity he developed a respect for other religions, and struggled against his natural reaction to the new and bizarre.

By 1979 Sting had begun to divorce himself from his strict Jesuit upbringing, much to the dismay of his Catholic wife. For both parties, spirituality was a moral crusade. Unlike Tomelty, however, Sting refused to yoke morality to personal virtue. There were no longer any taboos: everything was possible, with the exception of staying still. Whether indulging in sex, drugs or exotic rites, Sting was in constant motion. This was welcome in creative terms, but it pulled certainty from under the feet of those who knew and loved him. There was no longer a sense of security about what it meant to be Mrs Sumner.

There were, however, rewards. On 1 August 1979 Sting and his wife became co-directors of Steerpike Limited. The company's principal activity aimed for breadth: 'to carry on business as theatrical and entertainment agents and to enter into contracts for the appearance of groups, bands, singers, orchestras, artists, dancers, actresses and actors in clubs, licensed premises, theatres, halls, places of entertainment and sporting and athletic events'; essentially, the management of Sting's royalties. In the same month The Police formed Roxanne Music, a repository for their A&M money, which shrewd accountancy converted into long-term security. Keith Moore writes of the creation of 'umbrella organizations' to deal with the receipt of joint income and to 'pay the individual's business expenditure as well as a salary, [Roxanne] retaining the liability to the Inland Revenue'. What strikes the reader is how little the structure varied from that of any hard-nosed multinational. Moore also began to consult with Sting on investment policy in 1979. 'My advice was to the effect that the first transactions should be in ultra-safe securities and that we should not embark on riskier speculations until the bed-rock had been established': another eminently sane, orthodox strategy. By decade's end, Sting was a rich man. He needed to be, and never felt himself wholly set, but by the standards of most 28-year-olds, even those in his own industry, he had little to moan of. He was wary, well managed, careful without being mean, and always did the best deals.

As well as shares, Sting had banked his film salaries and still 'modest' cheques from Virgin, not a new story for him. More promising was the royalty flow from The Police's two albums. *Outlandos* had brought the band £10,000 overnight and went on to sell a million copies. Because they settled for low advances and high returns, Sting, Copeland and Summers each made a tidy fortune from *Reggatta*. An initial investment of £6,000 in studio time was transformed, almost incredibly, into gross sales of four million. 'I get twenty pence each,' Sting told the journalist Paul Morley. 'It's a lot of money, but I haven't seen it yet. I still live in a two-room flat in Bayswater. I don't have expensive tastes. Next year I'll be rich, and that's where the rot could set in.'

It did. For all his intelligence, Sting was a man of perpetual ironies: a wide-awake self-starter who was also prone to fits of pique and promiscuous dabbling that amounted to an implosion of the will. As Richard Branson says, 'he wasn't the kind of guy to spend all afternoon in a hammock'. Almost inevitably, that kind of nervous intensity brought lapses of judgement. Money exacerbated his restlessness. Sting reacted to wealth with a spree of drugs and sex while simultaneously writing in a new vein of realism, adding the one element lacking in his first, self-centred singles: a heartbeat. Not everyone cared for the songs on *Zenyatta Mondatta*. One reviewer wrote of the 'creeping trend to sermonize' in the lyrics. It was never that hard to distinguish between Sting-on-a-roll and a vow of silence. 'Most of his rants,' says a writer who knew him, 'freed journalists of the need to be any good at their jobs. A chimp with a tape-recorder could have made copy from him.' What the critics refused to realize was that Sting learned some brand-new facts about human nature on his first tours. He observed, investigated and made notes, with the gratifying result of a 'Driven To Tears'. Sting, in short, contained the paradox of a sane man sometimes as much on the lunatic fringe as the 'twerpy punks' he came to hate. He was the Catholic ascetic who snorted cocaine off lavatory seats; the socialist whose politics lapsed into a smorgasbord of Utopian–Thatcherite drivel; the self-critic with a tongue as sharp as his suit in *Quadrophenia*. Above all, Sting was the man of deeply held irony. 'I try not to disguise the fact that I'm a home-loving, average house-husband,' he told *Melody Maker*. 'I have a child. I have a family life that is quite normal ... I don't see any point trying to promote an image of myself as a kind of rebellious playboy' – a claim he illustrated in the paper by posing with a fishnet-clad model other than his wife.

Sting was also capable, gruff, and sucked up to no one, including his friends. In September 1979 Carol Wilson and the Virgin lawyers were served with a writ alleging the firm had made 'fraudulent use of a dominant position' – a charge they denied – in their dealings with 'Mr Summer' (*sic*), claiming damages and a reversion of all copyrights.

Virgin, as Richard Branson says, 'made every effort to accommodate Sting', but were stumped. The company first offered to improve the deal to a 75–25 split in the artist's favour. This Miles Copeland refused, apparently because Virgin also asked that the term of the contract be extended. To Branson, however, it was 'hypocrisy of the worst kind by Miles, who was plainly out to sign Sting's publishing himself'. Exasperated, Virgin sent an intermediary to Leinster Square to try and bypass management channels and speak face-to-face with the man Branson calls 'the best mind in rock'. Sting lasted only five minutes before he lost his temper and stormed out, refusing to return. From there the dispute simmered for three years, at which point it boiled into the law courts.

The money was coming, *Reggatta* was selling, Virgin were on notice. Now Sting's immediate goal was to conquer America. The tour that began on 27 September 1979 took full advantage of The Police's earlier, madcap visits. Thanks to steady sales of 'Roxanne' and the rest, they already had a cult following; thirty-six dates – including a captive audience at Terminal Island prison – lifted them to true celebrity, in the peculiarly American sense of the word.

By then, the whole post-punk fold, including such mutants as Blondie and the Pretenders, had become more than a blip on the fringes of the cultural radar. In cold terms, they *were* the culture: quasi-metallic bands that dared to be tuneful, unblushingly pegged to midwestern tastes. The Police generally and Sting particularly came into similarly realized focus. Like the Beatles before them, their music was engaging enough to carry the odd dud, and reaffirmed what was likeable about them in the first place: their angular but catchy riffs, the wholesome image and, of course, the sharp – and often funny or poignant – lyrical turns.

Nineteen seventy-nine was his year, and a new, or nearly new, Sting saw it out. It was at this heady moment of his career that, buoyed by the smash of *Reggatta* and *Quadrophenia*, he made the gaffe that would haunt him for years. Informing the world, 'Given the choice of friendship or success, I'd choose success' was one thing. But Sting went too far in skewering both his family and himself, telling a friend, 'I don't much like me.' He wasn't alone in this. Sting's brother retaliated, and the uneasy sibling truce shattered. The younger Sumner's comment about 'megalomania' was obviously wide of the mark, but nonetheless expressed a certain quality people saw in Sting. There were mutterings that the raw foot-soldier of 1976 had become a 'little Adolf' just three years later: a narcissist who saw life through a fog of reflexive vanity, his stock in trade a pseudo-literacy and vicious barbs at everyone and everything not meeting his expectations.

On a material level, he could hardly have asked for a better year. The Police sold five million singles and two million albums during 1979. With the multi-platinum coup of *Reggatta*, they traded on level creative terms with the likes of Wings and Fleetwod Mac and would leave Ian Dury, ELO and Boney M in a cloud of dust. Much as the group worked on a confluence of random, mutually beneficial fads following the punk uprising, their figurehead and focal point was the man voted by *Record Mirror* 'the face of '79'. That Christmas the mainstream press squeezed themselves into a snug Police T-shirt and reported on the band's mobbed progress between two adjacent London venues in Beatle-like vernacular. One story, a cover, was head-lined STINGOLA, and a phenomenon had its name.

The following night he fought with Copeland and decided it wasn't good for them to be alone. But the truth was that he raged at everyone: at Miles, Virgin, at anyone within snarling distance, which, in Sting's case, meant several dozen yards. When rational, he began examining his behaviour, whether in wry asides or the self-confessional digs in his diary. Sting's public outbursts and personal insights seemed almost to come from two different people. In a sense they did, and in the 1980s his double life took on new poignancy. He began to speak of himself in the third person. 'I'm quite interested in finding me again,' he admitted. 'I used to be the same sort of guy on stage that I was in private life, but now it's a kind of monster.' His career read as a morality tale of mercurial rise and guilt pangs about making it; of the clash between mere ego and being treated as a god; of despair tarted up with sex and money. Sting was about to pay the levy of fame on success.

4

I Cared What You Thought of Me at Breakfast

THE YEAR-LONG ODYSSEY THAT BEGAN three weeks into the new decade was a triumph of size and revenue, as well as of musical enterprise. 'I happen to believe in the values of our western society ... I don't pretend we're perfect, but we certainly are better,' Miles Copeland told the world. He plotted The Police's itinerary through Greece and Japan, as well as such virgin rock territory as India, Egypt and Mexico, with political zeal. There was no higher office, he felt, than exercising the moral imagination necessary to mould the sentiments of the masses into the form most receptive to his global crusade. It was Miles's genius to sustain the same entrepreneurial flair guilty for the group's first, cut-price American foray – almost incredibly, just fifteen months ago – but now on undreamt-of scale. Professionally shot by the Burbidges and released on video, *Police Around the World*'s features were the routine ones of nomadic rock: fans at airports, polyglot brawls with stewards, logistics, ethnic colour, random music and the overall sense of an army on the move. Edited from the film, but obvious to those on the ground, was the gradual disintegration of Sting's character.

The circus began at the State University of New York and eventually wound down, eighteen countries later, in a tent on Tooting Common. The first American dates, in January and February 1980, stuck close to the blueprint of the previous autumn. It was never easy being a clever lyricist when few in the audience could understand, or even hear, what you were singing about. But, at his best, Sting pulled it off. Depending on Kim Turner's legerdemain and the halls' acoustics, sound quality ranged from under-amplified clutter to an empty roar. At the Showbox in Seattle, the start was delayed because the group's equipment was lost. After the Specials had sapped their two-song repertoire, Sting ran on, cued in the power chords of 'Roxanne' and gave a vulpine leer to the girls up front. A near-total absence of stage lighting only added to the intimacy. By 'Reggatta De Blanc' he no longer had to ask fans to join in; most of the crowd had already become a chorus. Stage right, Summers and Copeland were silhouettes, filmy, transient figures in the giant shadow of the star. By 'Peanuts' Sting was laughing and dancing, his head bobbing in and out of synch with the surrounding chaos. It all came together on 'Can't Stand Losing You', which jammily dissolved into a long, whooping riot of shouts, yodels and swirling bass runs. Later, Sting spent forty straight minutes signing autographs at the stage door.

From Hawaii, the group flew to Japan, Hong Kong and New Zealand, where Sting promptly lost his voice. They played dates in Australia and became the first rock band ever to work in India. The two nights at Homi Bha Bha auditorium, Bombay, were memorable not just for their novelty, nor for the occasional dark irony ('*Shit*,' spat Copeland, as amputees rushed The Police's hired Cadillac. 'Can you imagine showing your deformities to everyone?'); they also showed why Sting enjoyed a press that raised interest in the group as well as his own profile. One of his basic tenets was that 'no man can lead [without] communicating down'. He was proud of his command of the English language, photographed like a god, and knew how to tease a hack. It was 'Stingola' exquisitely controlled.

After meeting the previous August at Wembley, Sting and *NME*'s Paul Morley held their next summit at the Bombay Inter-continental Hotel. In the meantime, all The Police had cultivated the media, especially the senior names. Journalists who covered them would find themselves treated to long, in-depth theses on their music, decoded by the men who made it, the band them-selves. For all their willingness to debate melody and kinetics and polytonal arpeggios, Copeland and Summers came across essen-tially as engineers. It was Sting who used the press to send a message.

First, he flattered the messenger. ('I care about how I present myself,' he told Morley. 'Like this morning when we met, I cared very much what you thought of me at breakfast.') Next, he might engage in a show of winning, spot-on analysis. ('The *Gestalt* of the music is very simple. Three blond hairs, the macho name, albums that have a very camp title ... It's very cleverly put together. I'm quite proud of it.') Finally, Sting would deliver his mission statement, the keynote of his whole career: 'I'm a workaholic. I could never stop working. When I stop this tour it's great to be back with the wife and kid, but pretty soon I want to be back on the road again.' He would 'do anything' for the fans. Exotically illustrated by a picture of Sting in native garb, sprinkled with one-liners and acid, epigrammatic barbs on rock, he used the interview to smoothly ram home his dominance of the group. Both Copeland and Summers, notwithstanding their own good looks, could just as easily have adorned a story about professional footballers. Only Sting knew instinctively what to say and how to say it, when to pout and when to frown, why to seduce Morley, and the *NME* editor, like other editors in future, could scarcely avoid giving him the acreage he craved.

As the year and the tour wore on, The Police became evangelists for anarchic, feelgood pop, even if fuelled by economics, not a moral fit. Marketing became a kind of vocation with them. Every town and every outpost eventually fell to their drive to nudge both themselves and their fans into new audio playgrounds. In cities like Bombay and Cairo, logistical blunders gave way to the general feel of hip young explorers throwing a rave for themselves. Bobbing, weaving, hip-thrusting, Travlota-stepping – and playing great songs – Sting was the fleshly god to a vast Third World province: his subjects responded like dogs fresh from the leash. It was the end of civilization as their cultures knew it, and they seemed to feel fine about it.

The Police were conquering the world. And all the time they were doing it they were at war among themselves. Copeland's characterization of his feelings contains a good deal of truth. Sting 'wasn't a scumbag', but that was the perception. More than ever, he was a being apart from the others, on terms of cordial loathing with his drummer, civil to Summers and Kim Turner, his twin defences a Nikon and a minder named Larry Burnett, his hobby whatever shapely female killed the time between gigs.

It was the bunker syndrome: everyone around him was clicking their heels, the saluting guards had highly polished boots and beautifully creased uniforms. But as a rational human being Sting was disintegrating. He was prone to black moods, especially with those who encroached on his time and good nature. He embraced the dark, literally, rising at noon and going to bed towards dawn. For the first time, drink and drugs became his constant companions, his most loyal friends. He later admitted to being 'catatonically depressed' throughout the year.

One man was fully alive to the differences between the old Sting and the new. Andy Partridge, of XTC, had been one of the first, unrecognized sources of 'reggatta de blanc' – his dub version of 'All Along The Watchtower' virtually invented the style – as well as the author of three albums and a hit single. Now XTC, merely by opening for The Police, illustrated that cults of their day would inevitably become grist for the ironic patronage of those who followed. Partridge remembers the tour fondly:

> We all shared the proverbial bus. Even offstage, Sting was the tough guy: he used to humiliate you at backgammon and come up with surreal words in Scrabble – 'Iqba' – that he dared you to challenge. He was an odd mix, half school-bully and half crippled by shyness. Before gigs he'd get dressed up in overalls and a fake beard and wander around stage, just to get used to the audience: it was either professionalism or stage-fright on an epic scale. He could freeze you out with that leonine stare [as when Sting asked what The Police should call their next album and Partridge suggested 'Yet More Of The Same-a' or 'Get Yer Yo Yo's Out'] or come across as an affable, fun-loving bloke. On the last night in America I walked on in The Police's set, sprayed Sting with foam and pretended to shave him. He loved it. I'll say this for him – in the right mood, he could give a stunning performance as your best mate. I actually liked him.

Partridge also notes that Sting and Copeland fought 'wildly' on tour, with Summers either in the intermediary role or 'totally shtum'.

After riots in Italy, Spain, Germany and the Low Countries,

The Police played nostalgic shows at Newcastle City Hall. There was a note of festive homecoming as Sting walked on, to full-blooded roars that turned to quizzical shrugs, and dedicated 'The Bed's Too Big Without You' (gasped, rather than sung, in the chorus) 'to the ghost of Roland Barthes'. He went on from there to deflate his self-importance and deliver the expected package of anthemic punk, old–fangled pop and lilting reggae beats. The whole event raised tens of thousands of pounds for charity. Jeff Griffin, who recorded both shows, recalls them as a triumph. Yet it was a strangely hollow victory. Although Sting held a large party afterwards, he was never mobbed. He'd alienated too many people, spoken too freely of the failings both of those who trusted him and his whole Newcastle life. His old cronies had admired him for his songwriting, his persistence and his pop savvy, and still did; but his put-downs and mythologizing in the press left a legacy of shock and horror. Sting's later psychological goal was to relieve these stresses with a burst of frantic bonhomie. Softened and trained by long years of Jungian analysis, he was the master therapist of the friends he left behind.

Aside from Newcastle and the unrepeatable mayhem of Bombay, the year's most memorable night was in late July, in Milton Keynes. The Police halted work on their third album to headline the one-off 'Rockatta de Bowl' in front of 40,000 fans. Unlike other, botched efforts to play outdoors, the lighting and sound quality were both meticulous. The sight-lines were exemplary and nobody needed binoculars. Sting appeared with a new toy, an upright bass he named Brian, and ran through a relentlessly upbeat set, convivially mixing the old with new tracks from the studio. Fans screamed as the band kicked off 'Walking On The Moon', hitting its riff simultaneously with two zaps of white light from the twin PA towers. That one track alone made up for the reflexive-Teutonic gloom of the words 'Here's one off the new record.' For the main, the band eschewed stage effects in favour of straight-ahead, joyous stomps and mutual horseplay with the crowd. With an authentic festival atmosphere and the euphoric singalongs of the best tunes, the event billed as 'the greatest party of the year' nearly lived up to the hype.

Predictably, there was a backlash. In India, Miles had spoken of his belief in the values of 'our western society'. In practice, that meant not only exporting capitalism to foreign markets, but milking his star turn in a way that would have made Colonel Parker blush. There were murmurings and near-mutiny among the photographers at Milton Keynes when Miles insisted they each sign a contract waiving copyright of their pictures of the group. The print media (whose hastily built shanty collapsed in the mud before the first chord) responded in kind. Here the complaint was that the band, though rabidly successful, seemed not to be going anywhere. The very formula that brought the crowds both infuriated the purists and narked new-wavers. For *NME*, 'They left me utterly cold, and yet I'm not unhappy to see The Police where they are – they're unique and sharp and original, and their frontman projects a humane, responsible kind of stardom, demonstrating his total control of the event with an admirable assurance. All the same, during those leisurely, strung-out tunes, I could feel my concentration wandering, to be shortly followed by my feet. It was no place for the undevoted.' To *Sounds*, a torch-bearer for The Police in 1977, it was 'a reliable if not electrifying performance'.

A fortnight later they were back in Europe, whistlestopping through France until they came to the bull-ring in Fréjus. Here Sting showed his competitive, creative and aggressive edges in the space of a few hours. On arrival he visited the town's Roman ruins, which he deemed 'crap' compared to the fort at Wallsend – forgivable, but churlish, given the trouble to which his host had gone. Waiting to go on stage, Sting then called for a double bass to be sent to the dressing-room. Where other musicians might have passed the time in endlessly varied combinations of sex and drugs, Sting began to strum. Within five minutes he'd written the basic riffs for two tracks on what became *Ghost in the Machine*. Within ten more he was threatening to 'rip the fucking arms off' a fan who tactlessly offered him a drink by heaving a wine bottle at his feet.

He ended the year in North and South America, urging the one '*not* to vote for Ray-gun' and blanching at real political oppression in the other. On 17 December The Police left Argentina for London. There they played on Tooting Common using an arena-sized tent which, as with press facilities at Milton Keynes, was both structurally suspect and cramped. As before, the media retaliated. 'Just because The Police were in India,' rumbled *NME*, 'there was no reason to turn the tent into a simulacrum of the Black Hole of Calcutta.' On that note, after a curtain-call at Bingley Hall, Stafford, the world tour ended.

As well as jetting around the globe, writing and playing massive hits and rapidly becoming tabloid fodder, Sting launched his own charity; gave money to causes from music therapy to Amnesty; jammed with old friends like Chelsea and Jack Bruce; recorded and released *Zenyatta Mondatta*; and left Bayswater for homes in Hampstead and the west coast of Ireland. A small empire of companies controlled by Keith Moore – Illegal, Steerpike, Roxanne Music, Roxanne Music (Tours), Roxanne Music (Overseas) and the evocatively named Megalo Music – all shielded him from excessive tax. In cash and property, Sting was over a million pounds richer than when the year began.

The other thing he got from the tour was a practical insight to go with his theoretical knowledge of the world. Sting was repeatedly astonished, even astounded, by what he saw. Bombay he quite aptly described as 'flabbergasting'. He now realized that American political conservatism 'reflected abysmal ignorance' among the public. The sight of baton-wielding police in Buenos Aires was one 'burnt into [his] skull'. In an ill-advised lark Sting had told a reporter before flying to Tokyo, 'We'll be able to find some interesting ethnic music to rip off.' He meant it as a joke, but there was no denying the tour's effect on the bleak drone mesh of his early lyrics. From *Zenyatta* on, almost all his songs became variations of psychoanalytical broodings on life. Self-obsessed tales of broken love gave way to richer, darker topics beyond the superficial workaday world. It was 'protest' music, but with a solid refusal to preach. Like the best of the original bluesmen's, Sting's words rose and dipped in intensity, and never lost the simple joys of narrative to surrealism. The man leaving England in January 1980 was a gifted popsmith and lyricist. The one returning eleven months later was, in his touching on universal themes, an artist.

Paradoxically, Sting also went quietly mad while on the road. His self-portrayal as 'a monster' was no fictionalized rendering but a direct observation of his double-dealing, conceit and raging ego. Not coincidentally, he drifted further apart from his wife, who, though glimpsed on a few European and Latin American dates, chose her old life as an actress. (Tomelty starred alongside Peter O'Toole in the Old Vic's notorious 1980 production of

Macbeth.) After four and a half years of marriage and four of fatherhood, and after talking for endless hours of his wife and son while on tour, Sting still had a hard time either accepting or grasping his role in the family. A friend compares him to 'a castaway sitting on an island, shrieking to be rescued, who after an hour in civilization would be pleading to get back to the island. He never made up his mind whether he was Gordon Sumner made good, or a rich and randy rock star.' After a year's globetrotting he must at least have known that the fabric of life as husband and wife had been torn apart, and there was no way to stitch it up again.

The gradual breakdown and the unreality of his life on the road were defining events for Sting. They profoundly affected his attitude towards the old friends who still, bizarrely, kept in touch, reducing him to childlike dependence on his entourage at a time when he might have exerted the full powers of a mature artist. It was never a question of Sting slumping slack-jawed while minions came and went bearing drugs, pizzas and comic books. He did, though, throw himself wholeheartedly into the fame machine. Responsibility for day-to-day marketing of Sting's wares – his public image – fell squarely on Miles Copeland. It's been said to Miles's credit that he was prepared to oversee parts of his clients' lives which other managers tended to avoid; it can also be said that he exploited his talent more than another man might have had the gall to. Starting with 'Roxanne', three Police singles were reissued as pricey badge-shaped discs, and numerous other satellite goods launched, the first salvo in a strategic year-long blitz that would make 'Sting', like Warhol before it, a virtual brand name. Even he would object to the spurious *Six Pack* anthology concocted by Miles in May 1980. This singles box, accompanied by dubious curios and pressed up on blue vinyl, was widely panned as a limp retread of old glories, a recycling normally reserved for bands in their second or third decade. 'A rip-off' was the *Sounds* verdict.

Miles had already alienated much of the music press by his tight-wad tactics at Milton Keynes. By late 1980 he'd also fallen out with Nigel Gray, thousands of fans riled by *Six Pack*, most of his suppliers, sundry car-hire firms, hotels and stores, and even a Hong Kong tailor who threatened to sue over a bill. For his slavish trust in Miles, Sting's reward would be to see his name ruthlessly worked to the public, whether on vinyl or a plague of merchandising. With a knack for persuasion amounting to hypnosis, Miles reached the hearts, minds and yawning wallets of fans of all races and climes. Naturally endowed with 'front', clarity of thought and lucidity of expression, he developed these gifts by indefatigable trial and error until he became a master of the dark arts of salesmanship. In sum, he made Sting a star. The negative side of his crusade was that Miles asserted himself as a moral equivalent of Larry Burnett, a brick wall between his client and the world. Sting's public persona was all too often warped by his manager's, and because of it he was tarred by association. It was a mixed blessing.

On the surface, at least, his career was making a meteoric up-hill curve. Sting's singles and albums were in the charts around the world. Night after night, thousands bawled his name, and through TV and the Burbidges' videos millions more knew the sound and look of The Police. Not everyone claimed to like the band, but everyone began to talk about them.

It was, above all, the physicality of the group. The two vertical players illustrated the act by a non-stop frenzy of squats, thrusts and karate-style jerks; seated, Copeland was among the most ferally exciting men in rock. As a group, they were a landmark in matching music and motion. Sting's sinewy body language – the low, predatory crouch and the writhing with which he under-lined a particularly tart riff – was spice for the main meal: the chorus of soaring vocals that lost none of their studio fire or force live. Between bouts of laryngitis, Sting's voice was still the lush, vibrant organ of 'Roxanne', sounding as if it had been stewing in port since the days of Sam Cooke and Smokey Robinson. Never have two octaves been better mined. Amazingly, despite the calisthenics, he still had the one thing a singer needs most – breath. Other musicians, like Eric Clapton, give endless examples lauding his control as a vocalist, never straining for the top notes even after jigging through a solo. It came, in part, from his years as a local track star, just as his stage persona followed his life as a teacher. Sting agreed that his time at St Paul's had given him the three key ingredients: 'Learning to stand up in front of people and not be an arsehole, although I might seem like one . . . Self-confidence . . . Entertainment.'

Sting liked to play, but writing was his *métier*. And once he learnt how to weld the classic I-VI-IV-V chord sequence to a telling lyric, he shrewdly guessed that he could 'have [his] finger on the pulse of a nation for a few weeks, and literally have everyone whistling my song'. This, he'd explain, was the result of an 'epic bloody apprenticeship'. Someone once asked him how long it took him to write a three-minute hit. 'About twenty years', he deadpanned. Actually the process could take as little as an hour. As with all tunesmiths, certain songs seemed to 'happen'; a riff or a groove wasn't reached – it came. Sting wrote 'Walking On The Moon' after waking up from a schnapps binge during a visit to Eberhard Schoener in January 1979. In an effort to clear his head he began pacing the floor, humming and muttering, 'Walking round the room ... I hope my legs don't break ... walking round the room.' Summers' guitar bolt and a rhyming dictionary teased the idea into a hit. More typically, Sting would sit either with a synthesizer or his new Ibanel bass, writing, he said, 'backwards ... building a song around a hook rather than starting from A and working to Z'. The process was hard learned. For most of the 1970s Sting had been filling up memo pads and diaries with song notes. 'Scrawling, always scrawling,' a friend recalls. Even after playing a show he was apt to indulge his greedy, sensual enjoyment of his art. Midnight would find him slumped at the piano with a metronome, jotting lyrics and noodling melodies that others translated in the studio. Summers would remember that Sting 'didn't like to use a big formal system'; or radically hone his first drafts. A second musician believes that 'at least two or three of the smashes would have been stillborn without the engineers'. Some of Sting's best songs emerged in the world premature, before being rushed to Nigel Gray like a sickly child to the incubator.

Until *Zenyatta*, Sting's first source material was books ('Exposure to literature is one of the mainstays of my life – I read all the time'), low-life pleasures (as when he trawled the Pigalle district or 'checked out' King's Cross in Sydney) and, as a given, his own pain ('Loneliness hits me a lot. I glory in it'). Essentially, the formula was a familiar one: a miserable life made for great art. Pragmatism ruled supreme. When a blow fell 'you just got on with it,' said Sting (avoiding the use of 'I', which would make the statement too personal). Thus with the end of his marriage he'd return to the self-referential mood on *Synchronicity*. In the meantime, *Zenyatta* (1980) and *Ghost in the Machine* (1981) flowed on interior musings, Jungian at the edges, like man's insular nature and the need to rehumanize. However worthy itself to trade up to adult themes, Sting's major feat was to rationalize the creative process as a necessarily random affair. 'If you're trying to be original, you can't come up with a brilliant idea every day,' he said in 1981. 'I used to go through months and months of paranoia about it, but the more you worry about it the worse it gets.'

Once the words squared with the music, Sting worked at wild pace. He recorded his vocals at a gallop and demanded similar haste from the sidemen. *Reggatta* had passed in a blur. *Zenyatta's* 'Driven To Tears' took on quite literal meaning after a dig at Summers' flubbed guitar solo. Sting rode himself hard, as he always had. Even with time and money on his hands, he kept pressing to a clean, professional finish. According to Nigel Gray's successor, 'whenever we agreed to a day off, by six in the evening Sting would be back in the studio, bored with relaxing and wanting to work'. Philosophically, he regarded his efforts as self-serving, even if strategically yoked to the group. 'I'm out for myself and the other two know it,' he revealed. 'As soon as the band is no longer useful for my career I'll drop it like a stone.'

That the formula worked was shown not only by The Police's unprecedented success (their three albums spent a total of 116 weeks in the chart in 1980), but by the tetchiness of those in the new-wave fraternity. In their view Sting, an admittedly raw talent, had betrayed his musical ideals, as if by becoming so popular, and thus by inference 'copping out', he'd in some way impoverished his gifts. This was a theory heard often in *NME*, where the Smiths' Morrissey trashed *Zenyatta* as 'a great big sloppy bowl of mush'. Another sure sign that The Police had ceased to be a band and become a phenomenon was the number of sound-alikes suddenly staking a claim to their turf. The Australian group Men At Work were a clever parody. Others were mere clones.

Sting's professional motives were mixed, if not confused. The creative urge bulked large. According to one of The Police's producers, 'the tunes would just fly out of him'. Hundreds of songs went down on tape, some clunky and monotonous, others smash hits waiting to happen. The need for money was another factor: money for Sting, but also for 'the industry that's appeared suddenly around us', as he put it: the vast apparatus of managers, accountants, lawyers, agents and road crew, not to mention record tycoons, who banked on The Police.

By spring of 1980 the band were tax exiles. One result was that, for the next few years, Sting enjoyed the lifestyle of an Irish rack-rent, looking out over his estate towards Galway Bay when not living in the world's best hotels. Another was that The Police moved from Surrey Sound and worked exclusively in studios beyond the pale of the Inland Revenue. In July 1980 they convened in Hilversum, south of Amsterdam, where, in a month of insanely tight deadlines, wedged between tour dates, they recorded *Zenyatta Mondatta*. The album sounded strained, partly because it often was. As well as his responsibility to his own sub-industry, several of Sting's relationships, notably with Tomelty and Nigel Gray, were falling apart. Under the circumstances, it was odd that he produced an album at all, let alone one as catchy, if flawed, as *Zenyatta*.

The name (etched on the cover under Sting's immaculate, Mount Rushmore profile) came from the Sanskrit for 'top of the world'. His natural talent for pomposity was, in truth, no more than the band's literal due, though the title and *Zenyatta*'s lyrics were ironic jabs at worldly success: there was metaphor in Sting's madness. The music, too, followed down a line from *Reggatta*, whose fare would be reheated time and again, but the victory was never just one of formula. *Zenyatta* wasn't merely a good album, but something more – a collision of varied styles, a test of the compatibility and strength of diverse noises. At base, it marked a first step away from reggae and roll towards a slick, if oddly bland, sound Sting would profitably explore in future.

The songs still reigned supreme in the realm between pop and new wave. It was just that this time round, Sting decided to push an agenda as well as boundaries. Basically, *Zenyatta*'s lyrics were elliptical and world-weary instead of linear and self-absorbed, though Sting still dabbled in autobiographical plots such as 'Don't Stand So Close To Me'. On one level *Lolita* with a back-beat, on another a flashback of life at St Paul's, the storyline (hammed up in the Burbidges' video) was about the forbidden love of a teacher for a teenage girl. The song baited the listener with a low drone and Summers' guitar-tuning, then slowly turned anthemic, climaxing with a Wings-like pop chorus. 'Don't Stand' was a megahit on both sides of the Atlantic.

On 'Driven To Tears', Sting moved from a cosy, conversational tone to a bitter critique of Third World poverty. That he included himself in the rock-and-roll-call of those shirking responsibilities was heard in the lines: 'Hide my face in my hands, shame wells in my throat / My comf'table existence is reduced to a shallow, meaningless party' – though Sting's guilt, at this stage, fell short of direct action. 'When The World Is Running Down, You Make The Best Of What's Still Around' (neatly cannibalizing 'Bring On The Night') showed both Stings, the spry social critic and the egomaniac: the idea was that he was the sole survivor of a holocaust with all his favourite things still intact. As usual, the music was engaging enough to carry the conceit.

Elsewhere, *Zenyatta* ranged from the expertly harmonized ('Canary In A Coalmine') and hardcore ('Bombs Away' – in which Summers hit the sweet spot on the Fender), to the languid groove of 'Voices Inside My Head'. The second single, 'De Do Do Do, De Da Da Da', as well as boasting one of pop's silliest titles (in the school of 'Da Do Ron Ron' and 'Doo Wah Diddy'), also contained some seriously inept rhymes: a juicy chorus that meshed Copeland's sledgehammer drums to jangly guitar made it a hit. Summers' 'Behind My Camel' won a Grammy for best instrumental performance which even its author disowned. 'Man In A Suitcase' was Sting's self-centred but sly take on life on the road. Copeland's tuneless 'The Other Way Of Stopping', a jam with minimal aim and no point, was engineered by Gray into a three-minute filler.

The only real problem with *Zenyatta* were the compromises between The Police's three house styles. Competition for song-writing credits, and thus a slice of publishing action, meant that the album was mired in cheesy guitar and drum workouts that sounded ominously like soundtracks.* Where Sting took centre stage, the music was better than it had any right to be: energetic, moody, fuelled by the carnal–spiritual tug-of-war in the lyrics

---

*Nigel Gray also fought for a share of the all-important 'points' from *Zenyatta*. Sting and Miles Copeland turned him down. The producer left, under a barrage of threatened writs, and fell into steady debt until he sold Surrey Sound in 1987.

and the sleek vocals. Despite critical lumps and snide comments from the band itself, *Zenyatta* was subsequently discovered as a classic, high intelligence applied to low art. It made number one in the British chart.

After the tented fiasco in Tooting, Sting spent Christmas Day 1980 jogging with Larry Burnett before joining Tomelty and Joe for a rare meal together at home. Though he was unstinting in the time he lavished on The Police, he still made an absentee's hash of relating to his family. Sting was also driven by his hatred for his own childhood and for the idea of childhood most adults have. He was a generous and, within the vast realm of it, 'good' father; but his generosity lay in treats and elaborate gifts rather than the daily trivia of Joe's welfare. Visitors to Hampstead would speak of a congenial but strangely formal atmosphere, as if the home were a family hotel of which Sting was manager. According to one Wallsend friend, 'as head of the house, he was either gone, knackered, or just gone. What Gordon hated most about himself was what he hated about Newcastle, the blue-collar cringing, the petty morals, that whole Victorian bit. He was hellbent on not becoming like Ernie.' Paternally, Sting was a boy who never went home. As a symbolic break, both his son and wife were asked to call him by his stage name.

What Tomelty objected to were the very qualities of icy self-containment that thrilled others. She'd been insufferably loyal for unconscionably long to a man who couldn't bear to be in anyone's debt – not even a woman's. In spite of her own career, she'd nearly always been there. Tough, discreet, unselfish, cool, a good organizer, Tomelty had scored consistently highly as both mother and father to Joe. Though she enjoyed saying 'we' about herself and Sting, she wasn't proprietorial. She did things her way. But renewed self-confidence in her life as an actress made her more demanding in her relationship with Sting. When he belittled her by saying, 'Jesus Christ, I feel lonely making love to my wife', she wasn't inclined to smile pliantly. By the end of 1980 Tomelty was at the end of her long rope. The same friend recalls a day when 'Gordon and Frances sat in the lounge, both gazing up into the sky', unable, apparently, to find common ground. By the time Sting flew to America early in January, there was no longer any pretence about his pattern of scheduled promiscuity. There were literally dozens of lovers on the road, 'always discreet, but always visible' to a man like Andy Partridge. With Tomelty on the far side of the Atlantic, Sting was free to split leisure and domesticity between groupies and wife. He was lucky to keep hold of a woman who still made herself available whenever he needed her, though he was mostly unavailable in turn. Sting, says the Newcastle friend, 'would stay put, if not faithful, till there was a flesh-and-blood choice on the scene'. She emerged in 1982.

When The Police announced that they planned to play Madison Square Garden in New York, some of the fans and most of the press were cynical. American pop critics, no less and perhaps even more than the British, had trouble fitting the band's work into familiar categories rigidly fixed by new-wavers and rockers, from the Sex Pistols to Pink Floyd, the Clash to Springsteen. This mental confusion, and the shock of novelty, led to sneers that the band's reach had exceeded their grasp. In the event the venue sold out in two days. All went well on the night until the third number, when a fan buried a bottle of vodka in Copeland's drums. While repairs were made, Sting came forward to the lip. 'A real supergroup would go off at this point. We three arseholes just stand here,' he quipped, before leading the crowd in an off-key rendition of 'The Yellow Rose of Texas'.* It got just the ripple he seemed to be after.

Next day The Police played to an overflow audience in a nightclub. Sting then recorded Bob Dylan's 'I Shall Be Released', the theme for a TV film called *Parole*. Philosophically, if not musically, he followed in a line from Dylan, Woody Guthrie and Pete Seeger. He was the most receptive and acquisitive of rock stars, and made his own those human-rights causes which garnished his radical views. Sting made it a point to go to Amnesty meetings in dingy church halls instead of sending money in the customary pose of regal hauteur. A small act in itself, it gave a sense of concern and direct participation that was never allowed to die. It took a man of staggering self-possession to be simultaneously the rabble-rousing stage idol and a social worker. Sting's altruism showed the paradox at the core of his double life. From 1980 he was regularly involved in projects for other

---

*Sting, too, had worried about the scale of the New York show, and told Ian Copeland he wanted to 'humanize' the event. He did.

people's benefit. He worked just as hard when there was no chance of profit as when there was. Sting, as he said, believed that 'there's a purpose in the universe'; identified his own purpose with it, and made the achievement of that purpose an act, not of self-sacrifice for himself, but of self-realization. Hence his activism.

From New York The Police criss-crossed America until California. The guarantee of the Burbidges' cameras added to the gaudy spectacle at the Los Angeles Arts Theatre. Everyone that night, including the crowd, the press, the road crew, the MC Jools Holland and even Miles were issued with ratty blond wigs. It was a novel form of self-parody. As usual, Sting (whose own hairpiece was black) was the ringmaster of the circus, flicking out his tongue and jerkily pumping his arms like an evil troll marionette. The tour then headed through Japan, New Zealand and Australia. Somewhere over Perth, The Police learned that 'Reggatta De Blanc', recorded in an era of almost archaic remoteness two years before, had won a Grammy. With heroic audacity, even their duff songs were winning fans and influencing people. Thoroughly bemused, they returned for dates in Europe.

Friends weren't optimistic about the trip. They found Sting near clinically depressed, partly through fatigue, domestic problems and too many drugs. It was clear that he'd have to make some kind of change, and Tomelty urged him to take the summer off. She worried that he was close to a breakdown; it only confirmed her suspicion when, a short time later, the band cancelled their British shows. It had been two and a half years since the first American tour and nearly two since fame struck. Sting was worn out and, as usual when under stress, had trouble with his voice. He self-diagnosed cancer. He was examined by a specialist in London. The x-rays showed swollen nodes but no tumour. Sting remained unconvinced; it became part of his martyrdom.

Amazingly, as Sting had moments of startling insight into the flash-burnout cycle of most rockers, he failed to realize that his analysis of others read like a computer printout of his own symptoms. He never resolved his ambivalent feelings about the paired universe of his childhood, the unsatisfactory marriage of the Catholic woman and the man who was treated like a god. His anxiety gave rise to the brutal demands he made on himself – his pursuit of fame, his manic work ethic. In the early months of 1981, even as he trotted the globe, Sting weighed five Hollywood offers, including the villain's role in *For Your Eyes Only*. Eventually he settled on a BBC telefilm called *Artemis 81*. Principal photography began in the Midlands on 1 March.

The job came at a chronic time. He and Tomelty had all but split and The Police pressure-gauge showed red. The band were at meltdown. In need of change, and probably flattered by the proposal, Sting took only days to agree to *Artemis*. He settled for the standard BBC fee, £1,000. In keeping with other pop deities like Jagger and Bowie, whose CVs he studied, he'd basically worked himself to a standstill after three years. Straight, but creatively painless acting gave him a chance to regroup and, not incidentally, wring plaudits from the heavyweight press. *Artemis* employed him and legitimized him. It did not, however, do much for his mental health.

Sting, at first excited by the script, soon began to see signs of implausibility: cod-classical plot twists; druidical costumes; the bizarre contrivance of his own role as Helith, Angel of Love, whose fate was to save the world from the evil power of a stolen relic. The part had all the Hellenic credibility of a cartoon. Nor did Sting ever rumple his robes in order to find a joke in the folds. On one of his first day's filming, he was standing in the rain for hours in a disused quarry with the director alternately shouting 'Less!' and 'More!' and technicians fixing scenery so skimpily constructed that a whole set once crashed around him. The shoot itself was a remorseless and self-flagellating slog. 'A balls-up' was Sting's own confidential description of the project. Within a week he was home in Ireland before surrendering to location work in Denmark, Suffolk, Birmingham and north Wales later in the spring.

Most highbrow scorn of *Quadrophenia* was shattered by *Artemis*, the soupy and freewheeling surrealism of which was exactly to the taste of papers like the *Guardian* and *Observer*. Others felt the script's follies and the alien landscapes worked against audience involvement. Sting himself looked suitably angelic but failed to flesh out an underwritten role. The film's downward spiral into accidental comedy was the blunt instrument which the tabloids used to bash *Artemis*. The sub-*Star Wars* plot was, they said, overheated, but Sting's mere presence offered its own rewards. His all-white get-up and albino hair achieved a stark visual impact: the dazzle was more eloquent than the words. For one critic, Sting brought Helith a physical charm that 'neither offset the film's flaws nor insulted his own intelligence'. *Artemis* just barely worked as the breathing space he needed.

Throughout the early summer, Sting was drafting songs under a management-imposed deadline and on money from the platinum-selling *Zenyatta*. He promised Miles an album's worth of material by early June. As well as writing, he was reading (Arthur Koestler's work would surface in his new lyrics), using cocaine and enjoying a varied life apart from Tomelty. With his smoky voice and feline good looks, not to say his worldwide fame, he was a fixture on the social A-list, a rock aristocrat who, says one hostess, 'mingled as easily with us in the Ritz as with the minder taking him there'. His only outer show of stress was in his periodic though undiagnosed illnesses. Audrey Sumner had always been fussy about her elder son's health. She pampered him and at the slightest sign of a cold kept him home from school. Sting, who had a tendency to hypochondria in later years, learnt the tactical value of ill health at his mother's knee.

From the tone of their wranglings after *Zenyatta*, it was clear that Sting and Miles Copeland on one side and Nigel Gray on the other would never work together again. Over the winter of 1980–81, a number of new producers were sounded. Finally, on a tip-off from Andy Partridge, Sting hired Hugh Padgham, whose collaboration with Phil Collins, *Face Value*, was about to enjoy an unbroken run of 270 weeks in the chart. On 15 June, The Police and their court arrived at George Martin's studio on the island of Montserrat. It was a stunning realization of Sting's adolescent fantasy of living in the Caribbean. Every evening he walked on the beach under skies streaked with red and purple, eating *al fresco* before settling in to twelve hours' solid work. As dawn came he might jog up the coastline with Larry Burnett or drive into Plymouth to comb the local market for records, books, clothes, cheap jewellery and native bric-à-brac. He slept in the best hotel.

At the outset Sting urged that the band 'wing it in and out of the studio', but he proved sadly inept at doing so himself. Despite the toney facilities, lush surroundings and visiting glitterati, there was trouble in paradise. He later recalled the scene as something other than the hoped-for tropical idyll: 'Very horrible. Very dark. Miserable. Our marriages were breaking up, [The Police's] marriage was breaking up, and yet we had to make another record.' Effectively, Sting managed the rare feat of combining a work trip and a guilt trip. Personally and creatively, it was, he said, 'a nightmare'.

Financially, Sting was in full revolt against everything his socialist and egalitarian politics stood for. He saw it himself. 'You have to stay hungry at the same time as you've earned a fortune,' he said. By 1981 he'd describe balancing his various accounts as 'not maths [but] astronomy'. With a hit album on both sides of the Atlantic, steady sales in the Far East and his performance fees and merchandising, Sting was a seriously rich man. By most estimates, The Police were earning upwards of £5 million a year: fortunately – or unfortunately – their accountant, Keith Moore, managed to create a Byzantine portfolio of stocks, shares and domestic and foreign bank accounts on their behalf, in so doing setting up a mutually dependent link between himself and the band. As he says today, 'At an early stage The Police determined they didn't want Miles involved in the administration of their business or personal affairs, nor in the receipt of their income. I encouraged this spirit of independence . . . Over time I was, for the most part, the means of communication between the group.'

It was the beginning of a decade-long boom-to-bust cycle in which Moore opened some seventy accounts in Sting's name,* primarily at Coutts, with other funds on hold in New York and Los Angeles. With the healthy cash flow from *Reggatta*, they began to invest in property. Sting left Bayswater and took up full-time residence in his fame. His home at 108 Frognal, Hampstead, was modest in comparison with other rockers' mansions, though it became the scene of continuous and costly renovation. The décor was more exotic, the shag pile deeper and the lighting more arty, but the house retained the same vampire's-lair look of Leinster Square. There was a bookcase, a Teac tape deck, a toy toucan and children's mobiles swinging from the ceiling, but,

---

*The figure of 108 accounts given in the press was, claims Moore, put forward 'in order to attempt to demonstrate how difficult it was for Sting to keep his "finger on the pulse".'

apart from the framed photographs of Sting, nothing that gave it a human touch. In the two years in which he visited the home, a family friend never once saw the curtains open.

Sting also spent £60,000 to buy a three-storey, whitewashed villa on the far west coast of Galway. It was an isolated spot, and the local village of Roundstone boasted only four pubs, two artists' garrets and a post office unaccountably filled with pots of shrimp. The estate itself was surrounded by Roundstone bog and the uncompromising bulk of Errisbeg mountain. Sting made his home there for eighteen months, less than one of which he spent under its roof. One evening in March 1982, drained from yet another tour and about to go to war with Virgin, he walked into the largest of the pubs. In virtually all of the several versions of what followed, the atmosphere is pictured as edgy, much like a stranger's arrival on the scene in an old Western. There was little to break down the starchiness of the occasion but beer. After a second or third drink Sting tried to leaven the tension with a few jokes, which fell flat. He then offered to buy a round for the house. At that stage a man approached and asked for 'a minute of your fine life'. The two stood out of earshot in a corner of the bar. Whatever the man said in the allotted time, it was enough to persuade Sting to leave Ireland for ever. Most accounts agree that the warning was along the lines of a veiled threat against the Sumner family. It may have been followed up by an anonymous letter. The house was quickly sold to a local businessman, another milestone down the road of Sting's mental crack-up, and thus, of his marriage.

Sting's numerous companies also engrossed him, though their day-to-day administration fell on his accountant. They conferred on broad strategy, but the initiative was all Moore's. By 1980 Steerpike, Sting's nominee firm with Tomelty, was turning over hundreds of thousands of pounds annually in royalties and ancillary rights. Roxanne Music administered joint Police revenue. And on 14 March 1980 Sting became a director of Roxanne Music (Tours), a receptacle for performance fees from Miles's exotically bold plan for world domination.

A year later, on 16 March 1981, a property company named Letoll became Magnetic Publishing Limited, channelling lucrative songwriting money to Copeland and Summers. Even though he was sacrificing part of his own cash by agreeing to the set-up,

Sting went along. Three successful albums (and the three individuals' natural competitiveness) had inevitably sparked a duel for royalties. Magnetic was an attempt, as Sting later put it, 'to keep the band together by giving a portion of my publishing away . . . Everybody wanted to be a songwriter.' As late as 1992, the company was turning over close to £4 million yearly and earning a gross profit of £100,000. For fans who wondered what the fuss was about inside The Police, Magnetic's books held the answer.

Since he was still taking the lion's share of the action, and it was unlikely that his net income would ever fall below £1 million annually, Sting's gesture was both safe and shrewd. It was also vital. The situation was particularly dire with Copeland, who more than once threatened to decamp over the well-worn 'musical differences'. The compromise scheme worked, though at the cumulative cost of fanning stress between the group. Magnetic's inevitable result was that, over time, Sting's peers became his slaves. His magnanimity was in thrall to his conscience, but also in the service of industrial relations. The end of the one-for-all band ethic was part of the repeating drama Sting enacted later in his career. From the mid-1980s on, musicians were his employees, generously treated but subject to hiring or firing like any paid help. Sometimes he stated his reasons for sacking a colleague, sometimes he didn't, but usually the less intimate friends were given an explanation of why they were being banished. One man was accused of 'bringing back bad vibes'. Evidently he'd not responded well to Sting's songwriting, thus committing the one cardinal sin.

Miles Copeland, meanwhile, consolidated his own *ad hoc* management interests into Illegal Music, IRS Records, Firstars and Talent Bank International. Illegal Songs administered Roxanne and Magnetic in the US, as well as supplying a shelter for Sting's overseas assets. The irksome deal with Virgin Music survived until 1982, and wasn't fully dissolved even then. Sting also turned his sideline hobby of photography into a full-blown company, Kaleidoscope Cameras, which if nothing else provided equipment on later Police tours, like the 'hot head camera' used in 1983. All of these interests turned a healthy profit, or provided goods and services beyond Sting's grasp a few years before. All were scrupulously accounted, audited and signed in his curiously stilted and schoolmasterly hand, 'G. M. Sumner'.

Charity was hammered to expediency when, early in 1980, Sting began to carp at the pernicious top rates of British tax. That March he told *Melody Maker* that The Police's next album (*Zenyatta*) would be cut outside England, 'for reasons other than artistic ones – it just makes more sense to make a record in Germany, Holland or somewhere'. By April the band had formed their own philanthropic trust, Outlandos, fronted by the Tory MP Anthony Steen. Receipts from The Police's two Newcastle shows that spring were earmarked to 'help youth projects' and 'encourage kids to learn a trade, particularly musical'. Despite mumblings that Sting's virtuous populism was, in fact, an ingenious tax dodge by his manager, Outlandos undeniably pumped thousands of pounds into the Northumberland Association of Boys' Clubs and other worthy groups. It was also true that, between them, Sting and Keith Moore erased the nominal separation between artist and accountant; from 1980, all The Police's projects and Sting's own solo outings were tackled with one eye on the creative imperative and the other firmly on the bottom line.

Sting's draconian bloody-mindedness suggested more was at psychological stake than circumstances openly showed. Desperate to have his sense of self confirmed, he never risked feeling undermined: whether thrashing Andy Partridge at backgammon or striking the train-robber Ronnie Biggs as 'bloody keen not to let me win at ping-pong' on a trip to Rio, he had the dynamics of a bullet in flight. Sting had only the poorest of relationships with his rivals, which worsened after his fame turned celestial. The creative grudge was mutual. 'I'm sorry. Somebody should clip Sting round the head and tell him to stop singing in that ridiculous Jamaican accent,' Elvis Costello told *Melody Maker*. The two most frequent press criticisms were that he was cold ('A private meeting is like being locked in your car, the windows shut, with a good-looking scorpion,' wrote Jean Rook. 'Sting is intelligent, brilliant and ruthless') and pretentious (on tour he played the oboe and read Jung). His pronouncements on high art were among the characteristic qualities of a Sting interview: an avalanche of ideas, half-baked theories and unblushing self-promotion made for a tone of breezy superiority and heavy-handed cleverness.

Sting post-fame was like Sting pre-fame. He made the same well-meant gestures, showed the same willingness under stress to drop ideas and people he'd once been wed to, the same Gibraltar-size chip on the shoulder. But he was also the most eloquent and innately bright man in rock. Few stars in any nook of showbusiness have been so winningly free as him of morbid inanity. His typical mental state was alert, well briefed and not lacking in nerve. Many of his views on art, sex and religion weren't just provocative – as when he ranted about the Pope – but those of a polished actor. A 'leading' remark would be followed by a 'suggestive' grin. They gave him the excitement of intellectual discovery that comes with being shocking. Sting relished it. He had theories on everything.

For all Sting's volubility, he still managed to keep aloof. The regal demeanour (he was 'a self-made man who worships his creator', sniffed Rook) was one part of his elaborate defence mechanism. Swelling vanity was another. By 1982 Sting had affected an ear-stud and paid a cosmetic surgeon a small fortune for a nose job. His hair retained its bleach-blond shine. He'd long had a quiet, half-shod elegance; now he was a designer grace note. If his mental and physical conceits appalled – one ex-lover sent him a narcissus bulb for Christmas – they attracted, too. His airbrushed publicity shots (fluffed up, he once admitted, 'to look like *Penthouse* centrefolds') loomed from every tabloid, trade and fanzine. The issue of *Interview* with Sting on the cover was the biggest seller in the magazine's history. Thanks to his gym regime and post-show massages (one of the perks of platinum-album sales), his body was more like an Olympian's than a ravaged drug-tooter's. He was king of a vast hill. The words 'rock' and 'star' hadn't been in such close proximity since the salad days of David Bowie. This was boom time for Sting, and he was mad for it.

Like Bowie, he became a cultural polymath. Sting had his music and film careers, his causes and now a children's book based on the lyrics of 'Message In A Bottle'. Even his critics conceded he was good at what he did: nobody got so lucky so often. There was also a vein of charm – what some called 'Stingola' – to go with the vainglory. He was no less anxious to be liked than before, but at thirty he was old enough to seek favour on his own terms. A&M's Derek Green learnt to admire Sting for his masterful handling of the company. He made the inevitable trade-offs with his label, but he refused to 'try to soften the band to make it acceptable to even more people'.

Above all, Sting was the pop psychologist's dream, the man with sub-personalities for every occasion: a lean, impish figure, sly and devious, with bright button eyes, always game for a smirk, but also on the lookout for enemy attack. The photogenic cool was all a front. 'I don't believe in it,' he'd told *Rolling Stone*. What some saw as swagger, he put down to shyness. Sting enjoyed the leeway his protective masks gave him. 'The press are pretty confused about me,' he said. 'They think on the one hand I'm an arrogant bastard, and on the other I'm a do-gooder ecological bum ... But I have a lot of freedom because there's no consensus. I exist between the extremes.' His real need, his wife insisted, was for people who'd relate to him as Gordon. He often spoke of coming to terms with his own self-image by inventing a parallel life. 'It's Sting who's the superstar,' he told a reporter. 'He has all the fans, not me.' On occasion, he deflated his alter ego by referring to him, in the third person, as 'Stingo'. Other times he was merely evasive. Rik Walton, the Newcastle photographer who befriended Last Exit, found himself next to Sting on the set of Channel 4's *The Tube* one night in 1982. 'He admitted, with great glee, how he'd told The Police's official biographer a pack of lies,' says Walton. Sting clung to the notion that he was really two people, one a megastar, the other a Geordie who liked to watch football and bevvy with the lads. 'I often find myself looking out at the audience and wondering how I got here,' he told a second biographer in 1982. Fifteen years later the sense of shock remained. 'Sometimes I look at myself and my position, and I think: how on earth did I arrive here? Me ... a person who came from the worst part of one of the worst towns in England.'

Sting's capacity to be 'a person from one of the worst towns in England' had begun to show signs of wear, and his marriage with it. A friend believes that the sheer affluence of his life with Tomelty brought restlessness rather than stability. 'Frances was either banged up in Ireland or forced to compete with all the arseholes and hangers-on. Even when she went on the road with Sting, they ended up rowing. Everyone would be knackered, tempers frayed and it took its toll on the relationship.' Despite

Tomelty's own career, Sting's life and work had taken him into a
different orbit. They grew, but, as the friend says, 'they didn't
grow together'. His success resulted in other forms of friction. At
some point Tomelty rebelled against her husband's casual affairs,
and that became a factor in the break-up. By 1982 it was obvious
to outsiders what insiders had known for a year: home, for Sting,
was only a place he dossed between tours.

Some thought he travelled equally light politically. 'I'm a
socialist and I care passionately about people,' Sting told one
writer. That he made the announcement with a hollow laugh,
according to the interviewer, perhaps showed his ambivalence on
the issues. But Sting undoubtedly felt for human rights. His
recording of 'I Shall Be Released' was followed, in September
1981, by an appearance at a London gala for Amnesty International. His haunting versions of 'Roxanne' and 'Message In A
Bottle' weren't just among the night's show-stopping moments.
They were the vanguard of his solo career. Without turning
his back on his core audience or lapsing into cuteness, he
summoned the testimonial power of the songs' moving, cogent
lyrics. After hearing the numbers, even a blues diehard like Eric
Clapton, not one to tout what he calls 'bubblegum', was heard to
mumble: 'Sting has arrived.'

He followed it up by playing a set with Chelsea, in which he
guested on the band's angry anthem to the times, 'Right To
Work'. Despite the fact that he railed against the 'apathy and
arse-sitting' of old left-leaning friends, Sting still professed to be a
socialist, if not a fellow-traveller. Early the next year he was on
hand to judge a Battle of the Bands contest staged by the
Workers' Revolutionary Party. He continued to rant at the
apparently wilful suppression of Britain's youth. 'It's a deliberate
economic measure, creating unemployment to keep inflation
down . . . It's a disgrace, it's immoral.' Whatever the merits of the
argument, Sting's efforts to help the jobless were at least of a
piece with his liberal credo. Elsewhere, his activism seemed to be
a mixed bag. He helped fund a 'subversive astrologer' who
knocked on his door in Hampstead one morning, and attended a
'psychic seminar', with Marxist readings and metal-bending
experiments, at London University. In February 1982 The Police
donated funds from a San Francisco show to the ailing Laker
Airways, the carrier that first brought them to America. Between

times, Sting also paid £150 a year to help raise a young Kenyan orphan named Achira.

With an eye on the IRA hunger-strikes and his marriage to Tomelty, it was inevitable Sting would take up the ideal of a united Ireland free from the yoke of British rule. The Police's 'Invisible Sun', a hit in September 1981, was morally ambiguous – the lines 'I don't wanna spend the rest of my life / Looking at the barrel of an Armalite' could have been a sniper's or his victim's – but his willingness to speak out won Sting respect, as well as a BBC ban. (The single's release was the trigger for Sting to tell Derek Green, 'I'm glad you supported it, and proud to be with A&M.') In his mind, the purpose of 'life's first battle' was to preserve human rights. In May 1981, he wrote 'One World (Not Three)', ostensibly a protest at Western greed, but also at the nationalist Bobby Sands' martyrdom.

It was part of the irony of Sting's politics that he wasn't always appreciated by the very groups he propped. Thus, only six months after 'Invisible Sun', he was forced to hurriedly quit Ireland for fear of a terrorist attack. Not all his friends in Amnesty applauded when The Police played in Chile that winter (and Sting declined to read out a message slating the Pinochet regime). On other issues, like unemployment, many of his beneficiaries regarded him as a sort of patriarch; but they were also hero-worshippers, and never bothered much with contradictions. Whatever the mixed result, it was still to Sting's credit that he backed certain causes not necessarily in his own, or his family's, best interests.

Nor were a number of his other hobbies. Sting's various interviews touched frequently on drugs, a taboo only a year or two earlier. In a rare trip to the confessional, he told one friend he had a 'distant relationship' with cocaine. Above all, he wanted to distance himself from the wasted rock-star stereotype. 'Most bands just don't make money,' he said. 'They squander it on producers and coke and lots of other bullshit, and it's disgusting.' A year later, in 1983, he told *Rolling Stone*, 'I don't take drugs any more . . . They're so insidious and available, and when you're feeling vulnerable, they're there. But you mustn't. It's wrong, and as puritan as it might sound, they're not even that much fun.'

All of that was true, but Sting concealed the extent to which he conformed to the addled pop-caricature. He was on nodding terms with pot and uppers as early as the mid-1960s, before graduating to cocaine as a working musician. One associate at the time of *Zenyatta* recalls him creating a 'virtual one-man Colombian export boom' and dozing through a debate on the 'morality of dope', in which he took no part. In 1978 he struck up a professional but problematic friendship with Nigel Gray. Gray's secret life as a rock producer assumed new poignancy when he took a message at home one night that the drugs squad were about to raid Surrey Sound, and would he, as duty police doctor, join them? Lightning reflexes and quick-wittedness saved the day. Nothing suggests that Sting made *Outlandos* or *Reggatta* on anything more than a wave of adrenalin. On the other hand, however, the long nights at Surrey Sound did have their particular mood, and the dealers who haunted the shabby hallway went unmolested. The Police certainly weren't Keith Richards-style suburban zombies, but the stuff was there.

By 1980 the signs of drug use could be seen in the increasing brutality of Sting's moods, his alternate rages and introspection, and the oriental magnificence of his fits of self-promotion. Andy Partridge remembers a day when a roadie handed Sting a bottle of Quaaludes on the tour bus. Hours later, just before showtime, he was still comatose. More handlers had to be sent to the dressing-room to wake him. In the twilight zone of life on the road, sights that not long before would have left Sting's friends numb with wonder left them droopy-eyed with boredom. The bulletins about his behaviour read like weather reports, subject to local variations. Most journalists, interviewing him backstage or in hotels, for instance, would remark on his intellect, self-restraint and unshakeable cool. Those who saw him at home in London or Galway knew they crossed the Rubicon dividing his public, iceman persona from that of a man cracking under stress. Finally, even the fanatically loyal triad of Miles Copeland, Ian Turner and Larry Burnett were forced to recognize the symptoms of a breakdown. It showed in both drugs ('I've used cocaine to get me on stage when nothing else would,' he understated), drink (according to a Montserrat staffer, Sting reviewed one studio playback by 'belching a rum counterpoint for three minutes') and generally succumbing to the lure of megastardom.

The angst was also leavened with a good deal of high spirits and indiscriminate sex.

As well as dressing up and liking to do it on dining-room tables, Sting told *Interview*, he needed to make love each and every night. Friends failed to see how he and Tomelty could have slept together while on different sides of the Atlantic; but it was nothing to fret about. Sting certainly liked to fill out the dead time between shows. One midnight he took a young fan on to the roof of his Los Angeles hotel, where he promptly took steps against the girl catching cold by surrounding her with his own clothes. He had, all in all (in the words of one ex-lover), 'more models than General Motors', but he still seemed lost for a role. 'I'm a very serious father,' he insisted, and there were other reports – not denied – of him ringing his wife in tears. Tomelty for her part took the party line: 'There's no such thing as an open marriage between us. We're both jealous as hell and utterly monogamous.' For years Sting had liked to tell reporters it was the Jesuits who were 'responsible for my venomous nature'. He meant it as a joke, but others thought he was all too seriously at war with Wallsend. His Los Angeles fan remembers that as they left the roof Sting remarked, 'Sex is a kind of suicide. I love it, but the old Catholic in me disapproves.' To the various problems of his friend's life on tour, Andy Partridge plausibly adds another: guilt.

Sting was becoming a slave to the new tyranny of excess. The drugs and sex did nothing for his self-esteem, and, democratically, he was just as down on others. Sting told *Rolling Stone* he had 'very few friends' and 'couldn't think of anyone offhand' he respected. He went on from there to tell the Copelands he was 'topping' The Police. All three brothers were sceptical. They knew his moods, his habit of suddenly quitting only to smoke out his enemies, and they also knew that, as Sting went, so went a multi-million-pound industry. Over dinner Miles was able to talk his protégé back on side. Sting pretended to accept the position reluctantly and remained in the fold.

Other friendships were equally brittle. Contact between Sting and his Newcastle cronies sputtered for a while and then failed. Although his ex-colleagues cultivated a sly indifference, they were no doubt perplexed and hurt. In later years, when members of Last Exit occasionally broached Sting, trying to revive old vibes, they got nowhere. Like most of his Geordie friends, they never admitted knowing why he snubbed them. One credible theory is that Sting didn't actually ignore the various letters and calls. He didn't even know about them. Miles Copeland and a whole train of bodyguards, secretaries and flacks shielded their client from his past. In granting access to some and aggressively rebuffing others their jobs became variations of Colonel Parker's classic bouncer role. Miles, in particular, bulked as a kind of Janus, ruthless, utterly unsentimental, a master of organization and logistics, the bedrock on which Sting's whole career was founded. It was the legitimate inheritance of his father's CIA days. One result was that, with several rare exceptions, tours ran to plan, literally everything was done for Sting it wasn't vital he do himself, and no one bypassed 'channels' to get to see him. Another result was that he began to lose touch with the very people who helped launch him in the first place. When The Police played at Gateshead Stadium in July 1982, only 11,000 fans turned up instead of the expected 30,000. An MC appeared after the encore to light-heartedly urge 'all Sting's mates' to leave quietly, but there was no problem – most of the thin crowd had already shuffled off.*

Sting worked hard towards improving his family relations from their low ebb of 1980. After flaying the Sumners in print as 'losers' he was forced to take a flow of angry letters and calls from home. Sting's compelling urge to distance himself from his parents was no doubt a response to his snub of them as mediocre. But that hardly explains the bile he occasionally allowed to rise to the surface. Even in jest, his put-downs could be slashingly cruel. Now, from the far side of fame, he began to reverse himself. He visited the north-east several times in 1981–82. He sent cards and gifts. He knocked himself, for his blurtings, as 'a wally'. And, Sting told Patrick Deuchar, chief executive of the Albert Hall, he was 'chuffed' when, during a performance there, he looked up and unexpectedly saw his mother watching from a box.

By then, Audrey and Ernie Sumner had divorced. Their elder son achieved some sort of rapport, if only a cursory one, with

---

*The BBC producer Jeff Griffin reports that even Miles spent the evening 'asleep in the dressing-room'.

both parents. He arranged for them to sit in the front row of his concerts, along with his grandmother Agnes (still attending his Newcastle shows today, aged ninety-one). He was supportive when Angela Sumner went into hospital for back surgery; he hosted his other sister's wedding. Relations with his brother also slowly thawed. Phil Sumner, still doing a milk-round in North Shields, bitterly paid the price of fame by association. 'Everyone talks about Sting and I can't always face it,' he said in 1983. The two men became steadily closer after that. By 1990 Phil had bought a bar and grill on the beach at Whitley Bay, where he regularly played host to Sting's fan club and signed the odd autograph. A wary affection began to show through the earlier venom. Compared with his sisters' total indulgence, which Sting took for granted, his brother's new warmth was evidently appreciated. He told a mutual friend in 1997 that he and Phil were 'mending fences' and had 'never been closer'.

By 1982 Sting was still married to Tomelty (with whom he had a daughter that April), but a new woman was coming up behind, fast. Trudie Styler had first caught his eye when they passed each other on the street in Leinster Square. Like her predecessor, she was an actress. Born in January 1954, Styler had been living in digs and working as a 'bunny mother' in the Playboy Club to pay her way through drama school. Even this modest ambition had shocked her parents, a dinner-lady and a labourer living on a Birmingham council estate, who had wanted their daughter 'raised up high', so high that she'd never need to scrimp and grub and lean on a man. They wanted Trudie to work in the local brush factory, the most respectable job in the area.

Instead, Styler ran away to London and had plastic surgery to fix a cheek hideously scarred in a road accident. Roles in fringe theatre and a stint compèring a topless floor show opened up her career, and with her West End début in 1980 she hit semi-fame in *Macbeth*. This was the same production starring Tomelty. During rehearsals Styler was rushed to hospital with a burst appendix, but recovered to take her role as one of the witches.

She wasn't a pretty girl in the classic sense, some would sneer, with her damaged face, her unruly blonde hair and her long-lipped mouth. But Styler was, nonetheless, a beautiful woman. As *Macbeth* began its run in September 1980 she became accustomed to the nightly arrival of Sting backstage. Within weeks a triangle had formed, the unmarried young woman becoming the friend of the older actress who was married, visiting husband and wife at home in Ireland, and then innocently and doggedly setting out to win her man. It was, says one of Tomelty's camp, 'the oldest trick there is'. But for at least a year Sting and Styler were just good friends, in every sense of that satirical phrase. He was on tour, recording or filming *Artemis*. She was at home in London. Styler would later take tabloid heat as a home-breaker and speak of the transition as 'a very dark time [in which] we were put on trial', but she alone wasn't guilty.

It was the beginning of a nightmare. 'I was terrible to work with or be around,' Sting says today. 'I was unsympathetic, aggressive, mean, selfish, egotistical.' And prolific. As usual, Sting found therapy in art. The songs he wrote in 1981–82 moved steadily nearer the *sui generis*, winning hybrid of his solo work: they not only veered from the formula, they embodied his mood. Music and words conspired in doleful self-exposure, pushed home at high energy. Twee soundware gave way to dark masterpieces.

Ghost in the Machine was released in October 1981, the same month that Sting turned thirty. It was, by that simple token, the work of a mature man. There were other faintly tedious signs of ageing: the Arthur Koestler title, the Led Zep-type cover logos (a digital image of the band) and the almost parodically turgid press notes, in which Sting apprised his public of the news that, 'I've lost faith in the political process to solve our problems. I think the answer is in our own heads. I'm disillusioned with order.' It was this observation – and other sub-anarchic pranks – that excited the pop cognoscenti and tabloids to concoct an image in which everything Sting said or did from now on could be classified as the ravings of, as he put it, 'a pretentious git'.

His saving grace was his ability to aim again and again; instead of analysis, Sting's method was construction. He never classified and categorized in submission to anyone else's ideas but was always willing to start over, regroup, edit, revise, adapt. He never fed on himself. While *Ghost* featured some gleeful plagiarizing, it was also a boldly assured leap in a new direction, with ska and pop ousting rock and reggae as the principal points of departure.

What hoisted the record above Madness or the Specials was a

batch of quirky, melodic songs, some of which made the debt to Sting's R&B roots plainer than others. 'Spirits In The Material World' combined bone-crushing rhythm (and honks of Sting's sax) with a classic pop chorus. Another genre lark, 'Every Little Thing She Does Is Magic', squeezed fresh juice from hoary love lyrics and a rippling piano, with Sting's high, dramatic voice soaring above like a stunt pilot. 'Every Little Thing' was unexpected, beaty, irreverent, with a joyously racy playout. (It was also, as with all Sting's best songs, ambiguous: lines like 'Do I have to tell the story / Of a thousand rainy days since we first met / It's a big enough umbrella / But it's always me that ends up getting wet' suggested that all love stirred fears of heartbreak.*) 'Demolition Man' started out as a track from *One Step Beyond* before swerving, via a blues guitar, into the outro of the Stones' 'Can't You Hear Me Knocking'. 'Too Much Information' was equally influenced by James Brown and the calypso groups from whom Copeland was constantly borrowing beats. 'One World' twisted Sting's vocals around riffing saxes and more Caribbean rhythm. 'Secret Journey' kicked off like something from Kraftwerk but ended up a classic, low-fi rocker; using just a few hooks, Sting made the tune as catchy as a Wings or Abba. Plenty of other acts married the big melody to minor-key, *musique concrète* modes, but few did it as well. Like most of *Ghost*, 'Secret Journey' pulled together a unified sound, firmly anchored by the vocals, running the whole pop gamut.

For more than a year, Sting had been agonizing from various throat sores. Several shows were cancelled. There was a moment at the Amnesty gala when his voice cracked into a gruff rasp. By late 1981 he was practising the Alexander method – lying on a floor for twenty minutes to get his back level with the ground and (thus) relax the larynx. He ate special diets and breathed steam through a facial sauna. None of the problems were audible on *Ghost*. Sting worked the husky low end of his register to specially good effect; like the best of the old soul merchants, he'd grown more authoritative with age. Less successful were the horns, centred on a reedy sax that propped half the tracks. Sting had recently been taking lessons and, like a spoilt child transported into middle age, over-indulged his new toy. On the

*To make the point, Sting sang the exact same words on 'O My God'.

other hand, the writing was, for the most part, wry, sharp and universal. Philip Norman, the Beatles' biographer, believes that *Ghost* 'stands comparison, in end-to-end quality, with *Revolver*'. It was a number-one hit in Britain, number two in America.

Two of the album's three singles were bouncy, foot-tapping tunes, with solid R&B momentum provided by galloping drums, twangy guitar and revved-up bass. 'Every Little Thing' and 'Spirits In The Material World', each with a video shot by the Burbidges, made number one and number twelve respectively. 'Invisible Sun' cast a darker spell. Not only was it relentlessly downbeat, Sting denying the riff access to its anthemic potential; the video was banned by the BBC. The song was a British number two and never saw light of day in America.

What galled some, but impressed most of the critics, was The Police's arrival as a musical crusade. Their sales from albums and merchandising were impressive enough. But what struck home even more, if feasible, was their growing number of highbrow gongs. In December 1980 they scooped the *Evening Standard* top band, top singer, top album and top single prizes, and the equivalent categories in *Le Monde*; Sting was best male rock star in both papers' polls. The following February, the group won their first Grammy. In May 1981 Sting was named Songwriter of the Year at the Novello awards held at the Grosvenor House in London.

Within twenty-four hours in February 1982, The Police won the Best British Group title at the first-ever Brits, then Grammys for Best Rock Vocal Performance ('Don't Stand So Close To Me') and, as in the previous year, Best Rock Instrumental ('Behind My Camel'). 'Every Little Thing' scored a Novello. The band took the tributes quite seriously, declining to turn the ceremonies into a sideshow when they refused to play or even appear. By 1983 the various honours began to appear as logos on their press releases, much like royal warrants. The 'one-man cocaine boomlet' now swayed domestic markets. Miles and the other courtiers all spoke, repeatedly and not without truth, of The Police's contribution to the export drive. A letter from the Department of Trade confirmed this. They were nothing if not big business.

The band relished the recognition. A *Melody Maker* writer remembers an interview with them in the summer of 1981, when Sting tried to persuade him to write an article not on the 'second

British invasion', but 'a whole puff piece on The Police alone'. The band won respect for hitting their marks, but they took critical flak, too, for the same reason. Even with the Grammys and Novellos, they were one of the most polarizing acts in rock. When the press dissed them – knocking them in *Sounds* as the Bleach Boys – the tone could be bitchy. Eager to mute rather than dignify the attacks, the band loftily ignored certain titles (though Sting still liked to fire off broadsides at his critics),* with the inevitable result that paranoia soured their already spiky press relations. By *Ghost*, The Police were a storm of warring reactions to their fame: vain, wary, a band torn between duty and self-destruction. They imposed a harsh life on themselves. That December they played British dates, including three nights at Wembley Arena; zig-zagged Scandinavia and Europe in the New Year, before digging in for three months in North and South America; did the festival rounds in July; and then meandered back through America that autumn, until they hit Montserrat in December. As well as writing and recording, Sting was obliged to make good his promises to star in Dennis Potter's *Brimstone & Treacle,* and develop his own screenplay. According to one of the entourage, 'It got so that he couldn't read a letter from his mum, or take a crap, without it screwing up the schedule.'

If the heat was beginning to tell, the band were a model of surface calm. 'There was a period when we argued a lot,' Summers informed the *Sun* in 1982; 'but there's a different feeling between us now.' Copeland would loyally claim that 'I can do whatever I want and I like that amount of room.' He was speaking musically. Personally, The Police were on terms of intimate mutual loathing. After Paul Morley's critical orgasm in *NME*, Sting admitted Copeland and Summers were 'livid . . . They thought I engineered all that publicity. I did, in a way, but I was just doing my job. I had no sympathy with them when they got like that.' At a photo-shoot that spring, a picture editor remembers Sting 'front and centre, with his elbows digging into Andy and Stewart, and his face only inches from the lens. When

---

*He upbraided one woman who mocked 'De Do Do Do, De Da Da Da', 'It's an articulate song about being inarticulate – something you should know about.'

the others moved up, he leaned forward until he was virtually nutting the camera.' There were other signs of creeping stress between the group. Sting had to be the best, outrun the pack, and win at almost any cost. He balanced his actions against the wisdom that he was 'just doing a job', leading The Police, and some of the worst rows touched on the band's sound. Around the time of *Ghost* they recorded a track called 'Low Life', originally written by Sting alongside 'Roxanne'. Celebrating his love of the instrument (and anticipating his whole solo career), he scored in a jazzy sax solo. Copeland and Summers bridled. The composer was adamant – and turned out to be right. Summers felt all Sting's wheeling and dealing on behalf of the band was really a cloak for personal glory: daily, constant efforts to coax others into 'his bag'. Muttering ironically about a 'police state', the guitarist (and later Copeland) gave in. A friend of Eberhard Schoener's duly played the sax, giving 'Low Life' an edgy, contrary feel that cut right to the heart of the band's identity crisis.

It was hard to know, meanwhile, what qualified as a crisis between Sting and his drummer. There might conceivably have been fans left who raised an eyebrow over the reports of squabbles and brawls, but far more, probably, who would have regarded a mere punch-up as heroic self-restraint. Copeland had once said of Sting that 'not only does he hate humanity, but every human within the species, except his family'. The inference was that, as far as Copeland went, the feeling was mutual. By 1980 the ill-will had moved into mythology. Parodying a local saw, Copeland told a reporter in Japan, 'Sting's superior to me, because I'm less humble than him. *I'm* an arrogant twat.' As so often, the smallest things triggered the biggest scenes. Sting's push-ups and incessant stretching routine in a cramped American dressing-room prompted Copeland to flick a well-aimed drumstick at his head. A merry row then ensued, circling, like most of their fights, from the specific to the general. By the time of *Ghost*, they were at swords' points. Copeland joyfully slated his rival's songs; Sting's favourite and most effective reprisal was the use of the *reductio ad absurdum* to taunt his enemy's playing. 'If you sped up any more, you'd fly up your own arse,' he told Copeland one night at Wembley. Although musicianship was often the spur, the feud ran on much more than just beats per minute. Sting overwhelmed his two colleagues. He needed to be the frontman, to outdo everybody, to 'go to the studio with twelve songs and get those songs on the record' as he puts it. The caricature of him as a driven, overbearing, self-centred Rasputin/tsar captures only part of the man; but it was enough for Copeland to go on.

Sting's paranoia, or at least his anxiety, was rampant. Locked into the notion that he was being treated as a myth, 'not a man', he began to distrust his friends, too. But if a person chose misery, there were grounds for it to feed on in 1982. That spring, Sting wound up yet another American tour. Within a week he was forced to sell his Irish seat and simultaneously put his Hampstead home on the market: the marriage to Tomelty, who had just given birth, was over. In a sorry piece of timing, Virgin chose that exact moment to license 'Don't Stand So Close To Me' for use in a deodorant commercial. For nearly three years, the company had taken pains not to risk their legal position in self-serving business deals. By May 1982, with a date for Sting's 'fraudulent use' action scheduled in the High Court, Virgin decided to cash in on their star asset while it was theirs to loot. It was the last straw.

The eleven-day hearing that July saw Sting seek victim status, claiming he'd suffered from 'inequality of bargaining power' when signing the original deal with Carol Wilson in 1976, a stand supported by readings from his diary and, movingly, by Tomelty. At stake was the copyright of fifty-four of his songs, which Virgin said had paid Sting more than a million pounds in royalties (and he swore had cost him £700,000). The presence of Wilson herself, ready to testify that 'inequality of power' had never been an issue, added an extra level of interest. Outside, in the mid-summer heat, fans mingled, swarmed and occasionally sparred with police. Each day, ten minutes before the start of proceedings, Sting arrived, a pale, scowling figure moving through the spectators like Moses parting the sea. A hushed silence came over the hallway as he made his way towards the courtroom's swing doors wearing an Italian suit, white shirt and tie. His face was ashen and pasty as he stared straight ahead, seemingly lost. He was accompanied by Miles, his barrister Andrew Bateson and a bodyguard. They took seats in the front row, immediately beside Wilson and the Virgin lawyers.

After a week and a half of argument and £300,000 in costs, the case ended in an undignified huddle in the corridor. Under the terms of the settlement Virgin agreed to pay Sting a lump sum of £200,000 and up his share of future earnings. In turn, the company would publish the next Police album and insisted on keeping the song copyrights for their expected lifetime, which they estimated at 7–10 years. Both sides claimed victory, if only pyrrhic. After a glib announcement by Mr Justice Mars-Jones ('If I'd known you were going to take so much time [in conference], I would have written a couple of tunes while I was waiting'), and the mutual acceptance of costs, Sting and his manager left without comment. After months of quietly wooing the press, they had no more use for them. To Richard Branson it was a 'sensible deal . . . Sting will do another record for us and we will give him something back in return.' After days of elaborate testimony, with accountants offering their different spins on royalty rates and residuals, neither side had the stomach to go on. As one legal expert put it, 'Both Sting and Branson regarded it as vital that they win, as much for principle as money. Rather than risk a crushing blow to the ego, they settled for a draw. It came down to an old-fashioned British compromise.'

From the High Court Sting and Miles drove to the House of Commons, where they had trouble getting into a party in their honour. Copeland said a policeman 'took some convincing' before letting them through. By the next day, 28 July, Sting had regained his sang-froid with the media. 'Any kid with a contract should go to a music lawyer,' he said ruefully. 'I didn't . . . and it cost me millions and far more in heartbreak.'

That was nothing compared to his eruption on stage at Friar's Club in Aylesbury. Sting broke off from one song to harangue his audience from behind a beer bottle. 'I'm going to tell you a story about when I was young and innocent six years ago, and I signed a contract to an arsehole.' Warming to his theme, he told the crowd he was 'pissed off' about the misuse of his wares. 'Do you want to hear a Bodymist ad or "Don't Stand So Close To Me"?' he asked, without a trace of a smile. Even Branson's urbane civility wilted in the face of Sting's tirade. 'Although we shook hands after the case,' he told reporters, 'no action can ever be totally amicable.' Virgin, he added in private, had been forced into a deal largely because Wilson, their star turn, was potentially mutinous. (Branson and Wilson then fought a mini-war of their own, over her severance pay.) There was scathing criticism of Miles Copeland. Even today, Branson says he thought his rival – whose terms with his own acts made Virgin's with Sting seem lavish – 'something of a shit'. However, 'not being one to hold grudges', Branson reconciled with Copeland two years later, when they discussed a joint venture. He also made up with Sting, with whom he exchanges 'pleasant notes' and 'the odd Christmas card'. Branson and Wilson didn't speak again.

At the same time as Sting divorced Virgin he left his wife. On 17 April 1982 Tomelty had given birth to their second child, Fuchsia Katherine (Kate), in the Royal Free Hospital, Camden. Sting's quote from New York that he was 'bowled over' concealed the certainty that his marriage was over. Later in the spring the couple's two houses were put up for sale. Tomelty and the baby moved into a home in Antrim Road, Hampstead. On 25 July, during a break in the court action, Sting flew back to London after attending a Riviera party thrown by the arms dealer Adnan Khashoggi; another moment when his Amnesty credentials needed careful polishing. He was with Trudie Styler.

Straight off, at the airport, there was tension. It centred around Sting's bodyguard and a tabloid photographer, who somehow mutually fell down a flight of steps, breaking the camera. Sting, still in his Monte Carlo garb of white ducks and shoes and striped blazer, then announced: 'My wife has been with me all the time. Leave me alone. I'm extremely tired.' His escort, coyly named in the *Sun* as 'resembling green-eyed actress Trudie Styler', denied being anyone's girlfriend. A week later, at Stringfellow's in London, Sting left hardened showbusiness hacks muttering among themselves in disbelief. Styler, he now said, was 'my mistress'.

She was much more. As early as 5 March, she'd moved in with Sting; by mid-1982 she was his constant companion, lover and ally against the world. Even a friend of Tomelty's came to accept that 'Sting and Trudie were like a tuning-fork, always aquiver'. Others credited Styler with greater insight than her rival into the stresses of Sting's career. 'She was the one relationship that saved me,' he said in 1996. 'She knew me and, despite knowing me, she loved me. When I talk to other people who saw me through that period, they say, "God, you were a bastard." And I was.'

Sting, according to this thesis, hadn't just been on the run in 1980–81 from the Inland Revenue. He was also severing his moorings to Gordon Sumner. A harsh, libertine fanatic with an unnecessarily large number of intrusive key feuds – not least with his family – he'd estranged potential friends and fans. Future history would be kinder than Sting's contemporaries, still finding him 'a bastard', but with extenuating circumstances. Both sides agree that his rehabilitation began from that dire summer.

Within days Sting was back on the road in America, along with Styler. Over the next month The Police mounted a coast-to-coast tour that made insiders fear for the group's sanity. The carefully orchestrated stunts of Miles and the crew assured that the band played to sellout crowds. Advance men informed local DJs of when Sting would hit town. A few days before his appearance, press kits landed on the desks of print and TV media. Newspaper ads and word-of-mouth did the rest. As tightly run as a military advance, the late-summer push won record receipts, as well as high-margin spin-offs from merchandising and souvenirs. Ironically, probably the only people not elated by The Police's financial bonanza were the band themselves. Both Copeland and Summers had begun to fret at the hectic itinerary imposed on them from above. Over the spring, the drummer had declared that stigma of the frustrated artist – a solo project, writing music for the film *Rumble Fish*. The guitarist's marriage had folded. Each man had something to say on the sense of emptiness that heavy drinking, drugs and vacuous one-nighters couldn't feed. For Sting, also in demand as a spokesman on everything from Amnesty to abortion – and, thanks to tabloid attacks on his treatment of Tomelty, now a moral issue himself – Styler was the anchor. While they rarely spent a quiet evening together and often devoted late nights to partying, she supplied him with a kind of sanctuary from himself, a well-organized haven where her calm balanced his volatility. 'She was the one relationship that saved me' was no more than Sting meant.

On 3 September 1982 The Police headlined on the first day of the US Festival, a composite concert–trade-fair held in the foothills of the San Bernadino mountains near Los Angeles. Promoted by the Apple computer guru Steve Wozniak, the event's chief characteristics were the usual ones of festival rock: extreme weather (heat, for once, not cold), traffic, drugs, deaths, and a fifty-seven acre site which, for most of the dense crowd, reduced the performers to the dimensions of ants. It also featured some robust pressure by Sting and Miles Copeland. Other top draws like Fleetwood Mac and Tom Petty were paid $500,000 apiece for their services. 'We offered the Who a fortune to play, but they turned us down,' says Wozniak. 'And The Police . . . Well, there was a problem getting The Police, and their price did go up' (to a million dollars, in most estimates).

Miles, above all, won Wozniak's grudging respect. Nothing Copeland did was illegal or unprecedented in the strong-arm world of rock management, where everyday work habits would have raised eyebrows in a Mafia den. Yet corrosive tactics had played a major part in Miles's business plans from the start. Wozniak wasn't the first to mutter about 'Police brutality' in Copeland's assertion of the band's fee. Literally no ruse was too cruel, no caper too *outré* in his virile protection of his assets. As Keith Moore puts it, 'Miles has long taken the view that to be of assistance to others in connection with "his" artists is to deny himself a potential source of income.' Copeland may have done little that Colonel Parker or Allen Klein hadn't done before him, but as a metaphor for his times he was peerless. The one-time punk avatar and *Sniffin' Glue* editor had become a Thatcherite mogul, a brilliant if narrow tactician whose *laissez-faire* monetarism matched even hers.

Miles was equally vigilant of his clients' extracurricular projects. By 1982 Sting was well on his way to a solo career. He saw nothing incongruous about pursuing his 'own thing' within the group format. Like other chameleons before him – his heroes Lennon and Bowie come to mind – he began to record an oldies collection, a homage to his favorite R&B hits from the past. In the end, for commercial reasons, he never released a nostalgic LP, though his version of 'Tutti Frutti' graced the soundtrack of *Party Party*. Reverting to his St Cuthbert's persona, he then toyed with starring in *Ghost Runner*, a film about the marathon star John Tarrant. He also wrote an adaption of *Gormenghast*, Mervyn Peake's fable of 'a kitchen boy who tries to gain control of a castle [but] is undone by his pride and innate evil'. Despite the autobiographical nod, and flickering interest from Hollywood, the script remained unfinanced. It did, however, provide a reference point for Sting's next role in front of the cameras.

Seven years earlier, Sting had starred in *Hellfire*, an amateur Newcastle musical in the incendiary tradition of Arthur Brown and Kiss. Some of the same theme, if not the pyrotechnics, must have come to mind when he read Dennis Potter's teleplay *Brimstone & Treacle*. Both Bowie and Malcolm McDowell were offered and refused the lead role of Martin Taylor. Sting then met the director Richard Loncraine at four o'clock in the morning – a time when he rightly judged the latter's faculties 'a tad impaired' – and landed the part. Filming began at Shepperton in the autumn of 1981.

Although Potter himself was enthused, during and after shooting most film buffs were cynical. Real drama, to them, had never been an obvious part of most rockers' repertoires. Andrew Smith caught a mood when he wrote in the *Sunday Times*, 'Being a pop star is about the projection of the ego. Good acting, of a type any self-respecting rock icon would aspire to, is about the ego's submersion, its subservience to character and text. The two processes are mutually exclusive.' Even Sting's success in *Quadrophenia* was largely a matter of faith, a submissive respect for dead-eyed style, rather than a sober view of his performance. *Radio On* and *Artemis 81* had similarly tossed stagecraft for sheer cool. Real indignity had befallen Sting's cameo in *The Great Rock 'n' Roll Swindle*.

If Sting had seemed depressed during the *Artemis* shoot that spring, his mood was no better on the set of *Brimstone*. He began the four-month job with ample reason to hope it would pull him out of his downward spiral. His confidence was soon dashed. Like many a rock star before him, he carped at the long delays and 'interminable arse-sitting' of most location work. His revival of 'Spread A Little Happiness' for the *Brimstone* soundtrack did give him a first solo single, and a Top Twenty hit in Britain; but the rest of the score straddled the line between clunky and bovine, and, in the words of one critic, 'should have been bulk erased by a public-spirited engineer'. For the most part, Sting's screen work was all bits and pieces, scraps of action that never jibed, and clashes with his day job in The Police. At one point he injured himself by plunging his hand through a plate-glass window, forcing him to give up the bass and sing with his arm in a sling for a dozen dates.

Brimstone's plot was uneven but unmistakably Potteresque: Sting ingratiates himself into the home of a married couple whose only child, paralysed by a hit-and-run driver, writhes comatose on her bed. In a neat twist filched from *The Caretaker*, he plays off father (who hails Sting as 'a mealy-mouthed, pasty-faced ninny') against mother (seduced by his go-to-church haircut and choirboy smile), eventually moving to their daughter's sickroom. Stripping the girl's bedclothes, he fondles her nude body; as he mounts her she lets out a falsetto scream. Potter's critics, and many of the converted, balked at this sequence, which was played out over the song 'I Burn For You'. Sting's character exits via the window and goes off in search of fresh meat, 'a kind of nice boy,' he said of Taylor, 'well-mannered, but also quite nasty. Like me.'

The BBC banned *Brimstone* three days before transmission, though it traded briskly as a cult on video. In the final edit, many of Sting's best lines (including a take-off of Styler's role in *Macbeth*) were left on the cutting-room floor, and pundits were sufficiently shocked by the rape scene to maul writer and star alike. To Ivan Waterman, *Brimstone* was 'sick, sensational and bound to anger the parents of every handicapped child'. The *Mirror* branded Potter 'Britain's pornographer', and other Fleet Street moralists joined the consensus.

Sting himself was 'very proud of it . . . It's quirky and weird and unusual.' He was attracted by the ambivalence of the character. Audiences weren't sure whether Taylor was the devil or a mummy's-boy with a sideline in kinky sex. Sting played him as both, regarded the part as 'shifting from genuinely religious to demonic' and won highbrow praise for his shady, mixed sprawl of emotions. *Brimstone*, Grand Prix-winner at the Montreal festival, became a minor *succès de scandal*, a dark comedy people either loved or hated. What intrigued was the conflict raging in Taylor's head, bringing with it the verdict: flawed film, fascinating role.

'I'm just trying to find out who is the real me – is it this monstrous character or someone more normal?' Sting asked in 1982. A year later, the question was no nearer solution. His intelligent, sensitive side still jarred with an ego hardy even for a rock star. A MONSTER CALLED STING ran the headline in *Rolling Stone* in

September 1983. The piece gave full vent to his divorce, the Virgin suit and the obligatory 'pop star scuffles with photographer' to-do at Heathrow. The magazine's view: 'Sting finds the action in his own head more engrossing than most of the people he meets and he is singularly self-contained.' To some it seemed that *Outlandos, Reggatta, Zenyatta* and *Ghost* were the core work that followed a slow start and apparently preceded a long decline. Court actions and dubious solo projects were only the latest signs of a personality, if not a career, in freefall.

Yet between his *mea culpa* in 1982 and The Police's culminating triumph a year later, Sting drove himself night and day. As well as touring, enjoying his own money and disbursing funds from his Trust, acting in a $50 million film, developing his screenplay, drafting a book and dabbling with a symphony, he found time to write the songs that became *Synchronicity*. Full of nervy ennui one minute, stunning charm the next, Sting's cynicism and idealism were inseparable, both of a piece. Like Martin Taylor, he was a study in schizophrenia.

Over the winter of 1982–83, Sting and Styler rented a house on the north coast of Jamaica. Known as Goldeneye, it had been built in the 1940s by Ian Fleming, author of the Bond novels, on thirty acres of land formerly used as a donkey racecourse. It was and is an idyllic spot, with steps leading to a small private beach. As Fleming wrote, you could live there on the fruit and coconuts from his trees, and the fish from the sea just beyond the reef. The house itself was a bungalow, white-stuccoed, with three bedrooms and, in Fleming's words, 'shower baths and lavatories that often hiss like vipers or ululate like stricken bloodhounds'. Most afternoons Sting sat at the author's two-tier desk made of bullet-wood, scrawling lyrics on yellow foolscap and strumming his guitar. By March 1983 he had the first draft of his master-piece.

These rough efforts were far from what *Synchronicity* would become. Yet the basic idea was there: by nailing wily tunes to lyrics about love-gone-awry, Sting touched raw nerves like precious few other pop megastars. 'I do my best work when I'm in pain and turmoil', he once said, and from 'Can't Stand Losing You' to 'Every Breath You Take' the hits kept coming, gloomy words with sweetly grainy riffs and a snappy beat.

Ambition, charm, compassion, affection and self-confidence

were all part of Sting's make-up, but by late 1982 they were muted by the blows of the past twelve months. By the time he hit Jamaica, he not only faced the daunting job of writing an album for which 100,000 British fans had laid advance orders; he also had to adapt himself to a change of public image from a swaggering popster into a home-wrecker who sued his colleagues and brawled at airports. Much later, he described himself as having behaved 'like a complete cunt' during the year. For all her devotion, Styler still looked askance at that side of Sting's life. In private, she told a friend it was like 'living with nuclear fission', never knowing when and if 'the whole thing will go up'. In public, she hid her feelings and took a detached, loyal view of Sting's volatility. 'He's a genius,' she said. And, 'Sting knows he's cute. How many years can you take your shirt off onstage and not think you look great?'

Styler also saw that, inside and out of reach, there was still a part of Sting forever Gordon Sumner. This was the streak at work when, for instance, he murdered pub songs on Noël Coward's piano at Goldeneye, or rang home to get the football scores. Though it was six years since he left town, Newcastle remained a place on his map. It taught Sting to be an outsider, a role he still played every day. 'I've no idea what my place in showbusiness is,' he said. 'I'm sort of a misfit.' He was an essentially private man who only felt 'truly alive' when he was alone with his guitar. Yet he only wanted to be alive that way a few hours a day. Stories of his introspection did the rounds. Later in the 1980s, a backlash against Sting's various crusades would also take its toll on his good name: it was the negative perception rather than the positive reality of his Rainforest Foundation that shaped the media view. It would be a decade before he mastered the art of bluff congeniality, and took his place alongside family favourites of the likes of Phil Collins and Elton John. In the meantime, Sting – the populist who genuinely wanted to do good – would be seen as a man apart from the people, a kind of icy-fey potentate who ruled from a great height. They were interesting years.

5

King of Pain

STYLER LEFT HIM ALMOST IMMEDIATELY. The crisis came after Christmas spent in their rented villa on Montserrat. A member of the entourage visiting the island remembers Sting 'totally up and down ... completely comatose or running round in a cloud of dust. He couldn't stand not being the centre of attention. He had to be top dog ... And people had to do what he thought they should do. Sting was just a basket-case in those days.' Another plausible explanation is that he felt guilty at quitting his family. Whatever the cause, the effect was that Styler flew home to London, telling her friends there had been a 'bust-up'. She came back again, having made her point. From then on Styler never subordinated her interests and needs to Sting's. She resumed her career as an actress and, later, a producer of documentary films, including *Boys from Brazil* (a study of transvestite prostitutes) and *Moving the Mountain* (about the student rebellion in Tiananmen Square). Her bid for independence made both parties think twice about their future. In time, children, and a shared commitment to the rainforest, would provide a fixed mutual love. Sting and Styler reinforced each other's strengths and blended their differences into a productive partnership; but in early 1983 the affair could as easily have ground to a halt.

As Styler adjusted to life with a rock star, Sting focused his energies on recording *Synchronicity*. It was a protracted, ugly, emotionally draining business. As usual, both Summers and Copeland fought for their own songs; their two tracks to make the cut were, the drummer says, 'concessions, like on the Hendrix albums where there'd be one Noel Redding tune'. No one expected the sessions to be easy when all three men imagined themselves fighting in a death-struggle for not only royalties, but their own egos. Even so, *Synchronicity* was a slog – 'the hardest album we've made,' as Sting put it. From Montserrat, the band and Hugh Padgham flew to Le Studio in Montreal. There the rough tapes were mixed to give *Synchronicity* its sleek edit: sparse, melodic hooks; rubbery bass lines; and, of course, the voice.

Sting added one last song. Unable to sleep one night in the tropics, he began humming and plunking Coward's piano. Within a minute he was singing the melody-line of 'Every Breath You Take'. It was the same as when he wrote 'Walking On The Moon': he picked up sounds like a satellite, polishing the tunes and beaming them back to millions. 'I'm very musical, but it all ends at the wrists,' he says. 'I need other musicians to interpret my work. I give it structure. They give it colour.' Writ large, that nuance was the difference between a working wage and millions of pounds. Summers duly wrote the riff (a homage to Bartók) that helped make 'Every Breath' a number-one hit in both Britain and America.

By spring 1983 Tomelty would gracefully admit what the tabloids had known for nearly a year. Her marriage was over, and 'there's no question of us being reconciled. I want to bring to a close a part of my life which is finished for ever.' After filming *Dune* on location in Mexico, Sting emerged at the Château Marmont hotel in Hollywood. Styler was with him. The couple presented a happy front, though one guest felt it was 'more of a merger than a romance'. Both spent hours talking on separate phones, cutting film and music deals, and treating each other with 'formal protective respect'. Sting refused to discuss Styler when *Rolling Stone* came to call, telling the reporter, 'The important things I have to say are in the songs in a veiled, symbolic form. It's true there is a lot of damage around me. But I hope it's not directly because of me.' At this, Styler nodded.

Though neither Sting nor Styler was ever likely to ring the Samaritans, they both came to a certain amount of grief in 1982–83. She had another set-to with her family in Birmingham, as well as taking her lumps from the *Sun*. He wrote tunes, notably 'Every

Breath' and 'King Of Pain', that showed he still made an artistic link with the brokenhearted. 'My personal life is in my songs,' Sting said. 'Many of them seem quite contradictory, and I seem to be two people: on the one hand, a morose, doom-laden character, and on the other, a happy-go-lucky maniac. I'm [like] the character I played in *Brimstone & Treacle*, and I didn't have to delve too deeply into myself to excavate him. He's definitely an exaggerated version of me.'

Although Sting's live act was still a celebration of hedonism, pomp and kick-splitted excess, his music – particularly on *Synchronicity* – was no longer the province of the flash but of the deadly earnest. There was a sense in which he wasn't only the 'happy-go-lucky maniac' of 'De Do Do Do, De Da Da Da', but the King of Pain himself. Without that personal connection, he could never have written with a control that now verged on repression. Sting knew exactly what it felt like to be contrary. He loved adventure, but wanted order; liked other people, but needed to be alone. Not unusually for a robust, pumped-up type, he suffered from poor health. There were other, chronic contra- dictions. Sting made his it's-all-there-in-the-music claims his means of spreading the enigma. As head of a multinational busi- ness, he had responsibility for writing, recording and flogging the 'product', as well as for the livelihoods of his band, manage- ment and crew. Yet he found it hard to cope with the problems of everyday life. Moody, irritable, mercurial and easily bored, he was deeply dependent on his lover and close friends, and notoriously uptight about living the rock-god myth. Like any intelligent pop star, he never quite lost the taint of self- consciousness. The songs he belted from the stages of arenas and football stadia were actually rooted, for the most part, in the folky tradition of a James Taylor – an artist Sting praised for treading 'the thin line between enchantment and madness'.

He balanced his own superstardrom equally finely. On one level, Sting clearly enjoyed the prestige and money. On another, he rued fame's hassles and potentially dangerous trade-offs. In the summer of 1983 he spoke of *The King of Comedy*, Martin Scorsese's film in which a deranged fan nags and stalks a TV chat-show host, played by Jerry Lewis. 'I walked out of the theatre, and there was a crowd of people waiting to come in. They all started to shout, "Hey, it's Sting!" . . . I'd just seen Lewis brutalized by a fan, and I felt vulnerable.' Sting himself was menaced by a disciple trading as 'Roxanne Sumner'. Among the last lyrics on *Ghost in the Machine* were the lines, 'Instead of worrying about my clothes / I could be someone that nobody knows . . . Life was easy when it was boring.' (The words were Copeland's, but Sting made it a point never to sing material without an engaging sincerity.) He particularly resented the prying eye of the media. 'If I could get away with it, I wouldn't do any more interviews,' he told *Trouser Press*. '[Publicity] can go too far,' he added. 'I've seen that become genuinely destructive, not to me, particularly, but to those around me, and it's no fun.' Nearly five years in the front line had given him grounds to protect what space was left. Above all, Sting took a dim view of the notion that success would be the point-man for joy. 'It isn't, and I don't think anything is. But I don't think happiness is necessarily the reason we're here . . . We're here to learn and evolve, and the pursuit of knowledge is what alleviates the pain of being human.'

There was a lesson here on fame, and Sting seemed willing to both grasp and give it.

Not surprisingly, his assertiveness, a tendency to crow and a steely perfectionism galled some of his colleagues. Speaking of the new album, Copeland told *Musician*, 'After five formative years and five records you grow apart. Now, the only thing that the three of us have in common is on stage and on vinyl. That's the only place we achieve synchronicity.' Sting for once echoed his drummer. 'It's not easy to be in a group. It's like marriage without sex. The only lubricant we have is music.' For all his love of *Synchronicity*, Sting remained unsure about The Police, and more often spoke of his screenplay and acting career. He was of two minds even about them: he told one friend early in 1983 'he wanted to do another tour and a movie as a pension plan, and then retire to the country'.

The film was *Dune*, a would-be epic shot by David Lynch, cult director of *Eraserhead*, *The Elephant Man*, and, later, *Twin Peaks*. Sting took the part after being told he was a 'gothic anti-hero', and a sure bet for screen stardom. It was a personal commitment, and the reply was personal. 'I'm doing *Dune* because of Lynch and for no other reason,' Sting said. 'I didn't really want to do the film, because I didn't think it was wise for me to be in an enormous movie . . . Then I met David, and I loved him. He's a

madman in sheep's clothing, and I just felt I had to do it because
I know he's going to do something extraordinary.' With a $50
million budget, three hundred special effects and a shooting
schedule of eighteen months, *Dune* certainly raised high hopes.
Sting's role as the evil Feyd – clad in black rubber and an outsize
codpiece – occupied him for six weeks, between mixing *Synchronicity* and the global tour to sell it.

Filming to a deadline in Mexico was never the ideal way to
enjoy the 'total peace and quiet' Sting said he wanted. He was
under psychoanalysis at the time: 'What it taught me,' he told *Q*,
'was that you can actually work on yourself. Instead of running
like a rat on a wheel, you step aside.'

In fact, most of Sting's demons pursued him on location. As
well as the tensions steadily building with the press, there was the
adjustment to life with Styler and the usual mutterings by The
Police, again shunted aside on their leader's whim. Then there
were the day-to-day ineptitudes of life in central America. Much
of Sting's personal music collection vanished in transit at the
airport. Along with most of the cast, he suffered breathing
problems and nausea from the smog, altitude and suspect food.
For some scenes, over a thousand extras were hired, all herded by
Lynch, whose humour wilted under a barrage of production
delays and soaring costs. Besides script and language hassles,
what no one had calculated was the so-called Fleece Factor –
namely, just how local merchants cashed in on the show. One
drinks vendor was supplying 5,000 bottles of water a day at a
dollar each. If logistics and petty theft weren't bad enough, the
film's crew then had to contend with the weather. Fierce heat
alternated with monsoon, and in late spring there was a down-
pour that lasted for eleven straight days. Sting spent most of the
delay shut up in his hotel. The gossip that, even there, he was
friendly with a number of extras, mainly the young and female
ones, was obviously a wicked calumny. Most of the Mexican
women in the film had minor, nonspeaking parts, but there was
one role of substance: the actress Sean Young, cast as Chani.
Young seemed to pursue Sting 'like an Exocet', as one colleague
puts it. Even this one-sided affair made a splash in the tabloids,
and set up a recurrent rumour – of Sting's involvement with his
leading ladies – regularly aired on his later films.

Lynch's script was adapted from a best-selling novel. Over the years, the director had had the savvy to treat his material like a good book, with exposition and narrative, where the pictures actually built on the story. *Dune* wasn't one of these films. The three-hour version of Frank Herbert's already overblown yarn was cringingly inept: intergalactic power-struggle takes place on an arid planet (inhabited by giant sandworms) over a magical spice. That was the plot. It never kept the real world on the edge of chaos in the way the low-budget *Eraserhead* did. *Dune* was all front, with flashes of hallucinatory brilliance but no real depth. It didn't 'come off the page' well. By the time Sting made his entrance as the judo-kicking Feyd, *Dune* was already lost in confused and confusing rewrites, bizarre effects and needless detours. It took wing from there.

On a personal level, *Dune* at least achieved its objectives. The image of Sting, in full Feyd regalia, made headlines in Britain and America. Stills of him dressed in his black fetishist's garb enjoyed almost iconographic status in the years ahead. Several, if not many, gay men adopted him as their cover-boy. To some, he *was* Feyd, a villainous feudal lord with a soft side, like the schizophrenic Taylor in *Brimstone*. Sting himself savoured the experience of casting and rehearsals, up to the actual time of shooting. 'It's all good stuff,' he told one reporter. In later years he tended to join the negative consensus of the film, which Styler pointedly called 'the flying jockstrap'. 'I hope you understood it,' Sting told one fan. 'I certainly never did.'*

Dune was released in 1984, two full years after Sting first signed on. The studio's publicity apparatus had begun cranking in advance, trying, desperately at times, to plant stories that would take the edge off the indignant buzz about the film's cost. Gossip columnists had already linked Sting and his co-star. A photo of him apparently ogling a bare-breasted Mexican woman was hawked around. Perversely, certain critics actually praised *Dune*'s scale and overkill, incessantly quoting statistics like the number of trick shots. The alternative view was taken by those who saw Sting as the last in a long line of rock idols unable, apparently, to cope on film. 'In his latest farce, he leaves every spell unbound,' wrote one. 'I hope this waste of celluloid comes back to haunt him.'

* Sting also revised his opinion of David Lynch, whom he later panned as 'a monster, a geek from the Midwest'.

It didn't. *Dune* not only absorbed Sting and paid him, it brought him a steady flow of scripts from producers keen to cash in on his name and cinematic looks. Dino de Laurentiis offered him the lead in a remake of *Mutiny on the Bounty*. Sting turned him down. Next came *The Bride* (another *Frankenstein* mutation) and *Plenty* (which, with Meryl Streep, Charles Dance and John Gielgud, lacked for neither talent nor originality), both of which he shot in the next twelve months. He had a stab at legitimate stardom. Sting's acting may have been low on range, but his professionalism and all-important name-appeal made it fly.

Dune itself died at the box office, though money trickled down on the video stores. It garnered a single Oscar nomination, for 'best sound' by the AOR group Toto. *Dune* also spawned a host of imitators, including *Tremors*, and other larval sci-fi clones. Like *Heaven's Gate* or *Waterworld*, it became famous as a morality tale of epic spending and glut, where costs rose in inverse proportion to quality and only the extras had fun.

Once in London, Sting and Styler took possession of a seventeenth-century home at 2, The Grove, Highgate. The manor house cost them £250,000, and almost as much went on repairs. The happiest, and most productive, time of Sting's next few years was to be spent there – a long, three-storey mansion situated in a semi-private lane between Hampstead Heath and Highgate cemetery. As Sting told his sister, it was an ideal place for work, and his main early additions were the state-of-the-art tape decks and Synclaviers without which no rock star was expected to function. The home studio looked out on a garden, through beech and laburnum trees, on to the heath. From the front door Sting could see the village green and the spire of St Michael's church.

The Grove enjoyed the advantage of being both city and country. There was a wavy gravel footpath, and an old-fashioned coaching lamp lit the brick façade. Though only five miles from central London, the house stood among winding lanes in a leafy, tree-lined row. Highgate village lay just to the north: a time-warp of red Gilbert Scott phone boxes, family-owned shops and thatched pubs, seemingly frozen *in situ* since the 1930s. Sting maintained the 'arty' traditions of the place. Both Samuel Coleridge and J. B. Priestley had once lived in The Grove; among the contemporary neighbours was the violinist Yehudi Menuhin (and Keith Richards' elderly grandfather). In the months ahead, dozens of local poets, painters and members of the Highgate Literary & Scientific Institute were among those given Sting's unlisted number (340 6669), and asked to visit.

On a tour of The Grove, the *Daily Express* wrote of the couple's home as 'fabulous ... with its sumptuous and comfortable large rooms, old pine-panelled walls, endless shelves of books, comfortable sofas and welcoming fire in the grate'. As well as the musical equipment, the house soon overflowed with baby ephemera, potted palms, thick rugs, thin blue delft china, electronics, clothes, and strangely formal, stylized etchings. It was all a long way from Wallsend, though some of the clutter of Station Road remained. One visitor thought it an 'odd mix of calm and chaos'. Unlike Sting's first home there were, for instance, plenty of bathrooms. But, despite the extra facilities, the water pipes burst, the boiler was often out and members of the household went for days without washing. A primitive central-heating system pumped hot air into the hall; elsewhere wood fires belched black smoke from the chimneys; in winter there were faded patches of damp, and the books in the library curled.

Despite the lavish scale, Sting's new house made another link to the past. It was one of his articles of faith that Station Road, and all Wallsend, had been walked by the ghosts of Roman centurions. This was a key saga of Sting's childhood. The Grove, he believed, was similarly possessed by the spirits of a mother and child. One night early in 1984 he woke to see the two wraiths apparently standing in his bedroom. In a second incident, he 'looked into the corner of the room and, clear as day, there was a woman and child ... I heard Trudie say, "Sting, what's that in the corner?" I just went totally cold, icy cold.' In time the family called on the services of a spiritualist. As Sting's early Catholicism lent credence to the idea that sexual infidelities beget grief, so the exorcism argued an intimate relationship between guilt and obsession. Even after the house had been purged, Sting claimed to be visited by strange phenomena: on one occasion a kitchen knife rose from a table and embedded itself in the wall.

Sting and Styler also bought a New York apartment from the singer Billy Joel. The two-million-dollar duplex, on Manhattan's Upper East Side, commanded a view of Grand Army Plaza and

Central Park. Here the neighbours were Placido Domingo, Luciano Pavarotti (who became a friend) and Frank Sinatra. Styler liked to refer to the place as an 'accommodation address'. It was indeed close to work, Broadway and Masterdisk studios, as well as the film production office both parties haunted. Like The Grove, the New York penthouse soon filled with books and musical paraphernalia. Other touches came from the designer Alain Mertens, the man behind London's DM Gallery, who had the skill and imagination to embody old rooms in new construction. It was here that Sting wrote parts of *Nothing Like the Sun* and Styler doodled on her scripts.

Early in 1984 the couple had their first child, a girl, Brigitte Michaela. The birth made waves in the British tabloids, riveted on Styler as they never were on Tomelty. In the West London Hospital, paparazzi skulked and squatted in laundry hampers, swarming the family when they left to drive home to Highgate. A month later, Sting and Styler were mobbed when they walked into Joe Allen's restaurant in Covent Garden. For most of the rest of the decade, other private trips would become unexpectedly public when press and photographers hounded them on the streets. Styler, in particular, enjoyed the prestige of the scarlet woman – 'Sting's honey' as one card put it – her gossip-column stock rising as her film career dwindled. She later told the *Daily Mail*, 'I was a successful actress before I met Sting and then, in 1989, I had a year of not being offered any work at all. When I complained to a girlfriend, she said: "But darling, you're just perceived as a jetsetter." ' In Hollywood, to enjoy life, as opposed to work, is to be branded a social outlaw. Styler's career revived as a result of her charity drive with the Rainforest Foundation and her first feature film, *The Grotesque*, in 1996.

Long before then the two had taken their place among the Jaggers and Geldofs as rock's most photographed double-acts. When Sting spoke of socialism most people never realised just how social his life with Styler would be. The two went out of their way to be seen with all the trappings of screen-idol glitz. They made great copy. Rumours regularly drifted about of their separation, and when the broadsheets went to profile A-list couples, they knew where to look. In time, they became famous merely for being, rather than anything they said or did. While Sting had once craved the coverage, by the mid-1980s it had become intrusively pesky. Once in the tabloids, he found, it was impossible to get out. Long used to being written up in *Melody Maker* and *Sounds*, to be pilloried in the *Sun* was a novelty. His reaction was indifferent in public, but exorbitantly crisp in private. Sting began to carp at being 'treated like Princess Di'. Under the veneer of worldly cool, he had to clutch hard at his good humour in the face of constant media barbs. It was to his credit that, with the sole exception at Heathrow, his relations with the press never came to blows.

Meanwhile, *Synchronicity*, The Police's fifth album, was released in June 1983. The title (also prompted by the ecologists' slogan 'It's all connected') came from Jung's theory of collective consciousness. Sting expounded on the theme in a high-minded interview. 'In the past, I've often suspected myself of deliberately manufacturing unhappiness. I didn't have that problem this time.' At its self-indulgent nadir, *Synchronicity* was the composer holding up a mirror to himself. Yet Sting – who could think, brood and click his fingers in the same phrase – was too canny a popsmith to saddle the tunes with the kind of angst that got Leonard Cohen a bad name. The album showcased neither a style, an era, nor even the high-blown, sub-Jungian lyrics. The theme was woven into its stately melodies, its elegant guitar twists and full-throttle vocals. What emerged was slick mood music. *Synchronicity* may have ultimately fulfilled some deep, aesthetic need, but you could still hum it.

It also marked the band's further move away from the pop-reggae clip that made them famous to start with. The Police glossed their sound partly to put blue water between themselves and their mimics, but also in a bid for dramatic economy. They were growing older, and as they matured they began to value worldly influences like jazz and ultrasmooth balladry. Derek Green, head of A&M, was 'bitterly disappointed' with *Synchronicity*, which he felt caught Sting 'flat between The Police and a solo album'. But elsewhere reviews and sales were all that could have been hoped for. There were few qualms about a thoughtful record that dared float sweet, keening rhythms over a booming beat as a complement to the lyrics. As one critic said, 'Sting had our attention. With *Synchronicity*, he got our respect.'

The album's lead-off track, 'Synchronicity I', offered a curt, take-no-prisoners salvo of quasi-punk excess, and inhabited the same universe as the Stones' 1978 hit, 'Respectable'. After the riot of drum vignettes and staccato verses, Sting lowered the heat on 'Walking In Your Footsteps'. Flutes, sound effects and congas set up a (factually flawed) anthropology lecture and featured some fatally, even palaeontologically, lumbering rhymes. The song's own evolution was in the general direction of Sting's solo career; if ever there was a statement of future intent, this was it. Side one was blighted overall by the creative rift at the album's core. 'O My God', with its Beatlesque bass riff, neatly fused funk and R&B. For once, the pummel came off as more than a pose. The drums snapped, the guitars had bite, and Sting flung abuse at a parting lover. Here was the attitude, passion and skewed wit the sidemen could only feebly approximate on their own two cuts. 'Mother', Summers' gnarled *Psycho* pastiche, began life as a 'little thing I did in my kitchen studio', where it thus amply fulfilled the classic pop-writing adage: great songs should be baked, not microwaved. Banal harmonies, added for sweetening, dished Copeland's 'Miss Gradenko'. Sting's 'Synchronicity II' broke no new ground, but at least recaptured the mood of purring Cadillac-rock. It also showed his skill for sleight-of-hand and metaphor: here was a domestic scene ('Another suburban family morning / Grandmother screaming at the wall') juxtaposed with a monster emerging from the ooze of a Scottish loch. Somehow, alongside the bazooka blast of bass and drums, it worked.

Synchronicity's enduring moment was, of course, 'Every Breath You Take'. In terms of creamy arrangements and flawless renderings, it was a model song: four minutes of muted guitar (cribbed from Bartók, and a distant relative of 'Invisible Sun'), cocktail-bar piano and a swelling, hummable chorus. 'Every Breath' also enjoyed the advantage of ambiguity. The message, treated by most fans as a sugary greetings-card, was loaded with a mix of self-pity and venom worthy of the most twisted stalker. The lyrics dealt with Sting's marital crack-up. 'I consider it a fairly nasty song,' he told one paper. 'It's about surveillance and ownership and jealousy.' Sting touched on universal themes in the imagery, but the words still bullied the listener, insisting on the writer's control, satisfying vanity rather than exciting response. The song's trite rhymes were almost completely uninvolving, not just in terms of story and emotion, but even at the level of the phrase. Sting later tended to disown the hastily coined lyrics, but stood by the song. He was right to: his obsession with failed love had never been in such gorgeous context.

'King Of Pain' turned the same trick with an angular but agile melody, a dynamic AOR chorus, and a tune that went both to and fro, again linking Sting's roots with his solo work, the '60s with the '90s. The treacly 'Wrapped Around Your Finger' laboriously stuck to the formula needed to re-moisten hankies still damp from 'Every Breath'. The words were little more than a pretext to charm. It was, nonetheless, a tender, clever ballad in which Sting was cast as the young apprentice, 'seeking knowledge/ Things they would not teach me of in college', and one of the few pop songs ever to mention Scylla and Charybdis. Snail-paced chords and a sense of *déjà vu* (in its echo of the minimalist 'Walking On The Moon') nearly stopped 'Tea In The Sahara'* in its tracks. The first verse sounded like a strong wind could have blown it away. By mid-song, the tune had darted for the safer ground of a C-G-A-F rock chorus, and ended on an anguished, sustained note; 'depositing us at the edge of the desert, reaching skyward, our cups full of sand', in *Rolling Stone*'s vivid image. Dark humour, never far from the surface with The Police, broke out openly in the bonus track, 'Murder By Numbers', a marginal jape that wandered in jazz-rock borderland and evoked a smoky after-hours club.

There were no fewer than four singles – 'Every Breath', 'Wrapped Around Your Finger', 'Synchronicity II' and 'King Of Pain' – which were successively in the chart for ten months. Each came with the requisite video in which Sting preened, marched, cooed, strutted and, in one shot, swung apelike on a rope, his face rictal in a Johnny Rotten leer. Tightly scripted, lavishly budgeted, all four were a progression on the hand-held footage of the band's early hits. The new, sleek look was the essence of *Synchronicity*.**

In a neat coincidence, the album was The Police's crowning artistic coup and their major commercial triumph. It was number one in the UK and topped the US chart for seventeen weeks.

* The title came from a reading of Paul Bowles's novel *The Sheltering Sky*.
**The record's cover, on which Sting's photos were washed in yellow, was also much admired and endlessly probed for 'clues': was it a reference to his hair, some self-reproach, or was he just jaundiced?

By 1983 the roar of acclaim and public celebrity was constant, and it made Sting antsy. As a close friend puts it, 'It took him a while before he saw that that's what he was – a myth. He was so absorbed in himself he never looked around. With *Synchronicity*, he really heard the yells for the first time.' Sting himself offered a more stoic appraisal of what was happening. 'Being a rock star's little more than a joke,' he told one reporter. (It was, however, as Steerpike's books show, a singularly practical joke.) He took the same line elsewhere: 'It's ridiculous the amount of money I get paid, but that's not really my fault. I didn't create the system. I just laugh at it.'

Sting was a man of so many faces because it served his deepest need: to assert himself effectively, come out ahead, and wield power. He may not, as he said, have been much of an actor, but he used brain and body to fill the stage and hold an audience. Even as he was running down the 'cynical burlesque' of most rockers' lives, he was planning a year of continuous touring and sales work. Fittingly, it began with the release of *Police Around the World*, the film of the trio's global smash. From recording in Los Angeles and rehearsals in New York, Copeland and Summers flew to Chicago, where the advance opened at Comiskey Park on 23 July. It wound up again, via the US, Europe, Britain, Australia and a second American leg, nine months later. In sordidly material terms, as well as professionally, this was the band's shining moment. 'We've been through it all and we've grown with it,' said Sting. 'We crawled and then we walked, and now we're running. And we'll keep running till we fall.' The eighty shows that followed represented The Police's major contribution to mass culture, in every banal sense of the adjective: there were films, videos, photos, badges, buttons, posters, programmes and exclusive accessories – everything from socks to designer suits. If a teenager could wear it, Sting and the band were on it.

The group themselves rented their last communal home and the finest of all, a $50,000 per-month mansion on Long Island. Nearly a century old, it was surrounded by tall trees and gently rolling lawns whose ivy-clad walls had communicating doors. Security arrangements were elaborate. Video cameras swept the grounds and two armed guards stood at the door. The elegant façade of the three-storey house had high sash windows and a small portico flanked by columns. Equipped with a gym, jacuzzi and swimming pool, it also had a butler and three professional chefs on standby in the ballroom-sized kitchen. A private airfield lay just to the north. From there, the entourage jetted by Gulfstream to their east-coast dates, returning the same night, rather than subject themselves to hotels. 'This way they feel happy and comfortable,' said Miles, outwardly indifferent to the cost. 'It makes good sense.'

In keeping with the epic scale, the Chicago *Tribune* sent both arts and business correspondents to Comiskey Park. The night was a triumph for the entrepreneurial fringe, *ad hoc* vendors skirting the official sales force and the approaches to the stadium lined with jerry-built shanties. 'Hordes of males', the paper noted, arrived bare-chested at 35th Street and Shields Avenue 'to avoid that tacky look of wearing a concert shirt over another one ... The Police's slow-burn songs lit an incendiary sales fuse ... programs and souvenirs were both flying over the counter.' Ticket touting was brisk.

After no fewer than four oblatory groups, and MTV clips shown on a giant screen, The Police came on to a standing ovation. 'We took off the rough edges – got rid of the stuff that Middle America couldn't handle,' Copeland had said of *Synchronicity*. The *Tribune* critic agreed that, with 'Every Breath' and the rest, the band had not only perfected mass marketing, but discovered a mass market. 'In the past, The Police's mix of pop and reggae often seemed uncomfortably close to the sort of synthetic calypso one could imagine being played at Club Med. These days, the trio has broadened its musical base and sounds much the better for it.' It didn't hurt that they had the number-one album in America. The Police came armed with taut, crescendo-heavy tunes and knew how to deliver the goods. Sting's voice fused seamless verses with rock-and-roll choruses that ranged from seductive to mildly subversive. Add the pop nous of Copeland and Summers, visual punch and three scantily clad female singers, and it was easy to see why the crowd went home happy.

As ever, Sting's own looks and muscle-tone were the hub of attention. By mid-1983 he'd transformed into a gel-haired matinée idol – sporting what one cynic called a 'sub-Bowie, Barbie Doll cut' – eager to show his newly buffed torso and ever ready with a pose. Men like Bowie and Jagger had increasingly turned rock concerts into giant power-aerobic workouts, with themselves exhorting their classes to join in. Sting took the drill a step further by flouncing on stage with a trampoline. The sight of him bouncing up and down to Summers' guitar break was the night's most surreal moment, though the fans happily trilling the chorus of 'King Of Pain' ran a close second. Along with the garish lighting, the dapper costumes that served as a central metaphor and the set decked with potted palms, Sting's unflagging zip was the show's basic key. The energy level rarely dipped, and The Police never outstayed their welcome. After ninety minutes they were gone, back on Long Island before the last of the fans had left the parking lot.

The band travelled with a crew of seventy-eight. For the first time, as Summer says, 'we had people working for us whose names we didn't know'. A colleague once watched Sting at a sound-check before a New York gig; though he was perfectly civil, it was like seeing a medieval king receive petitioners and flunkies. Humble gaffers unfurled song playlists before him 'as if they were merchants with rolls of silk'. Little of the ritual was strictly necessary. They weren't offering information so much as obeisance. By the time of *Synchronicity*, Sting's staff had become his vassals, and The Police toured with a hierarchy of toadies, lickspittles and others whose precise status was hard to say. (So labyrinthine was their backstage area that Phil Collins took a wrong turn while watching them at Wembley and got lost.) There were notable exceptions: Kim Turner still moved in the zone between icy professionalism and personal warmth, and Sting's roadie Danny Quatrochi became a friend.* Relations with Stewart Copeland, on the other hand, hit bottom. Sting would publicly ridicule any gaffe the drummer made on stage, belittling his sense of rhythm, his tempos, his harmonies, or anything that put his back up. Copeland retaliated in a dressing-room brawl that nearly bucked the tour. Sting spent that night in a Minneapolis hospital, with what was at first feared as a heart attack. The later diagnosis was a cracked rib.

By high summer 1983, the band's manager felt bold enough to

---

*Turner and Quatrochi were duly appointed directors of Magnetic and Steerpike, respectively.

announce: 'We're the biggest group in the world – bigger than the Beatles.' In terms of accountancy, it was no idle boast. In only four years, The Police had sold more records than the Fabs had during their career. It was now that they crossed over into the land of American stellardom. The Police even sold out a gala at Shea Stadium, scene of orgiastic Beatle-fests in 1965 and '66. The *New York Times*, not one to tout new idols at the expense of old gods, was fulsome:

> Just about every Police song has a fleet, irresistible groove that might hint at reggae, African pop, funk, classical minimalism or rock ... That takes concentration, and the band's fingers were so busy that the players had no time for typical arena theatrics ... The musicians took out their virtuosity on rhythm and texture rather than on individual display. Mr Copeland ranged over a standard drum kit laced with exotic percussion to find the right click or bonk for each beat, while Mr Summers and Sting chased each other through some songs in such close pursuit that they seemed to switch rhythm parts. The concert was full of the kind of jubilant, daredevil group playing that is rarely heard on rock stages anywhere – much less at Shea Stadium.

It was, as Copeland says, a magical night.

Backstage, Sting – whose quip 'We'd like to thank the Beatles for lending us their stadium' had had half the 70,000 crowd clapping and the other half scratching their heads – held court until four in the morning. *Le tout* New York was at the party: not just rockers but cultural icons like William Burroughs, Truman Capote and, inevitably, Andy Warhol, the last of whom thought Sting looked 'tired and old'. Warhol might have been surprised. Sting later admitted that this was the night he decided to leave the band.

It was 18 August 1983, exactly six years since The Police made their début. They had, in the meantime, become the all-in champions of pop, shifting millions of units and playing in places beyond the range and reach of any other contender. Sting had achieved all his starting ambitions. He was rich and cosmically famous. Even his friends and family, one cousin says, 'related to him as a rock star, not as our kid'. Yet it was one of the peculiar paradoxes of Sting's life that, while everything got better, he saw it as having worsened. Never had he been more successful, never did he look more put-upon. Never had he been more popular, never did he seem more woebegone. Sting's 'loneliness at the top' was abject. He'd aimed to be an artist, but, like Bowie before him, found himself no more than a stylistic wet-nurse, while men of lesser talent and dubious motives pursued their 'own bag'. It was enough to give him pause. As Sting says, 'I personally [at Shea], during the performance, thought, "This is it. You can't do any better than this" . . . And that's the point I decided to stop.' Writ large, it was the same as when the eighteen-year-old had retired as undefeated Northern Counties sprint champion; his pedestal had made a precarious perch, and in both cases he quit rather than face a slow and sorry slump. Sting always walked before he was pushed.

The final tour won the best reviews and richest prizes of The Police's career. By the time they hit London that Christmas, the band had grossed $10 million in ticket sales alone, quite aside from the bonanza in high-end spinoffs. Miles spent $400,000 hiring Kevin Godley and Lol Creme* to film the tour, a video (in which Sting briefly turned a hand-held camera on himself, a self-allusive moment *New York* hailed as 'naked vanity') released in September 1984. It, too, swelled the band's royalty flow. There were literally scores of TV specials, features and rockumentaries, and heavy rotation of The Police's hits on MTV. *Rolling Stone's* Dave Marsh flayed the group for endorsing a pop-music station that 'ignored' blacks, and there was grousing elsewhere about the hype and cynicism of the sales blitz. But those were isolated voices. By the time *Synchronicity* hit the bargain-bins, it was in the realms of *Thriller* and *Let's Dance*. Despite or because of the fame, Sting spoke of getting out of rock altogether.

His first extramural projects were back-to-back films. *New York* had gone too far in claiming Sting was 'unable to walk down pop's hall of mirrors and avert his gaze', but he enjoyed appearing both before and behind a lens. Backstage at Comiskey Park, he ran into his friend Franc Roddam, director of *Quadrophenia*. The result was Sting's starring role in the ill-conceived

*As members of 10cc, Godley and Creme had first met The Police in the bygone era of Surrey Sound.

Gothic claptrap *The Bride*. He followed it up with *Plenty*, a film that was subtle, haunting and blisteringly highbrow. Meanwhile, Sting failed to find backing for his screenplay of *Gormenghast*. The adaptation was eventually put out on radio.

If Sting was a Renaissance Man, he was still also a business-man. Throughout the 1980s, he would insist he had 'no head for figures', that he was a 'singer and songwriter [who] found myself at the head of a multi-million-dollar corporation', that there was 'too much paperwork', it was 'so heavy'. It's true that Sting was an artist first and foremost, but along with the naïve awe at his earning power he kept a hawk eye on the bottom line. After *Synchronicity* he threw himself into the pursuit of wealth. At core, Sting was a marketeer and he found himself in 1983–84 with the knack of generating dizzying sums for virtually any enter-prise he chose to bless with his name. He picked his investments well, for the most part. His twin watchwords were latitude and diversity.

Keith Moore continued the daily management of Sting's port-folio and duly opened an account – Moore Sloane Re G. M. Sumner – to administer funds accruing from legitimate tax avoid-ance by the singer's key companies. (Contrary to reports that Sting himself never knew of the kitty, it was specifically listed in the affidavit prepared for his divorce from Tomelty in 1984.) To Moore and the other advisers, he wasn't a pop star but a Caesar. Sting was akin to a human cash machine, as royalties and tour receipts rained down in the wake of *Synchronicity*. The album alone sold more than twelve million copies. Still, to the experts in such esoteric matters, his income never qualified him as 'filthy rich'. His homes in London and New York were modest by the standards of Elton John and his ilk. Sting himself was apt to point out that he lived frugally, enjoyed eating steak and chips followed by custard, and that his favourite clothes, the oft-noted symbols of his decadence, were 'years old'.

Most humans would be content to motor along this way for a decade or two before taking well-earned retirement, but Sting's financial drive matched his musical restlessness. He was still a director of Steerpike (where Styler replaced Tomelty on the board in September 1985), as well as Steerpike Overseas, Roxanne Music, Roxanne Music (Tours), and Roxanne Music (Overseas); Magnetic, meanwhile, turned over more than a million pounds annually for Copeland and Summers. In later years Sting would add directorships of Pangaea (his own label for 'fringe' music) and the Rainforest Project (selling and distributing merchandise bearing the Rainforest Foundation name), two companies that aimed for philanthropy over profit. He may have had 'no head for figures', but he was quite cerebral enough to know his own worth. By the mid-1980s, rock-star fortunes were a declension of good, better and celestial. Anyone who wrote his own music could hardly fail to thrive in a bull market.

Sting wanted a piece of it. He was as adept at business as anyone, knew enough to delegate and always or usually got good advice. By 1984 he enjoyed what the latter calls a 'cordial relationship' with Keith Moore. With Miles increasingly pursuing his own life in Los Angeles, Sting relied ever more heavily on his accountant. Some thought the friendship cast doubt on his judgement, yet a closer reading of the facts shows Moore to have been an eminently plausible and well-qualified lieutenant. He was not, as later claimed, made bankrupt in 1975, nor had he been banned by the Institute of Chartered Accountants. Moore's reputation, it was true, had taken its raps in the form of misconduct charges by the groups Queen and Big Country – and fines by his own professional body – but for fifteen years he never gave Sting any worry. His strategy was orderly and logical. The major investments were in 22-carat securities, and only the savings from tax – money, in a sense, Sting could afford to lose – went on ventures. In every way he could, Moore schemed and shielded, organized and arranged, and became both provider and keeper of his client's purse. This was the co-dependent relationship that ended in headlines, court and, ultimately, jail.

Sting spent much of 1984 reaping the fruits of 1983. As well as his royalties and tour fees, the industry rushed to heap kudos on him. *Billboard* named 'Every Breath' the top single of the year. Sting and The Police won in no fewer than four categories at the twenty-sixth annual Grammys in 1984. The awards were for Song of the Year and Best Pop Performance by a Duo or Group ('Every Breath'), Best Rock Performance ('Synchronicity II') and Best Rock Instrumental ('Brimstone & Treacle'). Although, for some compelling reason, Joan Rivers was recruited to go to London and present a gong to Boy George, The Police themselves failed to appear either in person or on film. John Denver accepted for them.

In addition, laudatory reviews were still hitting the news-stands, most critics praising 'Every Breath' with the sort of gush reserved for a 'Yesterday' or 'Candle In The Wind'. Where Sting's early songs had found him probing his mind, soul and sense of purpose, all within the context of an unfeeling, even cruel, world, the newer works were more confident and mature, tempered by experience and psychological musings. He'd been a superstar for four years, but because *Outlandos* and the rest were mired in provincial and personal beefs, America was charmed rather than captivated. *Synchronicity* was global, both in terms of its themes and chords, and reviewers took note. To *Rolling Stone*, for one, The Police were 'almost unquestioned as today's best-loved band'.

'Every Breath' continued its critical sweep in April 1984, when it won Best Group Video at the American Film Awards and took Novello trophies for both Best Song and Most Performed Work. (It became a standard.) The single and album seemed to appeal to highbrow and lowbrow alike, and there were plays from *Top of the Pops* to black urban stations. In Japan, *Asahi Shimbun* admired the composer's 'dark work, full of literate intuition and irony', while in France, 'le Sting' was everywhere – on hoardings and posters, and staring down from a billboard on to the Louvre. The German and Italian press shared in the international reverence, almost pious, of Sting's songs.

Making money and exciting critics didn't assure him happiness, Sting quickly found. He'd worked non-stop for six years, written a dozen pop classics, and made a conscious bid to branch into TV and film. But all of these ideals were soon met by the harsh ennui of reality. In time, Sting would romanticize this era as his dark night of the soul before his personal and creative renaissance, yet it was clear from his mood that the spring and summer of 1984 offered a series of dire threats to his stamina and commitment to The Police.

He began the year by informing a stunned world that the band was 'on hold'. The crisis, and near-implosion, were euphe-mized as a mere family tiff about the 'vision thing'. Meantime, a planned live album was shelved. Recording dates in Montserrat were dropped. Though far from idle, Sting would learn that his new-fangled domesticity and accumulated wealth posed major obstacles to the self-flogging borne since 1977. Without challenge he couldn't work, and he went through a grim period of writer's block before he was again able to come up with commercial songs – and then in a radically new context. It also added to his already confused sense of identity. Was he a pin-up, a serious artist who happened to make millions titillating his pubescent fans, or a family man and father? Without a sense of self, he was losing his sense of mission.

The Police reared large in his worries. Here, obviously, the successful formula had become formulaic. Early on they realized that the band's hook was wiggy pop-rock of no fixed abode, with homiletic words. By *Synchronicity* almost every song was strangely familiar, and even the zanier tunes veered to the mainstream. The lyrics were deliberately anti-heroic, and the choruses tended to loom, announce themselves and then get off; 'old hams,' wrote *Village Voice*, 'yanked from a sketch running long'. Put otherwise, it was like a sports round-up consisting entirely of goals, or even a porn film – endless sex with no context. For Sting, if not the audience, it didn't take long for a series of climaxes to turn dreary. Bluntly, he was bored, frustrated and tired of burlesquing himself on stage. He'd become suspicious of adulation, and seen it fade like yesterday's rainbow. On the other hand, his self-esteem was starved. At the best of times, he tended to fret about what he saw as the average group's lifespan ('about three albums,' he told one paper) and discoursed gloomily on being 'the guy in Las Vegas with the balding head singing "Roxanne"' at forty. Some form of reinvention was urgent, if not vital.

His roles in *The Bride* and *Plenty* were part of this. 'I want to be offered more movies,' Sting said. It was a sane ambition, but it wasn't enough. He needed applause that was rooted more in character and emotion than in slapstick and special effects. 'I'd like to do stage plays,' he added, 'because I don't think I'll ever be respected – in England, anyway – unless I do.' No small matter was the fact that Sting was again living with a working actress. Styler encouraged and coaxed him, and undoubtedly whetted his competitive edge. He went for several auditions.

Sting also took a lively interest in the world around him. He was concerned by what he saw as the twin evils of the Thatcher and Reagan governments – social decay and military chancing, respectively. He discreetly gave money to the striking British miners and wrote a song, 'We Work The Black Seam', which nailed his Labour colours to the mast in the lines, 'We matter more than pounds and pence / Your economic theory makes no sense.' He then dubbed new vocals on to 'Every Breath', turning the ballad into an anti-nuclear tirade. The first most of the world had heard of him in twelve months was when the song became the theme tune of the satirical show *Spitting Image*. Fussy and easily offended, articulate and excessively opinionated, Sting continued to hold forth on topics from Aids to Amnesty, abortion to education. He made generous provision for Joe and Kate in the divorce from Tomelty.

A measure of Sting's concerns were his veiled put-downs of both his band and rock in general, as if, a workmate says, 'he was apologizing for his job'. Despite being inert, The Police continued to nag him, though Sting's spleen fell just short of bile. 'I don't want to only do the old formula, even though I know it works,' he said. 'I get very claustrophobic, very frustrated . . . My head can cope with more than one thing, so I'm keen to get away from the stereotypes and people's conceptions of what I am.' In the mid-1970s, Sting had hoped that music would help counter his crippling shyness. Instead, a decade later, it raised more questions and self-doubt. 'You don't have to have the intelligence of a brain surgeon to play rock and roll. The opposite is the general rule.'

As well as acting and civics, Sting filled out his time in regular sessions with a Jungian analyst. On her advice he kept a pad by his bed to record his dreams, some of which were worked into lyrics (and the title for his next album). Sting was also a man of infinite physical energy. Nowadays, he turned in late, got up early, exercised seven days a week, and had to be forced to relax. He ran incessantly. He liked to ride and bet on horses, enjoyed motorbikes and skateboards, and played Scrabble as if in a death-struggle. He went windsurfing and learnt to scuba-dive while working in Barbados. Once he ran out of air while eighty feet under the Caribbean. Locals had to wade in to save him.

Critics who wrote off the British film industry after *Chariots of Fire* were never likely to revive it on the basis of *The Bride*. The story, concocted by Franc Roddam, was itself a freakish hybrid of *Frankenstein* and *Pygmalion*: Sting makes monsters for a living and ends up a monster. The actual birth scene played like a *Carry*

On spoof, with the female creature lurching from a vat surrounded by beakers, tubes and flickering candles, delivered by a
frock-coated Sting and his gay assistant (Quentin Crisp). From
then on the film was funny when it tried to be hair-raising and
hair-raising when it tried to be funny. Bogus history and geography clashed with science to create a misbegotten mess.

Sting camped the part as an Edwardian fop, with wing collar
and floppy hair. His character was eerily consistent with the
chillier edges of his stage persona, leading to gibes that he'd been
typecast: the scene where he fired a housekeeper with the words
'Your employment here is terminated' rang 'several bells' for
one ex-minder of The Police. The line 'I wasn't thrown out of
university – I left' also suggested autobiographical procedures
were at work. A rant about creating 'a new woman – a woman
equal to ourselves' just sounded like warped racial propaganda.
The morality tale of Mary Shelley's original was lost in a long
series of colour-supplement shots and a laughable, sped-up
climax in which Sting toppled to his death from the castle keep.
Wooden acting and smoochy music from Maurice Jarre added
up to a film equally thrown away.

The legitimate press took exception to, or ignored, *The Bride*;
as Sting might have guessed, the tabloids targeted his private life.
He was said to have had a fling with his leading lady, Jennifer
Beals – even to have married her. Rumours of an on-set affair
were nothing new to Sting, but the gossip swirling round *The
Bride* was unusually rich. In one much-touted clip, Beals's
character slowly descended a staircase and stood frozen in front
of her master. She was naked. Stills of the scene enjoyed wide
circulation in Fleet Street and further fuelled talk of a romance.
One female friend quipped of this shot, 'Sting looked so bored
with [her] pussy, he might have been designing drapes to go with
the thing.' There was certainly testimony to his emotional
detachment from his colleagues. Beals herself went so far as to
say she found Sting 'fun, sweet and supportive' and 'in amazing
shape for an old man'. The tabloids were both elated and confused by the admission: elated because Beals's witty, tart remarks
were the perfect caption for the photos; confused because it
neither confirmed nor scotched the scandal.

The press entirely missed the real story. Sting formed a close
and lasting friendship with Quentin Crisp. The gay author

certainly had no sexual ambitions on his co-star. But, like Beals and the rest, he could scarcely avoid admiring Sting's musculature. Asked his opinion of the cult of physical development, Crisp once said: 'I think everyone should spend hours daily in a gym and I've often explained that a man cannot be considered handsome unless his neck is thicker than his head.' Whether an endorsement or a disparagement, Crisp's remarks concealed real affection. He and Sting met several times in Manhattan, alternating between the luxury duplex and Crisp's own digs in the Bowery. The song 'Englishman In New York' was Sting's toast to the relationship, so baffling to outsiders – the older man 'all front', the younger one going through social motions – until one realized that, for Sting, sense went with pain, and the victimized found truth through hardship. Behind this train of thought lay Sting's icy self-pity, but it drew him to those, like Crisp, he saw as fellow loners.

As a film, *The Bride* felt like *Young Frankenstein* without the belly-laughs. It didn't help that the picture lacked an actor who could carry it. Sting had the looks and the presence, but those were never the real problem. He simply didn't possess the technique to lead a two-hour epic. Much of his performance seemed passive, unreflective, without insight. His reliance on posing exaggerated the unwitting sense of farce. The original idea had been for him to play a cameo; critics would rue the change of plan, and the lack of subtlety or variation in the script. Sting's own view was both blunt and tinged with ego. *The Bride* was 'dreadful – I was the best thing in it'.

The Police gave a number of small concerts in early 1985 and decided they liked them. The shows, with minimal props and lighting, were seized on by audiences of a thousand or two who listened attentively to the semi-acoustic sets and found it hard to believe the legendary band were these quiet, ageing, serious-looking men with jazz-symphonic tastes. One of the final nights was at Newcastle City Hall. Over the years Sting had had mixed luck when playing his home town, notably in 1982 before a vitriolic and sparse crowd in Gateshead. This was no exception. An electrical fire cut all power to the hall and the audience, including Ernie and Audrey Sumner, were asked to leave. Before they did, Sting played a solo version of 'Roxanne'. Even in near-blackout conditions, he knew how to deliver the goods: the number was genuinely haunting, as was Sting's parting comment about 'end[ing] up where I began'.

A sure sign that The Police, creatively speaking, were on the way out rather than the way in was their award of a lifetime achievement gong at the 1985 Brits. Nobody close to them, not even Miles, claims they took the slightest pride in this dubious obituary. The ceremony itself was a mess – for *Melody Maker*, 'the presenter given the task of explaining it gave us instead a superb impersonation of Magnus Pyke' – and took a strangely funereal tone. Throughout the night's speeches, people paid tribute to the band's past glories, without paying lip service to the future. Sting himself failed to show.

Throughout the spring and early summer he stood aloof, neither fuelling nor denying rumours of a split. Sting's view of The Police was so mixed, the messages so vague, the party line so variegated, that it gave the word 'fusion' a new twist. He told one reporter, 'We haven't broken up, but we're separated by our own plans for ourselves for the time being. It's nothing more than that.' This equivocal promise was followed in private by rants at Copeland and Sumners. When Bob Geldof rang to invite The Police to play at Live Aid, Sting was crisp: 'No. I'll do it myself.' Keith Moore, meanwhile, seeing the 'process of disintegration start, and the nature of my responsibilities change significantly', began quietly making arrangements for the end.

It seemed to have loomed for years. Insiders and fans alike had long heard of the war between Sting and Copeland, and rightly guessed that musical differences were matched by personal ones. In 1978–79, Police tours had been notorious for their excesses, for egos run amok in one-night stands hazed over by unfamiliar rooms, drugs, strange faces in packed halls, sex, and enough hero-worship for anyone. By *Synchronicity* the air of unpredictable charm surrounding the trio had given way to one of steely professionalism, the groupies had been replaced by wives and lovers, and the operation ran like a mobile company. They were militarily efficient. Yet the stress at the heart of the band worsened with every unit they shifted. The songwriting money – which arrived thicker and faster than mere royalties – had long meant that Sting was no team member. He was player-manager of The Police, a man who frequently told Copeland or Summers 'your song sucks' and rode herd on them in the studio. There may have been, as the guitarist says 'hardly any broken hearts', but there were still bruised egos and cracked ribs. Summers admits to feeling 'we were becoming more of an accompanist to Sting's songs' by 1983. He also speaks of him as 'very talented . . . but Machiavellian. He calculates everything.' Copeland's own frustration had long since exploded with atomic force. The drummer stormed out of sessions. He fumed and fretted. He was a ranter of unusual persistence. Sting, notoriously able to hold his own in that field, failed miserably when he tried to shout Copeland down. Derek Green, head of A&M, believes 'Stewart, to the very end, saw himself as the keeper of the punk flame . . . He was never going to give up his say in the music, and Sting was never going to listen.' The whole thing, says Green, was 'like an ugly family feud'.

Copeland's elder brother, ironically, sided with Sting. In the search for scapegoats after the split, certain fans would blame The Police's manager for over-extending the band and himself. In one view, with his crack about the Beatles, Miles had 'finally caved in' to hubris. 'That was the kind of crass carnival-barking that broke The Police,' says an A&M executive who should know. Nemesis followed. Yet Miles had his own working credo. Contrary to popular belief, he placed the highest premium on loyalty, friendship, humour, trust. (Loyalty, that was, *within* the circle; outsiders weren't necessarily eligible for the same consideration, and stories of those who took offence at Miles are legion – and undoubtedly true.) He may have been ambitious, but he was also a deft strategist, an astute promoter, a cool judge of character and drove a hard bargain. With every breath they took, every move they made, he hawked The Police. No one was more vigilant on their behalf, or more bullish. As late as 1986 all questions about the band's breakup were parried with angry jabs of Miles's hand. It says much for his personal commitment that, even as he threatened to sue anyone who wrote off the group, he was vigorously pushing Sting as a solo act, dealing with the new henchmen ('They're saying, "How much money is on the table, man?" and I say, "Yeah, but that's Sting's table – not yours"') as he had the old.

Miles had surely flogged The Police. That he was also a realist, hard-headed enough to back his prime asset even if that simultaneously snubbed his brother, was also true. Miles had nothing to do with the music, as he was always the first to claim. His job, as he saw it, was to do the best for his star client – whatever family strains that meant – and so he invariably did. He wasn't, however, the man who broke up The Police.

Inevitably, and wrongly, blame also clung to Styler. Where Yoko Ono had gone, Sting's partner was thought to follow. Nineteen eighty-five represented the height of her own frustration, not only with her career, but also at the fact that he'd carved out a life apart from hers. Although she apparently shared him willingly in order to preserve what she could, Styler, in the world in which they lived, was never as free as Sting; nor was she above occasional petulance and envy. (According to Hollywood sources, Sting was forced to turn down the lead in a film of *King Lear* because Styler was refused a part.) But she, too, wasn't guilty of wrecking The Police. The band's internal stresses preceded Styler's arrival on the scene by five years. She supported Sting, defended him, and accepted the love he was willing to give her. He couldn't have been an easy person to live with, as he frequently said himself. Styler had no more than a walk-on role in the final crisis, whose roots were Sting's frustration, restlessness and need to dominate.

In June 1986 the group appeared in Atlanta for an Amnesty International gala and played a thirty-minute set. They had nothing to say to the crowd, and the promoter Bill Graham didn't introduce them as The Police. The following month they went into the studio to record their sixth album. Here, some discrepancy exists between Summers' account ('One track took three weeks . . . I did my guitar part on the first night and the rest of the time it was the others arguing whether the Fairlight or the Synclavier was best') and Sting's ('I fucked off'). In both versions, it was agreed there was no new material and no wish to write any. Sting's semi-serious solution to this impasse was that they should re-record their old hits. Things, already apparently at their darkest, then turned black when Copeland appeared with a broken collarbone from a riding fall. In these dire straits the three ground out a turgid remake of 'Don't Stand So Close To Me', which was released to a largely indifferent world in October. It barely grazed the Top Fifty. The album was scrapped.

The Police never died a formal death, and over the next few years A&M and others would try to revive the band in one form or another, but it remained more fantasy and fiction than a realized effort. The group's future was caught up in an old quandary: they didn't want to split; they did want their own lives. They loved the band; they didn't like the gang. Sting spoke of his ambivalence, couched in terms of mutual loathing of Copeland, to friends. In private, he was open in his analysis of the reasons for the rift. The band had been thrown together, and Copeland and Summers became the vehicle for his 'naked lunge', or so he said. He felt they were 'all clapped out – like brothers' – in the unique way he defined brotherhood – though the creative spark remained strong to the end. Derek Green, for one, believes The Police were a case of unfulfilled potential and 'could have made ten albums'. 'It was sneakily done . . . there was no closure,' says Summers. Years later, Sting would tell *Q*: 'None of us had run our courses musically. We were all getting better as musicians and writers, but the politics had run their course and it was becoming too difficult to be creative within that structure. I wanted more freedom.'

He continued to be a slave to The Police's multi-platinum success. Although the band broke up in 1986, their work was regularly recycled in the years ahead. After *Synchronicity* was released on video, a tsunami of reissues, compilations and studio leftovers – some good, some not so palatable – polished the legend anew. In October 1986 *Every Breath You Take – The Singles* hit number one in the UK, number seven in America. In 1988, A&M released an EP of *Compact Hits*, as distinct from 1992's *Greatest Hits* anthology and video. Next came a limited-edition, digitally remastered set, *Message in a Box*, with every track The Police ever cut. Sting himself had mixed views about the project, which he told Styler he wanted to see sold in an artwork coffin. (Critics were equally sceptical about *Box*, whose mastering sugar-coated some songs and made others sound as if they were recorded in a closet.) Finally, in 1995 Summers produced the much-delayed *Live!*, one side from 1979 and a second from their swansong four years later. The Police bandwagon, no longer bogged down in churlish in-fighting, then revved up with a best-selling video, *Outlandos to Synchronicities*, as well as a glut of dubious out-takes, fag-ends and collectables. With the plethora of nostalgic hits, bootlegs and repackaged collections of oldies, it was easy to forget how long it was since the band last recorded a new song.

Sting, Summers and Copeland had become some of rock's brightest and most durable stars. They were all gifted musicians. But their best instrument, the one they plucked and teased most effectively, was The Police's audience. Only five studio albums had set up a worldwide demand for more product. 'People hadn't got enough of it,' Summers says today. 'We continued to sell a phenomenal amount of records, and still do.' For a decade they remained the ex-fetishized pop-teen idols to beat. A tip-off of the band's popularity was the healthy performance, year on year, of Magnetic Publishing. In 1986, when The Police disbanded, the company posted assets of £1,327,179 and retained profits of £86,645. From there annual turnover rose to a figure of £2,753,406 in 1991 and £3,713,679 in 1992. In June 1995 Copeland and Summers signed the accounts with the words, 'We consider the level of activities and financial position are satisfactory.' They were far more than that; at no further pains to themselves, the back-liners had become fabulously rich. Roxanne and Roxanne Music (Tours), meanwhile, still contributed to Sting's royalty flow, and even Illegal Music, formed in the heady days of 'Fall Out', carried forward a retained profit of £500,000 annually. All three men made fortunes out of The Police, both from sales and the sharp deals cut by Miles. Each of the two aspects of their coup reinforced the other. They were among the first bands to opt for low advances and high returns, the 'points' that were too big even to squander.

Aside from board meetings and chance encounters backstage, Sting, Copeland and Summers rarely met again. They descended to a level of bare civility for five years. Sting and Summers guested on each other's *Nothing Like the Sun* and *Charming Snakes*, respectively. Active sniping between the two stopped. They made something of a fan-funded party of their next reunion; in 1991 the duo hooked up on stage in Hollywood for an ill-advised jam. All three men later mugged through 'Message In A Bottle' at a private party. Late in 1996, Sting broke off from a concert in Holland to casually introduce Copeland. They welcomed each other not with the traditional greeting of bared fists, but in a bear-hug. Ten years' distance since the break-up had helped to cool tempers once frayed by life in the studio and the bleak backstage rooms of American arenas. Sting now even had 'fond, nostalgic' memories of The Police. His fondness did not, however, extend to re-forming the group, as he once hinted he would, in 1997. Their twentieth anniversary went unnoticed.*

For all their fame and money, The Police had always persisted in showing their raw parts as brazenly as a Miss World on her climactic catwalk. Edgy brilliance on stage was echoed in volatile interactions away from the spotlight. Despite, or because of, seeming to be always on the verge of splitting, they were a true unit. The synergy of Sting's literacy and ear for a hook, and the sidekicks' virtuosity was The Police's X-factor. It was a marriage of convenience: as Sting says, 'We didn't all grow up together in the same street,' literally or musically speaking. But, at a time when rock had begun to take itself seriously, their blend of guitar pop, smouldering good looks and white reggae wasn't, unlike punk, isolating and depressive. It was joyful. As with most shrewd moves, only in retrospect did The Police seem inevitable – the missing link between new wave and finger-popping melodies. Sting had a flair for singing and a genius for song-writing, but his greatest gift may have lain in his consistent good timing.

Sting, like God, was everywhere in 1985. As The Police faded from view, he compensated with a work schedule that would have jaded a teenager, and accelerated with every pound he earned. He had no guarantee of making it. Rockers' failed stabs at self-expression were hardly news. Their faintly risible emblems were everywhere from the ex-Beatles down, and nothing would more vividly illustrate their special horrors than the undignified scramble to revive defunct groups later in the 1980s and '90s. Sting had usually had the happy knack of falling upwards. Pigeonhole fears had led him to take real risks with his career, constantly reinventing himself yet never plunging into vacuous trendiness. He had little experience as a solo act, and, he said, 'dreaded a pile-up' where the fans pulled him one way, his muse another, and market needs a third. But through a mixture of pop ambition, common sense and grit, he hit most of his marks. His first year of freedom was a step away from the musical-crumpet image to that of an enduring icon. It took guts for Sting to lose

*There were, though, two tribute albums out that summer: *Reggatta Mondatta* and, from the archives, *Police Academy*, a live set by Strontium 90.

the idealistic firebrand of *Outlandos* in his own need for excellence, so that by the time he played Live Aid he was essentially an artist-campaigner, his concerns social and aesthetic rather than selfish. It marked one of his greatest triumphs.

In late 1984, after being moved to tears by a news report from Ethiopia, Bob Geldof organized the cream of British rock into an *ad hoc* group he called Band Aid. Their first and only single, 'Do They Know It's Christmas?', had worldwide sales of ten million. Sting was among the first names canvassed. According to Geldof, his prompt three-word reply was: 'I'll be there.' Sting duly appeared at the session at Sarm West studio, London, on 25 November. The news photo of him arriving, grave-looking and carrying the *Observer*, marked a new high point for the idea that rock stars could be intelligent. Later, there was a picture of the band, all grouped round Sting; his own pose like a Victorian patriarch with his family. Boy George, for one, thought he gave the impression of being 'a giant among men'. Although he was only a shade over average in height and build, Sting dominated the shot. He had a naturally expressive face and what Geldof called 'a hit parade of drop-dead looks'. His sly grins, prodigal smirks and the way he bounced to the music were, says George, 'gorgeous'. The whole body was always involved. Even in a room full of Beautiful People, he was the best, the most stellar, the one the roped-off fans cheered loudest. Whether as beefcake or a gilded social worker, Sting had presence.

Eight months later he was one of the major draws at Live Aid, both playing solo and duetting with Phil Collins. Sting warmed up for the event by posing for a curious photo with Joe Cocker and Jim Diamond, whose hit 'Hi-Ho Silver' naggingly recalled *Reggatta*-era Police. The shot, which ran over four columns in the *Standard*, illustrated that has-beens and never-to-be's alike would become fodder for those who endured. He then watched Bruce Springsteen slay Wembley. A week later, Sting walked on the same stage and played a smouldering and slowed-down 'Roxanne' and 'Driven To Tears', featuring only his guitar and Branford Marsalis on sax. With Collins crooning along, 'Every Breath' was at once graceful and austere. 'Message In A Bottle' staked out a strip of terrain bordered by loud, electric rock and whey-faced folk. Both songs soared on classic melodies undiminished by time or familiarity. The way Sting skinned his best

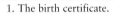

1. The birth certificate.

2. Station Road, Wallsend – a zone of light and heavy engineering works, bookies, bingo halls and the uncompromising bulk of the Swan Hunter shipyard.
The Sumners lived at Number 80, now over the Chinese takeaway.

3. Wallsend.

4. Newcastle and the Tyne Bridge in the 1950s; the place full of noise, stench and the sulphurous glare of the shipyard that Sting 'left but never escaped'.

5. The 'steady lad' at St Cuthbert's Grammar School.

6. Posing (fifth from left) with the Newcastle Big Band. As well as a residency in the foyer of the University Theatre, the group played impromptu in the nearby car park.

1976 Marriage solemnized at Our Lady and St. Oswin's Chapel, Front Street, Tynemouth in the District of North Tyneside East in the Metropolitan District of North Tyneside

No.	When married	Name and surname	Age	Condition	Rank or profession	Residence at the time of marriage	Father's name and surname	Rank or profession of father
38	First 1976 May	Gordon Matthew SUMNER	24 yrs	Bachelor	School Teacher	16A Heaton Hall Road, Newcastle upon Tyne	Ernest Matthew Sumner	Engineer
	1976	Frances Tomelty TOMELTY	28 yrs	Spinster	Actress	39a Dean Rd, London S.W.14	Joseph Tomelty	Actor Retired

Married in the Our Lady and St. Oswin's Chapel according to the rites and ceremonies of the Roman Catholics by Licence by me,
This marriage was solemnized between us, G. M. Sumner / F. E. Tomelty
in the presence of us, K. J. Gallagher / Rena Tomelty (Gallagher)
Thomas Cass (Rev.) R. C. Priest, R. Oldfield, Registrar

7. By late 1974, Gordon Sumner had a new address, a new job and a new stage name; and he fell in love. Her name was Frances Tomelty. They married on 1 May 1976.

8. In spring 1977, buoyed by his weekly £16 dole and casual modelling fees, Sting moved his family to a basement flat at 28A Leinster Square, Bayswater. It was an inspired choice.

9. The Police (l–r): Sting, Andy Summers and Stewart Copeland.

10. As well as an alluring mix of new wave and reggae, they always, or usually,
delivered the goods live.

11. The ex-*Sniffin' Glue* tycoon and future pop millionaire,
Sting's long-time manager Miles Copeland.

12. Sting as fame struck, 1979.

13. Miles would call The Police '10 per cent more rabid than other bands', willing to do almost anything for publicity.

14. Sting and his oldest son, Joe (b. 1976), now a rocker himself.

15. In the early 1980s, albums like *Zenyatta Mondatta* and *Ghost in the Machine* plotted the course of an unstoppable career. They also marked the break-up of Sting's marriage.

16. The megastar, with all the trappings of screen-idol glitz, enjoys a beer.

17. Despite, or because of, having no training as an actor, Sting launched himself into a decade of film and stage work. *Brimstone & Treacle* (1982) won a BBC ban and brickbats from the media.

18. As Feyd, the codpiece-clad villain of *Dune*. The movie bombed.

19. Atop Jennifer Beals in the ill-conceived Gothic claptrap *The Bride*.

20. Sting recovered with a cameo opposite Meryl Streep in *Plenty*, a film that was subtle haunting and blisteringly highbrow.

21. The latex rubber narrator of *Peter and the Wolf*.

22. Number 2, The Grove, Highgate.
Sting's London home enjoyed the advantage of being both city and country.

23. By the early 1990s, music and films had both taken a back seat to saving the rainforest. Sting toured the world with the Kayapo Chief Raoni.

24. With Bob Geldof, the feed in a drunken double-act that conjured visions of a 'fours-up' between the two stars and their wives.

25. As well as trotting the globe, having hits and generally being the rock icon, Sting was generous in his support of causes, whether playing for Nelson Mandela and the Aids Foundation or duetting with Elton John and Luciano Pavarotti for charity.

26. Marriage to Trudie Styler, 20 August 1992.

27. The church service two days later won splashes for the couple's outfits, and an ad-lib reunion of The Police.

28. Lake House.

29. The Sumners' friend Gianni Versace (second from right), shot dead in July 1997. Sting and Elton John sang at the designer's memorial service.

30. The 'sanest, smartest, most clear-eyed rock star' treading the boards.

tunes to the bone was a model of their resilience and his own artistic nerve. His set was one of the night's show-stopping moments.

'This is what rock and roll is all about,' Sting told reporters backstage. 'It's an event, as much as it's music.' Some of his tendency to harangue was on show at the press conference later. 'You can never, *ever* send enough money. You have to give of yourself.' Sting did. He was still in full possession of his pop faculties, and revelled in them. The fact that he was also capable of passion and concerned behaviour amounted to something of a small miracle of humanity. His handsomely weathered performance was perfect for the occasion. Live Aid expanded and extended Sting's fame.

From then on, he was a gloved fist pounding the final nail in the coffin of his bouffanted, rock-god image. Sting was a cultural roustabout whose projects also touched every base. They followed one of two tracks. Semi-furtively, there were causes, like his anti-drug 'Children's Crusade', his one-off collaboration with Jeff Beck on *Live! For Life*, and his continuing commitment to Amnesty. His other activities ran on more familiar lines. He worked with Phil Collins and Dire Straits; patronized U2 and Springsteen; and rose to the challenge of recording 'Mack The Knife' on a tribute to Kurt Weill.

At home in Highgate, Sting had a flash of insight unlike the stark visions he'd suffered through under the twin stresses of drugs and divorce. He imagined he was looking out on to the trim garden of his London home. Suddenly, dozens of blue crustaceans lurched into view. According to his Jungian analyst, the creatures symbolized shock, novelty, drama, and the next jump-start of his career. Sting made the inspired link himself. 'I had that dream at a time when I had doubts about my future,' he said. 'Should I stay with The Police and make a safe album? The [reptiles] said, "No."'

Within days, Sting had begun a stealthy transition from radio-friendly pop back to jazz. It was, he told a press conference, his true musical home. Yet even as his new genre made its visionary progress, there was the faintly depressing hint of calculation which offers the one key argument against his work. Jazz-rock was to the 1980s what punk-reggae had been to the mid-1970s. It did, it was true, neatly return him to type. After Last Exit broke up in 1977, Newcastle club-goers had first gone into mourning, then passed the next eight years wondering what kind of music the group would have made had Sting both stayed and matured. *The Dream of the Blue Turtles* was the answer: in 1985 he balanced the pop appeal of his songs with the improvisational fire of his band.

Using the journalist Vic Garbarini as a head-hunter and his booth at New York's Café Luxembourg as an office, Sting next hired a group. Branford Marsalis was an early recruit. Kenny Kirkland, a veteran of both Dizzy Gillespie and Elvin Jones, joined on keyboards. Sting himself reverted to guitar. Bass was taken by Darryl Jones, a man who 'really admire[d] Sting's skill as a composer and lyricist . . . I've never heard a song of his that was a nothing song', yet who presciently 'wasn't totally sure that this was a band where everyone had a totally equal say'. Jones's doubts were as nothing compared to his ex-boss Miles Davis's response. It reduced *Decoy* to a screaming-match. Davis made it clear that he considered his old friend 'too showbiz' and 'no better than an Uncle Tom' in joining the new line-up.* 'Go tell your shit to Sting,' he yelled at the hapless Jones, when the latter tried to explain his move. With the row still simmering, Garbarini quietly wormed Omar Hakim, ex-Weather Report, on to drums. He auditioned by rapping a knife and fork on a table at the Luxembourg.

The hired guns met in New York in January 1985. To Sting's friends and long-time cronies, the moment was emblematic. These were heavyweight, 'real' musicians with a language and slant of their own. At the first rehearsals Sting sat crumpled in the corner, silent and attentive, a listener for once. Having devoted himself to principles, to jazz in the abstract, he now had flesh-and-bone swingers to deal with. Sting's identification with black music stopped just short of total assimilation. He looked horrified when Marsalis gleefully hailed a new song as 'mother-fuckin''. But tensions with the group would go deeper than style. In the months ahead, problems about terms and conditions gnawed like a festering sore, needling star and manager alike with deputations over money. Marsalis himself soon uttered the fell phrase 'artistic differences'. This seemed to throw Sting into even

*The bassist also later played with the Rolling Stones.

higher paroxysms of self-promotion; without the give-and-take of a true band, he was more than ever on his own.

The group recorded at Eddy Grant's Blue Wave studio in Barbados, then gave a series of semi-secret shows late in February in New York. Sting mixed the album at The Police's old haunt in Quebec. By then corporate interest in the record wasn't merely intense – it was feverish. 'What's riding on it?' a reporter asked Gil Friesen of A&M. 'Sting's career,' was the quick-witted reply. With three phone calls, the label secured an equal number of cover stories, and jammed the A&M boardroom on Madison Avenue for a press preview on 29 April. It was unfortunate that, in his excitement, Friesen punched in a tape of Bruce Springsteen's *Born in the USA* rather than *The Dream of the Blue Turtles*. Sting laughed.

Sting and Miles Copeland functioned as partners in packaging the new group and puffing the album. They still made an odd couple. Miles struck Jeff Griffin as 'the ultimate capitalist', strangely out of place in rock and roll, and Sting seemed like a manager's worst nightmare, the restless, creative soul. Yet they operated smoothly as a team. Miles was a virtuoso at extracting seed money from the label, and spending or more often investing it jointly with his client. Overheads were low. Begging musicians were met with complicated explanations about start-up costs and outgoings, an almost hypnotic experience that, as one man says, 'left you stunned ... You went in [to Miles's office] asking for a raise, and came out thinking yourself lucky to know him.'

The system worked, mainly because of Miles's will to make it work, partly because of Sting's charisma. He was, after all, a star, and his job was to shine. Sting's leadership was impressive, his charm unquestioned, but his insistence on artistic control led to a gradual watering-down of the music. *Blue Turtles* only sporadically conjured up the fiery tone-colours limned by The Police. Certain fans insist Sting's real career to have begun with *Turtles*, his crisis of confidence a necessary lull between the fanatic he was and the entertainer he became. According to this school, the creative time-out brought his work, albeit on a higher budget, full circle. Others believe he never quite recovered from going off his head in 1982–83.

Sting's restless yen to experiment had led him to some strange associations, not least in films like *Dune* and *The Bride*. *The Dream of the Blue Turtles* straddled the line between eclectic and self-indulgent, an all-things-to-all-people confection one critic hailed as 'a mix of jazz and self-help manuals'. The album shunned strong-arm rock. Sting temporarily shelved the AOR hooks of *Synchronicity* in favour of a more ambitious musical hybrid of blue notes and jazzed-up improvisation. He covered the waterfront from muzak to punk, playing footsie with reggae. Echoes of Stax-era soul and riffing saxes vied with the canny pop of a cut like 'If You Love Somebody Set Them Free'. Sting's latest direction may have been born of extremism for extremism's sake, but *Blue Turtles* was ultimately saved by the lyrics' bitter wit and the musical adventurism. It managed a miracle: sounding both mainstream and experimental. The ringing slabs of funk were balanced by tunefulness and Sting's aching romanticism. Also, his sidemen had never sounded better, working up a blues/jazz groove that in its organic interplay recalled the early Police.

The album bowed with 'If You Love Somebody', yet more proof of Sting's ear for perfect pop harmonies, and a trans-atlantic hit single. Elsewhere, there were nods to some unusual suspects. Sting burlesqued his past in the outro to 'Love Is The Seventh Wave' with the ad-lib, 'Every breath you take / Every move you make / Every cake you bake'; on 'Russians' he quoted the *Lieutenant Kizhe* bass solo from Prokofiev. 'Children's Crusade' and 'We Work The Black Seam' mixed social comment with loungy tunes in an exotic medley. Other numbers like 'Fortress Around Your Heart' placed Sting in the pantheon of those unafraid to plumb medieval imagery – the same stew of a walled city, towers, flags and siege guns of an early Yes number. In 'Moon Over Bourbon Street' the key text was Anne Rice's *Interview With the Vampire*. Sting devoured the book and later dabbled with the idea of auditioning for the film in the role of Lestat.

'If You Love Somebody' and 'Fortress' were both hits, care-fully buffed for American radio. If 1979 was the year a hip market in New York and Los Angeles first discovered Sting, then 1985 would go down as the year he conquered the heartland, winning fans in towns and states previously aloof to The Police. He played numerous solo shows in the Midwest, where his popularity never seemed to wane. Time would see Sting evolve into a kind of troubadour, endlessly touring and polishing his gift for meta-phor against his next stylistic leap. Aside from the lyrics, his main flair was for borrowing sounds from a variety of genres and freeing them from their original context. At their peak, his albums were a breezy hopscotch between jazz-rock and classical argots.

The downside of *Blue Turtles* was Sting's own weakness: his gigantic ego; his Laytonian *poète maudit*, permanent-adolescent sense of rejection and alienation. As with 'Every Breath', some of the lyrics still bullied rather than evoked response. Much of the tension of thrashes like 'Born In The '50s' had been stripped from the music, too. At its worst, the album offered a testosterone-free mix of funk and sappy balladry all too remi-niscent of Last Exit. The misfires would have been less forgivable without the fresh creative spark of a 'Russians' or 'Moon Over Bourbon Street'. At its best, *Blue Turtles* achieved a balance between schmaltz and taut, turbulent musicianship. It spent sixty-four weeks in the British chart. Along with Phil Collins, Peter Gabriel and Don Henley, Sting joined the ranks of those to enjoy solo fame on level terms with that of their sometime bands. *Blue Turtles'* recording had made a Police reunion unlikely. Its success made one impossible.

That spring, Sting and his group began a year-long global tour in Paris. Though generally warm, and only rarely hostile, his audiences were less rabid than before. In 1983, Sting was accus-tomed to hearing drunken yells of encouragement from the crowd. In 1985, vocalization from at least some of the drunks took the form of heckling. Sting made music of such daunting sobriety and moody joy that it wasn't an altogether comfortable experience to find oneself swept up in it. That, of course, was his charm. The new songs were more crisply played, and more cunningly arranged, than the oldies, but the savage, snarling interplay of *Reggatta*-type rock was lost in the smooth but strangely inanimate tones of a jazz quintet. The tour was some-thing of a pet project for Sting, but most fans could appreciate a man who'd made some of the hottest sounds of the 1980s getting his long-sought chance to lay down some of the coolest.

In the frenetic weeks leading to opening night, Sting travelled with a retinue of crack musicians, minders, managers, sundry children, nannies and a full-scale film crew directed by Michael

Apted. Compounding the circus-like atmosphere was a heavily pregnant Trudie Styler. She experienced contractions as Sting stepped on stage at the Mogador Theatre. In the press conference to launch the tour and the album, he introduced his new band, fumed when one hack called him Gordon and ducked questions on The Police. When Sting spoke it was in short, laconic sound-bites rather than paragraphs. As a result, he 'edited' well both on Apted's documentary and local news shows. By the time he strolled on at the Mogador, French TV and radio were both accomplices in the strategic media blitz that also led to profiles in *Le Monde* and *Le Figaro,* and a by-lined article in the *Sunday Times*. Such publicity couldn't have been bought, particularly for a first solo album that dared to buck a formula.

The shows themselves combined rock pomp with jazz circumstance in three-minute anthems full of soul-tinged rhythm and Sting's vocal buoyancy. For years, he'd been in a state of chronic self-conflict. While maturing rapidly in the studio, Sting had been forced by Miles's tour schedule to slog the road, endlessly rehashing his bare-torsoed, raw-voiced pop persona. From the mid-1980s he tossed stagecraft (though not style) for substance. To some, the much-vaunted result was also a contradiction: the highbrow musical pretensions jarred with the audience-pleasing gyrations, and somewhat desperate urgings to join in. (Few French fans did.) For the upbeat numbers Sting played a serviceably choppy guitar. But the subsequent parade of largely acoustic hits was more cabaret than rock and roll. Even unplugged, 'Roxanne' still achingly – even radiantly – delivered its message, but Sting's modest musicianship was a mere shadow of The Police's electric virtuosity. Strangely, the full-band arrangements suffered from the same dire sense of self-control. Where The Police had been drilled, this group was regimented. Sting had rehearsed and blocked a routine where every step and nuance had been sanded down to the last detail. This approach worked on 'Low Life'. It grew tiresome in extended jams like the seven-minute 'Tea In The Sahara' (in which his voice went). The tunes still deftly swung from unapologetic power pop to funk-jazz, but there was no human touch or hard edge to the night. Sting came over as the consummate frontman, though never crossing the line between professionalism and shoutalong rock. Precision substituted for passion. Garage-group aesthetics gave way to a big-band swing and enough icy perfectionism to impress even the hipsters in the theatre. '*Un chat* "cool",' cooed *Le Monde*.

The *Sunday Times* had presented Sting as a man simultaneously raring to stress and discount his fame. He was, he enlightened the paper, 'a thirty-year-old [*sic*] millionaire living in a mansion, owning racehorses and with a record-buying public in millions'. Sting explained The Police as 'opportunists – we flew a flag of convenience which was: "We are marketable, yet we are part of this new revolution; take us on" . . . We were just there at the right time.' There was an engaging note of humility in his admission, 'It struck me as odd that one of the first interviews I did involved my opinion on nuclear fission. Luckily, I knew about it and gave a fairly coherent answer. But I thought – how funny; all I did was sing a song.' He had to laugh. One of Sting's greatest strengths was his capacity to achieve a sense of perspective by poking fun at the 'fame game' that, in another mood, he played like a maestro.

Above all, Sting was at pains to nurture his roots and domesticity. That March he invited his father to join Styler and him in the West Indies. Ernie's reaction to Sting's fame was as mixed as his son's. From a personal standpoint, he wanted him to succeed, and was gratified by the reflected glory he enjoyed around Newcastle. However, as a frustrated world-traveller, Ernie was poignantly aware of his own relative flop in life. Two years later, Sting would tell a reporter of having visited his father in hospital. Ernie was so gaunt that at first his son thought he'd been sent to the wrong bed. 'I was sitting with him and I looked at his hands – he had great thick fingers just like mine – and said, "You know you've got the same hands as me?" And he said, "Yes, but you put yours to better use than I did."' Sting continued to promote himself as a man consumed with his family. 'Apart from them, I've nothing firm in my life,' he told *Spin*. Later that spring his fourth child, Jake, was born in Paris virtually as the curtain fell at the Mogador Theatre.

In the past, when other rockers talked about the self-revelatory nature of fame, Sting had insisted merely that he was out to 'wing it'. As he got older he grew more serious. He developed guilt pangs about his wealth. 'There's a certain amount of "You don't actually deserve this",' he wrote in the *Sunday Times*. 'You can end up really hating yourself for that sort of trickery. It's another ingredient of self-destruction.' More than ever, when discussing his good luck he was unusually *piano*. He smiled 'almost apologetically' when talking money with Keith Moore. Paradoxically, Sting in his mid-thirties was also a man on the move, or so he said, living dangerously, never happy to do the same thing twice. 'One of the facts about my life is that I haven't the faintest idea what I'm going to be doing in a year's time,' he told one paper. And another: 'I feel I'm moving at the speed of light, relative to most people.' He had a provincial boy's thrill and manic glee at being presented with such a global array of treats. He gravitated to cities like New York, Paris and Rome; travelled constantly, for pleasure as well as profit; and felt his pulse quicken at the very names Armani or Versace.

Like his music, Sting evolved into a kind of symbol of innovation and change, a man who dared make his own career an art form, open to judgement and interpretation but never failing in its basic human growth. The very speed of his life meant that ironies could be made to surface. Early in 1985 he read *One Hundred Years of Solitude* and 'wept buckets'. His bibliomania was as strong as ever; it was therapy for a tortured mind. Yet, later in the year Styler would tell Michael Apted, 'He's lightened up a lot . . . he's not reading as many books.' While Dave Marsh continued to rap The Police for having exploited black music, Sting now insisted, 'Pop is dead. And one of the reasons it's dead is it's become reactionary and racist . . . My new band is an open challenge to that system.' Miles was worried about the strain on his client, forced as he was to be spokesman, singer, songwriter, leader and *de facto* chairman of a vast firm. Sting himself felt no pressure. An indication of his mood came as he walked down a hospital corridor, minutes after his son's birth, and heard an orderly whistling 'Walking On The Moon'. It was a 'great privilege', said Sting. His work was being hummed and sung by total strangers and, at its blander extremes, piped into lifts and hypermarkets the world over. It's possible that he was the most widely heard star of his day. Sting loved it.

Apted's film *Bring on the Night* was released in November 1985. It was an unusual idea – following its cast backstage, in hotels and rehearsal halls and even into the delivery room of the Hôpital Beclere. But in making Sting more accessible, it made the concept more pretentious. The moment the whole crew scrubbed up and loomed round Styler's bed was the moment queasy fans made for the exit. In spite of the slick stage footage and glimpses of Miles in Vesuvian eruption, *Night* was received by most critics with suspicion and dismay. Reviews by Sting's friends bristled with such adjectives as embarrassing, tasteless, tawdry, ballsy, brave, crass and cynical: an hour-and-a-half home movie from which a decent ten-minute 'short' signalled wildly to be let out. (It did, however, win a best-documentary Grammy.)

In the long preamble to Jake Sumner's birth, Apted seemed to lose faith in the script and desperately ransacked its minor characters for any available action. He was rewarded by a scene starring the band. Its rip was Marsalis taunting Sting as 'Gordy', while Danny Quatrochi blanched and the other musicians giggled uneasily. According to one of them, 'it was hard to know if [Sting] was laughing or gritting his teeth. Everybody kind of cooled it by playing *The Flintstones* theme. You had to have been there.'

Where *Bring on the Night* gave fans Sting through a magnifying-glass, the director Fred Schepisi offered an intimate downsizing, no less dramatic for that, in *Plenty*. The story was of a courageous and mulish woman, veteran of the Maquis, painfully adapting to life in post-war Britain. Meryl Streep gave her normal meticulous performance. Charles Dance, John Gielgud, Sam Neill and Tracey Ullman all filled out the five-way struggle for professional and sexual supremacy, as a potentially sinister black-marketeer (Sting) weighed in with a neatly detached, evil cameo. It was his best straight role since *Quadrophenia*.

Plenty was a volatile mix that Schepisi lit with a teasingly long fuse. The action was unobtrusive at best – all atmosphere and complicated, overlapping flashbacks – until Sting's arrival as the cockney Mick. In one vivid scene a nude Streep straddled him as the Queen's 1953 Coronation flickered on a bluish TV screen in the corner. Sting played it as a Shakespearean tragedy, with Mick as an Othello so driven by obsession and rage that he loses everything. Instead of chewing scenery, he invested a lewd spiv with quiet dignity. In Mick's sad, arch face, Sting caught his own yearning. The inner snap of the performance was impressive, but critics were struck even more by Sting's self-restraint. There was none of the crude hamming of *Dune* or *The Bride*. Where those films had been goosed with trippy effects and wild over-acting, *Plenty* persuaded with humanity, intelligence and dry wit. It seemed to point the way forward.

6

Metamorphosis

STING WAS OFTEN GIVEN TO MUSING on his good fortune. His *mea culpa* in the *Sunday Times* had included the line, 'In a sense [The Police] were very lucky, in that what we actually felt like doing coincided, historically, with what the market felt like buying.' As he again trotted the world with a hit album, Sting may well have pondered his rapid rise as a solo act. Only a year earlier, his own management had warned him off expecting to repeat the global smash of *Synchronicity*. Now he was touring with an LP that went on to spend fifteen consecutive months in the chart, more than any Police record since *Reggatta*. Luck had clearly played a role in his success, but there were other factors, including his hard work, his talent, and most of all his ubiquitousness. In 1986, like 1985, Sting was everywhere.

That February he presented a 'best record' Grammy to Quincy Jones for 'We Are The World', then performed 'Russians' at the same show; in June Sting duetted with Mark Knopfler on 'Money For Nothing' at the Prince's Trust gala at Wembley; he attended the Jerry Dammers-organized Artists Against Apartheid on Clapham Common (where he held his own with a narcotically voluble Boy George); and took part in Amnesty's Conspiracy of Hope tour, furtively reuniting The Police alongside U2 and Peter Gabriel. Sting's manic schedule and gadfly dabbling in outside projects were no accident. He was still driven, ambitious and with a sharp, wry mind. No one ever thought to describe him as an intellectual, even though, by his peers' standards, he was inquisitive and well-read. He wasn't liable to come up with any brilliant insights. But he had the ability to look at a situation or a problem and analyse it, see what alternatives there were, and pick from among them. He might miss some nuances, but he seldom overlooked major points. In general, he tended to back causes that would put power back in the hands of the people, and specifically those that championed minority rights. With time and money to translate his views into action, his various campaigns and crusades would become almost as famous as his music. He seemed to be on every soap-box, every stage and every platform. Sting spoke on his personal theory of socialism in other venues, too, always concerned with focusing his attack on problems he perceived, while making the issue more colourful, accessible and easier to grasp. His activism sparked ample debate, some dissension, and occasionally accept-ance. This response was more useful than the empty hedonism which changed nothing, so Sting kept up the fight.

Ultimately, there was a backlash. Where Sting's singing and songwriting had long been debated in the press it would have been bizarre, a year or two before, for a letter to *Rolling Stone* to have begun: 'How can you spend so much time on Live Aid and then practically forget Farm Aid? I guess at the *Stone*, if Sting isn't there, it's not worth talking about.' The editorial in the *Weekly* was blunter: 'Where have we failed that this half-baked social worker is our conscience? Who died and made Sting god?' The pretentiousness charge gnawed at him. He seemed to be struggling within himself about the relation of politics to art: when to preach, when to shut up, and perhaps most importantly, what he could personally do for his pet causes. Sting had to endorse only safe, mainstream projects and back them because others did, or opt for controversy. He chose action.

Sting's outspoken views, which he fancied to have weight and gravitas and which actually had some effect, were essentially the same ones he'd forged as a boy. There was no Pauline conversion. In Wallsend, he'd grown up in a Labour household, where a policy of state intervention was right and the market was often wrong; where Eisenhower's hand was behind most crises; and unilateral nuclear disarmament would have come as a blessing. To Sting, direct action was neither inconsistent nor illogical. Nor did he see it as a betrayal of his Sumner past to take a stand on moral issues. 'The song,' he once said, 'remain[ed] the same,' although later he turned up the volume to the point where it began to warp.

At 2 p.m. on a sunny day early in 1986, Sting was sitting on a folding chair at the front of a north London church hall for an Amnesty rally. He was dressed in jeans, a folksy Aran sweater and sandals. Six hours later, he'd changed into an electric-blue Armani suit for a sold-out date on the British leg of his *Blue Turtles* tour. In between, he'd talked to the *Guardian* and the *Sun*, first-drafted a new song, visited his doctor for a check-up, rehearsed with his band and walked the dog.

The transformation was pure Sting, a man with an epic ability to flip from one persona to another, one career to another, and one fad to another – making him an elusive quarry for enemies, as well as for the PR men. His chart-busting album and dramatic foray into politics had confounded those who thought he'd vanish with The Police. The music and the stands were both important, but so was the personality – strengths and weaknesses, vices and virtues, loves and hates – of the man who made them. In short, all that Sting touched he glamorized. His quip-laden interviews and photogenic looks were latched on to almost as eagerly as what he wrote and played. He led by example. Sting placed the key goal of 'hands-off' socialism in an inverted core of moral values and produced an arresting defence of self-help, a sort of intellectual Black Mass.

His very accessibility meant a sacrifice of privacy, on his own part and his family's, but it was a price worth paying. Sting was a conspirator in a friendly plot, whose other members were a rag-bag of record tycoons, managers and human-rights activists, to raise his profile and album sales. Sting himself was utterly devoted to these twin goals. It was a rare honour to be chosen as a spokeman for Amnesty, and an even greater honour to re-enter the rock arena and not be vilified for a vapid and corny performance. Sting would be remembered as one of the few men to pull off the coup of marrying art, politics and bouncing-clean pop, and remaining credible in each.

His British shows that winter attracted fans who, far from expecting Sting to be 'moving at the speed of light', admired him for exactly the opposite reason: his reliability. Few were disappointed. Though the odds were lengthening that Sting would ever write better songs than 'Roxanne' or 'Message In A Bottle', he was maturing as an all-round entertainer. The *Blue Turtles* tour brilliantly balanced irreverence, somnolence and passion. Sting's theatricality made up for the occasional blandness of the group. His weary, lovelorn vocals and spry melodies carried even the weakest tune. And Branford Marsalis prevented the shows from sounding too sterile by punctuating the set with rasping toots of his sax and bouncing riffs and jokes off the band. The gigs, by and large, were slicker than The Police (who, as Summers once noted, 'stopped rehearsing in 1979'), though the visually suggestive symbolism survived, subdued but fully intact. Sting set the tone by shuffling in and out of time with the beat, crotch-poking the guitar and jammily trading notes with the crowd. As always, he was a non-stop drill instructor, with enough cool to flash a wolfish smile to the girls up front.

The tour ended, where it began, in Paris. After the final show there was a poolside soirée at the band's hotel – an open invitation for someone to get dunked. Sting took the plunge, in his white linen suit, with a helping hand from Styler. Rather than fume (as he had after a similar ducking at the Chelsea Holiday Inn in 1980), Sting kept smiling. The critics couldn't kick. Wringing wet, he was still affable and polite. When Sting decided to be 'one of the guys', he did so with a sense of glee and abandon, even if that meant thawing his legendary cool. Nowhere was this truer than the way he dealt with the band. According to one of them, 'He had a great sense of humour, provided the joke was in the right context'; Sting wasn't above the odd whoopee-cushion jape, or sprinkling flea powder in Marsalis's pants. Others credited Styler with loosening up her partner. High spirits reigned for most of the year-long tour, and her addition to the circle had much to do with it. Styler was funny and independent, a 'crazy actress' as she sometimes put it, and would work her frustrations out by shaming the various members of the band into group skits. The high jinks of 1985–86 were in stark contrast to the mass neurosis of 1980–81, and Sting himself, says his colleague, 'looked like a man out of jail'.

It showed in the way he treated Styler, Tomelty (with whom the frost would steadily melt in the late 1980s), his children and the band themselves. '"Stick around and instead of social security, you can count on me for money, food and drink the rest of your life",' one man says of Sting's management style. 'He meant it, too.' There was a touch of the *patrón* about Sting, the big-hearted grandee who charmed and musically idolized his group. They met his fascination with friendship. There was another reason for the band to take him seriously as a boss. More than once, he hinted that he'd like to keep the musicians together, 'as a family', for years to come. Lastly, he made one other thing clear: he'd tolerate all sibling squabbles and frailties but one – disloyalty to Sting.

Bring on the Night, the live double album of the world tour, was released in June 1986. Measured against the freewheeling jazz of *Blue Turtles, Night*'s lean towards standard pop fare sounded, on the surface, like a bow to marketing. There were reworkings of The Police chestnuts 'Driven To Tears' and 'Demolition Man' and a reprise of 'I Burn For You', written in the hoary days of Last Exit. Among the newer material, high points included a piano-heavy version of 'Children's Crusade' and (yet) another take on 'Tea In The Sahara'. As an album, it was shot through with casual, if spotty, brilliance, full of dystopian irony and, as always, Sting's keen ear for a lick. It spent twelve weeks in the British chart, making number sixteen.

Night presented a unique challenge to its reviewers. For traditionalist hacks, it was an easy target to knock on any number of fronts: despite the pop undertones, there was little in the way of slashing guitars and heavy pounding drums. In one strained though florid notice, 'The album rocks back and forth on its feet like a dangerous drunk who's too far gone to cause any real damage and is about to start spouting poetry.' For Chris Welch of *Melody Maker*, the actual packaging let down the music: 'a combination of studied "throwaway" style design, including childish paintings and graphics, together with the minuscule type sizes make the information unreadable without heavy-duty magnifying glasses'. Not all critics were negative. There was praise for Sting's artistic gall. Compared to The Police's last hit, which worked a well-worn if lucrative blueprint, *Night* seemed liberating and novel. If *Blue Turtles* was the key that unlocked Sting's creative potential, then the new album was the musical rebirth. Although it was short (seventy-five minutes' music on a double CD), it cut to the bone, another deft change of tack of the kind fans didn't normally expect from a 35-year-old rock messiah.

That spring, meanwhile, Jack Healey of Amnesty International and the promoter Bill Graham had set about toasting Amnesty's twenty-fifth anniversary with a benefit tour. Sting and U2 were the first to sign up. Unlike at Live Aid, however, big names were hard to lure. As Graham said, 'waving Sting stationery in other managers' faces just wasn't enough'. He was asking acts to make a real commitment – two weeks for charity, at the height of the summer touring season – that some of them simply couldn't afford. In the end, after muscular pressure, the line-up would include Bob Dylan, Lou Reed, Peter Gabriel, Jackson Browne, Bryan Adams, Joan Baez, Bob Geldof and Tom Petty, as well as cameo shows by Miles Davis, Bonnie Raitt, Don Henley and Joni Mitchell. The star of the tour, which opened in San Francisco on 4 June, was Sting. At the end of a set that included 'If You Love Somebody Set Them Free' and 'Russians', he played a harrowing, solo 'Message In A Bottle'. In this context, Sting's earnestness worked. The caustic tone was perfect – and sounded it. Ten thousand lighters held aloft greeted the haunting lyrics about loneliness and solace. It was one of the most inspirational and ultimately timeless rock events that year. A rousing group finale of Dylan's 'I Shall Be Released' proved that, on this occasion, the mood was equal to the message.

From there the good vibes kept coming until Atlanta. Frantic fence-mending and robust networking by Miles found his brother and Summers amenable to an *ad hoc* reunion. The Police's brief set opened with 'Spirits In The Material World' and moved on to 'King Of Pain', 'Every Breath' and 'Roxanne'. Despite having nothing to say, the three musicians initially seemed to enjoy themselves. Coming off as more pop than rock, The Police had a lighter touch than the night's first offerings by Gabriel and Reed. They were less raucous and more moving than their own Mach-2 *Reggatta* days. Without the pressure of having to carry the night, the band deepened their songs with the help of Sting's witty, and suddenly wrenching, lyrics. 'Every Breath' became a metaphor and anthem for those protesting tyranny in all forms.

Inevitably, the goodwill turned to tension as, in a replay of virtually every Police gig since 1977, Sting and Copeland found themselves strangers to each other's tempos. Although the minatory words had been removed from the drums, the pique and sour looks remained. There was a moment in 'Roxanne' when all three men seemed to play solos simultaneously. But for the most part, the band's relative lack of fire – evident in both Sting's eyes-to-the-floor performance style and his clipped vocals – set the tone for a set that was more emotional than exciting. They played two final Amnesty shows together, in Chicago and Giants Stadium, New Jersey. Even their last, climactic exit was low-key. Midway through 'Invisible Sun', Sting, Copeland and Summers eased off stage. Their instruments were picked up by the members of U2, who finished the song; a symbolic, logical handover from one supergroup to another. In a last tribute to The Police, Bono then introduced 'Mothers Of The Disappeared', his homage to Chile's *disparus* and a companion piece to Sting's own, unrecorded 'They Dance Alone'.

The Police gave no interviews, showed for only a brief photo-op, and quickly left in three separate limos. With that, Sting hoped, the band would 'just snuff it'. But when megastars meet for neither love nor money, but nostalgia, the saga rarely dies easily. The music and national press sold the event as a second coming, and leadingly asked whether Summers and Copeland (at work on a solo album and *The Equalizer* theme, respectively) could afford to pass up a reunion. Sting kept his own counsel. It was one of his rules that, at charity gigs, he never sought publicity for himself. He saw to it that Amnesty got full credit, but failed to hype his own role or the band. Sting's new practice was either to say something nice about colleagues or not mention them, and he didn't mention The Police.

Sting's affability and new-found tact were in sharp relief to the clash that disrupted rehearsals and nearly derailed the show in Atlanta. The row between Miles Copeland and Bill Graham was one of those backstage scenes that confirmed all the comic hooks of *Spinal Tap*. Mushrooming from small beginnings, it became an implacable feud that poisoned the atmosphere of the tour's last three nights. It centred on wrangling over headliner status in Atlanta, Chicago and New Jersey; Miles lobbying for The Police, Graham for U2. The jockeying was brutal. Musicians, roadies and journalists goggled at this sudden crisis between two of the most powerful and headstrong men in rock. It looked like a fight to the death, with Graham spluttering at his rival and vowing to cancel the second leg of the tour. Faced with this edifice of threats, Miles's reply was curt: 'Fuck off.' This roused Graham to try and physically cut a switch sending 500,000 watts of power to the stage, while jostling Miles with his free hand; at one point he actually flicked the lever for a second, causing a Dylan song to end abruptly in a drone. Roadies ran to drag Graham away. He relented only when Sting appeared, and, calmly surveying the scene, said, 'Don't take it personally, Bill. This is business.' In the end, Miles's attack misfired. The Police and U2 themselves worked out the compromise formula. Both bands signed deals evading detailed mention of the headliner issue, and agreeing to contribute to a live album. Miles and Graham barely spoke again.

The same journalists who gaped as these two swore and snarled at each other found Sting to be shy, eager and near-adolescent in his buoyancy. He was always excited and effective when it came to helping Amnesty. A member of Graham's crew recalls that Sting tended to 'dance on the tops of the hills', leaving his handlers to hard labour on the slopes below. While they smoothed over every detail of his day, he was free to concentrate on the dogged pursuit of making music and raising funds. He did so with an enthusiasm and charm that seemed to be natural. Graham's assistant calls him 'the best informed, most consistent, least devious star on the tour'. Mike Noble, the ex-A&M executive now managing Joan Armatrading, spoke to Sting backstage in Atlanta and found him 'the nicest guy in the world'.

By any yardstick, the Amnesty tour was a financial and real success. A hundred and thirty thousand fans watched the six shows, while millions more saw the eleven-hour finale on MTV. Amnesty netted some $3 million; 25,000 new members joined instantly, and 100,000 more within a year. The live *Conspiracy of Hope* album (with Sting singing Billie Holiday's 'Strange Fruit') grazed the charts on both sides of the Atlantic. Miles failed to hint that, by some happy chance, his charitable work had introduced him to an unexpected terrestrial paradise. Bill Graham would front some of the first rock shows in Russia. Perhaps the most instantly satisfying result, though, was the release – just a

week after Giants Stadium – of the South African labour leader
Thozamile Gqweta, one of six prisoners of conscience singled
out by the organizers. Sting was learning the value of direct
action. The Amnesty tour showed that he was beginning to carve
out a fresh role for himself as an *artiste engagé*, rather than a pop
star who happened to back causes. His world was already
different from the one he'd conquered just six years earlier.

Sting strove to change history. 'He was the cutting-edge of rock
activism' in Graham's view, and 'wasn't scared' of putting himself out. Nor was he afraid of breaking with the past. A month
after the last chord of the last Amnesty show, The Police staged
their ill-fated reunion in a London studio. The farcical row that
ensued – Sting and Copeland debating the relative merits of one
synthesizer over another and ending up plunging into the drum
kit, discussing the point – was the mutual truculence of two men
who'd rubbed themselves raw. 'It was pathetic, as in truly sad,'
says one A&M staffer at the session. 'If you've ever heard a
married couple bickering about the toothpaste, you've got an
idea of what it was like.' Out of the fiasco came 'Don't Stand So
Close To Me '86', slowed down and saddled with a monotonous
disco beat, and a parody of the *Zenyatta* classic. Godley and
Creme's video showed The Police, aptly enough, as flickering
shadows.

Sting's disgust at the débâcle stayed with him. For the next
twelve years, he refused to work formally with Copeland and
Summers, or any other musician who did. Sting thought it
'unseemly' – a favourite word of his – and he couldn't understand how other ex-bands would come back from the dead. It
was a fair bet, he admitted, that The Police would prove as timeless as the Sex Pistols or Bob Marley, and that a spate of books,
articles and relaunched albums would assure them the same
exalted status. 'Our legend is intact,' he said. But he had 'no
interest – none' in writing any new songs. The need for creative
tension, once as vital to Sting as the creative spark itself, stopped
dead.

The Police took their past to the bank with *Every Breath You
Take* late in 1986. Sting had come to the band with a broad vocabulary – pop, soul, jazz, reggae and punk codified his style – and in
Copeland and Summers he found cohorts who could nudge him
into uncharted waters. So they did, and a star was born. The

compilation's title track had long become part of the atmosphere, and the rest of the album gave the listener no chance to rest: the ingenious hooks and bravura melodies kept coming. The celebrity cycle being what it is, The Police pulled a major coup in selling their wares – the songcraft, experimentation and infectious spirit – to a second wave of fans. In some views a timely reminder of old glories, in others a last-ditch cash-in, *Every Breath You Take* was an essential, even universal, primer of proven pop values.

From there things went downhill. After *Every Breath* reporters treated The Police as they treated the royal family, an attitude they didn't discourage. By 1987, wary civility had given way to bitchiness. 'I haven't got time to follow everything Sting's doing,' Summers told *Rolling Stone*. 'I lead my own life.' Copeland spoke constantly of the old days, reworking the tall tales of creative disputes and broken ribs. When asked, later in the 1980s, to take part in yet another Police reunion, Sting himself promised to call back: and he still might. Miles continued to verbally maul anyone who said the group had ever split. He was probably the one person to deny it. In the years ahead, Sting, Copeland and Summers never said anything which suggested that the band wasn't shut down for ever in 1986, like Chernobyl. Only their manager carried optimism to the point of self-delusion.

The crossroads of encroaching years and creative fulfilment found Sting a more mellow, relaxed soul. He learned affability as he went along, dictated by the realities of middle age. In 1988 the BBC's Jeff Griffin met Sting and Styler at the British Festival in Los Angeles. Like his client, Miles was geniality itself when Griffin requested an interview. Sting, in turn, was 'warm and friendly, talking about Amnesty with a passion that sounded genuine', even if, to another man, 'Sting and Amnesty used one another for their mutual benefit – each wanted an endorsement.' Later that year Agnes Miller, last seen at St Paul's, Cramlington, a decade before, met Sting at a funeral in London. He was 'utterly changed' from those days, 'a first-class family man and good friend' who drove his old headmistress back to her bus in his jeep. He saw to it that medical expenses for another ex-colleague were paid out of a special Roxanne company fund. When that was depleted, Sting asked that the bills be sent to him personally in Highgate. He gave generously, and quietly, to several relatives in Newcastle.

To most if not all of his old clique, Sting was the antithesis of rock pomp and pretension. He visited the north-east often in 1986, returning to his birthplace to star in the stark, stingingly low-life film *Stormy Monday*. When he drove to his boyhood haunts, he had a habit of warmly shaking friends, fans and even the St Cuthbert's staff by the hand, and he quietly rebuked minders who 'tried to treat [me] like the Pope'. If Sting walked into a pub, he'd buy a round and talk sport with anyone who cared to join in. His new, dedicated concept of stardom rejected ostentation, snobbery and vanity. For the role of the thug club-owner in *Stormy Monday*, he reverted to a thick Geordie brogue, and kept up the act for weeks afterwards. For all his ambiguity about his roots, he claimed he was 'fiercely proud of coming from Newcastle'; without any particular empathy for the place, he puffed, praised and defended his home against those (like his co-star Melanie Griffith) who slated it as 'a total dump'.

But for Sting, Newcastle meant more than nostalgia and a chance to show how far he'd come. The thing that scared him most all his life was loss of control – anyone else's, but especially his own. The roots of that fear may have lain in his hazy child's impressions of his warring parents, as well as his more vivid memories of brawling with his brother. Something, Sting once told a close friend, had 'locked me up' emotionally, had given him a 'lethal dose' of self-containment. His solitude was made all the worse by his need for domesticity. Sting craved family stability as only a person to whom it's been denied can crave it. In some of his adult dealings with the Sumners, he said so openly. 'I should have made my peace [with them] sooner,' he told a reporter. And Sting's sister Angela insisted, 'Gordon means the world to us, and he'd be the first to admit his family means the world to him. We are all so close.' Yet the goals toward which he worked remained murky. Sting was loud against 'drift' and no less noisy in favour of 'hearth and home', but exact definitions of the terms were hard to come by. Thirty years on, he still fought sporadically with his brother. 'Every time I say anything in the press that's stupid or gets twisted,' Sting rued, 'he gets it in the neck.' After reading an interview critical of their youth, one Sumner rang Highgate to complain. The four-word message ran, 'You fucking stupid cunt.'

Late in 1986, Sting learned that his mother and father were

both dying of cancer. He travelled back to Newcastle at Christmas, visiting each parent in turn. Pictures of him surrounded Audrey in her hospital bed; an early photo of herself holding him in her arms; portraits of him at home and school; and a snap which made them look like brother and sister. The small tape recorder in Audrey's locker sometimes piped him in. She looked forward to every new album, she told the nurses, and always listened intently, nodding and smiling to herself as her son's earnest, smoky voice filled the room. Across town, Ernie was still being treated at home. More guardedly fond of his children, he still fretted at his own lost opportunities in life. As he grew weaker, Ernie said, he sometimes liked just to lie back 'and brood about the whole thing'. This was the man, only fifty-seven but resigned to the end, of whom Sting said, 'He died angry, and I was angry with him.'

With the recent flurry of family visits, film work and nostalgic trips around town, Sting became a familiar figure on the streets of Newcastle for the first time in a decade. He made pilgrimages to all his houses and to Julie's nightclub, scene of impromptu rave-ups by the Big Band, where he queued at the bar unrecognized. Sting filmed one scene of *Stormy Monday* at a bus stop where he'd stood waiting to go to St Cuthbert's. And he drove to the school itself, 'still get[ting] that feeling of horror in my stomach' as he went through the gate.

Even friends, Len Forin says, 'couldn't guess at the grief caused him by his folks dying'; but the tenacity with which Sting clung to every surviving link with his childhood proved the pain went deep. He kept it to himself. He went about town, alone or with Styler, the soul of goodwill and warmth. Then one night, in a bar, someone innocently showed him a photo of Audrey Sumner taken when she was a young girl. Tears filled Sting's eyes. He murmured that he would like to be left alone. The other man made his excuses and went. None of his old friends had ever seen Sting cry.

When not making sentimental journeys around Wallsend and Tynemouth, Sting added more homes and offices to his collection. Since 1979, hardly a year had gone by without him visiting Malibu Colony Drive in California. In 1986 he spent $1.5 million buying a seaside home there once owned by Barbra Streisand. The grey, shake-sided mansion was, like the Highgate house, on a semi-secluded street hidden by a brick wall and thick trees. A sign read 'Patroled by Brinks Security'. The upper floors with their high windows and skylights were, however, fully visible from the road. Standing on a neatly manicured lot landscaped with a trellis and bushes, the three-storey house enjoyed a view over the beach on to the Pacific. Hollywood pharaohs like Warren Beatty lived nearby. After buying the property, Sting spent a small fortune adding a gym, sauna and heated pool. Special attention was given to the open-plan studio, a study in airy, state-of-the-art technology. With the electronics, antiques and security systems Sting installed in the mansion, it was said to have cost a total of $3 million. It was the Malibu home that was nearest his heart, the childhood dream that he was realizing with his energy and his millions.

Actually working at the beach was another matter, and Sting never made much more than a few brief goes of it. For three months in 1987 he holed up in his New York duplex, writing the songs that became *Nothing Like the Sun*. His quiet enthusiasm and creative spark were infectious. There was an intriguing sense of suspense whenever he sat down at the piano, since no one knew what would happen next. The Guv, as he was coming to be called, worked quickly, spinning raw tunes that Marsalis and the rest rubbed into hits. Newly civil in what a friend calls a 'courtly, old-world way', he never gave a blunt order but always expressed himself in the form of a polite suggestion, saying 'please' and 'if you don't mind'. He never got angry. He never raised his voice. Sting often changed his mind on matters like what clothes to wear and which colour to paint his homes ('He's a Libra,' as Styler says), but in the studio he got what he wanted through sheer force of will, charm, and shy obstinacy. He was democratic, and he was kingly. When a problem arose, he was apt to listen to his producer and band, then calmly make a decision grounded on 'marketability', the same musical virtue that drove The Police. Sting had stunning powers of reasoning and persuasion with an unbeatable track record to anchor them on.

Although both Sting and Styler valued their independence, friends had no doubts about their long-term prospects. He had a solitary side. She provided the space, the leeway and the tact to protect it. With rare exceptions, her strategy was support, not competition. They made a good-looking and evidently happy couple, whether kibbutzing with friends in New York, attending premières and openings, or ambling hand-in-hand on the Malibu beach. Even when Sting made a rare public snub of his partner, telling a reporter, 'Of course I'm not going to marry her,' Styler kept her cool. 'I'm not so insecure that I need constant affirmation he wants to be with me,' she said. 'I suppose he might go off with someone else – but then, I might, too.'

Styler, in short, rolled over for no one, including her partner. While Sting wasn't oblivious to her beauty, he was struck likewise by her smarts, self-confidence and relish for the absurd. There were no dull moments when Styler was about. She was easy on the eye and she made him laugh, two things Sting prized. By 1987 they seemed to have been together far longer than the five years since the days of the Virgin suit and brawls at Heathrow.

Sting recorded *Nothing Like the Sun* at Air Studios, Montserrat, home of *Ghost in the Machine* and *Synchronicity*. Early in the session he took a phone call from his brother. Audrey Sumner had died, two years after being told she had a month to live. Sting's response was to write 'The Lazarus Heart', a model of intelligence, intensity and impenetrable lyrics, and to dedicate the album to his mother. Within a year, his father had also succumbed to cancer. The cumulative effect of the two blows was to send Sting into a depression. His emotional slump, which got worse instead of better, worried him. He had a recovery plan that did him credit, broad-based, liberal and altruistic, and over the next three years he threw himself into a welter of *ad hoc* projects. There were Amnesty shows, films, tours and one-off collaborations. Sting became a human sounding-board for the grievances and remedies of the Third World, which he tried to weave into a practically, if not politically, coherent programme. But philanthropy was only one part of his personal syllabus. He worked with everyone from Ziggy Marley to the Chamber Orchestra of Europe. He starred on Broadway and visited the Kayapo Indians in Brazil. He did not, however, write any new songs.

Looking back, Sting would rationalize the breakdown as a response to 'the usual mid-life sort of stuff', as well as to his parents' deaths. 'I hadn't done as much as a rhyming couplet, much less a whole song. I was suffering from what they call writer's block ... I took long drives, long baths, long walks, but not one line of lyric – nothing.' He was no stranger to this creative agony. 'If you're going to be original, you can't come up with a brilliant idea every day,' he told a friend in 1981. Then, a relentless tour schedule and looming deadlines for *Zenyatta* and *Ghost* had been enough to force the next forward jump in Sting's career. Now, he faced a disturbing and demoralizing crisis. His frustration always came out in the same way: Sting would lurch from one job to another, aiming for width, not depth. Worse, although he was aware of the trough, he couldn't see his way out of it. One of his greatest strengths, and not the least of his weaknesses, was an ability to grasp his own predicament. It was inconceivable that the most self-analytical of all rockers didn't know that, for more than three years, he was trading on his past. He obviously knew.

Sting's wanton dallying in outside projects included wrapping his role in *Stormy Monday*; hobnobbing at the Cannes Film Festival; hosting *Saturday Night Live*; attending the Umbria jazz gala; hanging with Gil Evans and Cab Calloway; launching his own record label; taking the lead in Stravinsky's *Soldier's Tale*; playing at Nelson Mandela's benefit in London; co-headlining an Amnesty tour; and starring as Macheath in *The Threepenny Opera*. Between times, *Nothing Like the Sun* scored a number-one hit in Britain. The album brought one smash single, 'We'll Be Together' (taking one of funk's first giant steps across genre lines); a second, 'Englishman In New York', that stalled at number 84; and a third, 'They Dance Alone', a commercial flop that won an Ivor Novello award in 1989. The last was also a backdrop to the BBC documentary *A Prisoner of Conscience*. Even from the creative doldrums, Sting was the great pop hope of human rights, a dependable campaigner and tireless doer of good works. In December 1987 he agreed to visit the Brazilian rainforest, an involvement that dogged him for years. Never before had the motive been so noble; never before had attacks been so barbed.

Sting's stamina, social conscience and passion for causes had long since made him a conversation piece. From Rio to Rome he was an object of discussion, often heated, aimed at settling the issue once and for all: was he a nomadic, creative soul, or, as *Today* put it, 'a whiny sod'? While fans and foes debated

the point, Sting also found time to tour North and South
America (hearing of his father's death just as he was about to go
on in front of 200,000 people in Brazil), as well as criss-crossing
Europe and ending 1988 in Japan and Australia. A planned live
album never appeared, but that was the sole job he failed to
tackle.

Sting was learning. The pursuit of fame, he was coming to see,
was less important than what one made of it. Good could be
done – and his own career advanced – by chasing goals he would
have passed up during life with The Police. The narrowly selfish
issues that exercised most rock stars didn't tax him at all. Sting,
says a friend, 'genuinely didn't give a toss' if his face appeared
on the cover of *Melody Maker*. From 1987–88 he was consistent
and effective only when it came to causes. On the basis that
'happiness is equilibrium', says his friend, 'Sting shifted his
weight'.

He enjoyed his balancing act as a campaigner and happy
family man. Even the longer-than-usual lulls between albums and
tours suited him. Settled comfortably in front of the Highgate
fire with a good book, Sting was able to cut himself off from the
sleeve-tugging around him, to lose himself in literature. True to
form, he read everything he could lay hands on. There were
literally thousands of volumes flung around his three homes,
many of which found their way into song or album titles. As new
issues arose, they were met with new aphorisms.*

Uncoincidentally, he was maturing as a thinker and social
theorist. Middle-aged, a multi-millionaire in the thick of a
second, wildly successful career, Sting came as close as he ever
did to setting out a philosophical case for his politics. 'Our generation, the largest in history, is just about to come into power,' he
said. 'The Reagans and Thatchers are on the way out. It's their
last chapter, just as South Africa is the last chapter of slavery.' His
tropisms included awkward echoes of Wallsend, and his efforts
to exculpate his vast wealth seemed strained. But it showed that
he was starting to carve out a fresh agenda, always ready to see his
own life as being of universal significance – a mark of genius.
From the mid-1980s, he was equally at home in art and politics.

---

* For *Nothing Like the Sun,* Sting filched a line from Shakespeare's Sonnet
CXXX, and Anthony Burgess.

Musically, his name was so secure as to allow experiment, erratic fertility, and the odd pricking of the myth. Rock and roll, Sting said, 'is a bit like Las Vegas ... guys dressed up in their sisters' clothes pretending to be rebellious and angry, but not really angry about anything'. His work in 1987–88 was full of nooks and crannies of offbeat novelty. Sting collaborated with his old friend Eberhard Schoener in a Brecht and Weill gala in Hamburg. He played with the Gil Evans Orchestra at Umbria. And in September 1988 he took to the road with Bruce Springsteen, Peter Gabriel, Tracy Chapman and Youssou N'Dour for an Amnesty tour that kicked off at Wembley and touched India, Zimbabwe and Brazil, exchanging amorous triviality for songs, like 'They Dance Alone', that expressed pain, idealism and piety totally without irony.

Meanwhile, chafing at the long delays of most film work, Sting made a switch to plays. In late 1988 he put up £20,000 to help stage Ibsen's anti-fascist fable *An Enemy of the People* in the West End. A year later he was starring in *The Threepenny Opera* on Broadway. In his screen cameos Sting had found a working role that other would-be actors might not have shucked. The *Opera* once again brought sneers that he was over-reaching himself. Such barbs underestimated Sting's ambition, versatility and need – almost a compulsion – for change. His Macheath, if strangely hieratic (a stage name for boring), won raves in the New York *Post* and played to semi-full houses. There were better and braver thespians around, but few capable of changing hats as easily.

Sting also kept up a social life. While in New York he cut a cool dash at Nell's nightclub, where he discussed mutual plans with Andy Warhol (just days, as it happened, before Warhol died). Between tours and plays, his working-class roots might not exclude a week spent on the ski slopes in Aspen or Gstaad. He also won fame for his Cerruti suits and his designer garb generally. In choosing his wardrobe, he gave fresh spin to the classic modernist dictum that form should follow function. For trade-press interviews or mainstream TV like *Saturday Night Live*, he donned strict rock ware: black T-shirts and denim. For more spectacular set-pieces, he chose leather or silk trousers, wafer-thin sleeveless shirts (his muscularly displayed pectorals doing for Sting what cleavage did for Styler) and heavy make-up. At Amnesty or Rainforest gigs he appeared like the teacher he once was – all sandals and crinkly jackets. He often wore glasses.

The writer's block, ironically, accelerated Sting's already varied life in several directions. He took a new look at theatre. He upped his charity work, notably for Amnesty. He made his first trek to the Amazon. Sting's most visible 1987 moves were, however, commitments rather than a genuine extension of his career. He made his second solo studio album, *Nothing Like the Sun*. And Mike Figgis's film noir of the caring bosom of Newcastle clubland, *Stormy Monday*, bowed in July.

Neither the screen nor stage roles were mere whims. They were ends Sting chased with the implacable fury of his ego. One of the keys to his locked-in character lies in the rage with which he wanted things. It was a brute force beyond his control. In sheer intensity, Sting was freakish, judged against other waxen-faced, wasted rockers. Among his chief ingredients was narcissism – a legacy of his childhood and of an iron will transmitted through Audrey – as well as a dour refusal to laurel-sit. The pressure of his ambition, rarely curbed, never thwarted, drove him incessantly. It explained the self-seeking things he did, and the altruistic. It explained the vast energy he threw into all his jobs. It explained his capacity for work – when he could have spent his time in well-oiled sloth.

Stormy Monday began when Sting re-met Mike Figgis, a trumpeter on the same provincial jazz circuit in the mid-1970s. From there the film grew, via a British and Polish conglomerate, into a weird mix of local talent and imported Hollywood names, principally Melanie Griffith and Tommy Lee Jones. Sean Bean played a shady drifter, Sting the owner of a dive plausibly based on Julie's and the Club À Go Go. The picture teemed with references, visual and verbal, to the jazz *demi-monde* of the day: double basses, shiny suits, thugs, bungs and sinister property spivs. This was the vanished world of Last Exit. Add a rumbling sub-plot about encroaching American culture – made flesh by Griffith and Jones – and the film took aim at everything Gordon Sumner held dear between St Cuthbert's and The Police.

Sting wasn't afraid to play a monster. 'I don't like being pushed around,' he announced early in the film. He illustrated the fact by smashing his rival's arm with an iron bar. Sting's character was a blithe psychopath who rationalized immorality as part of the job. Predictably, there were hints that the fictive club boss was all too close to the real man. Sting clearly knew his way around the fantasies of bullies. And his continual demand of Bean to 'get a receipt for everything' echoed the real-life drama being played out with his money. *Stormy Monday* reflected all his off-screen qualities of charm and menace, and gave him a critical and popular hit.

Reviews were mixed on the film as a whole. The story reminded some of *The Long Good Friday*. To others it was a pale shadow of 1971's seminal *Get Carter*. Most papers recognized immediately in *Stormy Monday* at least a worthy British entrant into the world of Scorsese-type mayhem, and the première was one of the year's most glittering nights. Sting himself attended the opening. Shyness underpinned so much of his life, it was surprising how often he got out. He was at his best at public events. Sting's charisma was legendary. For more than an hour he signed autographs and delighted fans with his tart, droll quips on the film. That the charm could never be taken for granted was shown when a woman approached and mildly told him, 'I'm from Surrey Sound.' 'Great,' said Sting, in a witheringly sarcastic tone. 'I *must* make my next album there.'

Sting, of course, was as likely to make another record in Leatherhead as he was in the Antarctic. *Nothing Like the Sun*, out that October, had a budget Nigel Gray would have died for: as well as the high-rent studios in Montserrat and New York and guest appearances by Eric Clapton, Mark Knopfler and Rubén Blades, the lavish design and smoochy, pin-up photos of Sting himself all marked an end of the creative gamble of *Blue Turtles* in a hail of Grammys and platinum discs. Sting relaxed on *Nothing Like the Sun*. Facing a shortage of genres to blur, he refined his stylistic adventures into a slab of bass-pumping funk and meaty guitar. As an album, it was neither too dangerous nor too safe. The testy angst of 'History Will Teach Us Nothing' was matched by the gauzy, intimate romance of 'Sister Moon'; the abstract tune of 'Fragile' by the salacious stomp of 'We'll Be Together'. Armed with perverse, catchy songs and a sultry voice, Sting shelved the jazz-rock workouts to forge a ballad-charged pop blockbuster. With *Nothing Like the Sun* he finally downed tools in the hit factory and became an 'album guy'. Balancing the moody and the danceable, *Sun* paved the way for every AOR star to come.

The record repeatedly shifted gears while staying firmly on track, with the exception of the Gil Evans-led detour of 'Little Wing'. 'Englishman In New York' and 'Rock Steady' were power-houses of bent melodics; 'History' neatly cribbed 'Driven To Tears' and a touch of Paul Simon; the chugging party groove of 'We'll Be Together' (later disowned by Sting when it was used in a beer commercial) was at once derivative and oddly clever: musical ecumenism forged by Peter Gabriel's 'Sledgehammer'. 'They Dance Alone' was the most contemplative track – and most complex. Sting's sombre, understated vocal evoked a pro-test in which the Chilean regime was flayed in a wry and intensely heartfelt lyric, later an anthem for Amnesty. Closing the album, 'The Secret Marriage' soared on the strength of the double bass and piano framing Sting's Pinteresque vocal pauses, turning a classical melody into a slice of theatre.

At its worst, *Nothing Like the Sun* was a jumble of maudlin dirges (the word 'Heart' recurring in three titles) and cloying, Valentine-card lyrics. On at least half the tracks, the music was let down by the bathetic, self-obsessed words. Autism was the charge the critics made in the face of a brilliantly performed and affect-ingly personal hit. Sting was a man 'living in the shadow of his own ego', according to one. At its best, the album wore its passion proudly on its sleeve – literally so, judging from the stubbly, come-hither shot of Sting on the cover. Drawing equally from '60s soul, '70s pop and '80s AOR, *Sun* mixed and matched all three schools (often in the space of a single song) with a breezy snub of tautology. Sting's voice was again the unifying link: a rich, slick and full-toned instrument, achingly irresistible on the ballads and bluesy on the belters. Though shedding the jazz skin of *Turtles, Nothing Like the Sun* more than maintained momentum and market share. The album bulldozed any linger-ing doubts about Sting's solo career, lifting him to true celebrity and finally burying The Police.

A clutch of indelible videos made Sting a major star of MTV and did no harm to sales. In 'We'll Be Together', he played both insider and outsider, a prancing nance and a besuited diner somehow embroiled in a restaurant brawl. For 'Fragile', he aptly appeared pale and barefoot, hunched alone with his acoustic guitar. 'Be Still My Beating Heart' and 'Englishman In New York' both saw a rank blend of sentiment and surrealism, while

'They Dance Alone' was relentlessly downbeat until the happy, partified ending. The five films, shot by four different directors, were as stylistically contrary as the album. Production values were lush throughout, but Sting consistently cut and changed his type. In 1987–88 he wasn't sure whether he was a bare-chested rocker, a crusader or an actor who played at being both. Some of the schizophrenia came through in the videos, which flew on star presence over the thematic vacuum (and vacuousness). They went into heavy rotation on TV.

Nothing Like the Sun was a British number one (spending forty-seven weeks in the chart), number nine in America. It took 'album of the year' at the 1988 Brits. Sting also won a 'best pop and rock singer' Grammy. The record even stole into the *Playboy* jazz poll, bringing a mordant sigh from Miles Davis: 'What Gil Evans did for Sting's shit is a motherfucker – for Sting, that is.' In South America, where a Spanish-language version of *Sun* sold millions, the critics rushed to heap honours on him. From Santiago to San Salvador, people who hadn't heard of another pop star suddenly knew Sting's name.

However he expanded, Sting would never admit he was spreading himself too thin. After wildly successful gigs in Brazil, hitting a climax at the Maracaña stadium in Rio, he made a mid-life assessment. Both his parents had just died. Although the live shows and films kept coming, he had chronic writer's block. In December 1987 he was thirty-six, not young, in rock-and-roll terms fast approaching fossil status – 'an old fart', as he called himself. It was in this febrile mood in Rio that he met a Belgian photographer, Jean-Pierre Dutilleux. A decade before, Dutilleux had made an Oscar-nominated film about the plight of the Xingú Indians. He arranged a private screening for his new friend, providing a glimpse of a life rarely seen this side of *National Geographic*. Within days the two men, along with Styler and Mino Cinelu, the percussionist in Sting's band, were shoehorned into a plane of dubious vintage, heading north.

Environmentalism had already bulked among the roll-call of Sting's causes. For a year or two, his name was linked with the Sierra Club in California. He was heard to rue the ancient American forests falling daily to the chainsaw. He was an early champion of recycling and conservation. 'We can't live here and be happy with less / With so many riches, so many souls / Everything we see we want to possess', he'd carped on 'If You Love Somebody'. Closer to home, he'd spoken archly of 'attempted [land] rape by planners and speculators', a recurrent sub-plot of *Stormy Monday*. All the Sumners had protested the mad refurbishing of old Newcastle into the 'Venice of the north'. Now Sting made it plain that ecology was no longer a side-issue but a burning passion. Within hours, coached by Dutilleux, he could quote the salient facts and figures: the Xingú land was being ravaged; before the white man arrived in South America, there were six million Indians, now a meagre 200,000; the forests themselves were the highest, densest and most verdant on earth, despite their infertile soil.* To inexpert eyes, everything was uniformly green. But, for the native, the Brazilian jungle was a lush and endlessly rich world offering up raw materials for medicines, swarming with 1,600 species of birds and 30,000 of insects, the largest natural laboratory and bio-genetic preserve on the globe. This paradise was being razed, through slash-and-burn agriculture, logging, mining and road construction, at a rate of sixty acres a minute. An unholy alliance of government planners and local farmers were on the move. In 1988 alone, an area the size of Belgium would be eaten out by this spongiform mass.

Much as it took guts to fly into the interior, Sting's initial reaction was wary. 'Dolphins, penguins, who gives a fuck, J-P?' he asked as the cargo of fish-hooks, knives, fishing lines, torches, pots and pans was being loaded on the plane. Perhaps sensing the savagery of the backlash against him, Sting himself would write of the trip, 'If we can succeed in our plan and convince as many people as possible that there's something they can do, then I'll get out from under the feet of the ecologists and get back to singing.' Nor, at first, did he suspend the disdainful cool with which he habitually met strangers. In a weak moment in the jungle, Sting stuck a McVitie's biscuit in his mouth in mockery of the huge plates stitched into the Indians' lower lips. (Seeing this, one tribal chief took a knife and offered to give his guest the real thing by a quick slit under the chin.) To his credit, Sting intuitively realized that there was no earthly prospect of 'saving

---

*The vital nutrients are found in the jungle plants which grow, flower and fruit the year around.

the rainforest' overnight. The more the debate raged, the clearer it got that the campaign hadn't been thought through. Mavericks like Dutilleux were good at aspirational logic. They were less good at detailed planning, on which Sting thrived. In early 1988, the whole project resembled an elegant-looking parcel, beautifully wrapped, ribboned – and empty.

Sting and Styler spent several days in an Indian village of thatched huts, squatting over a meal of piraracu fish in the red dust, bathing in the river and playing football with the native children. They slept in hammocks under the stars. Even at night, the jungle was never quiet: the visitors heard birds and the screeching of animals, lying plagued by gnats and terrified of snakes. At dawn feathered warriors from the Kuikuru, Kayapo and Meinaco tribes – secretive, dangerous and normally highly territorial – performed the dance of the river spirit. Sting in turn sang 'Fragile', Cinelu using a pan for percussive effects. The Indians were pleased by the number. Sting then had the symbol of the snake god daubed on his chest and back, a charcoal and red dye design that, as his partner said, 'made [him] look like a bloody firework'. It was an impressive spot. They all came to learn the meaning of 'He was swallowed up by the jungle', the last line of a famous Latin American novel. Compasses were useless in the rainforest. Strangers could walk in circles forever.

Before leaving Brazil, Sting promised Dutilleux he would speak to Amnesty about his experience. 'My faith in man has been restored,' he told his guide. Friends agreed that Sting and Styler were taken by the place. 'They'd talk of nothing but the jungle. There was no other subject worth discussing,' said PolyGram's PR girl, Gilda Matoso. Sting spoke in almost mystical terms about the rainforest. 'It's not the noble savage I have a sense of, but the nobility of the species,' he wrote. 'In some ways Western man is in reverse evolution. We've forgotten our real potential. The Xingú can remind us of what we really are. They must survive.' He talked about the jungle the way others did of a religious experience, sex or war. Even his bedtime reading reflected his passion – he bought dozens of books on ecological theory and history.

While few doubted the sincerity of Sting's fad, there were those who thought him 'emotionally gaga' and 'unable to cope' with his parents' deaths (he attended neither funeral), dangerously volatile and all too eager to embrace a plausible chancer like Dutilleux. (The two men later fell out.) A more cynical interpretation of his safari was also forthcoming. Seen in a different anthropological light, Chief Raoni and the rest were very far from noble or savage. Sting had accused the West of corrupting the Indians with Reeboks and Levi's. One Brazilian's glacial reply was that it was the Xingú who were corrupt, precisely because of their materialism. During the visit, Dutilleux had arranged for a dozen chiefs from various villages, and from different clans – 'people who, last time they saw a white man, killed him' – to meet Sting. The actual summit was a parodist's dream, an attritional war of weird demands and internecine squabbling. Naked warriors found themselves sitting next to inveterate thugs with a fetish for guns, Rolexes and Sony Walkmans. An unholy row broke out when, on a future visit, Sting declined to buy his hosts a helicopter. 'In a sense Raoni manipulated me rather than the other way round,' he later said. Sting struggled to walk an uneasy path between the practical demands of the Xingú and the ethical absolutes of saving their land. He salved his conscience by doing as well as he could for the Indians while battling both passion fatigue and the media.

'Being a public figure helped get the whole [project] off the ground,' said Sting. 'At the same time, the scrutiny was intense and everybody was pooh-poohing us.' Even in a creative slump, Sting was one of the most polarizing names in art. At the highest extreme, he was the thinking-man's rocker, dressed down, horn-rimmed glasses slung low on his nose, reeling off facts about deforestation and global warming. There were limits, though, to how many good deeds the public could take from its pop stars: Live Aid, certainly; benefits for the Xingú Indians, less so. Sting's 'bungle in the jungle', as one wag put it, brought a furore. Those who, for whatever reason, had silently disliked him now shouted their contempt from the rooftops. A campaign began attacking him for patronizing both the Indians and his long-suffering fans. At the end of the 1980s, *National Review* ran a list of the 'five biggest bores' of the decade. Sting came in third.

The other potshots came from fellow musicians, like one who thought the cover of *Nothing Like the Sun* made Sting look 'a precious little fuck' and another who skewered him as a 'Geordie twat'. Rod Stewart took the trouble to carve the words 'Where's your fucking sense of humour, you miserable sod?' into a table on the private jet both men used. (Sting retaliated by padlocking the front gate of Stewart's mansion, leading to ugly threats and, ultimately, a conciliatory bunch of flowers.) Mick Jagger was heard to snigger about Sting's 'saving the bloody planet'. Even Kurt Cobain spoofed him as 'the environmental guy'.

There was something poignant in the speed with which Sting quashed suggestions that he was (as he had it) 'a pretentious git'. He was neither humourless nor pompous, he told *Q*, though 'perhaps didactic'. Sting put much of the blame for his image squarely on the press. 'The stories are total fabrications ... People say they don't believe them, but they do, and [fans] get a received impression of you.' He pleaded not guilty to the charge of fanaticism: 'I was *never* trying to save the world.'

His efforts did, though, force the rainforest on to the mainstream liberal agenda. In July 1988 Sting gave a Washington DC news conference in support of his conservation scheme. He spoke of the Xingú and others from the stages of countless arenas. The missionary work paid off. In 1989 the Brazilian president announced plans to slow the creeping development of Amazonia. By 1990 a total of 328,000 square miles – an area roughly the size of Egypt – had been demarcated for Indian use. A major second step forward for the tribes was the dedication, in November 1991, of a continuous 45,000-square-mile homeland (as big as England) for the Yanomamis of northern Brazil. A Xingú national park followed two years later. The reforms gained speed as a result of government initiatives to protect the environment, including new laws, the revision of tax incentives and an emergency order executed during Brazil's long drought to counter illegal clearings and burnings. By the time of the Earth Summit in Rio in June 1992, the tribal lands were being monitored by satellite, and domestic efforts reinforced by the international community through a pilot plan, sponsored by the European Union, and a model for preservation projects in other countries. Frankly, many or all of these schemes could have been pushed through by a somnambulist merely parroting his appointed lines. Most Western leaders, witness their presence in Rio, were ready to act. But Sting did much more than lobby guilt-ridden governments. His own dogged efforts made a more poignant success story than the usual self-promotional blitz; they were also far better adapted to real change at a time when people were tired of set-piece pop extravaganzas. He always stressed the tangible results of his efforts, rightly so. He helped form the New York-based Rainforest Foundation, sat on its board, and donated upwards of £1 million annually by giving benefits. To speak of such things with pride wasn't just bragging.

It was also here, in his famously high-profile crusading, that the common view of Sting darkened. As well as jeers from *National Review* and the likes of Rod Stewart, there was a widespread theory that he enjoyed the publicity, though few openly said it. No one had ever mistaken Sting for a Trappist monk. He'd dropped The Police as soon as he had enough songs for an album and quickly established himself as a hot solo act. A general criticism, even then, was that Sting's lyrics tended to focus over-intensely on Sting. The composer was a presence in almost all his own work. At its best, *Sun* and the rest allowed for a confessional mode which Sting defined – exposing the seamier side of life that most rockers, schooled in the comfort of the omniscient voice, would rather die than acknowledge. But the regular holding-up of a mirror to himself, professionally as well as in his campaigns, could begin to cloy. Over years, that constant presence, the insistence of his 'I', meant that Sting, as *Sounds* said, was tainted as an 'eco-pillock, tosser and something of a berk'.

Something of a berk. That the stuck-up view of Sting was a crass simplification was shown by his many private acts of charity and his love of raunchy pop; and well into his forties there were traces of old, unreconstructed, Police-era antics. He might have narrowed his field in sex but he remained quietly engrossed in drugs and rock and roll. Travelling in the rainforest in the early 1990s, Sting was introduced to a herb called ayahuasca, made from the roots of a jungle vine and boiled into a tea. Effects of this brew on outsiders are notoriously mixed. Where the Xingú feel themselves to be possessed by the spirit of his or her shamanistic animal, most first-time drinkers of the tea are violently sick. Sting spoke of his own experience in semi-reverent terms. 'When you take Dead Man's Root you die, basically,' he told *Q*, 'and meet your God. The first hour and a half you're terrified . . . Then I cried, physically wept for two hours. I went through my whole life. I was involved in stories in real time that took years, and then for two hours I was beatific, in ecstasy. A sort of sainted state. It's the whole basis of holy communion as a drug.' In 1995 Sting made a chance remark to a Swedish paper, suggesting that Ecstasy should be legalized. This – shortly after the death of British teenager Leah Betts – led to him being mauled by the *Sun* and slated by the girl's family. 'What surprised me is that, in a democracy, just expressing an opinion could cause such problems,' said Sting – 'a tad disingenuously', according to a friend. The same source still recalls 'what were probably cigarettes' being toked at Highgate.

As befitted a workaholic, Sting cared about nothing more than the shows, specials, and one-off benefits that served as the daily substitute for actual writing. On 20 January 1988 he began a forty-six-date US tour in Florida. That ran through to April. Over the spring he played in Britain, Spain, Holland and Italy, and managed a side-trip to Cannes. In June he opened the globally broadcast Wembley concert to celebrate Nelson Mandela's seventieth birthday. (The day itself polarized opinions, again putting Sting at the heart of a loud debate about rock's attempts to raise international consciousness. The backlash against the show was instant. 'Many will be offended,' rumbled *The Times*, 'by this latest manifestation of the new banality which yokes pop fiestas to political crises or national suffering, trivializing serious issues.' In the event, the day raised £1.8 million at the gate and TV receipts of £10 million, at least some of which found its way into ANC coffers.) After a hasty set, Sting and his band were on a jet to Berlin, where they played again that night. A round of summer festivals followed. After the Amnesty tour, Sting wound down with shows in Japan and Australia, yomped back through Britain and Europe and began mixing a live album. He narrated *The Soldier's Tale* for Pangaea, his own label. He slogged away most of the year, playing the old hits while the new ones wouldn't come – going home to rest, but then irresistibly lured back on the road, a twitchy, charismatic figure in his Italian jacket or leather vest, a more or less permanent sight on posters and billboards glued to a million walls; you could see his mournful pose on the back streets of Delhi and the *vias* of Rome. A huge advertisement of him got up as a poltroon broke out in New York like a rash.

Sting also worked hard to live a normal life. When he walked round Highgate he was as anonymous as a man in Cerruti gear, bleached hair and stubble can be. The very title of his last album had been suggested by a chance encounter outside a pub. Waylaid one night by a drunk who asked, after a titanically deep belch, 'How beautiful is the moon?' Sting's sharp, if not totally original, reply had been to quote the sonnet: 'My mistress' eyes are nothing like the sun'. A second man who met him around the same time thought him 'genuinely nice, folksy compared to most megastars'. Most mornings when in London, Sting made a point of walking his two springer spaniels on Hampstead Heath. No doubt the gesture was calculated, but it also showed the man still struggling inside the icon. Sting enjoyed both fame and money, but he also relished his citizen's right to stroll about town. 'The thing about success,' he told *NME*, 'is that you become a victim of a cell structure. You travel the world with a pod of people and you never meet anyone else. It's good to step outside that and talk to different types.' He was by far the most 'real' of the pop glitterati. Although Sting shared most of his peers' foibles, he was a keener observer and had a defter mind, and in the end rose above the intellectual fray of mere blokeism. Nice as he was, his public forays were still a rigidly controlled PR biodome; ever vigilant, he'd zap the first flare-up of trouble for his family or home. Within that limitation, Sting was open and affable.

Occasional jaunts to the pub or shop weren't, of course, anything new for celebrities. They all did it. Still, seclusion and petulance were corrosive and ultimately lethal to the man-in-the-street broodings that were everywhere on Sting's albums. He was doing more than cutting an image. He 'really meant it'. Sting was studiously genial even at concerts. Jeff Griffin found himself backstage at a German gig in 1988. 'Instead of the usual bullshit of the crew eating one place, the VIPs another and the star at his own table, there was Sting elbow-to-elbow with the gaffers and roadies. He looked happy there.'

Virtually from the crib, Sting had wanted an open, pluralistic society in which everyone would be 'free'. Precisely how this would be accomplished remained a bit fuzzy. But by his late thirties he had a workable personal agenda: for, if not amnesty and acid, then at least universal justice and 'the kind of drugs that connect you to the world'; against prejudice and brutality. He began to talk more and more of gay rights. When *Nothing*

Like the Sun took 'album of the year' at the Brits, Sting gave a long acceptance speech roundly attacking 'mean, fascistic, homophobic' government policies (a rant edited by TV to a quick grin and 'thank you'). In an interview with *NME*, he again talked up his friend Quentin Crisp. 'He's one of the most courageous men I've ever met, as well as one of the funniest . . . He was a homosexual in England at a time when being so was physically dangerous, and he was himself, with no apologies, in such a flamboyant and brave way that he was an example to everyone.' Sting's outspoken views weren't only shaped by his prying mind, but, for all his worldliness, strangely suburban and trite. He loathed, for example, 'seeing actors with guns – there they are on every movie poster, looking like complete dickheads'. Despite starring in non-Disney titles like *Dune* and *Stormy Monday*, he 'couldn't bear' macho posturing. 'I *hate* this fucking Stallone shit,' he said.* He detested violence.

Sting's attitude was as ambiguous as the bare record shows. He was devoted to worthy if abstract campaigns like the environment. But his chief flesh-and-blood cause, the one he turned to time and again, was himself. Throughout the late 1980s he kept his *pro bono* work in thrall to his day job of notching up smash albums and sold-out shows, and generally being a star. As part of his quick-change act between roles, he kept a mad schedule. That short hop between the Mandela birthday bash and Berlin was schizophrenia superbly handled, the social worker spouting a rock star's forked tail, then shedding it again later to play for Amnesty. Sting's double-life became more pronounced as the crusades and solo hits kept coming. It was a subject he discussed often with friends and family.

Neither gold discs nor fawning crowds meant a thing, said Sting, without a vision. That meant continuing work for the twin totems of his social conscience, Amnesty and the rainforest. A life with causes was controversial, but life without them was impossible. Sting's 'do-gooder' phase became the subject of endless acres of newsprint. Most commentators agreed, in milder terms, with Rod Stewart's private quip. Sting's high-profile, often wearisome, campaigns were always on the edge of satire. Yet

---

*In 1993 Sting supplied the title track for Sylvester Stallone's *Demolition Man*.

millions were quietly raised for his pet causes; men like Thozamile Gqweta walked free because of Amnesty; to many of the Xingú, Sting occupied a niche somewhere between saintly and divine. The reformist wedge he led made a difference.

Much as it was a feat in itself to have wrung changes in Brazil and South Africa, Sting's real coup was to balance his solo career and charity work, self-interest and disinterest, with mutually winning results. At a practical level, it meant that HBO viewers could watch the two sub-characters, the jigging rocker and the human-rights agitator, in separate TV specials that October. Increasingly, it also meant that Sting, his record company and the press, the last two with their yen to pigeonhole, were set on a three-way collision course. When, like him, an artist bucked the formula, the critics inevitably became grouchy. The 'pretentious git' school soon made it a point of honour to show their independence by knocking Sting. There were those, like Albert Goldman, who saw him as a symptom of a disease that had eaten away at rock's subversive power, mainly by affectation, for years; others who openly admired his passion and commitment. He suffered the fate of a symbol.

In early fall 1988 Sting began a seven-week tour for Amnesty, covering more than 35,000 miles in eighteen countries. Upfront, on opening night at Wembley, there was evidence of controversy. As at the Mandela gala, it centred on the newly consummated union between pop and overseas aid, much panned by, among others, the Tory MP John Carlisle. In the days leading up to 2 September there was a brisk debate on the marriage among British politicians (not one of whom, in the end, attended the show). Private frustration, too, broke out at certain key details of organization. Most Wembley fans never received their personal 'Human Rights passport' at the gate, and many were told that the £5 programme had already sold out before the first note was played. Sound quality was leaden. While other venues were experimenting with state-of-the-art, digital PAs, Wembley retreated through a sonic time-warp with its tinny, shrill tannoy. There was muttering, too, that the tour, the very soul of free-thinking individualism, was being underwritten by Reebok, whose sales executives took almost as many bows as the actual stars.

Sting turned in a seamless performance that divided his critics down party lines. To *The Times*, 'the careful blend of smooth rock-jazz' and buzz-saw pop sounded much like the ex-power trio who took Shea Stadium by storm. For *Melody Maker*, cultivating a niche as the bulletin-board of Sting-bashers, the set meant 'a lot of jazzy things, a lot of tinkering about with instruments, a lot of sensitivity and gentle noises and a lot of breathy singing . . . I like to think that Sting, perhaps, was deliberately interfering with the quickening-of-the-pulses as an experiment, or to be perverse, but he probably wasn't. He was just being . . . dull.'

While the show's energy sagged in the middle, Sting closed with 'One World' and the aching 'They Dance Alone', the closest thing to a torch song all night. By the final chorus, topless, Bic-flicking women were squatting on their partners' shoulders and, incongruously, a fight broke out in stage centre. It was like old times. What made the hassles of festival rock bearable were the brief moments when Sting engaged the crowd, tweaking the well-behaved thirtysomethings in his faux cockney, bouncing up and down, turning the stadium into a rowdy outdoor party. Families with nannies and picnic hampers, men in suits and grizzled hippies all joined in the massive campfire singalong. Even to *Melody Maker*, Sting came off as the 'consummate popster', unleashing bawdy call-and-response numbers alongside jazzy piano tunes, as safe, familiar, and, above all, catchy as classic-rock radio.

One by-product of the tour was a lasting friendship with his co-stars, notably Bruce Springsteen. The two men clearly enjoyed puncturing the loftier extremes of each other's fame. As well as semi-comic duetting on 'The River', they quickly developed a knockabout double-act on platform and stage, where Sting once stole up on Springsteen, in the guise of a pantomime villain, brandishing a vacuum-cleaner.* Despite tabloid sneers (including one suggesting that Styler felt jealous of the relationship), the bond flowed on genuine mutual respect. Sting had been a staunch, public admirer of Springsteen's ability to turn the iciest arena into a raunchy dive, a trick The Police themselves pulled off at Madison Square Garden. The two had something else in common: both were recasting their early '80s rock-messiah type.

---

*Variations on the same routine were on show at Sting's thirty-seventh birthday party, celebrated with Springsteen and Peter Gabriel in a Greek strip club.

This was, for Sting, the end product of the success myth for which he'd lived and become a poster-boy. Springsteen, too, found only 'ashes and muck' in being treated as a demi-god. In coming years, the two kept rooms at each other's homes. By the 1990s they were sharing holidays and even attending church together, with their wives and families making up a commune.

By November, when the Amnesty tour wound up in São Paulo, the Springsteen role had been taken by Chief Raoni. The sight of the Kayapo warrior appearing on stage to daub Sting with the Indians' traditional charcoal and dye duly provided the night's weirdest scene. 'I'm here because our land is being raped by prospectors and farmers,' the chief announced in his off-Portuguese. 'I want Brazil to respect the Indians, and the government of Brazil to protect us.' Sting got through the next number in his war-paint and headdress that shone in the lights like a bat's wings. Backstage, the two discussed the Fundacão Mata Virgem, or Rainforest Foundation, as a priority setting up a national park for the surviving ethnic tribes. Sting agreed to return to the Amazon early in 1989. Via the Orient, he flew to New York (where he somehow found himself partying with Jodie Foster and Madonna), then London. Here his atavistic fit struck a satiric note. Sting's gung-ho campaign and eco-crusade for the rainforest were laughed off, by some of his friends, as a put-on. 'Most of them thought it was a joke,' says one. 'They just couldn't believe that Sting could be that sincere and feel that strong about things. It seemed like a gag.' It wasn't: Sting may have envied Bob Geldof's knack of putting complex problems in simple terms – 'Send yer fockin' money' – but he was shrewd enough not to try to copy it. He was too intense to bring off Geldof's casual style. Thanks to Sting, the rainforest came to occupy the same nook in pop mythology as Ethiopia, and, like Geldof before him, he became a cause's patron saint. It was no act.

Somewhere between Sting's American and European tours that spring, the film *Julia and Julia* was released. He played the lead opposite Kathleen Turner. A lovelorn, low-velocity drama, fusing the clunky 'realism' of cut-rate camera work, the lethal chill of a Pinter play and the sub-porn writhings of the stars, the movie rarely tapped the potential of the plot: woman mourns her dead husband and son, only to find them mysteriously back in her life; was it all a dream? *Julia and Julia* never showed the imaginative spark of a film like *Diabolique*, yet it was more literally true to the haphazard drift of a sick mind than anything on screen since *Don't Look Now*.

Shorn of the big budget and star ensemble that propped, respectively, *The Bride* and *Plenty*, Sting showed a gift for cool threat and vulnerability, a mix that, as every good actor since Brando knows, can transcend even the flimsiest premise. If the set-up was ultimately facile, the performance had a grainy truth. As in *Brimstone & Treacle*, Sting caught the duality of the character – the low voice and morose elegance both lent a tremor of sorrow, projecting a wistfulness starkly at odds with his rock-god image. As in all 'arty' erotica, the stars affected a kind of inertia somewhere between sophisticated ennui and a general anaesthetic. Even so, Turner's couplings with her co-lead broke new ground in glassy-eyed torpor. Sex, according to this reading, was just another job, like doing a sound-check or overdubbing vocals. As a film, *Julia and Julia* relied too heavily on moody compositions and close-ups to fill the gap where motivation and character ought to be. As an actor, Sting played to his most compelling strength – his weakness – rather than to his macho pose. It was his deftest role yet.

Reviews for *Julia and Julia* veered from savage ('surreal, hopelessly silly') to sugary ('poised on the knife-edge between Roeg and Hitchcock . . . an ingeniously unsettling gem'). Critical heat was never matched by audience enthusiasm. Shot as a high-definition video rather than a full-blown feature, it grazed the clubs and art houses before hitting the rental shelves. Whatever *Julia*'s flaws as a film, Sting was magnificently right for the part. The character was an ideal antidote to the cold calculation and eye-zapping technology of earlier bombs like *Dune*. Instead of cartoon situations, cornball dialogue and cut-out characters, Sting and Turner mined a rich seam of emotions from a deceptively small quarry. *Julia and Julia* flopped; the two leads rode through on the strength of sheer grit.

As Sting kept making clear to friends and reporters, he was no spendthrift – 'except that I have some very nice homes'. For a successful man, still newly rich, he was almost ascetically frugal. He didn't collect art or sports cars; nor did he have upmarket tastes. Sting's idea of a good meal was a slap-up breakfast, wolfed down with pots of coffee. He had his designer clothes, but those were his one and only decadence. His austerity was all the odder in light of his earning power. By the late 1980s he was able to ask, and get, $1 million per film. His three solo albums had all busted the chart; performance fees were coming in to Roxanne Music (Tours). There were grounds to think that yet more funds would pour down from Police residuals like *Every Breath You Take*. On the basis of Keith Moore's calculations there seemed no reason at all to suppose the money wouldn't continue to roll in as it had in the past, perhaps at even dizzier speed. The job now was to consolidate the empire.

On 21 December 1987 Miles Copeland's key business, Illegal Music, became Bugle Songs, contributing a first-year profit of £101,691 to the books. Bugle Group was the umbrella concern. Two companies named for breakthrough albums, Regatta (*sic*) and Blue Turtle, joined the fold. In August 1988 Sting officially launched Pangaea Records, with the idea of recruiting new, left-field talent. Within a year the firm's ex-president had taken out a suit against Copeland. Meanwhile, following his backstage summit with Chief Raoni, Sting bought an off-the-shelf company called Tilestral and registered it as the Rainforest Project (UK) Ltd – he, Styler and their solicitors serving as directors. The business sold T-shirts and other memorabilia with the parent Foundation name. As a corporate HQ, and a home for Sting's burgeoning fan club, Miles took a lease on Bugle House off Oxford Street. The office, sandwiched between a pub and a boutique in one of Soho's busiest ghettoes, soon grew into a court, accountants, lawyers and sinister 'special assistants' all hanging around, Miles's voice blaring through the narrow corridors, his white shellsuit always seeming to precede him by a split second. Sting often visited while in London. Apart from a company name, Bugle House gave both men a base, with receptionists, secretaries and commissars, and a constant, soothing drone of faxes. Sting liked to walk from one room to another, smiling and shaking hands. A caller remembers him 'working the building, head down, sleeves rolled up, running along laughing, like an unbearably excited kid'. Richard Branson was right. Sting 'wasn't the kind of guy to spend all afternoon in a hammock'.

The pocket-size Kremlin in Soho was also home to Sting's core businesses, all serviceably fluid and highly profitable. As ever, he and Miles put their trust in careful budgeting, financial savvy and reporting. Both men watched the cash as tightly as if it were their own, which much of it was. Overheads were cut to the bone. Without fuss Miles and Keith Moore blandly swapped day-to-day control of a group for that of Sting's solo career. Other rock-management types would learn from their example.

For the financial year 1986, Steerpike posted a gross profit of £1,855,614 on turnover of £4,905,314; of the latter sum, £2 million apiece came from performance fees and royalties, and £634,235 from merchandising. Nearly half the total receivables originated from America, and a quarter each from Britain and the rest of the world. (Sting earned £112,786 from Puerto Rico in 1986.) Steerpike's accounts in 1987, the first post-Police year, showed a slump in tour fees to £54,228, and a profit of just £588,376. Sting's name, reputation and future plans were all, of course, major if intangible assets. In 1988, after a year of non-stop globetrotting, his company turned over £8,187,921, with more than £5 million in ticket sales. Royalties added another £2,189,100 to Steerpike's bottom line. Sting had been well off; now he was fabulously rich.

By 1989, Steerpike's profit of £774,717 meshed with turnover of £229,202 from Roxanne Music. Obeying the law of diminishing returns, The Police's Roxanne Music (Tours) added mere wisps of black ink to the books, with £12,389 in cash at the bank and debts of £6,377. Copeland and Summers were, however, still in the saddle. In 1988 The Police's rump company, Magnetic, showed turnover of £2,399,177 (though, curiously, a profit of only £50,000). For the next ten years, the two sidemen continued to reap the happy dividend of their past. Everyone and everything involved with the band earned vast sums, without ever being, as Sting says, 'anally attentive' to detail. Nor, however, were they inattentive: he, Summers and both Copelands were all clear-eyed, shrewd and well screened from the Inland Revenue. From 1986 to 1992 inclusive, Miles's music publishing business logged £1,240,578 in cumulative profit; offset against losses by a sister company, Illegal and Bugle paid just £814 tax over seven years. By the late 1980s, the one-time punk guru had roomy offices in Los Angeles and London and a well-padded home in Marlborough Place, off Abbey Road. Miles's comfortable rock-star income suited him.

Like a stagnant pond, calm to the naked eye, Sting's finances, apparently so flush, were inwardly teeming with dark, invisible frenzy. Nineteen eighty-eight was the first milestone down the road of Keith Moore's deception. Late that year, Sting's accountant began transferring funds from Steerpike (Overseas) into the Bank of Scotland and Lloyds. A jury would hear that Moore benefited from this by using £6 million of Sting's money for personal schemes, among them the ones converting Russian military aircraft and setting up a chain of Indian restaurants in London. Here, some conflict exists between the court's eventual verdict ('theft . . . carried out in gross breach of trust, of large sums of money used to pay your debts and finance highly speculative ventures of your own which came to grief') and Moore's defence, essentially that Sting knew of the relevant account, first mooted as early as 1983, and agreed in the 'general principles' of an investment portfolio. Whatever the cause, the effect was a haemorrhaging of millions in cash, followed by disclosure, confrontation, and, unhappily, jail for Moore.

It had been a heady decade for Sting, first dragging punk out of its puking years and then bolting toward the mainstream. His signature versatility set the blueprint for pop's whole collision with AOR. There were, however, some notably low points to the family favourite's progress. By 1988, Sting's muse had gone south. Whether blocked by the trauma of his parents' death, or by a failure of artistic nerve, it would be two years before he finished a new song. On stage, he was still capable of an urgency that his writing sadly lacked. Nor was he idle in rallying to causes. But Sting's creative slump and looming financial crisis bulked large, even in his subconscious. For years he recurrently dreamt that he was in a jet plunging towards the ground, wingtips scraping against buildings, about to crash. For a man who believed in Jungian theory, there was no mistaking the symbolism. The plane was Sting's own life.

7

The Soul Cage

IN FEBRUARY 1989 STING SET OFF for a private tour of the rain-forest, accompanied by just Jean-Pierre Dutilleux, the Sioux Indian chief Red Crow, a pilot, two photographers and a French film crew. Their stop in Brasilia went well. The police set to work on demonstrators (mainly poor farmers and miners, worried about losing their jobs) before Sting's arrival, arresting likely troublemakers, cracking heads and surrounding the San Marco hotel with marksmen. Instead of the slammed doors and visa hassles of their previous visit, the party found themselves picked up in limos and swept to conferences with government officials. Such was the lure of Sting's name. Before flying north, he met Fernando Mesquita, an adviser to the Interior Ministry, then the president himself. The one-time 'Geordie yobbo' and ex-punk was about to fraternize in a state palace.

Once inside, the group went to work, Dutilleux making speeches, the photographers and crew setting up their tree of lights. Brazilian TV took the feed. The meeting took place in the library. The feasibility of a privately funded Xingú national park was the easy side in the debate, and Sting eagerly seized it. After an hour of crossfire and map-reading, the president agreed that, in principle, he would back the scheme. Elated, Sting walked outside to sign autographs, answer questions and in between hum snatches of 'Brazil'. In those sixty minutes, he'd learned some-thing about the nature of government, brutal certainty giving way to wary respect for rival interests and a grasp of fiscal reality. There was, for one thing, the stratospheric Brazilian national debt. 'The main thrust of what [the president] said,' Sting told *The Times*, 'was that you can't stop the poor people exploiting the land when the economy is in such a state ... He can't just announce that he's internationalizing the rainforest.' Years later, President Sarney summed up his impressions of his famous visitor. 'Intelligence, a quick-hitting sense of humour, dogged ... a steel-like determination coupled with an almost compulsive tendency to press a point – that was Sting.' (Sarney's aide was less sanguine, panning Sting's 'post-kindergarten, pre-school' economics.) Both parties agreed the audience had been 'cordial'.

That night Sting met Chief Raoni on the banks of the Xingú, excitedly planning the national park over the traditional meal of piraracu and rice, then lying in a cot inside a thatched hut. This time there was no problem with snakes. The problem was the cockroaches. Next day Sting had a second master-class in the art of consensus politics. He earnt the high praise he won in Altamira, where an Indian protest against a new hydro-electric project was boiling up. Sting was level-headed, his composure doubtless affected by an ingrained solicitude for the underdog. He made no attempt to hector and, despite prodding by Dutilleux, refused to condemn the farm workers counter-lobbying for the jobs the dam would create. He never directly attacked the government and entered into no intrigues. Instead, he played a major part in seeing to it that nothing happened between the two camps. In this, as in many other ways, he was a model of propriety.

Sting's speech ran, in full:

I came to Altamira to ask questions. Is the dam the only alternative available to produce this power? I wonder if enough research has been done ... I don't believe in the internationalization of the forest. It's Brazil's problem and Brazil must solve it, but the world community has a duty to help Brazil in its struggle. I'm here to launch a campaign to raise funds for the demarcation of a Brazilian national park, which would be the largest nature preservation area in the world. To protect the Indians is to protect the forest, and to protect the rainforest is to protect the ecology of the whole world. The Brazilian people know this, the president knows this. We want the world to know it.

There was a silence. Some of the farmers failed to rise above their anger. The president's aide assumed a serious, worried look, implying neither agreement nor disagreement; merely a public sign that he was missing nothing. The Indians smiled and shrugged.

Sting played a key, defining role in explaining the complexities of the two groups' positions. What made this confrontation so much tenser than any that had gone before, including those between warring tribes, was the likelihood of violence. 'There was certainly an edge of danger,' Sting told *The Times*. 'The right-wing farmers had threatened to send 2,000 gunmen into town and shoot it out.' A remote threat, to be sure, but still Sting had to assume that the thought had at least crossed the white settlers' minds. In the end he managed a miracle: appeasing both sides, enlightening the public with the wisdom that 'there are many divergent points of view focused here in this little town'. During the visit, and in the weeks afterwards, the farmers kept discreetly quiet. The Indians honoured Sting with a nickname, *Potima* (or 'liver of a little armadillo'). It was a diplomatic coup. One of the Interior Ministry agents, no fan of outsiders, gave Sting his due: he was 'poised and restrained,' he wrote, '... a man of great power *not* being presumptuously or prematurely assertive. That wittily empty speech in Altamira was his finest hour.'

Consolidating his role as a mediator, Sting next visited a town in the heart of Brazil's cattle country. He impressed the local ranchers as calm, collected, above all in control; his horseman-ship, too, won praise from the tough, narrow-eyed gauchos. From there, Sting, his coolness under a red-and-white parasol only heightening the sense of a Victorian missionary, drifted by boat down the Xingú. After a celebratory tribal dance by the natives, naked except for beads and feathers, and a final plague of roaches, the party flew through heavy thunderclouds into Brasilia. The chase plane in their convoy crash-landed, without casualties, in the storm.

Sting's fame was deepened and broadened by his second tour of Amazonia. One of the Brazilian reporters told him he'd been 'sensational'. Latins, he explained, admired courage and were contemptuous of fear or timidity. Sting was to hear this character analysis from all sides during his trip, his tact praised equally with his machismo. There were real achievements, too: the presidential blessing for a park; increased global awareness of the rainforest; the Foundation. Sting was also at work writing 15,000 words of stream-of-consciousness that, along with essays by Dutilleux, was published as *Jungle Stories: The Fight for the Amazon*. This, too, would go to help the rainforest, though, in the end, the two authors fell out in a row over royalties.

Sting, meanwhile, began a fund-raising drive with Chiefs Raoni and Red Crow, a bizarre deviation from the standard pop tour that brought headlines from Tokyo to the Tocantin basin. 'The odd couple' was one of the kinder portrayals of the long-haired rocker and his friend with the labial plate. One Brazilian general referred to the pair's 'melancholy spectacle'. There was dark humour, at least, when the party put up in Highgate. Sting's neighbours' view of the chiefs sharing a peace-pipe in a makeshift camp laid out on the back lawn was the village's major talking-point, though the sight of Raoni calmly strolling up Hampstead Lane in his loincloth made a strong go of second place. Sting's role was to serve for the next two months as the Indians' spokesman, what Gilda Matoso calls a 'beautiful blue-eyed gringo' to front the crusade to the world. It came to him by default. Raoni's uncompromising look and Dutilleux's relative obscurity combined to thrust the job on Sting. Not that he minded. Working as the Indians' straight-man made him 'happier than playing in front of thousands of kids every night'. The campaign itself gave rise to a pithy debate on the morality of celebrity do-gooding, in which Sting took no part.

By 1989, ecology generally had come to occupy a central position on the Western scene. Its various strains were everywhere: from talk about the ozone layer and global warming, to recycling, to the profusion of 'green' products jostling for shelf-space. As usual, Sting's timing was flawless. His strategy was simple and blunt. Despite later barbs about compassion fatigue, he relished trotting the globe and did so with gusto. In Bob Geldof's characterization, he was a 'chronic campaigner'. Indeed, the only man who enjoyed campaigning as much was Geldof himself. Nor was Sting unaware of the kudos he won from *bien-pensants* on the left for his willingness to speak out; nor was he more at home than when peddling a cause. It was a virtuoso performance: Sting's overpowering self-confidence, his flair for hyperbole, his dour ambition and shameless flights of passion – all these combined to make him hated, and admired. He rifted the public more than any other rocker. That the split was almost exactly fifty–fifty was shown by the scores of editorials printed in the *Guardian* and, less formally, on brick walls chalked with his name and words like 'git'.

On a material level, the tour achieved its modest aims. At each stop on the route, Sting set up a small branch office to support the Foundation. Eventually, over a million dollars was collected to help fund the Xingú park. The rousing speeches raised not only cash, but awareness. People with no other brief for the environment suddenly knew about the rainforest, defoliation and the greenhouse effect. Not everyone backed the campaign, but everyone began to talk about it.

Personal charm was his watchword. Where earlier ecologists had tended to think in fixed terms and move cautiously in the rarefied world of the nattering classes, Sting was warm, personal, concrete and impulsive. He immediately recruited world leaders to the cause. It seemed he had only to knock and palace doors would be flung open. After their success in Brasilia, Sting and his crew met Prince Charles, President Mitterrand and the King of Spain. They had an audience with the Pope. Raoni cut through the latter's welcome with a wild chop of his hand and a rant that spun heads among the Swiss guard. 'My god is saying to your god that your missionaries should get off our land ... *Now*,' he added, for emphasis. There was a pause, ended by the Pope handing each of the men a plastic rosary and muttering, 'Bless you.' He repeated it several times, while backing away towards the door. 'It was a disaster,' Dutilleux told an interviewer. The brief encounter certainly meant nothing for the rainforest. It may have meant more as a feat of assimilation; the St Columba's choirboy and lapsed Catholic mingling on equal terms with the pontiff. Ernie and Audrey Sumner's thoughts could only be guessed. The triumph of ambition and perseverance that had, almost incredibly, led to this scene had begun nearly forty years earlier in a north England slum.

In June, after trips to Switzerland (providing the Indians' first sight of snow), a whistlestop of Australia, prompting a debate on nudism between the chiefs and the manager of their hotel, and a jaunt of the Orient, where Raoni privately briefed two girls on this, to him, mesmerizing subject, the tour ended. On each leg, Sting changed his style, droll and self-deprecatory one moment, brash and pumped-up the next. With an alchemist's knack, and the sure touch of the world-traveller, he turned local prejudices to his own good. But the basic message never varied. It was that 'the Indians have been fucked up the arse since they were discovered'. Sting made the comparison between the Xingú and North American tribes like the Sioux. 'The people who were given the job of looking after them, the Bureau of Indian Affairs, [were] the very people to shaft them.' When Sting said 'save the rainforest' it was from the novel perspective of wanting to protect the natives as much as the land. He devoted himself to people as well as principles.

As a footnote to the tour, Sting and Dutilleux signed and sold large numbers of *Jungle Stories*. While much was made of the book's charitable end ('All royalties go to the Rainforest Foundation' read the blurb), Dutilleux later admitted that he pocketed his half of the action. 'I'm a professional writer,' he said. 'I had to take the advance. We're not all multi-million pop stars.' Sting cordially returned his co-author's contempt. The two never spoke again.

A more serious criticism was that the Foundation itself was ill managed. Nothing illegal or unethical ever came to light, and Raoni dismissed the whole thing as 'stupid, a distraction from the Indians' cause'. Had it had another figurehead, the chief almost certainly would have been right. But Sting had set himself up as the soul of morality, and thus made himself uniquely vulnerable. One journalist wrote that the Xingú and Kayapos had 'fallen out, big time' with their sponsor. According to Amazonia's governor-elect, Gilberto Mestrinho, nearly a year after the world tour, the Indians had yet to get a penny. Later in 1990, *World in Action* went on air to accuse the Foundation of not properly accounting for the money it raised; failing to prevent the deaths of fifteen or more tribesmen from malaria; and leaving Raoni himself to fester in a slum. Sting's denial was robust: 'Last week I saw [the chief] for the first time in months . . . He gave me a big hug and said he was glad everything was happening the way we'd hoped. So fuck 'em! We're doing the right thing.'

Sting may have been quick to defend the Foundation, but he still moved like a sleepwalker through his quotidian job. According to a relative, 'it was rock-weariness, not world-weariness, that caused him to dry up' in 1989–90. Sting's problem conceivably lay in his being bright enough to diagnose his block, but not enough to think of a remedy. Through analysis, therapy and his own soul-searching remarks to the press, he seemed to have studied the matter thoroughly. In May 1989 Sting came forward, and subterfuge was the last thing on his mind. 'I can't think of anything to do,' he told Q. 'I can't think of anything to say that's particularly useful. I haven't really got a direction. It's frightening and at the same time it's quite relaxing. I'll just wait . . . I think things will calm down and I'll get over it, but at the moment I'm so blinkered about [the rainforest].'

Within weeks, groping his way back toward the limelight, Sting had signed up to play Macheath in The Threepenny Opera on Broadway. His motives for the job were mixed. For a shy man, the challenge of dealing with a sea of anonymous rock fans paled next to the nightly torment of relating to a small group of strangers from a stage. But the theatre had been one of Sting's whims for years (even if, in terms of acting, frustratingly patchy since the days of his school nativity play), a passion rekindled by his co-backing An Enemy of the People. Health also played a part. Most mornings Sting was up, running and working out, at a time when other rock stars were known to be finishing dinner. His compulsive drill was due in part to his fear of the disease that had killed his parents in their fifties. In 1988, Sting began to have blood tests every six months. They always came back negative. He was, however, agonizing from more problems with his throat. When doctors urged him to take a rest from rock tours, he hit on the compromise of Brecht and Weill's songspiel. Under the director John Dexter, the Opera was more dazzlingly visual than vocal, and had the added value of being highbrow. It was just the holding-action Sting wanted. The other persuasive voice in the casting was Styler's. 'She was very instrumental in it,' Sting reported. 'She said: "Before you're forty you should play Mack the Knife." I normally take her word. You only live once, and if you're given an opportunity like this you take it and see if you can pull it off.'

Sting's role followed down a line from other rockers' attempts to go straight, notably David Bowie's in The Elephant Man. Nor was Weill's musical virgin-crossover turf. Roger Daltrey had played Macheath in a TV adaption by Jonathan Miller. Over the years, everyone from Ella Fitzgerald to Jim Morrison had covered the German's jazz-inflected tunes. Sting himself sang on the Weill tribute LP *Lost in the Stars*. His choice of breathing-space was neither surprising nor illogical.

What *was* novel was Sting's regime of hard work and rehearsal. His portrayal of it was either impish or intensely professional: 'Walk to work, clock on, do it and walk home again.' He took body and voice lessons, and served as Equity shop steward for the show – all to the mounting respect of the cast and director, even on the one occasion he led a lightning strike against the latter.* To bind himself to such a routine wasn't mere play-acting. 'I've signed up with John for a year,' Sting told friends. It was a personal guarantee, and Dexter responded in kind. He worshipped Sting to such an extent that for the next few months he lobbied the Metropolitan Opera to specially commission a new work for his friend. Dexter died before plans could be made.

After try-outs in Washington DC (where the first night was attended by George Bush), *The Threepenny Opera* opened at the Lunt-Fontanne theatre, New York, on 5 November 1989. Sting walked in, under the white marquee with his name, changed, shook hands and went on. He played the black comedy as a farce. The tabloid *Daily News* gave the print equivalent of a standing ovation. Other critics had a field day lambasting the sickly sweet, fey production. Sting took his lumps from the heavyweight titles, none worse than the *New York Times*. Frank Rich, self-styled 'butcher of Broadway', said of the lead: 'He seems to hope that a large cane and smug, insistent pout will somehow convey the menace of a murderer, rapist, thief and arsonist.' Most audiences were respectful; most pundits were ready, like Rich, to praise the *Opera*'s sets, though their contrast with the acting remained an imponderable enigma. The New York *Source* on 7 November caught a mood. 'Sting's fame fans his ego ... The plot, which takes its time, defeats an actor who wastes ours ... At threepence, this *Opera* is overpriced.' From then on houses were thin, not to say gaunt. After a cast ballot (Sting voting to go on), the show

*Sting went to unusual lengths to reconcile with Dexter, a man who was brilliant, savage and castratingly rude, and whom he called 'critical, acid, funny ... He reminded me of my dad.' The two father-figures shared his next album's dedication.

folded on 31 December, eight weeks into an eleven-month run. The star kept smiling. On closing night, Sting managed a bit of business, lathering himself up (just as Andy Partridge once shaved him) onstage, taking deep ironic bows, then throwing a New Year's Eve party at his duplex. A week into the new decade, he was back in the jungle.

The Sting who met with José Sarney in January 1990 wasn't the political tyro of eleven months earlier. He'd grown wise to the ways of government. Sting had particularly matured in his opinion of Sarney. The president had failed to keep his promise to demarcate the agreed 19,000-square-mile park. He was, however, perfectly happy to receive his rock-star caller; indeed, cynics claimed that these high-level missions were the best PR ploys the Brazilian government could hope for. Unsurprisingly, Sting himself didn't see it so. 'I don't think I'm being used at all,' he insisted. 'If anything, I'm an embarrassment.' But Sarney's perfidy jolted him. One of the Foundation directors described the change. The president made Sting realize that 'photo-ops at the palace weren't enough to cope with the problem. He knew he needed to act.' While Styler proceeded to a hospital where Kayoma malaria victims were being treated, Sting organized an all-star benefit in California. The gala on 12 February raised a total of $900,000 for the ailing natives. Bruce Springsteen, Paul Simon, Don Henley and Herbie Hancock all lent their names to the Indians' cause. Rock-star support for the Foundation was still growing, but so were the barbs of its detractors. 'We've been naïve,' Sting admitted.

World in Action first aired doubts about the organization in April 1990. Almost overnight fresh twists on the charges appeared in the press. The media's use of the term 'sleaze' was harsh, but throughout the summer new and embarrassing facts on the Foundation's finances absorbed a public for whom do-good icons had become wearisome in their familiarity. In November the *Daily Express* splashed a feature under the begging headline WHATEVER HAPPENED TO STING'S RAINFOREST CASH? According to the story, '[Governor-elect] Mestrinho and others are raising concerns – like what happened to all the donations which have helped swell the coffers of the infant Foundation to $1.2 million in just one year.' Sting met the charges squarely, without trying to paper over his clash with Dutilleux. 'We certainly had a colour-ful cast of characters,' he told the *Express*. 'There's no doubt we had people who were, for want of a better word, adventurers and that doesn't work when you get this kind of responsibility.' He presented the Foundation as virtually back from the dead. 'The people we have now, particularly on the ground in Brazil, are the best you can have. If they can't make it work then no one can.'

In late 1990 the Foundation appointed Larry Cox, a fifteen-year veteran of Amnesty International, as executive director. He led a full-time staff of eight. Cox's confidence that the $1.2 million could be found was justified; it was, with over half going to build an Indian centre, offer legal and medical help, and finally move villagers from malaria-hit areas. Other funds were ploughed back into branch offices like that in London. The Rainforest Project (UK) continued to turn over small sums from T-shirts and merchandising, though sales rose from a bare £743 in 1990 to £6,314 in 1991 and £22,324 in 1992. All the books were kept by the City firm Stoy Hayward, who also audited Live Aid; all were signed by Sting and Styler. Fraud played no part in their handling of the funds.

Sting spent another three weeks in Brazil that winter. He met the new president Fernando Collor de Mello (whose wife, promisingly, was a Police fan) and again took up the cudgels for a national park. By now, three years after his first visit, Sting spoke of the rainforest, and the environment generally, in neo-spiritual terms. 'I've come to believe that we made a mistake in trying to imagine God outside of nature,' he informed *Rolling Stone*. 'We're not the most important thing on the planet, we're *part* of the planet, and until we realize it we're in [trouble].' Statements like that divided Sting's audience at a stroke. Even as a boy, he'd never been slow with a moral verdict. The dark thread was still present in his late thirties. No one doubted his tactics for 'saving the rainforest', merely his motives. To critics like William Buckley, it wasn't just that he preached – preached constantly, preached about big matters and small, preached so incessantly that he became, in a widely used phrase, 'St Francis of Wallsend' – but also that some character flaw *made* him preach. Even friends glimpsed ego as well as pity in Sting's sermons.

It was all a long way from rock and roll. For all that Sting was on sabbatical from his day job, he never meant to quit it. Apart from having three homes and two families to keep, there was the side of him visible since his days on the back streets of Wallsend, where, if he couldn't play centre forward he'd take his ball and go home – the quality which led one local to carp, 'If Gordo didn't score, he didn't play.' That aspect had been seen in The Police, too. 'He couldn't stand not being somebody – just could not *stand* it,' says Andy Partridge. Sting couldn't endure being one of a crowd; he needed – with a manic need – to shine, to lead, to bend others to his will. Above all, he needed to win.

With no new album since 1987, Sting's flame was kept alight largely through plays and sales of his back stock. There were the inevitable awards. In February 1989 he was nominated for two Grammys, and won a Novello trophy in London. Eighteen months later, he was given a British Music Industry gong for two million sales of 'Every Breath You Take'. Whereas the night's other winners came in categories like 'new' and 'début', Sting's song was introduced as a kind of holy relic. That sort of fame was far from what he wanted. Recognition and royalties poured in to Bugle House as fast as Miles could count them. But for all the honours, it was three years since Sting had seen the inside of a studio. He'd found himself beset by a swarm of distractions – stage and screen work, Amnesty, the jungle, and, of course, the death of his parents. He'd been 'blocked' before, but never like this. He tried everything: 'long drives, long baths, long walks. Got drunk ... the lot,' as he put it. Still the words wouldn't come. Even a self-imposed deadline failed to kick-start proceedings. Sting was thirty-eight, father of four (with a fifth due), earning $10 million a year. He still ground out tunes on his Synclavier, but mostly for his own amusement. Now, under record-label pressure, he had to kiss off his career or somehow rationalize his creative slump. He chose shock therapy.

Sting's third trek to the rainforest brought not just a meeting with José Sarney but a long debate with the Indians about death, not normally a staple of light entertainment. 'I realized that dying is something that's obviously important to them,' he told *Rolling Stone*. 'I figured that I'd have to go through some sort of process where I would get this stuff out. Once I'd worked that out, I realized I was going to have to write a record about death. I didn't really want to.'

Implicit in Sting's cultural epiphany was a strong but silent confession. He'd never grieved for his parents. When Audrey died he was working all hours on *Nothing Like the Sun*. A few months later, when news reached him of Ernie, Sting numbly went out on stage. He attended neither funeral. Only now, bowing to the Indians' way, willing to write if simultaneously the words acknowledged his loss, was he ready to mourn. Sting's grief suggested a theme. Remorse and guilt were real issues. They provided the same link to the past as a new child did to the future. He immediately went back to his life on Station Road. The album would be a sentimental homage to Newcastle.

'I decided it was time to reassess,' Sting told Q. 'What I turned to was my earliest memory . . . as soon as I got that down ["Billy was born within sight of the shipyard" was the first line of the first song] the thing was written in two or three weeks. It poured out. Although it was painful it wrote itself almost, free-associating . . . lines about this father thing kept coming up. Something was saying I had to deal with it.' Sting did, not for the first time turning grim experience into great art. In February 1990 he had no more than a few scraps of lyrics doodled in the jungle or backstage at the theatre. Within a fortnight, the creative recluse was converted into an amanuensis and medium for verses, choruses, couplets, rhymes and titles, actual and imaginative stories (some written in the very hotel where Marcel Proust worked), all elaborated and deepened, welling up from within. Now Sting was ready to go public.

The songs' emetic release took place in New York. Actual recording followed in Paris and Migliarino, Italy. While in the latter, Sting became a born-again football fan, swinging a rattle at the World Cup semis and urging England to put the boot in. What fellow supporters took as a show of laddish modesty was the spectacle of a pop star reliving his youth. For every night at the stadium there were a dozen in the £25,000-per-month rented villa outside Pisa. For every drink with the boys there was a champagne bash at the Versaces'. Sting enjoyed life on the Ligurian. Recording continued through July and August, the nostalgic theme punctuated by the crew at Villa Salviati: Branford Marsalis, Kenny Kirkland and Hugh Padgham all returning from Sun. (There was also a chance reunion with Summers, though no work resulted.) When Sting listened to the playbacks alone in the studio, he wept. 'I completely lost it. I felt better after that.'

Sting's efforts to resolve his past connected with a present-day need for roots and homeliness. His domesticity was very real. He walked the dog, received glitteratti guests in slippers and called Styler 'mother'. When not recording or crusading in Brazil, he spent months at a time in Highgate. His London base was no cloistered pop star's paradise. With two adults, a nanny, a secretary, Kate, his eight-year-old from Tomelty, Mickey and Jake Sumner, two spaniels and sundry actors, actresses, Rainforest workers and stray Indian chiefs, the house was a place of perpetual frenzy. Sting cut a genial, squirely figure. Dressed in brown corduroys and waxed jacket, sometimes carrying a staff or cane, he was a familiar sight chivvying Styler and the pets on to Hampstead Heath. A local boy named Daniel Morgan saw Sting striding out one morning. 'He seemed happy, normal and the friendliest man in the world.' Few who read his rants against Newcastle knew how family-oriented Sting was, in selective ways; how he longed for an idealized hearth and home; how much of his life was spent in search of a kind of padded domesticity that didn't involve waxing the car or brooding about the mortgage. During his mad years in The Police, he never found such a thing, nor could have. But by the early 1990s, he had a reasonable facsimile, replete with a lively extended family whom he loved and who were the objects of such paternal feelings as he had or cared to show. A visitor to Highgate recalls his host 'in front of the fire, wearing glasses, reading aloud in a quiet, dry voice, a baby asleep on his lap and a dog snoring at his feet'. It wasn't possible to dislike someone once you'd seen them like that.

Sting made a life for himself as a partner and father. He also worked hard to patch things up with his Newcastle clan. Anita Sumner had moved south and become a regular visitor at The Grove. Sting's other siblings, Angela and Phil, both admired the moody new songs, dense with images of dead fathers and sons, fatalism, loss and unrequited feelings, their brother played them. Sting made an emotional journey to his birthplace in December 1990. One Sunday morning the rock icon fetched up at the Dunes on Whitley Bay, found his first-ever guitar and strummed the early chords of 'Island Of Souls', his elegy for Ernie Sumner. Friends pressed close to the stage claimed they saw tears in his eyes. 'It really says what we all feel about our dad,' Angela said. 'Sting can express it ... we probably can't even say it to one another, but he can find words for it and I'm really pleased because it feels as though part of me's in what he's written.'

The last part of Sting's platform on the environment was an empty roar about over-crowding. 'I just don't agree with [procreation] any more. I think it's bullshit, and I think if we carry on thinking like that, we're doomed. We have too many people ... We're not the most important thing on the planet, and until we realize that, we're in deep shit.' Sting's common-sense plea for birth control didn't rule out fecundation on his part. His fifth child (third with Styler), Eliot Paulina, arrived in August 1990. Sting and Styler tried to obtain dual nationality for the Italian-born girl, known by her family as Coco. The authorities balked. Sting bridled. He had, nonetheless, a happy drove of healthy energy-hungry kids. A van from Harrods used to arrive at Highgate bearing a load of food, drink, nappies, toys and other paraphernalia. Sting's plea for austerity, in a word, didn't always cut very deep.

The contradiction had its pleasures. Life as a paterfamilias suited Sting. As he swung open the front door in Highgate in the evening, he'd be met by what his friend calls 'a flying wedge of brats'. Supper at the Sumners' long, narrow table, at which the children sat on benches down the sides, was a raucous free-form affair, only Sting himself homing in on the food. ('Like all northern lads,' says Styler, 'he was taught to shut up and eat his dinner.') Afterwards there'd be books and games. Sting also achieved a reconciliation, of sorts, with the victims of his one-time policy on love. Seven years' distance since the divorce had helped to warm relations with Tomelty. The two shared access to their children, Kate Sumner living chiefly with her father. During their ugly, protracted break-up, Sting had been apt to describe Tomelty as 'the rock missus from hell'. Time had reversed this bleak assessment. 'I'm lucky,' he now said. 'I have a very good relationship with all my kids and my ex-wife. I think we've done rather well. We're still good friends and we have something very important in common.'

The goodwill breaking out on all sides found expression in Sting's music. While his flagship product was the morbid song-cycle that became *The Soul Cages*, a second brand was the bouncy work dedicated to his family. In 1990, following the well-beaten path of David Bowie and others, he recorded Prokofiev's *Peter and the Wolf*. A year later he contributed 'Cushie Butterfield' to the Disney anthology LP *For Our Children*. He bought *Under*

Milk Wood for Bruce Springsteen's baby son. The rumour in 1991, that Sting was to host *Sesame Street*, was obviously a slur, but nevertheless expressed a trend people saw in him. 'He did everything but wheel out the kids on *Saturday Superstore*,' sniffed Jeff Bernard. Over the years Sting regularly appeared with his brood in public, earning reproof from some for exploiting an image, and praise from others for his willingness to be photographed holding formula and nipples. He had strong views on parenthood. All the children were encouraged to 'express themselves' (to call him Sting, for instance), to run harum-scarum about the house, laughing and shrieking, with none of the grim decorum of Station Road. At the same time, he swore by roots and tradition. 'I want them to go to English schools and have English accents. I like being English myself.'

The same accessibility that distinguished Sting from other pop gods turned ugly in 1990, when a series of notes arrived at Bugle House threatening to kidnap his children. One spoke of plans to 'slice the brats up one by one'. Sting promptly began to look for a home in the country. For several months, as he flitted from place to place, he became more like the 'typical paranoid rock star', says his friend. 'He almost literally wouldn't go out, because he felt he couldn't leave without the kids being hassled. He was truly tormented by it.'

Critics saw the change between the 1970s Sting and the '90s version in musical terms. *The Soul Cages*, wrote Paul Evans, shunned Police-style catchiness and tunes for 'vast swirls of sound that build to either musical or emotional crescendo'. Those who knew Sting in Highgate or his American homes saw the difference in human ways. He still burned with ambition, but as Jack Bruce says, 'there was a civility underneath it. He wouldn't try anything on.' That isn't what friends had said was 'underneath it' in the old days. At thirty-nine, Sting's narcissism had been leavened by the wisdom that 'friendship's much more important to me than what I thought success was'. His ego was, even in rock-star terms, still big – huge, in fact. The contrast between Sting then and now lay not so much in what he wanted, but in the way he wanted it. Ten years ago, he would have sold his grandmother for a headline. In success or failure, the key ambition was always touted. Nowadays, he puffed not so much the selfish facet of his work as its value as a movement. He balanced his actions against the trust he inspired – a trust that he had plans for others as well, that he wouldn't flog just himself, but also needy activists and starving artists. Among the many beneficiaries of Sting's patronage was Farid Haque, whose Pangaea-backed album made it to number five in the jazz chart.

An example that Jeff Griffin gives of Sting's maturity came at the gala show for Nelson Mandela's release. Due to safety by-laws, the gates at Wembley were thrown open that morning before the star turn had done his sound-check. Sting, says Griffin, 'calmly went on, with two or three hundred kids already jammed up to the stage, smiled, and told them, "When I come back, just pretend you haven't seen me." Then he played for a couple of minutes and went off.' A few years before, a similar scene wouldn't have been met with such poise. It was affable, and had the added bonus of being professional. Unlike most stars, says Griffin, Sting 'wasn't a drama queen . . . He seemed to relish doing away with the smoke and mirrors . . . All the effects used to prop lesser talent were tossed out. I admired that.'

Sting took his urbanity from a daily routine that reflected back on how he felt and acted. He'd always been health-concerned, if not obsessed, and had a lifelong interest in diets and alternative medicine. By his fortieth birthday he'd taken up ashtanga yoga. He practised it religiously, two hours a day, on the road and off. A special room was set aside in each of his three homes. When backstage, he was interested not in snorting drugs but in finding a spot for his exercise mat. 'Mentally and physically, it keeps me fit, helps me concentrate, relax and feel good,' he reported. The results could be seen and heard with every breath he took. Sting had never been in better voice. More pertinently, the yoga tapped into his affinity for self-growth. By 1991 he presented himself as cool and collected – 'centred' was the word he used – a man more apt to bury the hatchet than use it. His new-found aplomb survived even a three-way meeting with Copeland and Summers that February. For years, mere mention of The Police had ridden high on Sting's chart of dreads. Now he told *Rolling Stone*, 'I'm very proud of the work we did . . . And I'm proud of my association with Andy and Stewart. I've no regrets.'

A promoter who had dealt closely with Sting in the past found the forty-year-old 'more Olympian and detached' this time round. Another man who worked with The Police describes him as 'less high and mighty', though still 'restlessly stirring the shit'. His role in recent world events seemed to have given Sting a new aura. Workmates were dealing with a man whose name opened doors in the Vatican. More than ever, Sting bucked the first rule of rock careerism: instead of the trappings of mystery and illusion, he developed a personality. Not everyone claimed to like him, but most agreed he was fully human. They sensed the brain behind the banality – the swift mind that lifted Sting above trite melodrama towards something rarer. He was the first rocker to treat global issues on equal terms with topics like cars and sex, crossing all national and ethnic frontiers, yet still with a meaty backbeat. Sting was all things at once – concerned, snobbish, soulful, turgid, perceptive.

Sting himself was well aware of the various masks he carried around. His self-image was just as fickle as the one others had of him. A framed *New Yorker* cartoon in a bathroom at The Grove showed two men in suits drinking at a bar. One was saying to the other, 'Oh, I'm pretty happy – I just wish my life were more like Sting's.' In dark moods he sometimes laughed about the sketch as '*très* ironic'. He often had to strain for evidence of his good luck. Anyone trying to categorize him sooner or later bumped up against the contrariness of his make-up. 'It's the old ping-pong of wanting to escape and then having to go back and face it,' he told *Rolling Stone*. He was talking about *The Soul Cages*, but it summarized a mood. The patterned duality in Sting's thinking came through loud and clear in his whole take on the world. 'I like having people around, I like the house to be alive, but there's always Sartre's definition of hell.' He was still the outcast, shrieking to be rescued, who after an hour in civilization would be pleading for exile.

Over the years, Sting made it a fetish to baffle his critics. 'I don't really think that people know what to expect from me now,' he said. 'I don't think [*The Soul Cages*] is going to conform to any of their expectations ... If they're surprised, I'm pleased.' On 'Nothing 'Bout Me', he extended the theme into a whole song. More than anything, he dreaded the glib generalizations that passed for collective criticism of his work. He knew full well that perceived opinion tended to run down one of two lines, whole armies of pointy-headed nabobs warring with the likes of Rod Stewart as to whether he was, in fact, St Francis or a 'miserable sod'. Sting could see both sides, was prepared to acknowledge whichever suited him, and railed only when 'mob instinct' rode herd on solo thought. He made a strong plea against peer pressure. 'Men go crazy in congregations / They only get better one by one', he sang on 'All This Time'. For him, a bad review could be better than a good one, provided it came from the heart.

An album dedicated to his father, family reunions, a new baby – it was enough to make Sting maudlin, and it did. In December 1990 he took the train back to Newcastle. As late as 1979, his treks home had been cheap-day excursions, with no one to meet him at the station. Eleven years on, he travelled soft class with Tomelty, three journalists, a minder, two photographers, and a Channel 4 crew running backwards down the platform to film his arrival. 'I'm not sentimental about Newcastle,' Sting insisted – always taking care to gauge the distance between himself and 'professional Geordies' like Lindisfarne. It was, however, a romantic pilgrimage. It'd snowed during the night, the ground covered with a sleet that had frozen so that it seemed the slate roofs, the chimneys, all the wharves and the Tyne bridge had been varnished with ice. A Siberian gale was blowing. The minder jammed on a hat, 'as tall as a derrick' in a photographer's words. A fleet of limousines took Sting, Styler and the TV crew to Wallsend.

In the next few hours, Channel 4 was a spellbound witness to Sting's affinity for the cobbled streets with their Victorian terraced houses tilting down to the river. Back in the hotel, he found that Gerry Richardson, his old songwriting partner in Last Exit, was headlining that night in the lounge. An *ad hoc* reunion of the other surviving members was arranged. The Little Mo Blues Band débuted and folded that same night, jamming for an audience of starstruck businessmen and their wives. Even the Newcastle Architects' Association annual dance could have seen no odder sight than this: four middle-aged jazzers with the tandoori-tanned singer plunking down the riff of 'Every Breath You Take'. 'Something's going on,' Sting told the Q stringer at the bar. 'I was in a weird mood in Wallsend. Now having Gerry play here tonight – it's a circle closing. You can't contrive things like that.' Later he took a second writer to stare through the gate of his old school. 'Sting kept shtum as we stood looking in – so did I. I knew what he must have been thinking. "Revenge!"'

To say, as Last Exit did, 'No other pop star would have done the gig' wasn't to say that Sting met the group on level terms. Too many feelings had been hurt, too many failings of those who trusted him and of the whole town vented in the press. Some held that Sting's hasty summons of a band he largely wrecked in the first place smacked of neither love nor respect, but guilt. Others thought, for all his common-man affectations, he came over as imperially cool, having a roadie ferry ex-mates to his suite. According to this school, Sting's nostalgic effusion flowed from his belief that 'he'd made it – we hadn't'. It also stemmed from the knowledge that Last Exit and their ilk would never pose a threat. Sting was secure, self-confident, and could afford to be generous.

Elsewhere, the welcome was tumultuous. Local journalists had been tipped off to the trip and followed Sting about. The entertaining, if exacting, job of harrying him in and out of cars and the back doors of hotels contained a revelation: he was good with people. Sting was characteristically genial when fans approached. He answered questions and posed for photos. Nothing was too much trouble. Dave Wood was one of those who met Sting for a drink that weekend. 'The plain truth is, he was down-to-earth then [in Last Exit] and he's down-to-earth now. Sting isn't a druggy. He's not a loudmouth. Like everyone, he might have screwed up on occasion, but he never burnt his bridges. His reception showed it.' It seemed to some in his circle that Sting valued men like Wood both as a link with his past and as evidence of how far he'd come. Another old friend met him in his hotel and left impressed at 'how nice he was, [but] always with an edge. He was still Sting-the-superstar, and us the necessary proof of dull, everyday life. I was reminded of Gore Vidal's line: "It isn't enough to succeed. Others must fail."'

Over the next few days, Sting circulated through Newcastle, shaking hands with its people – and there were no airs at all. When he saw someone he knew, his lean, bronzed face would, in the words of one ex-lover, 'just *crack* up'. Sting would stride over, ungainly in his haste, and blurt out a name. 'Our Len,' he'd say. 'How you doing?' He'd put his arm around Len's shoulders. 'How *are* you?' he would say. Looking up at that face, seething with warmth, even the crustiest, most implacable foe would melt. Sting's charm offensive revived old contacts everywhere. The natives were friendly, and he heartily returned their affection. Even at potentially tense moments (as when one elderly man asked him solemnly, 'What've you been up to, then, lad?') he kept his good humour. After a rendezvous with his brother and sister, he took the return train south. He spent Christmas at home in Highgate.

The Soul Cages followed in the new year. Musically, his first album since 1987 caught Sting midway between the hot-licks showboating of *Reggatta*-era Police and the meditative woe of Lou Reed's *Songs for Drella* or anything by Nick Cave. Surprisingly, there were few or no allusions to his tours of the rainforest. ('I'm a little bored with the idea of singing for causes,' Sting said.) At least four tracks, however, drew blood with repeats of his childhood saga – 'Billy would cry when he thought of the future' – that cut to the emotional bone. Sting would later summarize his key audience in perversely fixed terms: 'First I need to amuse myself – to engage my own interest. And then it's really my wife and my band. And that's it.' To the millions outside the club, Sting's lyrics were at best wistful, at worst cloyingly soppy. *The Soul Cages* ultimately triumphed with fizzy, upbeat songs like 'All This Time', but only the erase button could have improved the forays into bagpipe-pumped angst.

Born of loud, electric rock and father to Sting's *Unplugged* work, *Cages* found itself stranded in a stylistic generation gap. Like his gigs, it swung from one extreme to the next, bouncing from brooding, classical prettiness to soundtrack noodling. To neutral listeners, the album couldn't decide if it wanted to return to pop's roots or join the alternative nation. History being cruel to those who can't find their place in it, a well-meant opus – appearing to be neither lifeless nor human, but only Stingian – would survive in genteel poverty: respected by many, politely ignored by more.

Sting was rightly admired for his dissonant, hybrid mood music. It was just that, this time round, he decided to push an agenda instead of boundaries. The best of the lyrics were achingly real, touching on universal themes like grief and guilt. The worst ones were plodding and cliché-laden. In the very first song fans learnt, to their utter amazement, that, on Tyneside, 'a working man live[d] like a slave', 'he'd drink every night' and 'money he never would save'. Similar felicities abounded on later tracks. The Romans, apparently, had built and occupied the north-east. There was a myth that a legion had marched off along Hadrian's Wall and been cannibalized by the wild tribesmen in the hills. This was the signal for a joke by Sting to the media. 'You see, they just loved Italian food.' *The Soul Cages* rattled with such drolleries, side-by-side with meandering spiels of lachrymose posing. The latter glaringly revealed the album's basic flaw – the absence of any attempt to explain the wider dynamics of childhood, or even of individual events, which alone could give meaning to the human rites so glumly harped on. Sting's yarns might have made perfect sense as a kind of therapy, but here they came across as gauzy and self-indulgent. For years, fans and critics alike had listened to his lyrics, full of shrewd yet icy self-doubt. Now, they eavesdropped.

After *Nothing Like the Sun*, Sting's public spent more than three years pondering what kind of music he might make next. *The Soul Cages*'s answer was instant. 'Island Of Souls', the album's first cut, began exactly where *Sun* left off. It was basically a shanty, though no rollicking tune, with a steady upbeat progression into three-chord country: the monochrome tone of the lyric was matched by the bell-and-pipe arrangement (early warning that *Cages* was something other than feelgood pop). Amidst the gloom, 'All This Time' flashed like a glint of gold in the pan. The album's first single started out as a hip Christmas carol before veering into Paul Simon-land. It, too, came with a message. If Sting undermined his sepia-tinged memories on 'Island Of Souls' with fey, comic-book couplets, he came off more convincingly here. 'All This Time' mixed a wry blast of anti-clericalism with a booming beat. The song's strength lay in its ability to filter rock riffs through a droll storyline, a trick not always pulled off on *Cages*.

There was more fun to be had on the album's first half. 'Mad About You' combined guitar, double bass and toots of Paola Paparelle's oboe over a jazzy motif, before hitting a lush, ultra-sexed chorus. Sting also came alive from his self-imposed coma on 'Jeremiah Blues (Part I)'; time and again, even the thinnest material was salvaged by the creamy-thick voice. Unhappily, two of the last three tracks needed all the vocal shoring they could get. 'The Wild Wild Sea' began like a Yes out-take before dwindling from that relative high into a shipping forecast. 'When

The Angels Fall' was, in the words of one critic, 'so boring it must have sent the drummer in search of oxygen to keep awake'. Between these dirges, Sting exploited his Peter Gabriel friendship by way of *Cages'* nasally poppy title tune, a meat-and-potatoes riff garnished with yet more lyrics about fog and fishermen, and one of his worst rhymes ever to make the final cut.

Meanwhile, a memorably silly Alex Proyas-directed film of Sting got up as a sailor, somehow climaxing in a Marx Brothers skit of life below decks, did the rounds of *Top of the Pops* and MTV. The video, for 'All This Time', seemed strangely positioned among the guitar-heavy, woe-laden bands hogging the airwaves, and even stranger in the bogus impression it gave of the album. The single was a Top Ten hit.

Had almost anyone else released *The Soul Cages*, they would have been ignored. Most of the paeans mischievously posing as 'songs' were colloquial, personal and vapid. Yet the response Sting had to face, especially in Britain, was more like hate. People were angry. The album took critical heat not only from those addled by the rainforest saga, but also from insiders like Sting's record label and manager, still both panting for 'another *Synchronicity*'.* From a man who constantly danced on the precipice of pretension, *Cages* practically dared critics to take a shot. Sting himself insisted he '[didn't] care what's written in the papers'. But even his newfangled poise must have been tested to the full by *Melody Maker*. The album, in Allan Jones's searing notice, was 'the sound of Sting rummaging in the undergrowth for his "roots" . . . quickly becomes morose, maudlin and whimpering . . . spluttering waffle . . . the kind of pompous self-examination with which Sting is now inextricably linked, and for which he deserves to be laughed at down the ages'. Other rants followed in kind. (Sting may have been above the fray, but coincidentally his next album contained a track listing the various denizens of hell. Among them were music critics.)

Americans, with their bottomless love of the confessional, were more forgiving. To *Rolling Stone, The Soul Cages* was 'highly serious and sonically gorgeous, Sting's most ambitious work –

---

*Miles Copeland would later take issue with Sting's breast-baring interviews to promote the record. 'That was a big mistake, and we couldn't correct it. If Sting hadn't said it was "introspective" it would have been better received.'

and maybe his best'. *People* admired the 'refusal to bow to commercial considerations'. Yet more than five million souls cared enough to buy the album. It hit number one in Britain, number two in the US. A&M kept up the hype, sometimes at the expense of credibility but never of sales. It said something for Sting's fan-base, scrupulously built up over the years, that even a relative dud could be a chart-topper. He emerged from his artistic crisis fully intact.

Sting's renaissance continued live.

Both in their proto-punk days and later, as they trawled the American dome circuit, The Police had sneered at glassy, smoothed-down acts like Fleetwood Mac, Genesis and the kids from *Fame*; their shows, they said – and Sting was one of those saying it – were meant to appeal to the 'great average'. Now he was back on the road, and Sting no longer mocked those bands' crossover dreams. He copied them.

There was one major difference. If fog machines and stage gimmickry were the centrepiece of a Genesis gig, they weren't at Sting's. His minimalist band worked before a black curtain and a light show that was downright quaint. Sting's craggy vocals and the group's pop flair with jazz arabesques were the nights' only effects. The tour's relative modesty was established by Sting's decision to play smaller American arenas. (No one was going to fill outdoor venues in February, not even the sports teams who ran them.) The shows were held in three- to five-thousand seat halls in the larger cities and, elsewhere, in theatres or clubs. Whatever the location, the setting was the same: a bare-bones stage bathed in stark white cross-beams of light. As canned music welled over the PA, the Volvos and Saabs would pull up in the rear, and whole families emerge, men in chunky sweaters, women in suits clutching children. These weren't people conspicuously seeking to have their buckles swashed. By seven, the hall would be full.

Promptly at eight, four figures would lope unannounced from the wings, three incognito, but the other, with his moussed-up hair and bulging black T-shirt, a part of their lives by now, tanned and sinewy in the lights. A quick bow, a count-in, and the band would swing into 'All This Time'. Sting's unflagging energy level kept up over two hours. The set-list became a *tour d'horizon*, rock guitar mingling affably with faux-jazz piano, whole brackets of time when the old and new fused into one. 'Roxanne', 'Purple Haze' and 'Message In A Bottle' all brought Police-era, fists-in-the-air frenzy. 'King Of Pain' was delivered straight from the 1983 playbook. The only hint of encroaching age came in the unheard cuts from *The Soul Cages*. Even Sting had to use an autocue for the words to some songs.

After just a month on tour, Sting had sufficient nerve to appear live in front of a TV audience of millions. He joined Gloria Estefan as co-host of the Grammys. A week later, a second show of self-confidence – one quieter and greater than the first – came in Los Angeles. Sting met Summers and Copeland backstage. 'Love broke out on all sides' was one man's verdict. There was good cause for celebration. Advance orders for The Police's *Greatest Hits* – latest in a series of nostalgic spin-offs – would add hundreds of thousands to Steerpike's and Magnetic's books. Thirteen years earlier, Miles's first, mould-breaking deal for *Outlandos* had seemed almost irrelevant, a technicality greeted by the band with a shrug. Since then, benefits had been discovered that had previously been ignored. By 1991, it was obvious that the group's royalty flow and residuals would add up in a way which few had ever guessed. Each of the three principals were millionaires. Sting and the others could well afford to be magnanimous.

Following in the steps of his Last Exit revival, Sting returned to Wallsend as part of the inevitable MTV *Unplugged* series.

The acoustic set at the Buddle Arts Centre that April attracted a capacity house of 150, including Sting's brother, sisters and grandmother. Dave Greider, a St Cuthbert's graduate who has 'mixed memories' of his famous peer, recalls that when the show was announced, 'that was just a *knockout*. It [the news] went round like wildfire. People were genuinely proud of him.' With his hometown homage, 'people were really chuffed about Sting. Everybody was saying, "That's our kid, I knew he'd do it. I knew he'd come back."' Additional reinforcement was, in some cases, provided by gratitude. The Arts Centre wasn't, after all, the only local recipient of Sting's largesse. Even the Newcastle City Council was advertising the town's virtues by using his name and sultry good looks on a poster. And, of course, in the fifteen years since Sting had left the north-east, ugly words and scenes had faded. The crowd swarming in front of the Centre that night was more than willing to embrace the prodigal son who'd grown up across the road.

If Sting's new songs travelled well, their homecoming drew out unexpected qualities. Shorn of their mannered, over-the-top arrangements, tunes like 'Mad About You' and 'The Soul Cages' were revealed for the mini-gems they were. Even the meandering 'When The Angels Fall' hung together. *Acoustic Live in Newcastle* was released, in a limited edition, late in 1991. The album showed the intriguing possibilities when overblown bilge does battle with stripped-down, folksy playing – an oddly happy marriage. *Acoustic*'s spry production and unconquerable soul revealed the true spirit of *Cages*. 'The Wild Wild Sea' was sung with a languor that can best be described as cosy. 'Island Of Souls' had a jamboree sincerity.

The album took more flak from the critics, not least Sting's nemesis *Melody Maker*. To them, the CD and accompanying ninety-page booklet 'may be bad news for the rainforest demolished to bring it into being, but good news for those in need of a chuckle . . . [Sting] expounds fifth-form truisms with the modesty of a soothsayer . . . A bit rich from an absentee Geordie who left the moment he could scrape enough money together . . . Terminally morose . . . An exercise in subliminal narcissism.' Special exception was taken to the volume's photos. Shot after shot showed Sting, bronzed torso bared, still cleaving to Styler's fond put-down: 'He knows he's cute. How many years can you take your shirt off on stage and not think you look great?'

Sting radiated confidence when he opened his world tour in Berkeley, California. As he walked on, a legation of women presented him with a gift-basket of flowers, lingerie, love notes and a child's toy four-winged insect. Their leader informed him (over the first chords of 'All This Time') that the last was a symbol of his being 'king bee' and his own name. Accepting it, Sting bowed archly, mugged through the song, and introduced the band. Vinnie Colaiuta, previously drummer with Frank Zappa and Joni Mitchell, had auditioned by flying himself from Los Angeles to London, walking into the studio and playing a four-shot roll that said 'this-is-my-gig' (just as Copeland's once beat a more dire tattoo), the same onomatopoeic technique as Omar Hakim's. Dave Sancious took the pianist's stool on the heady endorsement of Bruce Springsteen and Peter Gabriel. The guitarist, Dominic Miller, met Hugh Padgham, signed on, and quit his berth in the Pretenders all in the same day. Nothing in the first rehearsals indicated that the band was playing together for the first time, or the obvious fact that three of them were learning the old tunes from scratch. They gelled.

The tough, streamlined quartet had the bonus of mixing pop-classical drive with the freewheeling swing of Sting's favourite rag groups. This last virtue was only hinted at on *The Soul Cages*. But in concert the band were capable of a fire not always audible on vinyl. They barely surfaced for air during the monolithic (with the accent on *mono*) show that used songs old and new as launching-pads for solo forays. Sting had always said he wanted to do more than repeat note-perfect sets, night after night, as if plugged into a piano-roll device. Now he worked his theory into a manifesto. 'The album's merely a blueprint . . . keys, tempos, dynamics can all be changed, whole sections can be compressed or extended. Without this flexibility, it's impossible for the music to grow.' Much as it was exhilarating to hear the band stretch out into jazz-stoked overdrive, the ad-libbing also took its toll. It was quite possible, as some fans did, to nod off in the spongier passages. American critics seized on the stuttery pacing and perverse running-order of the early gigs. For *Billboard*, reviewing Sting in Los Angeles, 'things hit a wall of inertia when the vocalist launched into a song-cycle from *The Soul Cages*. This frankly self-indulgent, half-hour block of moodily introspective, melodically diffuse numbers stopped the show cold.' Even *Rolling Stone* was unmoved a week later, in New York: 'Hubris nearly got the best of Sting . . . He practically torpedoed the whole set by stringing four songs from *The Soul Cages*, including the longest and slowest ones on the album, into one protracted, thirty-minute endurance test . . . Everything dissolved into a somber sonic fog. By the time the comparatively sunny hook in "When The Angels Fall" eventually poked through the clouds, it was too little too late.'

It was impossible to watch Sting work a hall without being aware of the sheer effort he put into everything he did. The music itself may have been free-form and fluid, but literally everything else was blocked out: the set list and lighting cues, the seemingly spontaneous raps with the crowd. All the tour's early dates shared a touch of pantomime. Later in the spring, as self-confidence struck, Sting recovered his old sense of *sprezzatura* – the Italian art of making the hard look easy – particularly in the joyous reworking of old hits. To hear 'Roxanne' again, amid crowds cheering both the song and their own propensity to cheer, was to feel a jolting surge of nostalgia. In its stupendous, push–pull rhythm, both novices and initiates could understand why Sting was rightly seen as one of rock's defining writers.

A few surprises broke up the gigs' Vegas-revue pace. Sting's choral master-class dramatically punched up the hackneyed 'audience participation' segment. It was a mark of genius that he could make grown men weep at lyrics, like 'Fragile', which, written down, were almost risible. There was a moment when Sting got the fans to sing along to 'One World' which was moving and profoundly soulful. The spot where he traded lines on 'Message In A Bottle' with the band was wonderful. It took a rare talent who knew his material so well he could change the arrangements from night to night and make a virtue of healthy deconstruction. The old tunes were so sturdy they could survive even quirks such as funk-inflected riffs and retooled verses. More than a decade on, 'Walking On The Moon' re-created something of the past magic. Unfortunately, since it came after the soporific *Soul Cages* suite, it also brought home that Sting couldn't aspire to such powerhouses at present. While fans swayed along and held flames aloft during 'Every Breath', it was obvious that *Cages* was never going to compare.

'One reason that I wanted to play here instead of the Enormo-Dome was so I can see you,' Sting told the crowd at New York's Beacon Theater. Even that venue dwarfed the Lilliputian club in Buddle where British dates began in April. From there Sting crossed to Europe. While playing five nights at Staten Hall in the Hague he was filmed for an A&M video. He returned to America in the summer and autumn. Reversing the bingo-hall aura of the early shows, he played four back-to-back concerts at the Sports Palace, Mexico City, grossing $2,745,360. Sting was back in Britain in late November, weaving a loop from Scotland to the south-west. After yet more sell-outs in Germany and France, Christmas was spent in Highgate.

No tour lacked a frequent feature of Sting's jaunts on the road: some one-off or charity spectacular that offered an interstice between mainstream gigs. In January 1991 he hosted and played on *Saturday Night Live*.* Two months later it was the annual Carnegie Hall gala for the Rainforest Foundation. A slice of Sting's Dutch residency in May was beamed in to a televised benefit for Kurdish refugees, raising not just cash but *Melody Maker*'s hackles. July saw him at the Montreux jazz festival. And so the specials kept coming until he hit California. Sting celebrated his fortieth birthday on stage at the Hollywood Bowl, cutting an ironic dash in yellow and black, a nod to his past extended in a four-song encore backed by Summers. As the last number expired in a chaotic tone-cluster, a flare dipped and there was the thump of the first canister of a firework display, silver and red shells bursting overhead and the number '40' picked out in stars. The show was A&M's gift to Sting. Later, they presented him with a speedboat.

Sting's travels wound down with dates in the new year in the Far East, Japan and Hawaii. Taken as a whole, the tour stunned the naysayers. Sting had played orgiastically received sets on four continents. *The Soul Cages* was a hit in the British, American, French, German and Italian charts. In the sixteen months to 31 December 1991 Roxanne Music (Tours), virtually defunct in 1988–89, turned over £8,137,797. Only Eric Clapton, Elton John and Phil Collins were making that kind of solo money.

The well-heeled rocker had little in common with most recession victims, although his intoxicating image continued to be a talking-point. If, in 1991, you were in your thirties or forties and you liked brooding pop, your shining example was *The Soul Cages*. By extension, you either loved Sting or hated him. What few people did was to ignore him.

The greatest target for scorn and choler was Sting's ambition and the affectation to be found along the way. Neither of his last two albums excluded the possibility of humour, but evidence of it was sketchy. *Nothing Like the Sun* was almost satirically po-faced. Not only was there the cover-boy photo of Sting

---

*Even in this knockabout scene, Sting's knack for controversy was at work. For every fan who laughed at his gags about Billy Idol and *The Bride*, there were two who questioned the wisdom of the show going out on the very night the Gulf War began. Making every concession possible, there was a lingering suspicion that Sting was unhappily accident-prone when it came to playing the clown.

ostentatiously 'thinking', and the Spanish-language version hawked as *Nada Como el Sol*; the very title was suggested by his quoting Shakespeare to a drunk. *The Soul Cages* spoke globally but thought morbidly. Apart from his recent work, Sting's image yielded to the barb that he took himself too seriously, whether starring on Broadway or in his near-ludic remarks to the press. Thus 'Every Breath', in most views a stilted if sleek pop tune, struck its author as 'probably *the* song of the Reagan years – this idea that you'll be looked after by a patronizing, beneficent figure'. When a journalist asked whether, after all this time, he wasn't tired of his stage-name, Sting's reply showed just how far the milkman's son had come: 'It's no sillier than Beethoven or Mozart.' Later that year he broke off at a press conference to read from the Brazilian constitution. Even when Sting made light of his image he somehow managed to echo it. 'The whole idea of me being a pretentious wanker,' he told *Q*, '*is* kind of extant.'

In private, Sting was guided by the same aspiring zeal that infused his music. He spent his evenings reading poetry or watching foreign films. He attended the Royal Academy dinner. Where other *soi-disant* ex-punks might collect Fenders or Gibsons, Sting bought classical instruments, from lutes and harps to a spinet once owned by Samuel Pepys. Nobody better demonstrated how the hoary rites of pop had cracked under pressure to be upwardly mobile. Sting's assimilation into the jetset surfed to its peak in the 1990s on the wave of friendships with Princess Diana, Pavarotti and the Versaces. There was no denying that, when the mood struck, he could still give a winning performance as one of the lads. But because he eschewed the smashing-hotel-rooms mode of behaviour, it was easier to retain the vision of Sting the homiletic rocker. 'Indeed,' as Albert Goldman said, 'there's no other vision *to* retain.'

Sting's high-minded effusions were by nature bound to consist largely of laying down the law. He was rarely in the habit of deferring to public opinion. Had he done so in the late 1980s, he said, men like Thozamile Gqweta would still be in jail; to say nothing of the Xingú. Speechifying was an area where he felt more and more at home. Occasionally, Sting had a platform for his orations, as when he addressed the second annual Human Rights Convention at Faneuil Hall, Boston. Other times he kept up long skeins of monologue that seemed not to depend on the attentive presence of another party. It was enough that he spoke.

Critical gibes that he over-taxed himself with a raft of political and philosophical dead-ends left his millions of fans unmoved. Nor did they bother Sting. If anything, he revelled in the chance to be more than the stock one-dimensional rocker, whose personable, suave, ungifted remarks are accepted as holy writ. 'I've tried very consciously to break the mould,' he said in 1991; 'to do things that pop stars don't normally do. I'm willing to take a lot of risks, to the extent where I don't mind being ridiculed.' His career was a textbook case of dazzling exterior far removed from inner self. Sting's stage seductiveness was *acting*; he didn't feel seductive. His empty vessel was open to the projected illusion of fans who viewed him as an upmarket sex-siren, as well as to his own self-reproach. 'We're still living the myth of the "Dying God", the Icarus myth,' he said. 'The Elvis Presley thing, the Sid Vicious thing. Society wants it and craves it.' As he got older, Sting worked harder to defuse his legend. By 1998, so he said, he'd managed to do away with most of the things that defined the rock code in the first place. 'I do yoga; I play chess; I read a lot and I spend time with my family. I play music. Really, that's it.'

Sting's aversion to the Sid Vicious school of existence was one thing. Despite his newly professed disinterest in fame, 'he was desperate to be loved', says one A&M staffer. Increasingly, that meant compensatory bouts of looning to leaven his uptight, eco-warrior pomp. Among the first stabs at pricking the inflated balloon of his self-obsession was a 1989 cameo in *The Adventures of Baron Munchausen*. Sting followed that by hosting *Saturday Night Live*. He met Peter Cook. In January 1992 he guest-voiced with a song called 'We're Sending Our Love Down The Well' on *The Simpsons*. He let it be known that he enjoyed the definitive rock-and-roll spoof of *Spinal Tap*. He could take and make a joke. He called his bass guitar Brian.

Sting's efforts at levity eventually reached a sorry nadir in a boozy double-act with his mate Bob Geldof, published, sparing no coprolitic joke, in *Q*. The piece had a particularly sharp edge, as it turned out, becasue of a certain lewd trend in the conversation. Typical was a mention of Styler:

STING: Socially, I'm loath to go anywhere without Trudie. I don't like to go to a party without her. I don't want to do much at all without her. I certainly

> don't want to have a sexual adventure without
> her. If you have an affair with somebody, it means
> you exclude your best friend.

GELDOF: But would she go along on a sexual adventure
with another boiler?

STING: Yeah. If she was serious. Wouldn't Paula? With
you and me?

GELDOF: What? A fours-up with me and Paula? She
wouldn't want to shag you.

STING: But would *you* fancy it? I think Bob secretly wants
to shag me.

GELDOF: Fuck off.

Even Sting's publicist Keith Altham later rang to tell him that the
interview was a cock-up.

A good PR man would have known instinctively that it was
impossible to turn a reputation like his by stooping to farce; just
as it was impractical to right global wrongs by facile moral stands.
Shifting Sting's image, however maligned, required as much a
sea-change in his attitude as in the public's. For a full volte-face,
all traces of self-pity would have to be ditched, his introversion
cloaked and displays of slapstick dumped. The smaller his port-
folio of contentious opinions the better. There was a precedent.
Sting's crony Eric Clapton had so managed to bend public
opinion by graft and common sense that, in the late 1980s, he
emerged as a family favourite you couldn't hate. Full-scale
rehabilitation like that took more than a few laddish quips in the
press. Not many people could hear what Sting said when their
ears were ringing with what he was: a caring, civilized man with
an un-English bent for self-revelation. His next album, his least
autobiographical, was also his best.

To the knockers, of course, it seemed that Sting was employing
the worst of strategies, needlessly arousing antagonisms and hurt-
ing his own cause. So far as this school ever reached a consensus, it
was that, in the *Sunday Times'* words, the waggish, quick-witted
man had become 'an embarrassing, pretentious bore'. Actually,
Sting was following a shrewd enough course for one at his pass – a
self-styled 'Geordie yobbo' battling for changes against heads of
state. He might have set teeth on edge by the sheer enormity of his
passion. But he also boosted his causes in a way that was bound to

force debate, if not support, the world over. Those photos of him greased-up, on stage with Raoni, added the latest kink to his dire PR straits. They also helped raise millions for the rainforest. For most of his campaigns, Sting struck a singularly dead-eyed blow. If the Brazilian government turned him down, for instance, they'd seem to be caving to the will of the vested interests. If they went along, they would be acting not out of virtue, but from fear of a public sentiment he'd whipped up. Whatever the result, Sting himself couldn't lose.

He was famously free with his time and energy, not only out of conviction but because he understood the social forces that balked him; understood and respected them. 'My music may not move Pinochet,' Sting said. 'But it might do his kids.' Britain in the early 1990s was suffering some of the impact of a recession that had chimed with 'compassion fatigue' to sap funds from a galaxy of good causes. Faced with political hostility and mounting ennui at home, Sting kept at it. In the space of eighteen months, he recorded for the Special Olympics benefit album; puffed Amnesty in Uruguay and Chile; played for the Kurds; appeared on TV with Quentin Crisp; donated a vintage car to the Music Therapy Foundation; and co-starred at an Aids gala with Elton John.

Sting rallied to these causes with his usual efficiency. Improving practices inaugurated by lesser stars, he was always alert, well briefed and asked the right questions of the charities' officials. He insisted on strict accountability. Amnesty, for one, was widely applauded for its bare-bones bureaucracy, even by cynics. Sting saw to it. He travelled widely and met royalty. It was sometimes hard to credit that this sober, bespectacled figure was the same man who liked to quaff hallucinogens and visit strip-clubs. He particularly enjoyed the latter. A woman named Rose Macnab, part of the entertainment at his thirty-seventh birthday, has fond memories of a very different soul to the rhetoric-spouting misanthrope. Specifically, 'he loved watching girls shake their cakes'. Low-life pleasures, of course, had been in Sting's game-plan for twenty years. But the mammiferous yen somehow jarred in the would-be dispenser of sanity and justice to a world maddened by crass follies. Sting was a breast man. If he wanted to combine that with a mission of global service, he would.

Sting was a more flexible and a cleverer politician than most laymen, but also less airy and less vacuous. As the human monuments to his concern – the hospices, schools and parks – rose up and multiplied, even his bitterest critics had to own that real progress had been made. But, they argued, it was coming at too great a cost. The so-called 'pretentious git' stood accused on the basis of unsourced quotes and charges that were often flagrantly partial. He also stood accused by industry figures who hadn't always been strangers to ego themselves. Again, Sting kept at it. He was both principled and pragmatic in his crusades: stolid, dogged and up for the odd dust-up with the right. Above all, he was swayed by a sneaking sense of mortality, his own and others'. 'Contemplating your navel will *perhaps* move mountains one day,' he said. 'If you work on yourself, you change the world in a microcosmic way, but it's getting a bit late. I feel that with certain issues, like the environment, you *have* to be active. You can't just sit there with your legs crossed and hope that the air is going to be fit to breathe tomorrow. I think we don't have very long left, frankly.'

At the heart of Sting's work for the Indians there wasn't a romantic hope but a commitment. By 1991, it was a practical, hard-headed slog: he wanted efficiency, long-term planning, results. 'They don't need a bag of flour,' he insisted; 'they need an administrative infrastructure to protect them and ensure they can choose how and where they want to live – to give them political power, in other words. That's what our board is doing now in Brazil. They're anthropologists, doctors, lawyers, fantastic people, the best.' Sting increasingly traded Utopian stargazing for the language of the seasoned aid-worker. Mission statements. Line management. Function. His own family initiatives followed in kind. In March 1992 he threw his third annual rainforest benefit at Carnegie Hall. Two months later, Styler produced and starred in a London fashion show for the Foundation. Both these events quietly raised hundreds of thousands. More importantly, it was money that went on productive projects like medical aid and a programme which trained local teachers for the Indians. Sting and his colleagues succeeded where a host of quixotic do-gooders failed.

The crowning moment of the Foundation's lobbying came when the Brazilian government finally bowed to pressure for a Xingú national park. In August 1993 the Interior Ministry officially ratified the demarcation of a 12,000-square-mile area, less than the original plan but still home to seventeen indigenous tribes, as well as to farmers, loggers and miners. It was a major coup, especially as the scheme had been under circular debate for forty years. From then on, Sting gradually cut back his woad-daubed tours of the Amazon, though the set-pieces increased.

His popularity – outside the hard-core – was not, however, growing.

Unsurprisingly, Sting was the darling of the *bien-pensants* on the left, for the same reason he was, in the *Guardian*'s phrase, 'king of the jungle': not only because of his dour fundraising, his charm, his need to win and his skill in doing so, but because, as Bill Graham said, 'he was a male equivalent of the Statue of Liberty. Sting actually gave a fuck about the poor, huddled masses.' And, of course, he cared more as he got older.

Sting was fully alive to his image as a self-centred bore carrying the world on his shoulders. He made a study of it. For him, the media digs tended to take one of three lines. 'They think on one hand I'm an arrogant bastard, and on the other I'm a do-gooder ecological bum,' he told *Us*. 'And also that I'm a rich bastard.' Stewart Copeland had seen all this, and was forced to admit he'd thought his ex-boss 'a scumbag' – a phrase that was often taken up by Sting's debunkers and used out of context. What they failed to add was that the drummer's tone was teasing, amused and affectionate. High-handed as Sting was, Copeland later said, much of his bluster was a front for his insecurity and deep concern, concern not just for himself but for a horde of causes. This was the tack taken by those closest to him. 'He doesn't give himself easily to people,' says Styler. 'He's not a small-talker or a small-thinker. He has a wicked sense of humour, but he takes things very seriously . . . People misinterpret his shyness for may-be snobbery or coldness.' Sting himself joined the consensus. 'I think I'm naturally shy, and that comes across as aloofness. But that's all right. As long as the people close to me know me, every-thing outside of that isn't real. And people are generally nice to me to my face.'

The sang-froid might have irked *Melody Maker* and others, but it wasn't the least obnoxious to Sting's friends; to them it was as natural as Oscar Wilde docking in New York and scrawling 'genius' on his 'anything to declare' card, in the same way as lesser mortals wrote 'nothing'. On Wilde's part it was an assertion of special values, but it was also a pre-emptive strike; and the same went for Sting. Both men evolved an epigrammatic approach to their shyness. Twelve years earlier, when fame first hit, Sting had told *Rolling Stone* he came 'from a family of losers [which] I've rejected as something I don't want to be like'. In the same piece he went on to give his law on affection. 'Success always necessitates a degree of ruthlessness. Given the choice of [friends] or success. I'd choose success.' The brutal ambition of Sting's twenties had long given way to the inevitable compromises and equanimity of middle age. 'You come out with polemic statements like that because people remember them,' he explained. 'I wouldn't say that again. I believe the opposite now.'

Sting had come to this conclusion just in time to save several key relationships. He used to quip that life was 'a two-week holiday; at forty you're halfway through it'. He had no idea what this meant when he first said it. He was relating middle age to virility and his own physical fitness. But to use the saw in its more general sense, meaning a change of life, a critical shift in priorities and values, there's no doubt that Sting hit maturity in 1987, the year his parents died and he discovered the rainforest. Between then and 1991 he attributed other symptoms besides ageing to the process: an aversion to axe-grinding, a new moral code, and a gradual smoothing-out of the music. Synchronicity, after all, was his big theme, and he achieved it in and out of the studio.

As the new decade unwound, Sting's albums, soundtracks and wiggy collaborations mellowed into a *sui generis* mix of jazz, rock, pop and soul, with touches of country and even the Big Band beat of Fletcher Henderson or Glenn Miller.* Twenty years after he bred the punk-reggae mongrel of 'Roxanne', and a decade since The Police went off the beat, he still had typecast fears. 'To give yourself a label is self-defeating,' he said. 'I'm a bit of a gadfly . . . I haven't ploughed one furrow for the whole of my life, like just rhythm and blues or folk or jazz, but I use all those elements. And it creates its own genre.' Sting had come out of

---

*Sting worked the Miller style into a pearl on *Ten Summoner's Tales* in 'Nothing 'Bout Me'.

the gate as a gifted singer who was apt to write about pain. As he grew beyond the standard love clichés, his diffuse sound, quirky time signatures and world-wise lyrics revived a faith in intelligent rock largely lost in the reign of Guns N' Roses and Metallica.

When Sting tried to write *de profundis* on *The Soul Cages*, the result was a collection of motley improvisations on stale Geordie themes laden with both gale-force woe and offhand tunes. Somehow, his original mission statement – to supply an emotional pick-me-up for weary fans – had got lost. A re-launch loomed. Change was due. The first obvious one was that Sting stepped back from the mirror. As he said in 1993, 'the plan was to get out of the cycle of traumatic soul-searching and confessional records . . . I thought, "What am I – a songwriter or a psycho-analyst?"' With choppy guitars, strings and jungle rhythms thrown in, Sting's new work would leave lyrical angst and musical convention behind like distant objects seen from a rearview mirror. 'Something for everyone' was the slogan this global foray took as its own.

It paid off. Sting used to tell old friends in Newcastle that 'despite it all, I don't have serious dosh'. That was hyperbole. He'd made vast amounts of cash in the past decade. What he really meant was that his funds weren't bottomless and that without constant creative output he'd be down to a million or two. Money meant security and comfort. For an artist, it also meant time to work. During his long 'block', Sting had once told a relative that 'I try to be generous, but I need help in the way of indulgence and support to write.' His cash-flow 'wasn't that brilliant'.

Nor, however, was it gloomy – some $10 million a year from all sources. Illegal Music had wound down by 1992; Magnetic Publishing, though, netted £3,713,679, with over £2 million in cash and equivalents on hand. Roxanne Music paid each of its three directors between £625,000 and £630,000 that same year. Roxanne Music (Tours) flourished in response to Sting's non-stop itinerary in 1991, slumping to a turnover of £595,063 and £2,941,478 in 1992 and 1993 respectively. Steerpike posted sums of £1,094,883 and £3,117,242 during the same period. Sting's primary company had over £3 million at the bank and a healthy pension fund managed by Skandia Life. It employed a full-time staff of six.

During the past twelve years, Sting's material welfare had

hardly been skimped. With three homes, a fleet of cars, his Italian wardrobe and the sort of credit rating normally reserved for well-run governments or giants like Virgin, he could make fans squirm as well as clap. 'I'm pretty happy – I just wish my life were more like Sting's' may have been a good joke, but it expressed a view people had of him. It was obvious now that, between his advances and soaring tour fees, he could afford to lead life on an even sweeter level. There were his royalties and perked-up residuals from The Police. Another branch of the Sting industry churned out merchandise like posters, badges and calendars, and a £25 *Nothing Like the Sun* sweatshirt. Miles continued to preside over the palace at Bugle House. From the fourth-floor throne room he managed a global asset which grossed tens of millions annually. If Miles's reward for all this – the West End office, the St John's Wood mansion, the Bentley – was impressive, equally impressive were his tenacity, loyalty and willingness to go to the wall for Sting. The feat of risk-taking and consolidation that had led to their mutual Eden had begun a dozen years earlier with the scratchy demo of 'Roxanne'.

Sting could well be generous. But it was a measure of the man that, even when financially strapped in his twenties, he'd kept up a flow of donations and *pro bono* work. He was open-handed with panhandlers and cadgers and 'always [kept] a quid handy for those guys who clean your windscreen'. On a higher, administrative plane, he gave lavishly to the Rainforest Foundation. Sting's tour with Chief Raoni had raised £600,000. All-star dinners and shows at Carnegie Hall brought in upwards of £1 million annually. In 1991 Sting calculated that he'd put at least £150,000 of his own cash into the Foundation. He was also quietly pouring tens of thousands into Amnesty International, making loans to old friends in Newcastle and keeping Pangaea afloat as an act of artistic philanthropy. He funded literally dozens of charities.

For all the mixed reviews of his last two albums, Sting still found himself bankable merely for being, not for anything he said or did. He still got offers, but outside of his key deal with A&M he could pick and choose whatever suited him. In November 1990 he asked for a million pounds to write thirty seconds' music for a coffee commercial. 'We were staggered,' says Susie Galbraith of the agency Duckworth Finn. 'I can only assume that he didn't really want to do it and suggested a ridiculous figure to put us off.' Such was the draw of Sting's name that the client involved had, in fact, met at board level and put his fee to a vote. They chose to pass.

Rumours swirling about the rainforest money weren't so easily dismissed. As early as 1990, Sting had been forced to scotch suggestions that there had been 'hands in the till'. Wholesale reorganization had since turned the Foundation on its head. Exotics like Dutilleux had given way to seasoned administrators like Larry Cox. But many of Sting's friends didn't realize how bad the situation was and thought his blast at *World in Action* was mere spleen at unjust charges. Actually, Sting was deeply rattled that at least one part of his empire had been rotten under the skin. He moved quickly to 'kick arse', he said. 'If we have made mistakes, we've rectified them.' In fact, this taint of crookedness never quite left the Foundation. From his Belgian exile, Dutilleux continued to rant at the 'pathetic dinner parties [*sic*] Sting gives once a year to raise money'. His parting salvo was withering. 'I just wish I'd found someone else to save the Indians.'

The whole saga might have blown over but for the ironic light it cast on Sting's finances. Both here and in his other companies, problems were found that had somehow previously failed to surface. The gap, for instance, between how Sting's money was handled on tour (by a man called Jonathan Kessler) and how it was invested generally (by Keith Moore) wasn't just unusually wide, but cosmically so. Among the latter's more offbeat plans was the doomed scheme to open a chain of Indian brasseries in south London. As Moore says today, 'the restaurant venture started out as a perfectly legitimate short-term, fully secured loan with an option for equity participation ... Unfortunately, because of some chicanery involving, among other things, the diversion of funds ... the involvement was not a happy one.' Nor, as it turned out, was it unique. Moore's client was being bilked out of millions. In 1996, a justifiable pique, a self-pitying sense of victimization and a jailed accountant did more than put the flame to Sting's pent-up fury. They also lit the torch of a closer self-scrutiny. 'The problem was ... I found myself at the head of a multi-million-dollar international corporation,' he told *Us*. 'And it's so complicated, the way money is routed, there's so

much paperwork – you have to trust somebody.' That wily
rationalization lay ahead. In 1991, as fast as Sting's money came
in, it was quietly bleeding out again.

Sting hit forty in true celebrity style, in a small Hollywood
ceremony with his band, a Disney film crew and ten thousand
guests. Throughout the day, local fans, press and pickets whipped
up an atmosphere of Super Bowl-like frenzy, with two sets of
demonstrators, protesting California's environmental and sexual-
equality laws, mingling at the gate. The show itself ran squarely
within the festive atmosphere while featuring most of the
'difficult' cuts from *The Soul Cages*. On the slower tunes, Sting
was an unabashed purveyor of hangdog rock, looking like a man
whose family pet had just been run over. Musically, the set stayed
close to the acoustic strum of the last two albums, while exuding
stagecraft and pyrotechnics handed down from a bygone era. (In
People's words: 'The special effects were garish . . . Weren't they
listening when Sting sang on "Roxanne", "You don't have to put
on that red light"?') The concert went both ahead and astern,
linking reggae with jazz, Sting's new oeuvre with The Police.
Summers himself emerged for the encore. When the two men
hammed up 'Message In A Bottle', visions of their Beatles-tinged
glory days danced along. Robert Hilburn spoke best for the
consensus in the *Los Angeles Times*: 'Watching them side by side
again reminded you of how daring a move it was in 1983 for Sting
to leave one of the most successful groups ever formed to pursue
the artistic freedom offered by a solo career. Yet the excellence of
the music itself made it clear that the move was absolutely
correct.'

Sting at forty was a hybrid. He combined a deep sense of his
own value with a peculiar vulnerability and lack of self-esteem;
for all the platinum discs and Grammys, a sense of banality still
nagged him. He might well have worried, for instance, about
revamping a career his own son mocked as 'getting up on stage
and shouting'. Or about stumbling into marriage with Styler
after ten years – perhaps remembering his childhood and adolescence, in which Ernie and Audrey had brawled like two sailors on
shore leave. He was still struck enough by his upbringing to
agonize about it in public. At their highest level, Sting's efforts to
resolve his past were perceptive, wry and touched human truths.
'It's only when you have children yourself and look in the mirror

and start to see your parents in your own physical features that you come round to the fact that, yeah, I can understand that person ... I feel my father has in some way been mourned. I don't believe in any afterlife. But I get a feeling of something. Even if it's only in my own head. Something has fallen into place.' At its nadir, Sting's relentless self-analysis sunk into middle-age vanity. Nowhere was this worse than in his collaboration with the Slav artist Roberto Gligorov on a picture book of his lyrics. The illustration for 'History Will Teach Us Nothing', in which various sketches of Sting were doctored, like Warhol's *Marilyn*, in the guise of dozens of world figures, ranging from Hitler to Jesus, was only the most surreally inane.

Above all, Sting was the man who stressed long-term values over fleeting careerism. 'I don't want to be a star when I'm forty,' he'd said at thirty-two. Eight years on, he was just that, an icon, while being perpetually on the move. He'd drifted away from the assaultive school of rock aired on *Outlandos* through the social crusades of the late 1980s. His parents' deaths and his own swelling family had deepened him; witness *The Soul Cages*. Midway through life's 'two-week holiday', he'd managed to convert his fears and doubts into productive means of enjoying the second half.

To his band, his record label and the cottage industry based at Bugle House, Sting was a friend, father-figure and corporate boon. A&M were quite right to throw him a bash. On a sound-stage downtown, Jerry Moss handed over the keys to a vintage Riva speedboat; Pavarotti appeared on video; Sting's five children sang a Hawaiian-hula serenade. By dawn most of the guests were intoxicated, if not by numerous glasses of Dom Pérignon, then by the fireworks, the fellow VIPs like Dylan and Jackson Browne, and the room tricked up, bizarrely, to resemble Wallsend. After several hours of windy speeches and tributes, Sting might have been, as he said, 'the most knocked-out man in Hollywood', but Summers could have made a bid for runner-up. Late in the evening he was approached by Miles Copeland with a document insisting he legally waive all rights and fees from his live cameo. The guitarist signed.

8

Country Life

SPENDING MONEY WAS ONE OF STYLER'S KEY STRATEGIES for holding on to her man. When Sting was on tour in Mexico his partner called to tell him that she'd found the perfect house. 'He asked if I liked it,' Styler recalled. 'I told him I loved it. He asked why I wanted to buy it. I gave him a lot of reasons. There was silence. Then I told him that there was a 350-year-old tree in the garden. "Buy it," was the quick reply.'

Styler's enthusiasm meshed with Sting's own hankering to move his family out of London. The kidnap threats against his children continued through 1991. Having just signed a £16 million deal with A&M for four albums (and, the very week Styler rang, grossing $2,745,360 for four shows), Steerpike and the rest were cash-heavy; now more than ever, Sting had money to burn. Keith Moore remembers walking on the Malibu beach with his client one afternoon in October 1991. Sting pointed to a page in *Country Life* and told his accountant, 'That's the house I want.' The sale was closed early in the new year. Sting would later say, not without pride, that he 'got the place for a song, literally'. In fact, £2 million changed hands in a typically intricate series of corporate manoeuvres. By late 1992 Steerpike's two principals would list their official residences as 2, The Grove, and Lake House, near Salisbury, Wiltshire.

The sixty-acre estate lay on the banks of the river Avon, eighty miles west of London. Behind the stone house the land sloped

down to the water meadows, swans eddying round in the breeze
and the sun sending chopped-up light through the willows.
When the stream was running it was a rich blue, and there were
whirlpools along the verges. In the early summer, when Sting
moved in, the fields were ripe with crops; there were orchards of
fruit trees and beyond the river a church rose from a dip in the
hills with the downs beyond, browned in the heat and rolling
gently towards the market town. Lake House stood on the edge
of a weir. Sting liked to lie in a cot in his boathouse, listening
to the river, 'reading or meditating or maybe not even doing
that', humming the tunes churning in his head. It was a fair
stretch from the alleys of Wallsend. Sting himself would speak
of his mid-life switch from city to country, calling Lake House a
home rather than a glorified hotel in which to kill time
between gigs. 'It used to be all right to go away,' he said. 'Now
it isn't.' Moreover, with the nearby Roman earthworks and
dairy farm, the place restored two childhood connections in
Sting's life.

The mansion had been built in 1578 for George Duke, a West
Country wool merchant. It was enlarged in the eighteenth century
(when a broader staircase was needed to accommodate a style for
wide skirts), razed by fire in 1912 and rebuilt, and expanded again,
for a visit by Spanish royalty. There were eventually fourteen bedrooms and eight baths. After yet more work in 1992–93, Lake
House emerged as an elegant jumble of ancient and new. The
vaulted ceilings and formal library met with offices for Sting and
Styler, stereos, computers and what an engineer calls a 'sinfully
flash' studio. Windsor chairs joined an oak refectory table in the
combined kitchen-dining room, candelabra and fresh flowers
setting off a typical meal of pasta, home-baked bread and organic
spuds. The copper beeches pressed up against the mullioned
windows. Dogs and cats prowled the oak-panelled rooms or dozed
in front of the Gothic chimneypiece.

When Sting put down the money for Lake House, the plan
was to ease in slowly over two years. The clan would drive out at
weekends and then return to Highgate. In the event that idea
proved hopelessly drawn-out. Styler reports that 'he loved it so
much that he talked me into moving right away'. By mid-1992 the
seat was home not only to the Sumners but to a vast retinue of
professional and domestic help: there were nannies, secretaries,

architects, workmen and Sting's own band, in-house to cut an album. The designer Alain Mertens, meanwhile, set about restoring the property inside and out. There were some florid touches: the painted frieze by Jono Clive with portraits of the family and their pets; the Persian rugs; Italianate stencils; four-poster beds covered with embroidered velvet and silk. But Sting's most personal flourish was the 62-track studio in the dining hall once used to host the King of Spain. Throughout that summer he wrote and rehearsed the songs that became *Ten Summoner's Tales*. Although Styler had doubts about children co-habiting with long-haired rockers and their ilk, her lover's presence there appealed to her domesticity. As it turned out, family, musicians and builders all got on famously.

A special room in the garden would ultimately be fixed for Sting, but he always preferred to write in the boathouse, or strolling through the formal garden and pastures with their low hills, horses, goats and cattle grazing in the wetlands at back. In this rural idyll the songs poured out of him at the rate of one a week, and new tunes and lyrics kept coming throughout the summer. Although he was quite sure in April that he'd start recording in July, July came and went and the juices still flowed. Sting's only constraint was the near-constant accompaniment of hammers and drills from Mertens' crew. 'Writing is a solitary business,' he said. 'I like having people around . . . I'll be sorry when the last builders go, but there's always Sartre's definition of hell.'

A test of Sting's creative nerve came one morning early in April 1992. A slim package cryptically marked EARS ONLY was hand-delivered to Lake House. Inside was a demo tape combining guitar, piano and some twenty musical cues for the raw soundtrack of *Lethal Weapon 3*. It came with a note, urgently pleading for help, signed 'E.C.'. Sting had known and liked Eric Clapton for years. In 1991 mutual respect had deepened in the wake of personal losses. Following the death of his four-year-old son Conor, Clapton had found a scrap of solace in *The Soul Cages*. Sting in turn was moved by 'Tears In Heaven', the guitarist's requiem for his son (and angry anthem to Clapton's own survival), then riding at number two in the chart. He agreed to work up the guitar noodlings, cues and sampled clicks of Clapton's Zippo lighter into a unifying song.

Since The Police, Sting had spent much of his time in creative block or solitude, yet in some way shy of collaborating much with others: at home only with causes. There was also the fact that, as a film, *Lethal Weapon 3* was exactly the kind of 'dickhead' drama he'd roundly slagged in Stallone. Yet he rallied to Clapton in a flash. Abstract pledges to people as statistics and ethnic groups gave way to a personal commitment. It was a seemingly small, but significant, watershed in Sting's life. As he put it, he'd gotten 'real'.

Twenty-four hours later, Sting came up with a melody, a bridge and a key phrase that said: when everything else fails, at least there's one person still there, and 'it's probably me'. From that wry line, the track evolved, via an all-night session in New York, into one of the great buddy-songs flung on to celluloid. With its striking lyric, novel percussive twist and Sting's own vocal, 'It's Probably Me' wasn't just the perfect score for the movie, it was a hit in its own right. Sharp-eared critics would say that a major part of the singer's life seemed to emerge in the verses about fickle friendship and chary male bonding. Sting's accomplice took the pragmatic view that, 'He's fast. I've never worked faster in my life, he just wings it.' This casual gift from one pop icon to another would strike Clapton as the moment his friend was launched from the first division into the super-league, one of three or four men with the priceless skill to 'pump out a number-one smash' overnight.

Time and again, Sting would confirm the old adage about inspiration and perspiration. The natural genius whom his friends and fans saw still considered himself a tortured creative soul. 'As a rule,' he told *Billboard*, 'composing's painful to me; it's a *tabula rasa* in which I have to deal with who I am and what I think.' He may have disguised the sweat that went into his best work, but Sting had a flair for metaphorical writing that wouldn't have shamed a novelist. The sort of first-person-singular he typically evoked was droll, alert and fully human. He rarely stooped to hectoring or propaganda. Where most authors stretch a small idea into yards of print, Sting's great gift was compression. He might have written some dubious couplets in the past, but no one could say that lines like 'I swear in the days still left / We'll walk in fields of gold' didn't hit home. Among his creations, Sting himself was his best-drawn character, and his deftly spun yarns of love and loss struck a chord in millions. At his worst, he was turning rhymes. On peak form, Sting was translating the human condition into words of one or two syllables. Add an ear for a riff and it was easy to see why he straddled both highbrow and lowbrow, hovering between worlds and carving himself a niche as the great communicator.

Later that spring, the 78-year-old Larry Adler, sage, mouth organist, and one-time colleague of Duke Ellington, was invited to Lake House. His memories of the trip sum up the guileful charm Sting habitually beamed on older men. 'He wanted me to play on his "Shape Of My Heart". I told him I was too ancient ... Next thing, a beautifully worded note and a tape arrived on my doorstep. I loved the track. A week later I went up to Wiltshire and we did it. Sting later wrote an article saying that he'd worried Trudie found me too dishy ... He was funny and sweet like that. It's very seductive.'

One of the sources of error in this lavish tribute was a false assumption about the link between Sting's public and private life, and another about his relationship with Styler. Most fans' glimpse of their hero that summer came in the *Unplugged* video. Dressed in an African dashiki, his hair lopped to Last Exit length, Sting exuded his signature mix of ego and insecurity. He apprised the public, for example, of the wisdom that 'Most musical form is ghettoized ... I despise those categories ... I don't want to conform to any of them. It's my job to evade them and fight against them.' Yet the off-camera quips about his voice (he was suffering from mild laryngitis) and ingratiating bouts of self-deprecation both ignited that mischievously boyish smile 'that made it so hard not to like him', Adler says. A complicated man, Sting. Fully alive to his role as a genre-buster, he constantly reminded interviewers of his bold rejection of the straitjacket. Instead of sticking to well-trodden musical paths he wanted havoc, cross-breeding, transplants, anything that implied shock and novelty – a romp across musical borders. Yet the fact that he tried so hard to be radical is the surest sign that, by nature, he wasn't. Even unplugged, his songs stuck closely to the Beatlesque sensibility at their core. When the band toned things down on the more intimate, less steamrolling tunes, Sting could sound like 'Yesterday'-era McCartney.

The artistic clash between trial and order reflected the conflict being enacted at Lake House. The long-running affair between

Sting and his mate was going through a sea-change. Styler was thirty-eight; mother of three of his children. Her career as an actress–producer was stifled by well-meaning projects, like *Boys From Brazil*, that attracted rants in the *Sun* rather than critical raves. Audiences tended to see her as 'Sting's missus'. One or two *Guardian* writers rubbished her as apparently under his sway. Sting's tendentious do-gooding was set against an alleged refusal to marry Styler and a keen passion for bachelor impedimenta like strip-clubs. His life was run on two interlocking interests – in hearth and home and, as he said, 'tits and arse'. A certain moral duality had been Sting's trademark for twenty years.

The fundamental shifts which produced *The Soul Cages* were the symptom, he also said, of 'the usual [middle-aged] stuff', something akin to a male menopause. That put pressure on his home life. Styler knew it. Throughout the spring and early summer of 1992, she continued to massage him with flattery, in public and private. He was a 'genius', she had it. Sting heartily returned the kudos. 'I'm loath to go anywhere without Trudie,' he told *Q*. She was 'the first woman [he] hadn't wanted to run away from and go be a pop star,' Sting said. Friends who met the pair in Wiltshire or Highgate were struck by the obvious warmth between them. They were 'peas in a pod', says one woman. Adler describes them as 'epically devoted' to one another. A 'joint front' was yet another eulogy. The couple's unity was apparently unbounded. This mutual love didn't, however, extend to a joint policy on marriage.

That late spring Styler continued to push the issue in a way for which a decade's intimacy hadn't braced him. About their children, for one, they varied wildly, mainly because she thought they needed married parents, he didn't. Twice a day on average, she became eloquently persuasive about wanting 'security' in the family. When Sting told her in effect to knock it off and salted his reply with protests of undying love, she stormed upstairs and slammed the door.

Some of the strain of those months was at work on the music. One of the first songs Sting wrote at Lake House was a witty Broadway pastiche with the opening lines: ' "Seven days", was all she wrote / A kind of ultimatum note, she gave to me . . .'

In public, Styler insisted that 'Sting and I have made a spiritual commitment. It doesn't appeal to me to go into a register office and sign a piece of paper.' Yet when a schoolfriend told their son

Jake that he was 'weird', and the boy tearfully passed on the slur to his mother, Styler took the offensive. 'That decided us,' she told the *Daily Mail*; 'because we couldn't have the kids feeling upset.' No one denied that both parents' first priority was their children. But, like most couples pondering marriage, neither was untinged with personal agendas. Taunts of bastardy chimed equally with the workings of Styler's body-clock. 'She wanted to marry and have at least one son in, as she put it, "proper English style",' says a film friend. For his part, Sting's resistance began to wilt in the face of renewed lobbying by his seven-year-old and the boy's sister. 'The idea of having to get married was really quite alien,' he later said. 'But the kids would come home from school and say, "Are you two married? We'd feel better if you were because then you'd stay together." It was gradually wearing us down. So we started to plan a wedding.' This, too, was to woefully omit the part played by Styler.

Sting's inability to match his partner's high hopes didn't thwart his whole-hearted involvement in the ritual. By mid-July he, too, was speaking of a 'proper English' do. Late in the month plans swung into top gear, with a church booked, Versace briefed and 250 guests sworn to secrecy. Two dates, one for the civil and one for the religious service, were made for August.

Unlike the rest of Britain, which was in a state of moral frenzy over marital crack-ups in the royal family, Sting and Styler were in high spirits as the day neared. On the 18th (as photos circulated of the Duchess of York's poolside sally), they drove to Highgate. Next night there was a party at The Grove. At mid-morning on Thursday 20th they emerged for the town-hall ceremony in Camden. Styler dressed down for the occasion. The disparity showed between her black suit and almost chemically bright-blonde hair. Sting chose a dark T-shirt and check jacket. 'It was wonderful. I feel fantastic,' he informed reporters. There were just two witnesses to the fifteen-minute function, and a handful of girls waving confetti as the Land Rover pulled off up Chalk Farm Road. It was almost exactly a decade since the couple had made their first public bow together. Then it had been a snarling row at the airport. Now Sting played the genial celebrity. He seemed to get more and more comfortable in this role. It was as if he were finally accepting the consequences of his fame, which made him one of the top four or five rock stars in the world. Women loved Sting. His blunt solidity won fans every-where. Even people who didn't buy albums knew of him.

Starting in 1991, almost all of Sting's videos underscored his seigniory with hazy storylines about castles, damsels and white chargers. Some of the same medieval wet-dreams padded out his church wedding on 22 August. Whatever impression the guests had from Sting's films, nothing could have steeled them for the vision in the nave of St Andrew's, Great Durnford, across the river from Lake House. Styler sported an exotic £20,000 Versace number in ivory satin consisting of six underskirts and two silk overskirts. A diaphanous blue veil trailed down the thousand-year-old aisle. Sting himself wore tails with a black-and-white striped waistcoat (an upmarket copy of the Newcastle football strip), formal trousers and Chelsea boots. These baroque outfits, later auctioned for charity, would bring the Sumners untold media grief. When Styler mounted a horse to ride home across a ford, the animal shied at the weight of her dress.

After a knockabout turn by Billy Connolly, industrial quan-tities of Dom Pérignon, skinny-dipping in the Avon and presen-tation of the gifts (including a Jaguar XJS from Keith Moore and Kim Turner, and a bed from Miles Copeland), the Troggs took to a makeshift stage in the grounds. The band's singer Reg Presley, booked for this dazzling night by Sting's publicist, remembers it as 'the gig of a lifetime, which seemed to go on and on like a dream, until everyone was grunting along to our big number'. As 'Wild Thing' expired in a crash of mangled drums and chugging air-guitar, all eyes moved to the groom. Sting in turn located Copeland and Summers, also both lurking in the garden. Not without muttering, but yelled on by Connolly and the rest, the vaunted trio made their comeback. Sting would later say, with all the mixed emotions he had towards The Police:

We got up and we hadn't rehearsed or planned anything and we started with 'Message In A Bottle' and Andy starts the riff, he can just about remember it, and Stewart immed-iately starts fucking speeding up, as usual, as fucking usual, so I turn around and ten years just suddenly evaporate and there I am glowering at Stewart and he's glowering at me and Andy's fumbling with the chords and suddenly it'd all come back and Stewart and I caught each other doing it and started to laugh. It was very funny. It was actually a very warm moment. That tension was back immediately. People said that the atmosphere was electric watching it.

Although Styler would tell both guests and the media that 'we did it for the kids', that was to downplay her own central role in the wedding.* Nor did things exactly proceed in the improvised, let's-put-the-show-on-right-here manner suggested in the *Mail*. Versace confirm that the first sketches of the couple's garb were made in March, five months before the church service. The whole business captivated the press for a day or two, until the gossip-shoal reverted to the royals. On Sunday the headlines were HERE COMES THE BRIDLE and other quips on the word Sting; by Tuesday it was MY LIFE IS TORTURE, by Tragic Di. But for forty-eight hours, at least, Ernie and Audrey Sumner's son had vied on equal tabloid terms with the Princess of Wales. He seemed at home with his fame.

Sting couldn't have asked for a better life. His reverse humiliations on Newcastle and the world had long given way to a note of mild, stoic irony. He had a new bride; five children; a benign ex-wife; and a sense of awe at his good luck he characterized as '[being] in the garden and turning around and looking at this fucking huge house and thinking, Jesus! How did that happen?' The financial situation was golden. Sting was right in judging that his 'difficult' confessional LPs would do big business, even if artistically they didn't endure. Steerpike had over £3 million on hand. Sting's trusted accountant had long evolved into a friend, one who bought his client a £30,000 car on his wedding. Nor were the high spirits bursting out all over a front. However 'successful' a person's career may look to an outsider, what counts is what happens daily. Here, too, Sting scored highly. He clearly took pleasure in the routines of life, in raising his family, tending his homes, in the process of music itself, in conversation with friends, in walking, reading, writing or brooding alone in his boathouse under the beeches. Few men are so blessed.

The bubble was pricked just days after Sting's wedding. With

---

*'There's a word that's usually affixed to a rock star's girlfriend: "current",' Styler later told the *Mirror*. 'Now I'm a wife I feel secure.' Sting's own take on the day proved it. 'Nothing changed except that Trudie got more respect.'

money flung into high-risk follies like the Indian brasseries, Moore Sloane Ltd crashed in a slew of unpaid bills and ugly recriminations. A postscript to Sting's accounts on 30 September 1992 noted blandly that the firm had 'resigned as auditors as a result of the dissolution of this Partnership'. It was the next line that took the breath away: 'We confirm that there are no matters which require to be brought to the attention of members or creditors of any company.' In fact, Moore Sloane owed £13 million against assets of £650,000. Sting's very bagman would be declared broke with debts of nearly £9 million. Six million pounds was missing from the singer's own books.

Early that autumn Sting was eating breakfast at his home in Highgate. A large manila envelope arrived marked PRIVATE AND STRICTLY CONFIDENTIAL. Instead of tour dates or a demo from Eric Clapton, the package contained an eleven-page letter jointly written by a worker in Moore's office and an employee of Skandia Life. Slowly the blood drained from Sting's face. In neat, well-rounded terms, he was told of a systematic fraud stretching back over four years. 'I was with my wife, and she was saying: "Honey? Honey? What's up? What's up, honey?" And I said, "Someone has pinched six million quid off us." I thought it was a joke. But I called my lawyer and my manager and ... sure enough.' The money represented a quarter of his total wealth. On 25 September Sting summoned his accountant to Lake House. Even at this late date, both sides evidently hoped to avoid a public scandal. As Moore says, 'He asked me about the investments and the possibility of recovering the money. Sting shook my hand, said, "Goodbye" and we parted. I had no reason to believe that the next time I would see him was in court.'

Sting sat tight. Seeing his finances splashed in the *Sun* would be ironic, and unwelcome, confirmation of his own aside that 'I get paid too much'. A more likely idea why he found mediating with Moore attractive was his dread of going to law. Although Sting and Branson had made up, he still had bitter memories of the Virgin suit ten years before. He also knew what the press and public would make of a man so rich that he hadn't spotted a mere missing £6 million. Most of the dailies would (and did) have a bonanza. Certain titles had long had it in for him, and Sting knew what to expect of the tabloids. His media nest hadn't been completely befouled, of course. The heavyweights and the

Americans were still on side, and he touted himself to *Us* as a man reborn from the venal, grasping 1980s. '[The fraud] made me look very seriously at the idea of wealth,' Sting said. 'I came to the conclusion that it isn't about what you have in the bank. Your wealth is your friendships, family, health and happiness.'

Sting's apparent sang-froid was all on the surface. Though posing as cool about his losses, he was inwardly seething with frenzied damage-control. He was in near-daily touch with Miles, his solicitor Christopher Burley and his record label in September and October 1992. The result of this four-way axis was what Moore terms the 'so-called A&M settlement' of late autumn. Essentially, it was a chance for him to return the cash. When Moore declined the offer (on the unanswerable grounds that most of it was already lost down a black hole), Sting and his team changed tack. They began to negotiate direct with the two main banks involved in Moore's ruse, Coutts and Lloyds, with the happy result that both finally reimbursed much of the money. Sting also hired a private eye to try and get a taped confession of the crime. At that stage Moore allegedly broke down and wept. In November the accountant went to Holborn police station where he was interviewed by Fraud Squad detectives for six hours. Eight specimen charges of theft would eventually be made against him. In April 1994 Moore was struck off by his professional body. He went on trial eighteen months later.

By early 1993 Sting was already larding his song lyrics and interviews with sly references to the scam. His *Q* double-act that January established the following mutual peeves:

> Geldof launches into a fifteen-minute rant which starts and finishes with him declaring, '[The press] is the single most anti-democratic force at work in Britain today.' Sting's theory is that the tabloids have 'disenfranchised the working classes in the country . . . It's just beer and tits.'
>
> 'That's editors with too much power and not enough intelligence,' spits Geldof. 'Take 'em out and fuckin' shoot them. Them and architects.'
>
> 'And accountants,' adds Sting.

The same profession would join archbishops, cardinals, judges, barristers and pop critics among the infernal roll-call on *Ten Summoner's Tales*. And Sting privately told a friend he felt 'raped' by the man he'd worked with and trusted since the hoary days of 'Fall Out', sixteen years before.

Whatever his drawbacks – pomposity, self-rapture and a yen to lay down moral law – Sting was always ready with generous help, says Adler, quick to size up a man and bring him out; ready with advice and cash; willing to take a stand for starving artists (like those on Pangaea) if concurrently they caught his eye and ear. He had an epic capacity for work, was an unusually frank self-critic and debunked his tensely morose streak with a dry, mocking wit. If, as *Melody Maker* said, Sting's turgid navel-gazing excited scorn, he had a geniality and open-handedness that won the loyalty of his band, as well as a love of music and a sharp professional savvy. He worked hard to develop a beery, one-of-the-boys image, if never quite affecting, say, Clapton's sham laddishness. At forty-one Sting was warm, well spoken and eager to please. He had a new-age way of talking positively about himself and his art. Like half the world's rockers, he was shy but constantly daring himself to be extrovert. His stylized duality came out on stage and in the occasional well-meaning *shtick* in the press.

Commuters at Ladbroke Grove station, west London, were dealt an improbable treat one morning in January 1993. For an hour, travellers on the Metropolitan Line (as it then was) were entertained by a busking superstar. Slumped against the soiled brick wall, under the gum machine, Sting strummed his guitar and dragged back songs like 'Every Breath' and 'Roxanne' from the stadium to sub-street level. It was a neat, if contrived, piece of flummery, dreamt up by an unholy mix of Miles, a sharp-eyed PR man and London Transport. After boosting his personal fortune by 75p in tips, Sting joined his old sparring-partner Bob Geldof for lunch. It provided the second dramatic feature of the week. Moore's tearful breakdown had been a tragedy – this was a farce. The interview followed down a line from cameos in *Baron Munchausen* and *The Simpsons* and preceded another spot on *Saturday Night Live*. When Sting was 'himself' (cracking jokes with Adler and giving him a gold pendant in the shape of a mouth organ, for instance), his emotional discipline often gave way to acts of raw humanity. It was the set-pieces, ill-advised bouts of public looning, that misfired. Sting alone could be warm and witty. As a stand-up comic, he never quite lost the taint of buffoonery.

Witness his views on sex. Much sport would be made of Sting's pronouncement that, through Tantric yoga, he could sustain love-making for five hours at a go. This, too, started life as a jape with Geldof (who maintained that ten seconds was quite enough). Sting's description of his technique was arresting. 'I've begun to use [yoga] now where you don't spill your seed, you don't come. You retain it all and go on for longer. You stay erect and your stomach goes as near to the spine as you can make it whilst still allowing you to breathe . . . and you never lose control, you just keep going.' Later, after a thousand jokes at his expense, Sting tended to back off from his boast. There was a kernel of truth in it, he told the *Telegraph*, 'although the five hours includes dinner and a movie, of course'.

Sting had a libido. Everyone knew that. As well as his marathon couplings with Styler, there was his VIP membership of exotic clubs around the globe and rumours that he swung solo, with only *Playboy* or *Penthouse* as company, in his dressing-room before a show. Sting either had a potent sex-drive or was, as one workmate terms it, 'a chronic wanker'.

Then there were drugs. Sting had given up on recreational stimulants, with their threat of addiction and loss of control, in the 1980s. That didn't preclude a taste for hallucinogens like ayahuasca brewed into a tea. Doping for fun was out, but doping as a form of spiritual growth was a way of coping with life. While in Brazil, Sting ritualistically (and legally) took the tea in a syncretic Christian church called the Uniao do Vegetal, or herbal society. There were, he informed the *Telegraph*, two types of drug: 'the kind that separates you from the world' and the kind that 'totally connects you to it'. The only problem, of course, was that not everyone made the distinction. Following his crack about Ecstasy, Leah Betts' family, for one, in a friend's phrase, 'went mental'. Yet again, Sting enjoyed the prestige of full-bore controversy.

He still tried to make sense of prolonging a puerile career into adulthood: it was among his best traits. Occasionally it backfired, as when Sting – who even fans saw as rich and pampered beyond the dreams of avarice – harangued the world about money or drugs. He had views on well-nigh everyone and everything. Sting's bleaker didactic side doubtless had its origins in childhood. Ernie Sumner's frustration and refusal to stand up for himself in the hothouse of Station Road unnerved his highly strung son, whose own fear of failure still loomed in middle age. Unlike most people, he never fully got over his adolescent crises. Well into his thirties, Sting flogged himself hard. His persistent feelings of inadequacy led to bouts of depression which hit bottom in 1982–83. By forty, he'd not only throttled back on his ambition, he took a wry view of his fame and the pop scene as a whole. 'I don't know half their names,' he confessed after reading a rock title. Later in the evening of his lark with Geldof, Sting was back in Highgate, playing chess and sipping wine. He explained how his teenage son Joe wanted to be in a band. 'I've told him he should concentrate on his A Levels,' Sting sighed. He turned to his wife. 'Is that the right thing to do?'

To say Sting matured wasn't to say he rashly gave up on the past. The old still slept uneasily with the new. Promiscuous sex might have given way to voyeurism, a coke habit to natural herbs; but he intuitively, inveterately courted grief. With a typically perverse gift for self-mortification, Sting still, for instance, raged at his critics. He no longer wrote ugly notes to those panning him. He merely fumed at them in private. Sting berated the reviews of *The Soul Cages* as 'the revenge of the nerds'. He told a friend in Highgate that 'one of the reasons [the press] hate me is because I'm better than them'. His own revenge was the four houses and his cash in the bank. He referred to them often, with the anxiety, part justified, of someone who feared they could go just as fast as they'd come.

As he aged, Sting became increasingly a patriarchal figure, insisting on certain rights. Having a cloistered view of work, he demanded hours of privacy. Especially in a home teeming with children, he was apt to retreat to his boathouse or the Captain's Room, an oak-panelled haven named after a nautical ex-squire. Even when not writing, recording or trotting the globe, he always measured the distance between himself and regular parents. 'I'm not a normal father,' he said. 'I'm like a sailor. I'm here twenty-four hours, and then I'm away.' His growing family made him less compulsive about touring and more prone to relax. But, even at home in Wiltshire or Highgate, space was a concept he valued highly: space to read, meditate or, as he said, 'bug out'. He liked absolute quiet; his children wanted what their schoolmates and friends had – a normal pipeline to the outside world through, at least, TV. He also had an image of how they should grow up, as he said in 1996. 'The kids know they're privileged and that there's a responsibility which goes with privilege. You can't escape that. I've also told them, don't assume that whatever money I have is yours. I have long arguments with my ten-year-old about this. He says, "You've got plenty of money." I say, "Yes, but it's mine. I'm going to spend it all before I die" . . . I'm trying to get him out of the trap of thinking that he's a rich kid and he can just waste his life.' Styler had a similar take when her elder daughter once sneered at her grandfather's home as 'a doll's house'. Both parents expected graft, self-reliance and 'normality' within what was possible for a millionaire's brood – all as part of their strategy not to spoil their family. They set a good example. Sting may have been a coddled rock star to the outside world, but to Joe, Kate, Mickey, Jake and Coco he was also a plain-spoken, Geordie dad.

Thus Sting's sixteen-year-old, shelving his rock ambitions, would start college in Boston; Kate Sumner shuttled evenly between her parents; his three children with Styler went to the Church of England school in Salisbury. Sting's son Jake was treated successfully for dyslexia. A friend recalls fondly how genial and proud their father was, and how his affection grew in the years after his own parents died. Sting would frequently tell his sons, ' "Right now, I'm missing my dad" . . . I suppose I'm telling them they should appreciate me while I'm here.' He also worked hard to right the wrongs of his own upbringing. Sting was, in his unde-monstrative way, a doting parent. He kept the sprawling house-hold together, even as his need for solitude grew. He was a friend and playmate, a protective elder brother more than a Victorian morality figure, someone who arranged tour dates as best he could around school outings and breaks. Even as he remained essentially a private man, one who didn't bare his soul lightly, he sought out the basic familial joys. It took an act of will to scale down if not vanquish his furies and his own need for reinvention; especially for the son of Ernie Sumner. Sting was a model father.

As a struggling rocker he'd been uptight – 'like a clenched fist', said Copeland – prone to manipulating people's antagonisms more than appealing to their good. By 1993 the bratty neo-punk persona had long given way to that of a smoothie. With a few rare exceptions, Sting put down his cudgels. The endless loop of vanity and insecurity led him to try and convert, not rubbish, his critics: partly from the key need to ingratiate himself; partly from age. As Adler says, 'By the time I met him, he was wise, considerate, good company,' animated by a desire to 'do right by his friends and family' and a serenity that seemed natural. His *ex cathedra* pronouncements gave way to wonder-working powers of persuasion. This trait reflected, in another musician's view, a simple truth: Sting had chilled.

Some of this maturity and easygoing charm shone through in the music. *Ten Summoner's Tales* (a cross between Chaucer and a pun on Sting's surname) was released in March 1993. All soaring vocals and shimmering, radio-friendly MOR, it was the perfect résumé of Sting's genius, fifty per cent Police punch, fifty per cent solo-career craftsmanship, and no lachrymose lyrics about death. Miles would tell reporters that there'd been a plan to 'talk less about the new LP than about *Soul Cages* so that the public and reviewers won't have any pre-conceptions'. From the title on, Sting himself stressed the joys of story-telling. 'I didn't really want to write about me, to excavate another trauma,' he said. 'I just wanted to have fun.' In practice, that meant indulging Sting's gift for diverse, eclectic tunes that raged woozily between blues, funk, rock, country and soul. The days of whine and poses gave way to a pop classic. *Ten Summoner's Tales* was brilliantly inventive, even by the lofty standards of an artist who went from playing subversive punk-reggae to tinkering with jazz to writing funereal dirges within a decade. The tracks themselves were marvels of stylistic sprawl, yet surprisingly pithy and self-contained. Sting's all-weather mode never failed to honour a strong hook. As Jon Pareles of the *New York Times* wrote, 'no other Top Ten contender is so fond of odd meters or mid-song shifts of scene'. Hugh Padgham was also struck by the album's sweep. 'Sting writes these things with weird time signatures . . . It's always tempting for him to try new roads and discover things and people as he goes.' Such lyrical and musical ramblings could be a recipe for disaster, but *Tales* managed the feat of being organic, whole and fully fluent. Sting's catchy voice had never sounded better.

The album's stand-out track and first single found Sting fusing mainstream appeal and his creative muse. 'If I Ever Lose My Faith In You' revisited the scene of 'Spirits In The Material World' and the other sub-Koestlerian rants on *Ghost in the Machine*. The melody was slight but stately. It was the vocal, rather than tricky playing or studio alchemy, that made 'Faith' an indelible pop song, the delivery turning the trite into the transcendent. Along with a video rife with Arthurian-type jousting, flaming torches, jesters and keeps – sappy and pompous on paper, but deftly setting off the tune – it was a major smash. It also won Sting another Grammy.

From there *Ten Summoner's Tales* thought locally but acted globally, offering homespun yarns on hearth and home with a predilection for wacky, crossbred tunes. Thus 'Love Is Stronger Than Justice' matched funk with a countrified, touch-of-twang chorus; 'Fields Of Gold', Sting's paean to his new home, in the same teary-eyed tradition as *Soul Cages'* 'Why Should I Cry For You?', was a winning mix of Spanish guitar, churchy singing, sleek bass and swirling pipes. All the best tracks on *Tales* shared this sense of breezy gamut-running. Despite the varied emotional landscape, the album was never nebulous. Requited or semi-requited love was the key. It was when Sting took the short stroll from blues to R&B that things soared.

Nowhere was the formula more gloriously evident than 'Heavy Cloud No Rain'. As well as a generous beat-per-minute count, the song shared the disco groove of 'We'll Be Together', along with a lyric evoking the mystic easy-listening of Sting's friend Peter Gabriel. 'She's Too Good For Me' was akin to a 'Twist And Shout', call-and-response chorus with nursery rhymes; 'Seven Days' like one of Joe Jackson's early-'80s Broadway skits, but more so. The crafty, across-the-board allure of those six songs made *Tales* the best-rounded album of Sting's career. This wasn't music bound by genre but a rich, mercurial sound full of heat, heart and a love of the pun. And the best was yet to come.

After the bluesy snarl of 'Saint Augustine In Hell', Sting slyly reprised his own 'Be Still My Beating Heart' on 'It's Probably Me'. Here the point again became the ironic, neatly turned lyric, with its grudging oath of allegiance: 'If there's one guy, just one guy / Who'd lay down his life for you and die / It's hard to say it / I hate to say / But it's probably me.' This was soundtrack raised to a high art. 'Shape Of My Heart', used in the outro of the film *Leon*, took the same idea into the stratosphere. At a time when he could have played it safe, selling his poet's soul for more FM-friendly rock, Sting opted for a concept album whose key text – dry musings on human attachments – unfolded gradually in the second half. The closing salvo came in 'Something The

Boy Said' and the contagious 'Nothing 'Bout Me', Sting's defiant cocked snook at his biographers, set to a jumping-jive, swing beat. It was the final flick of the comb, the ultimate dab of the clothes-brush, a sort of thematic 'Fuckit'. Sting was loved by some, admired by many, but he remained semi-detached from most. His mixture of charm and seduction, froideur and tart wit was the album's stock in trade. Something for everyone made it a hit.

Tales was accented by toney, if not slick, production (perfectly tuned for Sting's voice, says Adler, unlike their later collaboration on *The Glory of Gershwin*); and frenzied hype. There were fulsome spreads in *Q* and the *Sunday Times*. Sting performed on *Saturday Night Live* and even hammed through *Top of the Pops*, before hitting the road and coming down with laryngitis. *Tales'* videos, in which the swords-and-sorcery fad of 'Mad About You' became a fetish, all went into heavy rotation. A live radio hook-up to the Albert Hall would be the highest-rated rock broadcast of the year. Above all, the album established the terms on which Sting would be reviewed, and revered, in his mid-forties. He was a man apart, a star and a survivor, and most critics paid court.

As usual, some of the headier touches that endeared Sting to fans made others cringe: his penchant for metaphor and cryptic allusions; his versatility; his striving to round every base. A few fringe hacks didn't just dislike *Ten Summoner's Tales* – they wished bad juju on it. Most fellow musicians loved the album. Mick Jagger, Eric Clapton, Tina Turner and Bob Geldof regularly included it in their 'best-of' lists. Even Kurt Cobain, prince of grunge and unwitting spokesman for a generation, liked *Tales*. The public joined the consensus, lifting it into the British chart for sixty weeks. With the exception of a few obscurely positioned sneers, even the press agreed. It was Sting's finest hour.

Early in 1993, Sting and his band began to gear up for a tour that would graze twenty countries in just over a year. The rehearsals went through countless changes, delays and shifts of emphasis. Running as a throughline was the matter of Sting's voice. Although he got through two TV shows in February, laryngitis forced him to pull out of warm-up dates in Florida. Instead he made a cameo at his annual rainforest gala in New York, went on, raw-throated, in France, Holland and Germany, and opened a season of six nights at the Albert Hall. One result of Sting's guttural problems was that, for several weeks, he rarely spoke except when spoken to; another was that, live, he concentrated on singing rather than interweaving his sermonistic views on life. Being Sting, he still made himself heard. As critics said, he was miked so closely you could hear him inhaling before starting a phrase, his voice seemed too low, and he slurred and sped up his best songs. This, added to amnesiac neglect of all but a few Police hits, made for mixed reviews. What was remarkable about the shows, though, wasn't the vocals, but the pacing and rhythms. The band stretched out in several frisky improvisations. Their virtuosity astutely moved the centre of gravity away from the woefully grunted lyrics to the spirit of the music itself. Ironically, the vocal lumps showed how sleek the songs were.

Patrick Deuchar, chief executive of the Albert Hall, like others in the business, was wary of Sting. He'd heard the stories about cracked ribs in The Police and read the profiles skewering him as cold and self-centred. The very virtues that were the soul of Sting carried the potential for his being a tough nut. Last-minute hassles due to the laryngitis had seemed to confirm his fame for being 'awkward'. Deuchar, in short, expected anything of Sting but the 'warm, sincere guy' who sat with him in the artists' bar discussing his family and band with 'a total lack of bullshit'. Much the same quiet charm was at work on his colleagues. Sting asked Larry Adler to guest at his London shows. The older man was so moved by the offer, and his wild reception by the crowd, he made a speech that turned into a mutual devotion spree. 'I'm too old to have kids,' he told his new friend, 'but if I adopt one, it'll probably be you.' 'Thanks, Dad,' said Sting.

Six months later, Adler began to make plans for his eightieth birthday party. Placido Domingo, Isaac Stern and Elton John all agreed to appear on his tribute album to the Gershwins. Out of the blue, Sting rang to ask if he, too, could sing. Again, says Adler, 'that was typical . . . He took time out from a schedule that would have knackered Henry Kissinger. Generosity was Sting's strong suit.' Perhaps even stronger was his aversion to doing the 'done' thing, such as re-forming The Police. Sting liked to act on his own whim, and, if possible, as a jolt. Then, in his uniquely spontaneous, affable way, he was at his best, and the warmth of friendliness he conveyed was unforgettable. It was an attitude that chimed with his deep love of independence, with his hate of being ordered or even 'expected' to do something, of having his goodwill abused in any way.

Along with his tenor rasp and new Fender bass, Sting then made the bravest move of a solo career known for quixotism. He played warm-up for the Grateful Dead. The stadium tour round America not only allowed him to utter the rubric 'Here's one off the new album' to 80,000 fans at a time, it also brought him to a crisis with his manager. Long used to his client being at the top of any bill he graced, Miles was aghast that he'd consider the 'no-hoper job' of vying with programme-sellers and hotdog-vendors for punters' attention. Others interpreted this ploy of Sting's as sheer arbitrariness. His own comment confirmed it. 'I want to see this Deadhead phenomenon. I want to see it first-hand.' In the event Sting avoided the fate of most support acts. His mini-sets were marvels of power and punch, the Heads dancing giddily to 'Roxanne' and offering the kind of rowdy whoops usually associated with a Bon Jovi gig.

From there Sting re-crossed the Atlantic, whistlestopped Turkey and Greece, performed with a hundred-piece orchestra for shows in Belgium and Holland, trawled Europe, revisited the Albert Hall, jagged between Japan and Taiwan, crisscrossed Asia, barnstormed Australia, zigzagged through America, blitzed the Gulf and sprinted to a finish in South Africa. By autumn 1994, Sting was back in the chart. His *Fields of Gold* anthology not only capitalized on his wanderings, it reminded people how good the songs had been since he lit out from The Police.

Sting knew that platinum discs and perpetual touring weren't the only means by which his career bloomed. He was friend and backstop to a bevvy of other artists, too. In January 1992 he'd recorded Elton John's 'Come Down In Time' for the compilation album *Two Rooms*. A year later, his collaboration with Clapton enjoyed a new lease of life as *Lethal Weapon 3* made the trip from cinema to video. Meanwhile, another one-off project, Sting's narration of *Peter and the Wolf*, was animated with latex puppets on American TV. It was a winning romp in *Spitting Image* vein, blending Prokofiev with end-of-the-pier humour. Sting survived being seen as a cravat-wearing midget, a cartoon caricature of himself he laughed at 'louder than anyone'.

One of the weirdest episodes of Sting's search for new horizons was his involvement with Luciano Pavarotti. This singular friendship had its roots in a mutual love of the rainforest and other causes. In September 1992 the Sumners attended a concert by the great tenor at Covent Garden. The event was richly symbolic of Sting's career as a whole: as he slid from his black car into the Opera House he could peer up Bow Street to the boarded-up club where, a lifetime before, he'd bawled 'Fall Out' into a gale of punk spittle. Affable and attentive, he then signed autographs and chatted for an hour after the show. Among the questions was one asking if he'd ever re-form The Police. He had 'no plan', said Sting. In fact, he made a principle of planlessness.

That night in London led to a joint appearance at Pavarotti's charity fundraiser at Modena. Sting, introduced as 'the ace British rocker', contributed 'It's Probably Me', duetted with both Pavarotti and Zucchero, then returned for the ensemble 'La Donna è mobile'. There was a ritual exchange of plaudits and gifts. Sting, said Pavarotti, 'carried off Verdi with style, [though] he thought he'd make a fool of himself'. Mutual family visits followed to Tuscany and Lake House. Pavarotti gave his protégé an antique music stand; he agreed to sing at the 1994 rainforest gala. The opera star followed down a line from Gil Evans and Larry Adler as greats of another era, and other genres, for whom Sting became a kind of mascot.

The all-things-to-all-people appeal of Sting, George Michael and James Taylor filled Carnegie Hall to the rafters in March 1993. Later in the year the breathtakingly dire *Demolition Man* meant a new recording of the hoary Police track, and a video – in which, ditching his Camelot fantasies, Sting reprised some of the meticulously orchestrated mayhem of 'Synchronicity II' – trailing the film. In November 1993 he joined Rod Stewart and Bryan Adams to croon 'All My Love', a hit single and soundtrack for a remake of *The Three Musketeers*. Sting would take on anything, and most of what he did, even off the cuff, was sinfully good. A forlorn few on *Melody Maker* still slated him, but a new critical respect was bringing up the rear, fast.

Sting then sang 'Nice Work If You Can Get It' on the *Glory of Gershwin* anthology. Of this Adler says simply, 'The track's arrangements worked against him. They drowned Sting out. Plans for him to do a second song were dropped.' His annual gala again packed Carnegie Hall, and raised a million for the rainforest, early in 1994. He then got a call from Hollywood, asking him to play guitar on Julio Iglesias's version of 'Fragile'. And so it went: he seemed to pick his collaborations not for their challenge or monetary rewards (Iglesias paid him with a case of wine), but for their sheer breadth. If you wanted a pop star who could sing opera, lurch from a random mixture of funk and maudlin balladry and simultaneously cover a thirties standard, before resuming his day job as a polymath rocker, Sting was for you.

Precisely because of his catholicism, Sting won high marks – sometimes grudging, but sincere – from most of his workmates. He also conveyed, in an oddly vulnerable way, a bottomless need for love. He still cared about the intellectual kudos of those he admired. Although he could be acid-tongued and flip, he was solicitous toward people he thought worthy of friendship. As he got older, the passion of Sting's efforts to turn cynics betrayed a genuine warmth as well as a gnawing insecurity. One cause of his willingness to fly thousands of miles to attend dinners or make speeches was a creditable urge to 'put something back' into the industry. One result was that Sting spent his time garnering laurels, acknowledging praise and accepting spoils as much as making music.

Thus Sting collected his fifth Grammy, for the 'Soul Cages' track, in February 1992. Two months later he was a sunny presence at the Novello awards in London. In September ASCAP, the American publishing firm, named Sting 'songwriter of the year'. None of these sideshows marred his work on *Ten Summoner's Tales* – they may even have spurred him. But it was a fact that Sting would periodically, as a musician says, 'piss off to Manhattan', leaving menial tasks like overdubbing to be done by others.

With *Tales* a new appreciation began, one that hoisted Sting to classic status (alongside Clapton, Elton John and Phil Collins as rock's 'great averages'), but then moved on from him as a relic. Nineteen ninety-two and ninety-three were the years when Nirvana and the ugly sounds of Seattle blurred the punk–mainstream divide. Sting clung on not just as a working musician, but a survivor. His longevity and high-stakes charity work had given him a charismatic sheen. At forty-one he was a sort of monument, admired not only for his hits, but for having lasted. He had the tunes *and* the crossover fame *and* the past. Some of these factors applied to other rockers. There was nobody, though, to whom all of them applied, and applied simultaneously. Increasingly, the trophies and gongs began to treat Sting not as a pop star but a legend.

Vox, for one, would include him in the title's all-time golden-greats group. The London Symphony Orchestra conferred that stigma of the fossil rocker, an orchestral tribute album of Sting's songs. His activism and willingness to tackle causes brought their own high rewards (if not yet the Nobel Peace Prize one credulous fan sought on his behalf). Sting's brilliance, creativity and vaunted politics were, after all, the coin of the realm in academe. In November 1992 he received an honorary doctorate from the University of Northumbria. Sting's citation spoke of his 'governing artistic niche' and 'role in world ecology'. Eighteen months later, it was the turn of Boston's Berklee College of Music. As a metaphor for social assimilation – the university dropout waving his diploma at photographers – the scene was classic. The key image was, again, one of survival. Sting was praised for having endured the fickle musical trends of twenty years. More such plaudits followed. It could only be a matter of time before rock's Hall of Fame fell to the bandwagon again rolling under the banner and flag of Stingola.

Meanwhile, as *Ten Summoner's Tales* led the chart, the industry remobilized to heap honours on him. Pundits now rushed to fête Sting. He was one of ten winners of the 1993 Mercury prizes in London. The following week he was nominated, and performed at the MTV awards. *Tales* went platinum that same day. In February 1994 he scooped up a hatful of Grammys, including Best Male Pop Singer and Best Pop Vocal Performance. (He also won in the categories of Best Engineered Album and Best Video.) He was Best Male Artist at the 1994 Brits. Sting then pocketed a Novello for 'If I Ever Lose My Faith In You'. Later that spring, he was lauded for his work in the rainforest and for special services to the music business. According to the Nordoff-Robbins organizers, who honoured him in June, Sting was proof that 'artistic maturity and mass popularity aren't mutually exclusive'. This latter aspect of his fame caused even the Department of Trade to cite him as a 'nonpareil exporter of musical arts' to the world.

The recognition changed Sting's life, and he had to come to terms with the differences. As a cultural icon, he found all kinds of incursions on his time. All the same, many of them proved novel sport. Sting's tendency to 'piss off to Manhattan' had always been done in style. Now his progress was little less than imperial. When Sting flew to New York he went by Concorde or chartered jet; limos met him on arrival; whole floors of hotels, under the inevitable aliases, were booked to ensure privacy. Nineteen ninety-four found Sting treated as a dignitary. He graduated from being merely a superstar and became a personage. *Fields of Gold* was one beneficiary of his new clout. The greatest-hits collection went straight in at the top.

Not everything changed for the better. Middle-aged, Sting was still fit, supple, with eyes and an edgy, cocky smile both between rugged and grim. He also had the kind of mind that allows the act to be followed by the thought. Sting made his move, and found the explanations and excuses later. Even at this stage, he had a near messianic belief that all his enemies could be converted. He was immovably convinced of his own charm. He was also a wheedler, one who knew how to stroke people's vanity, fuel their egos, play them off, and share droll put-downs of mutual friends. Not a natural socializer, he'd long taught himself to meet and mingle, and learnt how to handle starstruck guests. Sting was a flatterer. Even then, Copeland's gibe that 'he not only hates humanity, but every human within the species' came to mind. Sting's fabled ambivalence was an engine that never rested. 'You're not going to get anything out of me,' he told prying fans. They got very little. According to one woman, 'watching his attempt at seduction was as unnerving as having a pit-bull lick your hand'.

Beneath Sting's spiky façade, of course, lay a broad swath of insecurity. His unabated desire to win friends and influence people – almost a pathological need – proved that neither power nor wealth had cured the deep vulnerability inside the milkman's boy from Wallsend. So, too, did his sensitivity to attack, his obsessiveness and ego. Much of Sting's petulance was mere world-wariness. 'He was magnetic but withdrawn. Shy like a wild animal,' says the same woman. As he hit his forties, Sting worked hard to replace the previous air of jagged rage with one of glassy civility. By 1999 his key mood was evolving from paranoia to an unassuming and even self-deprecating warmth. Sting was still proud, but he was willing to take a detached, modest view of his work. He also appeared to make peace with his fame. In interviews he came across as a sane, self-aware professional who stressed the long haul. 'I don't have any more ambitions,' he announced. 'I don't need any more awards; I just want to carry on doing what I'm doing. I have this little margin that's mine, and there's a certain [joy] in accepting that, because I'd like to be a singer when I'm sixty.' He harboured a deepening sense of endurance. 'My life simply isn't over yet ... at least it's my intention to carry on for many years,' Sting told this writer.

The other side of longevity was ageing. Though enjoying generally good health, Sting still suffered all the tedious mid-life rituals. Witness his myopic scowl and chronic frown, his eyesight had begun to fail. His hearing, after years of exposure to pain-threshold noise, was indifferent. At about the time of *Ten Summoner's Tales*, he was diagnosed with tinnitus, a faint ringing in the ears that he claimed was neither serious nor career-threatening. He was losing hair. To his credit, Sting turned these mild ineptitudes into virtues. Walking his estate with his rimless glasses and cane, heavily belted against the cold, the effect gave him a curiously grizzled air; like one of the brooding tramps in a Stevenson novel. It was also the perfect look for his surroundings. Arcadia was something he took to like the stage. Above all, Lake House was where he gave his most human performances. The place not only relaxed and grounded him, it had the added bonus of broadening his values. He liked, for instance, to grow his own food there. Organic vegetables, beehives and cows meant he was virtually self-sufficient. 'That's important,' he said. 'Being able to feed yourself is real wealth.'

Sting also counted his family as a blessing. He stayed faithful to a code which treated his brood as friends. No matter how he seemed to strain traditional Newcastle *mores* of graft and respect, he remained basically loyal to an enlightened view of children, fitting them into roles which allowed them air to breathe. Sting appearing on the Saturday-morning show *Going Live* made no sense in terms of commercialism. But it made good sense in terms of fatherhood: a day out for Kate, Mickey and Jake, all of whom joined him for lunch in the BBC canteen. Sting even tolerated and encouraged his eldest son, now mingling his studies with apprenticeship in the punk band Australian Nightmare. Truly it seemed, as Joe spewed rock and grungy *noir* in the cell of a London club, that the wheel had come full turn; and Sting could only grit his teeth, or, to be fair, smile.

For years his own songs had been rife with seedy pleasures, and Sting retained a healthy love of sex well into mid-life. As well as the print kind, he enjoyed film erotica. He patronized topless bars. The owner of the Pure Platinum club in New York would speak of Sting as 'the best tipper we've ever had'. He befriended exotic dancers. He even took in an S&M nightspot, 'out of curiosity', he said: 'It was just people hung on the walls being whipped . . . It was interesting, but I didn't go back.' Sting's two sides, the country squire and the pop plutocrat, each had their rites, manners and codes of dress. He alternated between a sweaty, ragged jacket or coat and Versace leather: the clothes in one, his reshaped persona; in the other, his trade as a rocker. His favourite boutique was Browns in South Molton Street, Mayfair. Here he could buy both sets of garb, the work boots and the silk loon pants, the sartorial yin–yang of his life.

Sting also continued his relentless exercise regime long into his forties. As well as jogging and aerobics, he practised yoga under the tuition of Danny Paradise, a world-travelling guru introduced by Dominic Miller. Within a year, Sting was speaking of his daily routine in quasi-mystic terms: 'There's a development in my thinking. The deeper you get into yoga, the more you realize, yes, it is a spiritual practice . . . I feel there has to be a higher level of compassion, of understanding, than merely a human one. It's embodied in all of us . . . The Godhead, or whatever you want to call it . . . I think that, in deep meditation, I've learnt to trust in the power of love.' He went on to disown some of his more lurid advocacy of Tantric sex. But he was happy to discuss nauli and bandhas, Krishnamurti and the whole yogi ritual. It was no passing yen. Sting even consulted Issak Matthai, the celebrity holistic healer briefly famous for treating the Duchess of York. He instructed the singer in his own motto, 'Learn to give, not to take. Learn to serve, not to rule.' Nowadays, before he went on stage, Sting warmed up not with drugs and groupies, but with chanting and drills. The band did a minimum of ninety minutes' yoga before each show, bringing communal good vibes, if at least one muttered comment from the ranks.

Cynics who saw Sting as gradually yielding to new-age kookiness would have found proof to feed on at Lake House. He believed in crop circles. By 1992 his obsession with ghosts had hardened into the conviction that he was being visited by UFOs. Reg Presley reports that his friend was 'spellbound' by the subject. 'One day Sting was making a video up the side of a hill . . . He looked down and saw what he thought was a Christmas tree, until it shot off at 100 mph past his head.' There were a number of unexplained summer lights seen in the Wiltshire sky, as well as odd markings on the neighbouring land. Those who thought that Sting might have sampled his ayahuasca tea before such sightings would have been wrong: he was 'quite level-headed and sane' about the phenomena, says Presley. The two men shared a theory that some form of high energy was being passed through the cornfields on their estates. Sting liked to walk slowly round, listening to the buzz the crops seemed to make. When the ground was dry, he might bend down and put his ear to the turf. 'I hear music all the time,' he said. 'Sometimes it drives me totally crazy. I live in an aural world. It's never totally empty.'

Sting's journey from punk thug into an eccentric moonraker was partly a result of sheer age. It showed his aversion to cleaving to a fixed line of thought. But it was also linked to an innate kindness and maturity. He was one pop star who answered begging letters, gave help to struggling bohos and money to the rag-toting merchants who approached at red lights. He was also the most articulate member of a profession not short of glib verbosity. Because he harboured the dark fear that many of his giddier pronouncements on art, politics and ecology wouldn't command popular or critical support, he tended to be defensive about his role as savant-beefcake. 'I've been called everything under the sun – God, they called me pompous just because I've read Proust,' he said. 'I don't think I'm a genius, but I also don't think I'm a shit . . . I'm not looking for praise or blame.'

Sting continued to deny pretension charges with a vehemence strong enough to shake his whole body. He worked hard at being 'an entertainer', just as so many entertainers strove to be rock stars. As it was, the cameos on *Saturday Night Live* and the rest were, at base, a bid to blindside his critics, most of whom joined *Melody Maker*'s thesis that Sting was a humour-free zone. He could still be seriously high-flown. Some seized on his various outings with Pavarotti. Others thought his most bizarre trips were in his own head. Sting himself liked to tell a story of having climbed an Aztec pyramid in Mexico. This trek to physical and spiritual wellness occupied him for several hours. 'And when I got to the top,' he told the *New York Times*, 'there was this guy sitting in a lotus position, facing the view. Suddenly, without even turning his head, he announced, "You will find peace within, Sting."' Inflating the story, which even he knew sounded unlikely, the singer would add, 'He seemed to be expecting me.'

Sting's primary tactic with cynics, especially as he got older, was dignified silence. 'My life would have to be written a long way in the future by someone close enough to have known me – a very small group of people,' he told this author. 'He doesn't give himself easily,' says Styler. 'You'll still know nothing 'bout me,' Sting goadingly sang. Like a sorcerer's incantation, the coy phrases worked. Most pundits were reduced to looting the archives or rehashing lies from the tabloids. Yet anyone queasy about invading Sting's 'anonymity-obscurity' could take heart from the overdesigned liner photos, notes and lyric sheets that turned his albums into small books. What one biographer calls the 'arch-fraudulence' of Sting's Garbo pose could equally be interpreted as a mocking kind of jeer, a 'catch me if you can'. According to this school, his reticence was a come-on.

Sting's every utterance to press and public claimed total indifference to his image. He professed not to care what people said, yet made it a policy to read his cuttings and flay his critics. From 'So Lonely' through 'King Of Pain', Sting's songs had had one key element in common: their author was anxious, even overanxious, to be loved. And very nearly from the start, he had been loved – by the fans, if not the media for whom artistic growth and popularity were at odds. Even in the late 1990s, as he consciously pared down his vanities, Sting was still good copy for the 'stuck-up git' school of journalism. Typical was an item in the *Mirror*: 'Yet another example of Sting's pretentiousness has come to my attention. When asked on computer on-line system AOL which artist he'd most like to work with, he replied: "Leonardo da Vinci."'

At the sharper end of the scale, Sting's detractors liked to slag him as part of a manipulative, vain and greedy world of pop celebrities, their conveniently elastic scruples, and their deathless ability to patronize those who made them big in the first place. This tendency reached its nadir when, in September 1994, Sting played three dates in Israel. 'I think it's important to be sensitive to the complexities of political situations. I'm glad things are happening in the way they are happening, so I'm here,' he told the world. His troubling capacity to rationalize his every move, and then define it with godlike pomp, also found expression on tour in South Africa. In fact, his main grounds for having avoided such places in the past were neither moral nor ethical, but because of practical hassles. With The Police, principle had always come second to strategic qualms. Sting, like a distorting mirror, warped the truth. No one who had played shows in Chile could wear their virtue as a halo. Sting's classic policy of embargoing rogue states met its climactic test not in the nineties, but ten years before.

On the vexed question of compassion fatigue, he noted: 'I've got it about musical events for causes. They drive me nuts ... Like everybody in the business, I get calls every day about some worthy event. I'm bored with the idea ... I'm bored with it, the public's bored with it.'

The interesting thing about this is that Sting said it in 1989. His own reaction against kneejerk activism set in early on. Even so, Sting still rode a stable of hobby-horses. There was his work for the rainforest, as well as a glut of *ad hoc* projects and performances. In late 1993 he played a free concert in Boston in aid of the Walder Woods charity. Next month he was at the MTV 'Rock the Vote' gig in New York. Early in 1994 Sting headlined the 'Bushfire Benefit' at Sydney football ground. Even at this late stage, he was wont to take pleas for help seriously. In most cases, he still displayed a natural eagerness to play, even when it didn't redound to the glory of Sting. He was generous with both time and money.

He did, over the years, grow more fussy about how he gave them away. By 1994 Sting's rainforest galas shunned quantity in favour of high-rent quality. That was the year Pavarotti, Elton John and Whitney Houston joined him at Carnegie Hall. Closely linked to Sting's craving for fewer and better causes was his commitment to Aids research. He may have missed the Freddie Mercury tribute, the Concert for Life, but that was the sole set-piece he failed to make. In June 1992 Sting performed at an Aids fundraiser in Milan. He quietly gave funds to the Terence Higgins Trust. Late in 1994 he flew back overnight from Johannesburg to be at the Stonewall gay-rights benefit at the Albert Hall. Sting animated the proceedings by duetting with Melissa Etheridge, before stripping off his shirt to sighs from his female fans and wolf-calls from the males. He starred at another Aids extravaganza, this one in New York, in January 1995. To Sting's credit, even at a time when his career assumed regal dimensions, he also managed to be a model constituency celebrity. He was particularly acute at making himself known around Salisbury. According to one neighbour, 'He was always at his nicest here, whether dropping off jars of his honey or giving you a lift to the shops. He talked to you as if you were no better, and no worse, than him.' In 1993, Sting joined a group protesting development plans at Stonehenge, a mile north of Lake House. The local church was among the many recipients of his charity.

Sting's world-view was basically apolitical in any concerted sense; but deeply political from the personal angle that he believed in self-expression, in freedom as a given. In his pursuit of this moral or body politic, he had no time for bigots, fascists or the Thatcher government. He voted Labour, though as an arch individualist, he opposed many, if not most, efforts to meddle in the free market. He saw life, civic and human experience in atomistic terms: not as part of state or party, but closer to Buddhist law, each man in his dharmic armour doing battle with life on his and its terms.

Put simply, that meant making a difference. In lyric after lyric, Sting transformed a personal and political dilemma into a moral tale, making individuals count more than fanaticism. He had a shrewd hunch about global trends, and an unshakeable belief that man's lot was to take a stand. Here Sting himself scored well. His work for the rainforest had drawn the jeers, howls and catcalls of the mob. Yet the national park was demarcated. It existed: seventeen Indian tribes enjoyed life there. Sting found the more idealistic aspect of the liberal ethic a weakness in terms of forcing change on a reluctant world. He preferred the pragmatic way of graft, direct action, protest, anything that jolted the torpid and dead into life. If activism was judged by the simple accountancy of change, then Sting was the politician's politician. He got results.

That wasn't to say he enjoyed or expected mutual goodwill with all his constituents. Indeed, fellow aid-workers found that Sting's was one Foundation where independent thought was prized and sycophancy wasn't. He liked to be challenged on substance, and he enjoyed a good row. Sting's policy on self-assertion had already led, in part, to the bust-up with Dutilleux. Now, in 1993, Chief Raoni went on the attack. 'The Brazilian

Indians don't need Sting,' he said. 'It would be better if we forgot him.' The *Daily Mail* published a story claiming that both men had had a falling-out over 'vision' – the eco-equivalent of 'musical differences'. Sting himself was scathing about the Xingú. 'They're always trying to fleece you. They see the white man only as a good source of earning money . . . I was very naïve and thought I could save the world selling T-shirts for the cause. I'm leaving behind my days in the jungle.'

In fact, once various problems of context and quotation had been sorted out, Sting and Raoni reconciled. The Foundation's work continued. Sting, though, gradually reduced his personal commitment to the tribesmen. His visits to Brazil were no longer the spiritual odysseys of old. When Sting was in Rio in May and December 1994 he was interested not in going native, but in jogging on Ipanema beach and dining at Satyrico, a five-star restaurant on Copacabana. He kept a hawkish eye on the women. He also took the opportunity to renew relations with the Uniao do Vegetal and their ritualistic tea. Reversing the whole original pretext for drugs, this had nothing to do with decadence or escape, Sting said: just the reverse. 'You're forced to face issues in your life which you'd normally reject or hide . . . principally the fact that you're going to die.'

Despite this gloomy prognosis, with the boyish glee of the Club Med tripper and the leer of a middle-aged rake, Sting revelled in the attention of the girls on Ipanema. A fellow guest at the Palace Hotel remembers him 'on the terrace, with that flinty, "don't fuck with me" look of his, clocking the talent'. Julia Levy would recall Sting in conference with a female fan clad in bikini briefs 'the shape and size of dental floss'. While there was no breath of anything underhand in these seaside forays – and Styler herself joined him there – the general tone suggested a man far from the ascetic do-gooder of lore. Sting, in short, seemed not to care quite so much any more. At times friends were left with the impression that the former king of the jungle, as a journalist says, 'didn't give a monkey's'.

It was an idyllic life, but it cloaked a restless artistic temperament. On *Ten Summoner's Tales*, Sting had come close to his hero Proust's 'privileged moment', when a kind of frenzy takes over. His description of his state when he wrote – 'music just flows' – had some of the qualities usually linked with a religious vision.

Sting was a sort of transmitter and translator of the melodies constantly buzzing in his head. He couldn't completely give up composing any more than David Bowie could give up wearing dresses. Some of the best songs on *Tales* were a result of automatic writing, created under a spell and therefore outside his conscious control. That didn't mitigate against Sting's careful, conscientious polishing of the material. His genius lay in the infinite taking of pains. Even at a time when he could have afforded not to, he still spent long hours in the studio, working the tunes to a clean, slick finish. He made decisions at every stage. He loved to play live.

Sting began another British tour in January 1994. After dates in Birmingham, Sheffield and Cardiff, he took up residence at the Albert Hall. His four-night stand was well received. His home fans took him almost as seriously as he'd once taken himself. Sting opened his London season standing, stage front, scraping and bowing, flinging out his arms while holding a red rose between his teeth. Somehow the actual gigs never quite lived up to the entrance. Sting then flew to Japan, Australia and America before hosting a raucously incarnated bash in Santiago, Chile, on 27 March. As with the recorded work, there was a sense in which he seemed to crank out these sets on auto-pilot, securing his ovation with a glib professionalism: even his flip, suave asides sounded rehearsed. It wasn't that – as some sneered – Sting 'didn't mind'. Concerts as tightly blocked and routined as his didn't flow uncontrolled from the ozone. Sting himself felt transported, and part of that feeling came from the ecstasy of purging personal and family demons with music that bypassed the head to reach the soul (and getting paid millions to do it). He certainly minded.

Meanwhile, Sting excited his audience and made new fans with the inevitable greatest-hits medley, *Fields of Gold*. Elaborately wrapped – and bought in droves by those for whom CDs furnished a room – the set still possessed a precise, eye-of-the-needle imperative, to lure collectors with the dubious bait of two new tracks. 'When We Dance', recorded at Lake House in August 1994, was a ballad that, despite the touchy chorus, never quite scaled the food-chain to songhood. It came with an arresting video of Sting, in black, agitating his guitar on an all-white set. Though he slipped in and out of styles, humour was still his best shade. The second new cut, 'This Cowboy Song', was a hee-haw, would-be showstopper with, as yet, no show to stop. It, too, had a video – this one in

Blazing Saddles vein – that showed its soundtrack potential. Despite the stubborn refusal to 'bottle out' and play Vegas, one trait still distinguished Sting from his ageing rock peers: he was more settled, more centred, more loyal towards old and new friends. 'A big thank you to all the wonderful musicians I've worked with,' read the album's liner notes. 'God bless you all.' *Fields of Gold*, released in a blizzard of mixes and formats, wasn't only a public love-in for Sting's band, it was a critics' and fans' darling.

By and large, Sting enjoyed ever warmer and better press relations, even if *Melody Maker* and the *Sun* left him cold. Unsurprisingly, though he affected not to care, there was a good deal he didn't want aired; parts of his past life read like a soap opera and reverberated to no one's credit. If the tabloids had really loosed the hounds, they could have sniffed out drugs, drink, affairs, back-stabbing and perfidy. That would be for starters. They could have uncovered a moody, ambitious soul whose private life hadn't always fitted the public view of St Francis of Wallsend. Sting: 'I don't give a shit.' As it was, the press entirely missed his passion for crop circles, UFOs and psychic phenomena, yet zoomed in on his sex life. The upmarket titles still dwelt on Sting's love of his own voice, though they rightly bowed to his worldliness. As one pundit said, 'He seldom lets the conversation wander from the topic of Sting, but he's interested in the people around him.' And another: 'I've got a lot of time for him now. He clearly cares about mankind and all the chat isn't quite the self-promotion of old. These days, Sting even lets you finish a sentence.'

Still, he'd worked too hard for his enmity to convert all his foes. It's fair to say that, among a vocal minority, Sting wasn't just not liked, he was disliked. At bottom, he stood accused of cant, concealing the worst rock-star airs under a fragile veneer of altruism. There was always pathos in his protests to be a 'Geordie yobbo'. He travelled, for instance, in potentate style. In an unguarded moment, he once spoke of doing yoga in his garden 'with the staff all looking out'. That only hinted at the size of Sting's court. In interviews, his retinue – A&M tycoons, publicists, his minder-manager – positioned themselves strategically around the room, monitoring his movements with rapt awe. They chuckled as Sting joked and nodded gravely when he was serious. This sort of cravenness tended to be met by the noise of journalistic grinding of axes. Also widely slated was the 'preaching'; the rainforest and the rest; the dabblings with Jung and Koestler; the Versace wedding; the videos; and Sting's tendency to pout photogenically like a Page Three girl (with whom he shared a love of décolletage). Some of the photos sent out by his fan club flaunted the same topless pose of his glamour-victim pomp twenty years ago.

Most highbrow writers deferred to Sting as a creative genius, someone who'd vaulted musical styles for decades. By and large, he enjoyed this kind of puffery, filling out the time, as it did, when the songs wouldn't come. He had less truck with the lowbrows. But in a spurt of their own form of genius, they talked up Sting's sex drive. There were long stories about his 'astonishing technique' and 'five-hour staying power', once illustrated by photos of him romping in his jockstrap. That wasn't all. According to the *News of the World*, on his forty-second birthday Styler had 'thrilled' her husband by presenting him with a video featuring her lying on a bed dressed in pearls and a sheer black gown; shadowy figures could be seen pulling on their clothes in the background. Sting, the paper helpfully explained, was still curious about the 'dark side' of sex and often visited transvestite clubs. Somewhere between the two caricatures, the *Guardian*-reading guru and the priapic stud, a truth existed. Only the public, it seemed, could hold in its head simultaneously the ideas that Sting was a well-meaning man who liked to bare his breast; that he'd chosen to live a highly visible life; and that the price for this Faustian pact was his privacy.

One of the givens of Sting hagiography and hatchet-jobs alike is to see him as made up of separate parts that, somehow, fail to gel. Ironies have to be made to surface. In this view, Sting as musician, thinker, family man, campaigner and sexpot, even as farmer and country gent – all are pieces of a puzzle that defy a clean fit. The theory flounders, however, because then the creative spark seems to come from the ether. Sting does exist as a whole; all the parts do fit. The key lies in his whim to grow old gracefully, to extend his shelf-life and stay a nose ahead of extinction. Hence his periodic residencies at a Victorian concert hall; his gleeful mingling with Pavarotti and Julio Iglesias; his willingness to tackle the worlds of Verdi and Gershwin; above all his insistence that 'I like being offered jobs – I like to do journeyman work.' Sting, in other words, has managed to turn his gifts into practical ways of plying his trade and broadening his mind; and taking the risk that all this might pay off.

He wasn't, of course, the first rock star to branch out. But not many matched his pluralism; few retained core musical principles while lurching into new playgrounds; and none combined with fame and power such awareness of humanity and moral duty. On that score alone, Sting was unique.

While he was one of the most talked-about gods on Olympus, he was also one of the nicest. For all his entourage and rock-star baggage, he remained as approachable as a man in black shades can be. He frequently walked alone, for instance, through Highgate or Great Durnford. He was always ready with a quip and an autograph for fans. He never sank to forgetful hatred of the people who made him big to begin with. A woman who met him at Lake House (while noting that 'he casually looked me up and down, like a doctor') calls him 'sober, sane, down-to-earth, modest and self-mocking'. Mike Noble, Sting's old A&M friend, has 'fond memories' of a professional reunion in 1995–96. 'He was affable, kind, and all in all, a classic case of someone who got nicer as time went on. You can always shout "hi" at Sting across an airport and he'll shout back.'

The smooth running of Steerpike and the rest involved a lucrative mix of advances, royalties, stage fees, spin-offs, muscular cost-control and the cachet that came from one of rock's most marketable names. Early in 1993, Sting's management moved to Fulham Road, west London. From then on his personal hub would operate from Estate House, a pink-walled villa that, but for the Shell station opposite, could have graced a non-orthogonal village lapped by the Aegean. Miles and the rest of the agency stayed in Soho. By the late 1990s Sting was a director of only five companies: Steerpike, Steerpike (Overseas), Roxanne Music, Roxanne Music (Overseas) and the Rainforest Project. Other parts of the empire were streamlined in the wake of Moore's fraud. The rationalization suited Sting well. He spent more time combing fewer balance-sheets, and liked to visit his various offices. When Sting was in, the places buzzed with a cross of low-level terror and frenzy. He tended not to sit quietly in the corner. Instead, he paced around, padded in and out of Miles's eyrie, dictated faxes and made snap decisions. Most of his staff forgave the occasional folly because they recognized his enduring if contrasting qualities of passion and rationality and wanted to humour him. 'He hasn't lost his spellbinding charm,' says one. 'He gets immediate respect whatever he does.'

It was a firm commitment, and Sting returned it in kind. He often spoke of his long-term employees as his 'second family'. Men like Kim Turner and Danny Quatrochi had been on hand since the early days of The Police. Sting was still friendly with at least two of the three Copelands. He even reconciled with Henri Padovani, the guitarist sacked in 1977, now working as a European manager of Firstars. It was a close-knit crew, and Sting's high-handedness was softened by an undercurrent of warmth, a concern for his team that seemed real. He was a kind and considerate boss, the sort who lent money and remembered birthdays. 'Cards, always cards,' a woman recalls. With a distracted air, Sting wove from flashes of anger to compliments, from weary resignation to self-deprecating jokes. His staff learned to cope. He was also fanatically loyal to his band, to whom, as Dominic Miller says, 'He's very fair . . . Sting tells us what he thinks, all the time.' (This same quality of frankness had been noted by Branford Marsalis.) A second musician speaks of 'him treating us just like his kid brothers. That's corny, but true.'

Sting could inveigle, charm, tease and occasionally dazzle. But more important, at least in the case of Miles Copeland, he learnt how to co-exist. This 'odd couple' of rock celebrated twenty years together in 1997. At fifty-three, Miles was still a layer cake of contradictions: the icing a stern, dignified public persona; just below that a hyperactive deal-maker and militant Tory; lower still, a canny, bluff father-figure who went to war for his clients. It didn't take Freud to see the obvious attraction for Sting.

He still had mixed feelings about his old brothers-in-arms The Police. For years, the band was kept alive only by their archives, a booming collectibles market and chat on the Internet. After the *ad hoc* reunion at Lake House, fans were rewarded by the stock *Greatest Hits* album in 1992. Sting gave a resounding thumbs-down to the Police boxed CD a year later. Bizarrely, he claimed not to have even heard of the set until it was in the shops. 'I wasn't expecting it . . . once I knew, I wasn't looking forward to it,' he told *Q*. In spring 1995 A&M released the first Police single in years, 'Can't Stand Losing You', culled from the double live album out that May. Sting himself was cool, but for Copeland and Summers (who produced it), detachment ended at the bottom line. Magnetic

Publishing still turned over millions well into the mid-1990s.

One reason for Sting's indifference was that he could afford it. 'I don't care if the box set sells or not,' he said. 'Do you really think I need to make a few quid from some repackaged back catalogue?' At other times he was apt to tell journalists, 'I'm happy and healthy and I'm rich.' Keith Moore's trial would mark Sting down as the man who could lose £6 million and not miss it. Even by rock-star standards, he was seriously well off. In 1994 Steerpike carried forward nearly £3 million profit. According to those who helped handle his personal assets, Sting's other companies collectively turned over three or four times that in song royalties, worldwide tour revenue and fat one-off fees from playing privately for the Nomura Asset Company or the Prince of Brunei.

For all his seemingly unstoppable cash flow, settlement with his banks and studied nonchalance over 'making a few quid', Sting was acutely bothered about his money. He was in a virtual coma for two days after hearing of Moore's treachery. He displayed some wit both on *Ten Summoner's Tales* and in once changing a line of 'Every Breath You Take' to 'Every account- ant's mistake', but that came later. By then most of the funds had been recovered. Generally, Sting's need for order, structure and balance was given full rein. After 1992, it was never very likely that he'd return to his old ways of signing his accounts unread. He paid close attention to the books, was cagey without being mean and stressed one value above all others: control. He took personal month-to-month charge of his finances.

By the mid-1990s, not much of Sting's global income came from Hollywood. He was frank about his apathy to being a film star, though he leavened his hatred of 'la-la land' by exaggerated praise for pet directors: *Stormy Monday*'s Mike Figgis, for one, who enlisted him to sing on the soundtrack of *Leaving Las Vegas*. Sting wasn't exactly under a blitz of studio offers. Since *The Bride* and *Plenty*, his only widescreen roles had been cameos. At the time he married, his movie career was established but creatively exhausted – until he hitched up with his wife.

Dune and the other big-budget flops had been 'a good way to get the waters flowing', Sting said; 'but I'm not sitting by the phone waiting for Hollywood to call'. Such scripts as came invariably called on him to play the kind of dodgy rogue of *Brimstone & Treacle*, if not an outright psycho. He did take bit parts in *Resident Alien* and *The Music Tells You*, but otherwise what he called his night job – starring on Broadway and being a *Variety* idol – had been stalled for years. His videos, some at least as well plotted as *Artemis 81*, drew respectful, curious reviews, but didn't change many minds.

Late in 1994 Styler began pre-production of *The Grotesque*, a black comedy set in 1940s England based on a novel by Patrick McGrath. As well as Alan Bates and Theresa Russell, the film starred Sting as an evil butler; Styler herself as his mousy wife. *The Grotesque*'s strange tendency to flesh out the plot of *The Addams Family* with Agatha Christie was enough to coax backers to put up $3 million. Sting came for free. Location work began in Norfolk in February 1995.

The Grotesque wasn't a bad interim job for Sting, giving him down-time to think, read, dream and even work. (He wrote the single 'Let Your Soul Be Your Pilot' between takes.) He had few duties in handling such a slight role on such a small budget, chief of which was to look sexy with both Russell and her potential son-in-law, played by Steven Mackintosh. Sting proved incapable of doing either, but otherwise used the time well. In particular, he grew even closer to the movie's producer. 'The best thing about making it was that Trudie and I were in charge,' he said. 'We were together twenty-four hours a day, and our marriage not only survived, it was strengthened.' For once the satiric 'luvvy' ambitions of most film sets were amply fulfilled. By the time shooting wrapped in April, Styler was pregnant with the couple's fourth child, Sting's sixth in all.

With a Fledge (Sting's character), a Coal and sundry Limps and Giblets, *The Grotesque* was an aptly titled collage of silly names and wiggy scenes. Shorn of the sub-*Bride* décor, full of mist and candelabras, and without Bates's mad hamming, the film came off as cynical pandering, a self-consciously wacky mix of *The Servant* and P. G. Wodehouse.

Sting's extraordinary turnaround from foul-mouthed yob to genial eccentric was an odd enough saga itself, richly symbolic of its times yet transcending them, touching not just the late-1970s' reinvention of rock but its whole infiltration of the mainstream. By 1995 a mood of laid-back serenity prevailed, but beyond the AOR albums and home movies there were angry flashes on the horizon. Sting's next major role would be in court.

9

Legend

'IF YOU ASKED TEN PEOPLE IN A ROOM what they think of Sting, you'd get a fairly graded response. I don't think you'd get "Oh, he's a cunt" ten times. I hope not . . . I get a good response from other musicians, which is pleasing. I don't read the newspapers to check whether I exist every day, as I think some people do.'

Those who worked with him were certainly loud in touting Sting's candour. Dominic Miller was particularly impressed by the way 'he doesn't mind saying at the end of a show "this, this, this and this wasn't happening" . . . He'll just say "I hate that" so you know.' To others, Sting typified the complacent end of celebrity, not just by being unruffled but by being positively smug. He could give the impression, because of his unabashed new maturity, of taking life easy. Too often, Sting's clinical efficiency seemed like a cynical exercise in consumerism. His vaunted poise came off as self-obsessed. 'I believed you had to manufacture a crisis to be creative,' he said. 'Now I'm fighting that idea. I want to be happy and still make music.' Though pain had been the first source of his genius, he'd achieved a working balance between domesticity and the creative itch. Its most potent symbol was the home studio. That was only the sharp end of a globally well-upholstered lifestyle. Whether at Lake House or Malibu, Sting was waited on hand and foot. He made casual jokes about his growing addiction to luxury. In the rare moments he wasn't writing, touring or loafing on Copacabana, he plumped for time on a private yacht with his friend Bruce Springsteen. He enjoyed the best service money could buy.

Sting had long since dexterously charted his own musical course. He'd plied between lines of style and format. Now, he swerved toward technology. In 1995 he released 'All This Time' on CD-Rom. He kept up a chirpy correspondence on the Internet. He wasn't, however, a slave to cyberspace. With rare exceptions, he increasingly shunned recording techniques involving drum machines, sampling and computers. Nor was he ever likely to 'treat' work by dead artists like Bob Marley, for instance. (He found the Beatles anthology 'kind of shivery', thus confirming it.) As well as a mildly progressive policy on the future, he had a more relaxed view of the past. Sting merely shrugged when the A&M marketing machine ground out yet another Police set, this one 'digitally remastered', with zany collectibles and a paltry 'bonus track'. He endorsed Pato Banton's funked-up version of 'Spirits In The Material World' with the line: 'There are no sacred cows in my canon.' Nor were there rigid rock templates. As well as his love of American soul, Sting returned to three or four key albums. 'I play *So What* by Miles Davis almost once a week ... To hear John Coltrane play, and Wynton Kelly, thrills me ... I know every note. I like French romantic orchestral music, Ravel, Debussy, Fauré, Erik Satie. And I've really got into these Dominican monks singing Gregorian chants.'

Sting's suave tastes were a good indication that the one-time punk rude-boy had mellowed. The very way he admitted to having 'run out of charisma' proved it. He still didn't suffer fools gladly, as Miller knew, but he did suffer them. Faced with non-compliance or, more commonly, ineptitude, he resorted to charm and retreated into the gentlemanly mode he'd mastered in his forties. He tended to talk *de haut en bas* to the band, as he might a nanny or gardener. Sting never used force, even force of will, over his own children, and ruled by manipulating others with prods at their ego or integrity. He was magnificent in his role of first among equals. The cringing *South Bank Show* profiling Sting in 1995 rarely went under the skin. There was no hint, for instance, of Keith Moore. It did, however, reveal a man with an engaging sense of his own worth. 'If anyone described me as a genius, I'd laugh. I have my moments ... I just have to join them together.'

At the broadsheet and documentary level, Sting was respected if not liked. His frequent dunks in the tabloid trough tended to wallow in the causes, until sex and drugs took over. He was pilloried for his remarks about Ecstasy. Sting's home life also gave endless gigglesome copy. He still enjoyed voyeurism. He was aroused, for instance, by Madonna's book *Sex*, he told *Us* (and then posed for the same magazine in his bathtub). He held to the view that a woman's 'breasts and brains' were her best features. Variations on this motto would somehow crop up even in his highbrow monologues.

The *Sun* and the *Mirror*, meanwhile, trotted out reprises of Sting's Tantric stamina on average once a month. Late in 1994 he was asked to pose nude for a spread in *Playgirl* – an offer he refused, though not before it, too, was lapped up by the *Star*. In a 1995 *Q* diary Sting regaled readers about his love life with Styler, then recovering from a broken foot: 'I find her crutches incredibly sexy. They make her look so vulnerable.' Above the mantelpiece in the Captain's Room, he kept two framed articles from *Viz*. In one, Sting admitted to making such energetic love to his wife that her head came off; the other related to his stay at the Palace Hotel, where 'four-inch sex monkeys' masturbated into his tea. Sting, to his credit, got the joke, but both yarns spoke to an image people had of him. Whatever the future course of his work, and notwithstanding the Ph.D.s and Grammys, he was never quite able to live down his brag about 'keeping it up' for five hours at a trot.

However loose Sting hung as a bawdy sex god, he was still the consummate working professional. His skill at working a crowd was legendary, and no one adapted to foreign ways better. In January 1994 he halted a brawl at his show in Manila by cutting the music, facing the crowd and smiling: heads, one by one, popped up from the ruckus as if from a mole-hole; the row ended. Despite home sneers, his popularity abroad remained a phenomenon to British journalists. One wrote a long article quoting, without irony, Sting's own solemn explanation of why he liked touring Japan, Thailand and Vietnam. It was 'because you're rewarded more than you could be playing twenty-five basketball arenas in America'. Sting responded with such glee to Eastern culture that he became a kind of *de facto* ambassador. In Ho Chi Minh City, the National Assembly formally voted its thanks to 'this writer of many good songs'. The Japanese arts *Jimmu* greeted Sting with a bow. In Singapore, where most rock was heard only on bootlegs and seen not at all, his arrival brought a riot at the airport. Through most of the Orient you could see Sting's image, interviews and wares more often than those of any politician, general, pin-up or sports idol. At forty-three, he'd transcended pop. Sting was now a vivid fixture in the world's imagination.

In the face of such fawning, Sting continued to nurse a sense, not exactly of unworthiness, but, rather, mystified awe. He'd insist, for instance, that 'I hear tunes all the time' and 'I need others to interpret my music . . . What I get paid for is being famous.' This 'I-am-a-mere-vessel' self-image gave him at once an appealing outer modesty and a clear inner direction. In fact, for most of 1995 his muse seemed to have gone south. Sting admitted he had trouble making the familiar match of melodies and rhyming couplets. 'I hate having to face a blank page,' he said that summer. As in 1989–90, he felt spent, stale and blocked. He improvised by putting in long hours alone in his boathouse, then, when the spark came, 'wandering around, humming tunes to myself . . . first a line, a riff and then a song. It's a mysterious thing.' At tense moments during the process, Sting didn't shout, swear or kick his dog. He practised Bach lute suites. After three months of introspection, trial, error and classical noodlings, Sting had his material. Now he was ready to make the short move to the studio.

That September Sting rounded up the usual suspects. Dominic Miller, Kenny Kirkland, Vinnie Colaiuta and Hugh Padgham all met at Steerpike Sound, actually the dining hall at Lake House. Branford Marsalis returned. Indulging a boyhood fantasy, Sting hired the in-house Stax band, the Memphis Horns, on half the tracks. He even used his old Newcastle crony, Gerry Richardson, on organ. Recording took up most of that autumn. Sting gave a quick, impersonal pep talk on the first morning: 'I want this done in two months. If you've got any ideas, spit them out. Otherwise, let's get on with it.' He broke off from this regime to host his birthday party on 2 October. Sting celebrated with just his wife, children, band and the East London Gospel Choir. The *South Bank Show* was also there. This was the signal for another speech. 'I'm very fortunate . . . I'm very healthy, I'm very happy. My sanity is reasonably intact. I owe it all to my family. God bless you.'

The pandemic good vibes looming all over concealed an anxious and fraught time for Sting. As well as touring, writing and taking long hikes in the fields, he spent at least half the summer and autumn huddled with his solicitor, Christopher Burley. Sting had been called as the star prosecution witness in Keith Moore's trial for theft. As well as concocting the oft-quoted sum of 108 bank accounts, Burley was able to coach his client in courtroom ethics and the correct tone to take from the box. In the event, Sting performed well. His steady, caustic evidence was laced with a biting wit, as when he quipped, 'I'm a generous man – but not that generous', or answered the defence's barb, 'You can't have someone working for the Inland Revenue who is horrified by financial documents' with the droll retort, 'I'm afraid that's why I left.'

The trial established Sting as the man who still trusted Moore even after the bands Queen and Big Country, and the producer Gus Dudgeon, had sacked him for slippery practice. All three had lodged professional-misconduct complaints with the Institute of Chartered Accountants. To Moore, this made Sting a 'good 'un'. To others, it meant that he, Burley and Miles Copeland had all been asleep at the switch in not firing him earlier. The four-week trial was also an embarrassment for the man who liked to keep his financial dealings private. It was revealed, for instance, that tax had been waived on £11.6 million of Sting's earnings, provided he maintain a home abroad. He had, though, paid the Revenue some £20 million over the years, and just signed off on a bill for £691,000. 'It's not an unusual amount for me to pay in tax,' Sting said.

Moore denied the charges. His counter-claim that Sting had agreed in the 'general principles' of policy and that the Moore Sloane Re: G. M. Sumner account had been escrow, always at his client's disposal, brought the tart reply: 'Are you saying I agreed that all the money saved from the Inland Revenue should go to a fund controlled by Moore? My assumption is that once the Revenue had agreed to a deal, that money would go into my personal accounts to do with as I choose . . . not that it's some treasure chest that someone can dip into and invest for me. It's my money.'

On 17 October 1995 the jury found Moore guilty on all charges. Judge Gerald Butler told him that a custodial sentence was inevitable. 'You have been convicted of a series of offences, carried out in gross breach of trust . . . You are now a ruined man, who will never again practise as an accountant.' (Moore had already been struck off by his professional body, and his companies wound up.) 'Mr Sumner has recovered much the greater part of his losses,' the judge added. 'But that's no thanks to you.' He then sentenced the prisoner to six years. As the words hit him, Moore crumpled up and seemed to slump on the brass rail of the dock. His girlfriend Santosh Bangor collapsed in tears. As Sting was driven home to Lake House, his ex-adviser was hustled through the back door into a van and locked up in Wandsworth Jail, among the bleakest in a penal system known for its austerity. After bathing, delousing and barbering, Moore exchanged his suit for blue serge overalls and his £800,000-p.a. consultancy for a job in the prison library. 'I try to be useful there,' he says.

Sting himself, in terms that could only have been supplied by Burley, later told a reporter, 'This wasn't a civil action, but a criminal prosecution brought by the Crown . . . It's not for me to comment on the jury's verdict, except to say I am pleased it is all over.' Significantly, he hinted at his successful bid to recover his missing funds. 'Coutts have been my bankers for fifteen years,' he said. 'I'm confident in their ability . . . I have no intention of changing [them].' Both they and Lloyds confirmed that they had settled with their famous customer. Ex-members of Queen and Big Country, Gus Dudgeon and the ICA also each had their say. Perhaps the most compelling quote of all, however, came from Moore's mother Peggy, who 'bitterly regretted' his foray into showbusiness. 'He should never have got into it,' she said. 'That was his foolishness. Sting went to him and he was skint and now he's worth millions. Someone made all that money for him.'

Moore's trial took place amidst a welter of other criminal and civil cases. Actions against the Wests, the Maxwells, Nick Leeson and the alleged ex-Nazi Syzymon Serafinowicz, the O. J. Simpson verdict, and libels involving Gillian Taylforth, Terry Venables and Devon Malcolm all made a bonanza for legal reporters. Even in such lofty company, Sting's name wrung the biggest headlines. To the tabloids, he was the pop-star 'supergrass' with the dark suit and cropped hair. Both the *Mirror* and the *Star* led their stories with the inevitable STUNG. The *Sun* found the elusive sex angle. According to an anonymous source, 'Moore had a thing for young Asian girls. He'd get them in as temps and rush them off to New York or Paris for some bogus meeting . . . Most would be so taken with the excitement he'd eventually get his way with them. He lived like a king.' Thus Moore's real transgression had been to enter into the moral vacuum and financial twilight zone of a stock rock star.

At the very least, the trial made Sting, whose wealth became proverbial from then on, the man who could lose a fortune and not blink. Some of this stunning laxity came out in court. It was left to the Crown's Neil Stewart to butter up the jury, as barristers do, to make it more amenable to his view of events. 'The fact was, Mr Sumner was not aware that the money had gone. That may be indicative of two things: how much cash he'd made over the years, and just how preoccupied he was with other things.' As well as forcing a break in recording, and generally causing headaches and unwanted publicity, the proceedings raised questions about Sting's self-confessed 'control freak' image. In fact, as in his suit against Branson, he opted for victim status. 'I'm a singer and songwriter,' he said. 'But I found myself at the head of a multi-million-dollar corporation.' The icy, shrewd and fulfilled man whom fans saw still considered himself a virgin when it came to business.

Sting soon returned to more familiar roles, in and out of the glare of the Klieg lights. He finished his album. He became a father again. In February 1996 he played live sets on BBC radio and TV. Elsewhere, he presented himself as a happy man, relaxed, easy in his own skin, padding his estate in clothes expensively tailored to look casual. The *New York Times* stringer found him in his armchair 'near a desk strewn with books and classical CDs, sipping from a cup of hot water, talk[ing] about how his new-found optimism has begun to surface in his work'. He was so enamoured of Lake House, Sting casually told the paper, 'I plan to be buried here someday.'

Bland and bonhomous one day, shy and standoffish the next, Sting still had things to do and platforms from which to do them. That spring he donated a self-portrait for the Hard Rock Café's 'signature series', to be auctioned for Aids research. He launched his new album (and babbled about crop circles at the party). On 12 April Sting hosted another rainforest benefit at Carnegie Hall. A month later he was at *The Grotesque*'s première. That midnight found Larry Adler sitting between Sting and Elton John. '"I've gained two uncles," I told them. "Or, in my case, an aunt," said Elton. Sting slapped me on the back and roared with laughter. He may have been a cold fish, but that smile of his, that look, could light up a room. He's got that gift.'

Mercury Falling, Sting's fifth studio solo album, also hit the bright lights in March. The name was deemed significant. Sting himself had two takes: either that 'Mercury's a very potent symbol . . . it's mythological, it's astrological, it's a planet, it's an element, it's a metal, it's a liquid . . . There's a lot of symbolical resonance'; or, more prosaically, 'Mercury was the god of theft, and I've stolen from everywhere.' Some ascribed the same titular downward loop to Sting's own trajectory. According to this reading, the barometric pressure of his career had been in freefall since *Synchronicity*. The actual album lay somewhere between the wry twang of Lyle Lovett, the velvet romanticism of Neil Diamond and the cornball charm of McCartney, making it a quicksilver, not to say mercurial, collage of creaky hit-parade sounds. Sting soaked the whole record in the iconography of vintage funk and R&B. Finally, there was the nominal echo of the Rainforest Foundation's Project Mercury, a health-care scheme for the Indians of Gorotire and Kikretum villages in central Brazil.

As the title also unintentionally suggested, the album wasn't Sting's high point. The eleven tracks roamed the map from bossa nova to bebop, yet seldom exuded the dizzy, jack-of-all-formats charm of *Ten Summoner's Tales*. That album was diffuse. This one was disjointed. So far as there was a theme, it was the reformed rocker's pet one of redemption. 'I've written about the literal deaths of people I loved, or the death of a relationship,' said Sting. 'Now I'm at a point where I see death as a new door opening as an old one closes. So the songs really are about beginnings as well as endings.' (In practice, that meant he grafted an American-style, twelve-step apology for past errors on to a dry British wit.) It was that bad. And patchy: for every plangent, hormonally shot verse, there was a frankly naff, bloodless chorus. Ethereal, hymnlike ballads were offset by clean-cut, MOR rockers.

Most of the tunes were a tasteful crib of classic riffs, smooth, Steely Dan-type grooves and slick musicianship from the likes of the Memphis Horns, Marsalis and even, allegedly, Keanu Reeves. Sting had never been in better voice. Since the castrato croak of 'Roxanne', his vocals had swooped downward in register and ever upward in subtlety and sly phrasing. His uncanny ear and interpretative flair came good on several passable impersonations of Pauls Simon, Carrack and McCartney. There was also a nod to his friend Eric Clapton. Clearly indebted to the affable, low-key strum of *461 Ocean Boulevard, Mercury Falling* filched at least one riff ('The Hounds of Winter') and one plot-line ('I Hung My Head') from Clapton's album.* The two men had already collaborated on 'It's Probably Me' and shared a second home at the Albert Hall. For a time, Sting's and Clapton's minglings meant that, in the public's eye, they became linked as a single unit, a beloved family entertainer whose self-mocking demeanour and smartly honed tunes concealed an exotically charged past.

Mercury Falling bowed with 'Winter', Sting using the idea as a metaphor for old age and solitude. The orchestral moodiness of the band and the cat's-purr vocals made for a satisfying, if not exactly swinging, opener. In 'I Hung My Head' the lyrical debt was to Clapton and Queen's 'Bohemian Rhapsody'. Here Sting turned his talent for mimicry towards that other soft-rock staple, Phil Collins. (The 9/8 tempo might have done for Collins' range.) The headline news of *Mercury Falling*, and first single, was 'Let Your Soul Be Your Pilot'. This was a throwback to the horn-heavy tones of Aretha Franklin, Booker T and Wilson Pickett. Enticing as it was to revisit the lost world of Atlantic, there was also a tang of parody in the performance: 'The song tells you all about soul, while evincing none of its qualities,' wrote one critic; 'gospel lite', another. In rock, like other lively arts, some things defy fakery. Sting's melisma was no worse than Steve Winwood's, but even James Brown's scraping of the studio barrel was better.

So far, so simple-but-effectively-done. Time and again, Sting's voice and the knotty arrangements salvaged the material. 'I Was Brought To My Senses' was more creamy embellishment of a frugal tune, reprising the bucolic mood of 'Fields Of Gold'. As Sting said, 'I've come to the realization that not only is nature an amazing metaphor . . . it's a miracle in its own right. You can't separate us from the tree. We're part of the same carbon-based

---

* Off 'Let It Grow' and 'I Shot The Sheriff', respectively.

family.' With its arboreal hug-in and ode to Lake House, 'Senses' wasn't likely to change the image of Sting as a punk turned landed hippy. 'You Still Touch Me' did, however, bring boyhood reveries full circle as it gilded chords (and pillaged the intro) from 'Soul Man'.

From there *Mercury* was truly downward. Each track took turns to reveal itself as a narrative link to the album's 'I'm OK' keynote. Fifteen years ago, Sting had written of lost love in terms of revenge, self-pity and suicide. Now he sang 'I took a walk alone last night / I looked up at the stars / To try and find an answer in my life . . . Everybody's got to leave the darkness sometime.' Then, he'd flung veiled threats in 'Every Breath You Take'. Now, he goggled at his daughter's caprices in 'All Four Seasons'. Sting did one number like Guy Lombardo. He warmed over some of the nautical fare of *Soul Cages*. And he ended in the purple haze of 'Lithium Sunset', with its overheated, volcanological prose: 'Take this heartache / Of obsidian darkness / And fold my darkness / Into your yellow light.'

Fans and critics gave credit to Sting's evolution. He still won awards and gongs. His concerts were sell-outs the world over. But, after the creative boomlet of *Ten Summoner's Tales*, he did little on *Mercury* but wrap the lesser songs with a trainspotter's attention to detail. The one-moral-fits-all message stifled even the best cuts. Overall, it seemed, as Sting's mood lightened, so his sound became equally vanilla. 'One more bland, and at times yawningly obvious pop noise,' was the *Source*'s withering notice. Sting's Police-era rants had long given way to a sophisticated brand of mood music, and stylistic no-man's-land. On *Tales*, he'd virtually defined sleek, high-performance rock. With *Falling*, the tunes gasped and spluttered before veering to the centre lane. In the *Sunday Times*' words, 'they're mathematical exercises that will happily keep you company while you do the ironing or set the table'. If that wasn't bad enough, Sting's lean towards artistry and self-restraint brought one dread *faux pas*: he sang a song in French.

A&M held nothing back. Billboards, posters, specials, ads and mail-outs (most featuring the cover art of Sting, hand to head, broodingly studious) made for a bonanza. *Mercury Falling* was a tidy hit. It hit number five on the American chart a week after release. The album won a Brit nomination and two for the

Grammys. Eventually it sold over four million copies. Sting was beginning to realize that he hadn't just the best of back-up and management, but the most loyal of all fan-bases.

By the time the album was released, Sting had already hit the road. The tour that began on 9 March in Amsterdam would wind up, sixteen months and 200 shows later, in the mud at Glastonbury. In the meantime Sting played in Russia, Finland, Sweden, Norway, Denmark, Belgium, France, Italy, Romania, Germany, England, Austria, America, Canada, Japan, Hong Kong, Korea, the Philippines, Taiwan, Thailand, Vietnam, Australia, New Zealand, Ireland, Scotland, Poland, the Czech Republic and Switzerland. He made TV and radio appearances, was greeted warmly by Tony Blair, partied with Princess Diana, raised cash for the rainforest and launched his album and film. Between times, Sting negotiated a new, multi-million-pound deal with A&M. Years before, an ex-friend had said of him that 'he lived to work'. It was an apt tribute, and one he might have echoed two decades later, when Sting ran off stage and said it was 'good touring's such hell – I might get used to it'. This seemingly innate histrionism found so little reflection in his drawing-room self that most of Sting's court weren't even aware it existed. It did: it was the core of the man. Hampered by the self-imposed curbs of causes and trying to raise half a dozen children while devoting his professional life to the dreary details of demographics and target markets, Sting may well have welcomed the 'hell' which freed him from his own straitjacket.

Whatever the cause, the effect was that he trotted the globe, basking in the manic roar and shifting more units of *Mercury Falling* than even the dour A&M 'penetration men' had hoped. Fame, as Sting said in 1997, may have meant nothing to him. That didn't rule out using his name to his own good and to further ends. Whether touring with the Grateful Dead or duetting with Pavarotti, Sting was a wily career-mover. It took a rare sense of personal balance to be cool, dignified and dependable on one hand, and warm, matey and fun-loving on the other, all the while denying familiarity through constant mobility. This was the 1990s ideal of the rock star, and within the model it was unthinkable to behave professionally as one did with cronies. Sting's cronies were few, and he worked non-stop.

A second ex-friend, more cogently, realized that Sting had a habit of moving by 'inner light', had the ability to wait confidently until he saw his chance and then, lizard-like, to 'pounce and grab it'. That summed up how he wrote songs. It was also true that Sting was prepared to dally between tours – but that once one began, it had the self-restraining qualities of a war. Early in 1996 a familiar shudder, something akin to a communal hug or sigh, spread through North America. Full-page ads of Sting, staring in studied three-quarters pose, nuzzling a tree or nursing his Fender, hit the press. He followed in person in June. His tour was a composite. There were times when it came to resemble a high-stakes, high-speed campaign, with the candidate, naturally enough, a stickler for discipline. Sting's occasional grouses to Kim Turner or the band could blossom into open ugliness. On the other hand, he was endlessly accommodating. Mike Noble speaks about how 'flabbergastingly nice' he was, compared not only with others, but with his early days in The Police. Sting's set list showed the same bias for benign, mass entertainment over punk situationism. 'The Bed's Too Big Without You', 'Synchronicity II' and a thumping, singalong 'Roxanne' all stretched out in a salvo. Otherwise the show was dense with cuts from *Mercury Falling*. Sting encored with 'Fragile', an easy, not to say effete end to the night.

In the old days, Sting had manhandled or sworn at fans who tried to horn in on his act. Now he began asking for volunteers to step up and play with him. The gag worked, and even produced a star. A man named Ross Viner joined Sting on stage in Vancouver. He sang breathtakingly well. At the end of the number the crowd chanted 'Ross!' and held up lighters. In the wings, their hero signed a waiver and accepted the scale $1 fee from Turner. 'I didn't do it for the money,' he said.

Sting was in Seattle on 10 August. Backstage, he spoke like a man in recovery therapy, apologizing for past mistakes. 'Ten years [ago] I was involved in divorce, not only my marriage but the band. They were both destroyed by my will . . . I hurt people. I've spent the last decade justifying, if you like, that . . . pain.' (A view satirized by one writer: ' "I feel your grief," says Sting, right after causing it.') Onstage, he bounded into the natural bowl of a gorge carved between two hills on the verge of a river, squinted into the setting sun and gulped 'Wow' before cuing in 'The Hounds Of Winter'. As the local paper put it, 'Everything, from the songs, lighting and sets to the audience give-and-take, had a deliberate sense of design, designed to entertain. It was a gig without political pronouncements, only the drama and comedy of music.' It was also a night that proved, yet again, that theatrics, personality and skill can make even the most timeworn antics and tunes sound spry. Sting was that good. He made an aesthetic link to the '60s. His smoky vocals drifted out into the valley like incense.

'I don't want to end up as the guy in Vegas with the balding head and the tux singing "Roxanne",' Sting had said in 1981. If so – and it clearly was – he held out for fifteen years. Sting starred at the MGM Grand Garden on 1 September 1996. He was both burr-haired and happy to do his first hit. (He avoided the tux.) From there the tour ground down through Arizona, New Mexico and Texas. After yet another coast-to-coast epic, Sting was no longer just a fad or cult but unequivocally a Name, at least on a par with other monomarks like Bono or Madonna, admired, loved or positively loathed, art-with-a-heart, uncompromising, dogged, yet also free, loose and in the thick of life. On stage, he put on a silly hat. He made jokes and smiled. He got his brass section to bop from foot to foot. Vaudeville seemed to live on through the spirit of his shows, which were none the worse for it. Sting had managed a marvel: he was both highbrow and low, belting the songs but never missing a chance to flay the crowd, whether with easygoing wit or a funny walk out of John Cleese's repertoire.

Sting, meanwhile, had become a father for the sixth time. His third son arrived in London on 17 December 1995. In keeping with his parents' Italianatism, the boy was named Giacomo, 'Spike' and 'Fledge' having been vetoed. His birth fulfilled Styler's ambition of marrying and having at least one child on the right side of the blanket. The 'proper English style' she'd craved for her wedding was formalized at the baptism in April 1996. By then the argument about Sting – was he or wasn't he on the make – had been worn as smooth as an old 78 rpm disc, with as many cracks and grooves and hisses. What most people didn't realize was that it had ceased to matter. All the words geysering up in *NME* missed the point. Sting had already joined the Establishment. He'd copped in. Giacomo's bow at St Andrew's church (where guests in morning-wear sang 'Jerusalem') marked the last full phase of Sting's assimilation. The essential coolness was preserved. *Hello!*'s effervescent spread and the glossy photos of Sting in tails were just the most recent proof that the 'Geordie yobbo' had been deep-sixed in favour of the country squire.

The pram in the hall wasn't always the enemy of creativity. 'My children help me keep cool,' Sting said. 'Some mornings I feel *very* uncool.' He suffered the now common fate of the rock-and-roll father. His eldest son considered him a musical 'old fart'. (Their one mutual fixed point was Nirvana.) Sting discovered bands like Green Day and Pavement through Joe's patronage. His children also helped rouse what was left of his northern roots. 'Work defines you,' Sting told them. 'Work is your self-esteem. It's you. Find it and you'll be happy.' He punctuated virtually every family gathering with, 'I'm going to spend my wad. You'll be on your own . . . ', words which, cumulatively, gave the impression Sting was living like a pools-winner. He commented to Styler at length about everything from the kids' diets to their wet swimming-trunks. He wanted them raised differently to him: to feel at home and at ease in any company, to 'stretch their minds', to 'do impossible things'. Sting tried to convey egalitarian values he hadn't always been able to live up to himself, cautioning Joe and the rest against snobbery, and encouraging a stab at self-assertion he'd never lacked. He didn't want them kowtowing to any authority, even that of parent or teacher; he stressed consideration over crawling. Above all, increasingly, Sting was a toucher, a hugger, a father who actually laughed when his family ragged him. Everything he did was a conscious, if self-conscious, effort to thaw the icier memories of life in Station Road.

Though as an adult Sting rarely attended church and gave little hint of caring about organized religion, he did speak in hushed, semi-pious terms of his wife. 'She's my best friend, my lover, my companion, and I don't want to contemplate life without her.' By 1996 Styler had shaken her image as a home-wrecker to become, as she put it, 'Mrs Respectability'. She gave an interview to the *Daily Mail* in which, with the incomer's crow, she announced, 'My dad was a labourer, but now we're worth £20 million.' Styler produced Aids fundraisers and Sting's annual rainforest gala. Her Xingú Films bankrolled *The Grotesque*. She appeared as a staple in the 'people' pages and gossip columns. 'Mrs S. was a

tremendous hit here,' says a friend who sat with her in
committee. 'The only one who could talk to a tea-lady on equal
terms to a princess. She was terrific. *And stunning*. Improved a
hundred per cent in looks.' Styler's charity work further fed the
consensus. People began referring to rock couplehood not just in
terms of Sid and Nancy and Kurt and Courtney (and, as direly,
Posh and Dave), but also Sting and Trudie. They joined the
pantheon.

Both still made their forays into tabloid land. Most of the
music types were bad enough, but a few turns of the *Sun*'s screw
revealed a pair positively oozing sex, drugs and rock and roll.
Some went to incredible lengths for the all-important sneer. Thus
the 'pretentious git' with the *Kama Sutra* love-life emerged.
According to this school, if Sting was growing older, it wasn't
from the angle of someone blanding out totally. Most of his one-
liners still whipped up a storm. In 1993 he told the world, 'In
yoga, sex is a spiritual focus of energy . . . If you've gone on for
four or five hours, you don't really want to come . . . I enjoy sex a
lot more now. I think it's a constant source of imaginative
play.' The press lapped it up. Sting's boasts made him fewer
enemies than fans. (Several women sent polaroids.) The exact
reverse, however, applied to his spin on drugs.

Over the years, the chance remark to the Nordic press has
caused grief to even seasoned rock gods. In 1976, David Bowie
told a Finnish reporter, 'I believe very strongly in fascism.' A
Danish TV crew later aired slurs by John Lennon most of his
fans would have preferred not to hear. Sting himself chose a
Swedish paper to make his notorious quip about Ecstasy. The
quote, he later said, was taken out of context. He made some
socially valid points. A number of experts and voluntary groups
agreed with him. Even the reporter would add that Sting spoke
'in a shrewd, quiet voice'. The headlines squawked back in
falsetto.

Sting may have meant well. He was right to highlight a drug
taken by up to a million people a week in Britain. But his remarks
not only skirted the overdose death of Leah Betts; they somehow
failed to dwell on the kidney and liver failure, heatstroke, depression, anxiety and brain damage that go along with the four-hour
fits of euphoria. The *Sun* virtually burnt Sting in effigy. The
Mirror nailed him as a 'middle-aged star making music for people

more likely to get out of their heads on cocoa than cocaine'. 'A tosser' was one vivid put-down. Yet again, Sting was in Def Con 2 mode. Virtually every American publication devoted time and resources to the story. CNN and the other networks took up the cudgels. Without making any apology for past excesses – and claiming 'I don't believe you can get into the spiritual state without taking drugs' – Sting looked forward, not back. He did reaffirm his aversion to chemicals that 'separate you from the world', but his own primary allegiance, he made clear, was to the young. In the struggle for those interests, Sting cited his policy with his own family. 'If you don't have the ability to talk honestly, you're in big trouble . . . If any of my children had a drug problem, *I'd* want to deal with it, not the police . . . Drug abuse is a health problem, not a moral or a legal problem. The sooner we start thinking about it in those terms, the sooner we can hope to solve it.'

For any analysis of Sting's character, 1976 was the year. In the space of six months, he married, sired Joe and made the move to London. He later said of the era, 'I could see myself in twenty years, a little greyer, as the deputy head in the school . . . I wanted to take a risk with my life.' Two decades on, Sting's punt had paid off better than he, or anyone else, had dared hope. He was no chalky pedagogue but a demi-god who compulsively made hits, wowed the Fleadh festival and toured America with the frequency of twisters. To fans, he was genial, well intentioned, generous to a fault. The worst you could say about their version of Sting was that there was pathos to him.

Sting himself knew it. He was fully alive to the hatred certain hacks, despite or because of his self-growth, had of him. He seemed not to care. 'As a younger person I was much more confused and angry. I wanted to fight everything,' Sting said. 'Now I'm more willing to accept things.' His new-found aplomb included gritting his teeth when well-meaning fans wasted his time. In a TV interview to quell excitement for his Vegas debut, Sting could be seen taking astral leave of his body as the presenter, scrunched in her tight, low-cut dress, asked passers-by to scream his name. He kept his cool on the *Rosie O'Donnell Show*. (She thought he was Phil Collins.) He braved the Niagara of balm and banality known as Oprah Winfrey. He even joshed his way through an unauthorized biography. In August 1996,

Sting told *Entertainment Weekly*: 'You can end up at fifty still in your tight leather trousers with your hair plugs and your corset and pretending that you're in a street gang. I would find that undignified . . . I have a stake in being grown-up. I vote. I think I can make a difference in the world, and not just by posing around.'

If Sting possessed a genius, which he did, it was for self-critique. After disbanding The Police, he plunged into almost every known form of *Gestalt* analysis. He had the knack for relentless mono-logues on his life and art: music, books, films, theatre, causes. All were equal when it came to Sting's soliloquies. He also had a firm grasp of his place in the firmament, which, by and large, he puffed less as time went on. 'Fame doesn't enter my creative process,' he said. 'I exercise citizens' rights when I live in the city . . . I walk around London and New York. I don't invite hysteria . . . I like to be treated as a normal person.' Sting went shopping for baby clothes. He changed his tyre in the street. He ogled the skin at Stringfellow's. In a publicity-mad, celebrity-crazed culture, he became famous for his rationalization and renunciation of fame, for daring to prove that brains and popularity aren't mutually exclusive. He'd achieved a new level of spiritual or artistic harmony – music that no longer needed the ego validation of old. Now he made a matching bid for personal breakthrough.

First, he made up with the past. Sting sent letters or made amends to most of those he'd savaged down the years. Gerry Richardson, Frances Tomelty and Richard Branson were all back on side. He reconciled with The Police. By 1996, Sting was allowing he was 'very lucky' to have met Copeland and Summers, whereas for much of the past two decades he'd insisted it was precisely their luck to have met *him*. He even forgave Keith Moore. About the only hitch to Sting's mellowing was his being, in the *Mail*'s words, 'a crashing bore'. Yet those who no longer got a buzz out of him were guilty of their own kind of torpor. Sting had moved on; they hadn't.

Sting had a post-therapy way of building bridges back to those he'd burnt, all the time being a 'very tomorrow kind of guy', he said, not stewing in the past. 'I've tried to [settle] with the people I left ten years ago, the marriage and the band. It hasn't been easy. But I changed my life and my way of thinking and became a better person.' Significantly, Sting's best friends outside his court were Peter Gabriel, Don Henley and Bruce Springsteen, three stars who had had the guts to light out on their own. He 'was crazy' for those who didn't wall themselves in. Hermetic and self-referential work was out. Headway was all.

At the core, if not the nub, of his own growth was a new love of farce and slapstick. This was how, inadvertently almost, Sting found what 'count[ed] in life', as he played the clown. In 1996 alone he starred on *Saturday Night Live*; collaborated with Conan O'Brien in a TV spoof of 'We Are The World'; endured Larry King; sang on *Late Night With David Letterman*; and self-parodied on *The Larry Sanders Show* (where Elvis Costello urged one of the cast, 'Never buy *anything* from Sting'). All the sketches and beery send-ups about sex weren't, he insisted, strategic ploys to reboot his image. He was more relaxed; and, as he unwound, he began to value levity more highly. He teased self-expression into a manifesto. 'That's what democracy is,' Sting said. 'I won't be shut up.'

The same scatter-gun tactic marked his policy on causes. He might not have cared as much, but the late 1990s still found him tagged as an ultraist. Sting was everywhere; from National Condom Week to Aids, to Amnesty, and the annual rainforest gala (where, in a tabloid sub-plot, Wonderbra model Eva Herzigova met her future husband). All the same, he'd concluded that the days of personal jaunts to the jungle were over. He still corresponded with Raoni and the rest, but the letters were flattoned, like those from a man dead with fatigue. His health, actually, wasn't bad. Yoga had given him a new lust for life. There were just the minor blemishes. As well as sporadically losing his voice and his hearing, he was shedding hair. Sting responded with an unfortunate buzz-cut and goatee. He looked about as knocked-about as a man with £40 million in assets can; but the eroticizing Versace gear gave him an edge on his peers.

Sting was also changing artistically. To him, it was no longer about 'selling records or winning Grammys ... it's the satisfaction of having worked, of having tried your best'. He was still a fixture on the nights when, as *Mojo* says, 'the rock rebels give it some cummerbund' and the industry rewards its great and good. But he didn't seem to mind quite as much about winning. It was enough to play. 'The more you know, the less you know,' he said. 'Music, for me, is a kind of religion, a cult ... It gets more mysterious, more compelling.' In July 1996 he was again backstage as Pavarotti sang at Wembley. When Sting played the Albert Hall the ushers there bet – literally took odds, with complicated lay-offs and spreads – on the likely date he'd pool resources with an orchestra. They'd seen it all before with Clapton.

Just as Sting's career was heading for sweep, scope and *cinéma vérité*, Styler's vanity shoot, *The Grotesque*, was released. Due to budgetary curbs, filming had been kept to six weeks and editing to a few months; an early cut was screened as early as November 1995. The film as shown rearranged and roughened the original flow of Sting's role – described in the blurb as the butler who 'insinuates himself into the household, seducing the mistress and performing who knows what other dark deeds'. In the UK reviews were tepid in most cases, sardonic in others. Mark Steyn in the *Spectator* suggested that 'Mrs Sting, in casting her husband, made a mistake. Rock stars like stately-home dramas, because these days they're the only people who can afford to live in them . . . But the minute you put an ornate figure like Sting in a Gothic setting, the whole thing falls apart. Whatever the charms of the novel, the film looks like *Cluedo – the Rock Video*.'

Even the mild impact Sting made as the help-from-hell was diluted by casting Alan Bates in the lead. Styler sent him the script on a whim. He 'loved it'. In Bates's hands, aristocratic cool was a thin veneer probed for stylized laughs. As Larry Adler says, 'Alan took up ninety per cent of the space onscreen.' What remained was a threnody to farce. Under John-Paul Davidson's direction, *The Grotesque* took on the aura of a live-action cartoon. The other paradigm was *The Caretaker* (also starring Bates); it, too, had the master–servant blur, iffy pasts and brooding madness. In between, every cliché of the whodunnit was faithfully mined. The only real grotesquerie was the plot – absurd in all the wrong ways, and, even on the level of art films, making no sense. Most critics were polite about Sting, but mauled the picture. *The Grotesque* died; however, the butler didn't do it.

Sex was the crutch the film leant on for column inches. A half-nude Sting, and gay clinches, gave a new twist to a hoary tale. That single sweaty shot (done in one take) made *The Grotesque* a minor cult. But, being Sting, he also got the girl. 'As a non-actor, getting paid [*sic*] for making love to Theresa Russell all day is my idea of a good job,' he told *The Times*. Sting's producer's comment wasn't recorded.

The bottom line that vexed Styler was, of course, the $3 million budget. She had a knack for stretching funds, and, to her credit, *The Grotesque* rarely looked cut-rate. 'It was great working with Trudie,' Sting confirmed. 'She's fierce about what she wants, yet she's very understanding. As an actress and producer, she knows the business from both sides.' There were times in *The Grotesque* that felt like the upmarket home movie *Bring on the Night,* but there were also moments when 1949 England, with its ration books, demobbed spivs and distressed gentry, leapt off the screen. At its worst, the film was almost audibly creaky. At best, it was mildly evocative – gamely redressing the fad for Jurassic-era plots dolled up with *Star Wars* gimmickry – and, at bottom, no worse than anything involving Hugh Grant and Elizabeth Hurley.

In Britain, *The Grotesque* opened at an Aids Foundation gala in June 1996. (The occasion was enlivened by Elton John, at the climactic moment, squeezing Sting's hand.) It hit the video dump-bins at Christmas. *Gentlemen Don't Eat Poets,* as it became in America, premièred in New York the following March. The film's fortunes didn't improve with its alias. It did rate a mention at the Toronto Film Festival, where it was thought to show 'an ordinary but sinister man ... strafing the world with high-velocity, precision shells'. But, that virtue aside, *Gentlemen* preferred bombs.

Sting's US tour ran from the longest day of 1996 to the night summer ended. Following in the steps of other road rats like the Rolling Stones, he then wound a loop through the tropics, around Europe and back home by Christmas. There were, however, several new departures. Sting was one of the first-ever stars to rock Korea; and the last to play the Hong Kong Coliseum while the Union Jack flew aloft. That was nothing compared to the venue on 16 October. Sting headlined in Ho Chi Minh City. For weeks beforehand, the Vietnamese culture boss had scrutinized the lyrics of twenty songs faxed by the secretariat at Bugle House. When these proved sufficiently tame, an invitation followed from the People's Council. The band, crew and an international press corps duly flew in from Bangkok. This was the cue for a brisk debate on the Vietnam War between Sting ('60,000 American soldiers and countless others died for no reason') and ex-GI Ian Copeland ('We succeeded in our mission'). It was also a night of strategic frenzy in Phan Dinh Phung stadium, where thousands of papier-mâché fans became makeshift frisbees and girls in tight satin dresses danced with Mao-suited National Assembly men. Over twenty years, most American and even European towns had all clotted anonymously into Sting's recurrent tour. But even he was knocked out by Vietnam (which reminded him of the Amazon), telling friends he'd 'beg' to be invited back. He was.

Sting then made for Australia. In Sydney the scene became part Royal Command, part cabaret at a fundraiser for coronary research. Sting left the stage during 'Every Breath', waltzed into the crowd and sang gazing into the eyes of a blonde in a blue Grecian-style Versace dress. This was one 'close friendship' the mob had totally missed. It was the Princess of Wales. The relationship between them was sexual in that it could only have existed between a man and a woman. The reason why in Sydney some felt it went further was because of the way she treated him. She teased him. He blushed. She giggled. Sting, of course, never lost his deep fealty to his wife, but, increasingly, after Sydney, people talked.

The press were still doing so a week later, when he checked into the Golden Doors resort near Brisbane. He spent two days there indulging in gourmet vegetarian food, bush-walking, chanting, meditation, and his first-ever facial. According to the manager, Brian Locker, 'The guests came up and spoke to him – he was very easy-going and pleasant.' Sting told them he wanted to recover both his voice and equanimity by the ancient arts of tai chi and chiqong. It was, he said 'an honour, but nerveracking' to have serenaded Diana. Ten months later, he paid court on a more sombre occasion, as a mourner at the Princess's funeral.

The tour's final lap opened in Aberdeen on 22 November. Starting with a rootsy version of 'Hounds Of Winter', Sting stalked the stage, half graceful, half lumbering through a mix of well-worn ('Every Little Thing') and anthems-to-be ('All Four Seasons'). 'Let Your Soul Be Your Pilot' earnt him his first ovation, thanks to a fluid midsong shift into gospel mode. He mugged around during the newer tunes, but raised the fans' eyebrows, as well as his own, in the chestnuts. 'Every Breath' was deodorized by a spray of sterile, white-soul saxes. The familiar contours of 'Roxanne' came and went without upping the emotional voltage, either amongst the audience or the band. It was just as everyone knew it would be, and that was enough. They were content. Less than half an hour later, Sting had triumphed. He'd convinced the crowd that this competent, workaday set, judiciously weighted with Golden Greats, was grounds for dancing in the aisles. 'I don't know how he did it,' says one fan, 'and I was there. I still am.'

Most critics like their rock gods along the lines of Liam Gallagher, so it would be understandable if Sting had a doubt or two about his first major homecoming in years. In the end, notices were good. After two decades, there were almost as many spins on Sting as mood swings on *Mercury Falling*, from 'sod' to St Francis. Above all, there was his tardy sense of fun. As Giles Smith wrote in the *Mail on Sunday*, 'You can gauge the tone of the current tour from the fact that the show's nearly stolen by the trombone player, swing[ing] that carnival instrument around like a fool. His antics are, however, upstaged by our main man, unselfconsciously chicken-strutting across the boards. Sting, whose various incarnations have often failed to score high on slapstick, dedicates his latest appearances to having a lark.' 'Make no mistake,' chimed the *Independent*, 'Sting is a fun guy.' Hair, or its lack, was uppermost in everyone's mind at the Albert Hall. 'What do you think of it?' Sting asked the crowd, patting his razor-cut tonsure. 'You're like Bruce Willis,' bawled a fan. 'Bruce Willis dreams he's like this,' Sting chortled. Others thought the slap-headed look recalled Paul Gascoigne.

Like Gazza, Sting had a love–hate relationship with Newcastle. In recent years, time had brought magnanimity, and with it nostalgia, into play. 'Whenever I come back,' Sting told North East TV, 'I don't recognize the place . . . My memories are sort of bittersweet . . . I have some great memories and some sad ones and they all come welling back . . . I was a teacher for a while and I kind of miss it. I miss that responsibility. The routine.' During a gig at the Newcastle Arena, Sting announced 'Twenty-Five To Midnight' as 'what could have happened if I'd made a different decision twenty years ago'. Later that night, he mingled backstage with his 91-year-old grandmother, siblings, friends and ex-colleagues like Nigel Stanger, whose one-time view of Sting ('I

can't play with the guy – get rid of him') had given way to a
civility becoming the Arena's co-owner. Later still, he made a
sentimental journey down the dark streets of Wallsend. A man
named Chuck Grice saw Sting near the gates of the shipyard.
'There was no one else around . . . I wanted to catch up and say
hi, but I didn't. He'd stopped, like someone lost in thought,
gazing up at the old cranes. It was no time to butt in, so I held
back. I couldn't help thinking, Where was everybody? Where
were the heavies and the manager? . . . This was someone who
wanted to be alone, a guy with dignity . . . someone who was
catching his breath before turning back into a star.'

There, after dates in Belgium and France, Sting's *annus
mirabilis* ended.*

For all that he lightened up on stage and in private, Sting was a
hard man to know. Aloof, laconic, caustic, with neither talent nor
time for small talk, he could take long flights or shuttle between
homes without even speaking. One friend jokes that he
'expresses himself in few words. One's "yeah" and the other's
"no".' In interviews Sting often sat for an hour without making
eye contact, an arm drawn defensively across his chest. There was
a 'reek of reserve', says Griffin. After so long in the public eye,
Sting was jealous of what space was left. 'A biography . . . would
have to be written by someone close enough to have known me,'
he told this author, '[And that's] a small group.'

Sting's ultracoy act didn't conceal the core personality: an out-
wardly well-mannered if wary charmer who was inwardly a
martyr to nerves. Those who met him soon found a compensating asperity. As noted, Sting was also able and increasingly ready
to laugh. There was the pantomime figure who stalked the stage
and mocked his follicular problems. When he came to make a
new video he adorned his flat-top with a wig that looked more
like a ferret; the film itself saw him horsing around on a pony. A
journalist asked him if he hadn't 'choked with emotion' when, in
Vietnam, he sang the lines 'Nothing comes from violence / And

* The year-long offensive of albums, singles, soundtracks, films and tours also
had repercussions for Sting's business empire. Over Christmas 1996 Miles's
organization moved from its five floors at Bugle House into larger offices in
Camden.

nothing ever could'. 'No,' Sting said. 'I belched.' Early in 1997 he appeared in New York tossing off surefire one-liners from his comic locker. Sting held his own with Howard Stern, survived Rosie O'Donnell and hosted *Saturday Night Live*, where he sent up his eco-warrior past in the opening skit. During his show at Madison Square Garden, semi-nude dancers appeared behind screens during 'Roxanne' – buckets of sludge, feathers and a funny frog rained down from the rafters. When he sang at that spring's rainforest gala, he did so in a fluorescent-green hat. These weren't the actions of a man smarting with his own cool.

Sting failed to scoop any Grammys in 1997. He did, though, continue his relay through Europe and America before hitting the festivals that summer. It was this non-stop slog that enabled him, exercising his genius as role-player, to foist off an image of poise, wit and self-confidence, when he'd actually come to those things late on. It also allowed him to overcome his lifelong shyness. Sting was always or usually at his best on stage.

So the nightly raids continued. Whether with the carpet-bombing of tours or the precision-bombing of galas, Sting normally hit his mark. He'd come to look on globetrotting as a trial between self-expression and poignancy. He loved playing, but he missed home. That meant not only Lake House but California, its eternal sunshine, his glamorous friends and, of course, Malibu. Sting bought a new, 'must-have' villa in July 1997. The price was $6 million. Trimmed in grey, its furniture a child-proof hodgepodge of airfoam-slab sofas, overstuffed cushions and Native American rugs, the view was of a flat, absurdly white beach. He liked to walk along the coast with his family, a foot at a time, the fastest pace Giacomo could manage. When they stopped to watch the gulls strafing down, Sting sometimes stood there, face up, as though back among the Wallsend cranes. He seemed to have travelled far more than the actual distance between the two towns. His whole journey had been an epic haul. One of the quirks along the way was that he'd become several different people. His love of the *dolce vita* and odd guilt pang over money lay behind the other, less obvious conflicts (mainly spiritual) that played their part in his, at times, schizo-phrenic career. His admiration for droning, ambient music met with the Beatleness of his hooks. Sting's absolute devotion to his wife pulled against a weakness for strippers and seedy clubs. His inundation in the world of rations, quotas and Utility garb gave way to a childlike glee in dressing up, alternating with the crazy self-reproach he summarized as 'the worry of someone tapping me on the shoulder and saying, come on, we know where you're from – now fuck off'.

In short, Sting's bent for self-denial co-existed with a precocious capacity for the good life. Early in the 1980s he became fixated by Italian food, wine and design, notably Gianni Versace's. The two men grew even closer when *The Soul Cages* was recorded in Migliarino. Versace supplied the rococo outfits for Sting's wedding in 1992, not coincidentally wringing headlines the world over. He appeared for Giacomo's christening in the same church four years later. Versace's family visited Lake House and Sting's family visited Versace. It was all part of a larger picture: Sting was Italianate – people wondered whether some Sumner hadn't once mated with a Roman – and loved the lakes around Milan and the Tuscan hills. Yet the relationship not only served both parties, but also rested on real affection and regard. Already a neighbour and crony, Versace was doomed to become the stock father-figure – as he'd long been to Elton John – that Sting seemed to need even before Ernie's death. 'No doubt Gianni played the role of a surrogate,' says Larry Adler, who did so himself. 'They were inseparable,' adds a friend.

On 15 July 1997 Versace was shot dead on the steps of his Miami home. Sting (hours offstage after a show in Croatia) and Styler weren't merely shaken – they were stunned. They'd walked in and out of that very house with their children. Both flew in for the designer's memorial service. The couple were screened by Italian police before the ceremony in Milan Cathedral. Security was tight; Versace's killer (actually then trapped in Florida, hours before his own death) was thought to be on the run. Authorities even feared that he might make his way to Milan to revel in the scene.

On 21 July Sting underwent his first audition in twenty years. Versace's family had asked Elton John and him to sing at the obsequies. The two superstars duly obliged, and for fifteen minutes gave a private, unaccompanied rendition of the 23rd Psalm for 77-year-old Monsignor Migliavacca. 'I knew their names,' the choirmaster says, 'but it was necessary to be sure their voices were worthy of a solemn celebration of Mass ... It

wasn't a perfect execution but only because each was overcome
with emotion.' Long in revolt against the professional hauteur
and so-so talent of most stars, Sting thought this a 'generous'
verdict.

Throughout the next morning, 10,000 fans and paparazzi
whipped up an atmosphere of catwalk-type frenzy somehow
becoming the Princess of Wales. She, in turn, was followed by
Sting and Styler, the latter in a widow's veil. They sat next to the
family. After the fifty-minute ceremony the couple joined style
gurus Giorgio Armani, Karl Lagerfeld and Valentino, ski ace
Alberto Tomba, sundry models, friends and the merely famous
at Versace's nearby mansion. Sting signed the condolence book.
If it was proof that no major event was apparently safe from his
presence, the whole saga also spoke to his dignity. Sting was the
sole star there seemingly aware of his surroundings. Lynn
Vaughn, also present in the cathedral, says 'most of the "names"
were off in an ante-room changing and having their hair done
before making an entrance. It was a sick scene, [more like] a
fashion show than a funeral . . . Sting, though, just sat there. You
got the impression he was the one person actually grieving.'

After that Sting returned to the stage in Germany and Russia.
He sang at both the MTV and Country Music awards. He jetted
the Atlantic with the Spice Girls. He joined McCartney, Clapton
and Mark Knopfler (with whom he again duetted on 'Money For
Nothing') in a Live Aid-style benefit for the volcano-hit island of
Montserrat, scene of *Ghost in the Machine* and others; sang on
the *Very Special Christmas 3* anthology; donated 'I'll Be Missing
You' to Princess Diana's tribute LP; staged his eighth rainforest
gala; and covered a Noël Coward tune for charity. Early in 1998 he
went back to the studio, if that word befitted the dining-hall of
his home. Sting was at work on a live album, as well as recording
the sounds that, he said, 'drive me totally crazy . . . In absolute
silence I hear music . . . It's never empty.'

What was it about Sting that, in Dominic Miller's take, made him
an 'ace boss'? What qualities of character and leadership filled
the musicians, engineers and wizened roadies at Steerpike with
such awe that some had stuck with him for twenty years? Part of
his appeal lay in his utter devotion to his work – work of sheer
sweat. Sting had given the *Sunday Times* the impression that 'after

Christmas [1996] he'll take a year off ... No touring, no recording, nothing'. In practice, that evolved into a schedule that made The Police's seem woefully laid-back. Part also lay in Sting's idealism and in what one flunkey calls his 'lack of side'. As time went on, he showed new faith in his lieutenants and teamed with them more often. When, for example, Miller came up with the chord sequence of 'Shape Of My Heart', 'what Sting did, his skill or genius, [was] to edit it into something that sounds like a tune ... It went off into these elaborate changes [which he] turned into a whole song, which I never could have done.' It was Sting's role to extract a palpable essence of the rough-hewn or inchoate and make it play on *Top of the Pops*, a skill at which he excelled and which left old salts like Miller, and the whole crew, willing galley-slaves to his drum.

Even Stewart Copeland came on board.

As Sting grew closer to his old blood-brother, he also made nice to Phil Sumner. He was a regular visitor to Whitley Bay over the winter of 1997–98. The siblings cut an odd pair: Gordon like something made by a jeweller's art, body perfectly chiselled, facial planes expertly turned, large green eyes ornamented by black lashes. Phil was more caved-in. He looked like his older brother after 10,000 fewer trips to the gym. More to the point, their previous death-feud ended. Stress remained, but Sting was apt to defuse it with a self-mocking jape and a round of drinks. His humour won through. Sting's mind was manifestly sharp; he could bandy football scores as easily as Jungian psychology. And as he downed his beer, belched, smacked his lips, then clapped his brother on the back, his vital presence filled the room with rude health and radiant boyish energy.

Sting's moods became less fickle. Critics and the like still took heat from a man who stood up for his beliefs regardless of who was rattled or piqued. In terms of tongue-bashing candour, the status remained quo: as usual, Sting reacted spontaneously to anyone or anything he didn't like – though more now by the arch quip than the full broadside. Many still gave him a berth. Even Miles declined to enter into the briar patch of a row with Sting about politics. Mick Ronson, no stranger to dogmatic pop stars, had called him 'a diamond, and just as cutting'. But Sting was also a warm, virile, droll man who, despite the hot flushes, was quick to chill. He no longer froze. Friends noted that he was the nurturing parent, Styler the disciplinarian. If Coco woke in the middle of the night with a bad dream, it was her father who sang her back asleep. This mellowing followed down every line. The old Sting – confrontational, impulsive, tart – still existed; but the new – tolerant, cool, forbearing – was getting up speed, fast.

'Schizophrenic?' says another old friend. 'Totally. It defines him.'

Before Sting made it, he cultivated his hard-nut image; but some suspected he was really macho-by-pose. *Rolling Stone* and the rest became willing accessories to his stony, he-man act, eyes hooded, concave-cheeked, and an overall air of chronic bile. That implied menace soon melted around women, or at least one who knew him well. 'Sting,' she says, 'was actually very old-fashioned. He had old-fashioned values, and a strong belief in family life. He liked to talk about the kids ... The tiger was really a pussy-cat.' Sting certainly cleaved to roots and domesticity. He was also an autodidact, atoning furiously for a relatively poor education. The slit-eyed tough gave way, in private, to a chess addict and poetry-lover. He could quote Shakespeare by the yard. By 1998, it seemed as though he'd spent the second half of his life ruing the first. But even in the 1970s colleagues had seen the old man inside the young. 'Basically shy, with a pumped-up façade' is Andy Partridge's view. Sting's novel ability to see at least some good in mankind owed much to the palliatives of hearth, home and a busy career. Still, 'he hates everyone, except for his family' was harsher than Copeland meant. He'd never been as screwed-up as that.

Sting could manage anything. He was the non-actor who held his own in *The Grotesque* and enjoyed a mini-revival in *Quadrophenia*; who popped flashbulbs at the Oscars; whom the mob cheered loudest outside Graumann's Theatre. Relatively few friends set their heart on him, yet he took the time and trouble to charm even crazies at stage-doors. Unlike a Jagger or Bowie, Sting was ever-accessible to his fans. The ex-misanthrope was affable and garrulous with the masses, if not always one-on-one. The photos of him smiling or scrawling autographs fixed him in the public eye; the severity of earlier put-downs giving way to poetic saws that were increasingly human, benign and self-consciously prophetic. Money seemed not to have spoilt him. In July 1997 Sting signed a deal with EMI Music Publishing worth

£20 million. He was Croesus rich. But he was also something more, a self-made man who managed to convince himself he wasn't well off, but just happened to spend days gardening or dozing by the Avon. Sting was never going to buy a Lear jet or diamond collars for the dogs. His idea of self-indulgence was a good book.

To some extent, Sting's image flowed from his mental bent. His lack of affectation was perversely dazzling. Sting was fully aware of the box-office pull of his looks and name. But increasingly, he became that rare thing: a rock star without vanity. Here again, he was better or different from a Jagger or Bowie. When, in 1997, Sting took a stroll around Bedales School with a view to sending Jake there, he was mobbed by screaming teenagers. 'Oh, come on,' he said. 'I'm a balding yobbo.' Sting's snub could have been laughed off but for the fact he was blushing. 'I suppose for a man of my age, I'm all right' was as far as he'd go in print. At least one of the Bedales girls guessed what only intimates fully realized; that he was 'easily embarrassed' and, at heart, 'didn't think much of himself'. Neither Sting's skinhead crop nor his unlifted face were the sign of a man abandoned to his own pomp. In the summer sun, his epidermal slump showed. He reminded the girl of someone 'ageing on fast-forward', like one of the mutant extras in *Dune*. Sting's number-three cut, the style popular with army recruits, was seized on by the press. According to *The Times*, he 'now join[ed] the select group who suffer from Samson Syndrome – once shorn, their good looks and much of their power go, too'. Tony Parsons in the *Mirror* was blunter: 'he ... looks like a walnut in a condom'. Nineteen ninety-seven ended with two of Britain's oldest and most popular papers arguing the toss about Sting's haircut.

Opinions on him personally were equally charged. A man backstage that April at the rainforest gala in New York (where Sting co-starred with Elton John, Stevie Wonder and James Taylor) found him 'up and down ... his soft heart and hard head both in evidence', the latter dominant. Daniel Morgan encountered Sting at a Pavarotti show in Covent Garden that summer. He was 'a jerk'. Nor was Sting's strenuous do-gooding employed without cost – in tense relationships with the media and numerous others. The *Sun* still accused him of being an 'eco-bore' and claimed he was motivated by egomania rather than real concern. At *Melody Maker*, he'd long been known as 'a wanker'.

If so, he was the sanest, smartest, most clear-eyed one treading the boards. And self-possessed. 'I'm not Phil Collins!' he yelled at Madison Square Garden after the Rosie O'Donnell débâcle, grinning broadly. A week later he took buffoonery to new heights with a send-up of himself on *Saturday Night Live*. (Viewers were treated to a 45-year-old icon posing on TV in red bikini briefs.) Conceivably, Sting could have managed the odd lacerating jape ten years earlier. What distinguished this from previous, half-cock efforts at humanization was the joke's butt – the rainforest. He could never have knocked, say, Amnesty in the mid-1980s. *Pace* Parsons, Sting's stubble-haired look not only took gall, it made a point. He knew full well he wasn't a permanent fixture. Sting admitted he was getting on, and wasn't planning to be cryogenically preserved. Accepting the obvious, and acting his age, gave him the right values. He was kind, genial, capable of gracious behaviour and bullseye self-insight. He had no illusions. His final diagnosis of his success: 'First you get lucky, and then to sustain that, you get smart.'

Sting's other virtue was his versatility. For twenty years, he'd subscribed to no package-deal of sounds. Preferring global to parochial jargon, all his albums had fallen into two camps: those for everyone and those just for fans. *The Soul Cages*, for one, belonged to the Sting-Only Club, though it also became a calling card for his forays into muzak and soundtrack. There'd always been a protean side to The Police, who borrowed from rock, reggae, punk, jazz, ska and the kind of Latin rhythms Copeland explored on *Synchronicity* – often all in the same song. But from the early 1990s Sting traversed a staggering range. He was fully alive to his reputation as a gadfly. 'I look at music as being a very broad church,' he said. 'I like the whole thing ... I even like classical music. It's one common language.' Albums like *Mercury Falling* were packed with Sting's stylistic allsorts, from witty cribbing of pop-soul riffs to smooth, 1970s-style hooks, from old-school melodies to hoary yarns about love. The flagship products were eclectic enough. But Sting's secondary brand – a steady output of jingles, duets, covers, mood music and film scores – showed he'd not only crossed his cultures, but mastered the art of fusing them. He was no virtuoso. But he played a giddy array of instruments (bass, guitar, mandolin, piano, harp, sax, flute, drums) and listened to virtually anything with notes. He loved to work, ruled nothing out and was always or normally for hire. He got around.

Thus, in 1995 Sting serenaded Prince Hakim, the Sultan of Brunei's son, at a private party, and pocketed over a million dollars. He performed 'Sisters Of Mercy' on the Leonard Cohen tribute LP *Tower of Song*; collaborated with the Irish folk band the Chieftains; wrote a protest number called 'Nuclear Waste'; recorded 'The Wind Cries Mary' (nominated for a Grammy) with John McLaughlin; saw his *Peter and the Wolf* revived on TV; worked with James Taylor and honky-tonk singer Toby Keith; and fund-raised with Clapton and McCartney. In March 1997 he took part in a Carnegie Hall gala called 'From Greig to Gershwin'. Later that summer he sang 'Waters Of Tyne' on *Carnival*, a children's album produced by Styler.

For years, one of the best-kept secrets in rock had been how happy top names were to risk their cool by appearing in lucrative foreign TV commercials. Sting may have turned down Duckworth Finn's offer of a coffee ad in 1990. But five years later he was happy to accept a reported £500,000 to promote the Saegaia golf complex in Japan. The irony of a man known for his hard line on ecology helping plug a resort that locals complained hurt the environment wasn't lost on his foes. By 1996 Sting's hostility to licensing his wares had faded, and he went on the prowl for corporate partners. 'Englishman In New York' was duly used as a vehicle to sell Rovers. Reverting to his male-model days, Sting himself showed off a range of Vitra furniture. For a while, he seemed to do little but pout floridly in magazines. In July 1997 the one-time *Sniffin' Glue* pin-up appeared, in spats and a monocle, adorning *Vanity Fair*.

Sting, though, was doing more than simply regressing on a bigger budget. Just as a yawning generation gap opened up in rock – even the Stones and U2 taking a popular hit – he shrewdly extended his shelf-life. He not only played with or patronized bands like Sonic Youth, The Verve and Oasis, he turned his talent for mimicry to a host of modernist, or post-modernist, dodges. Thanks to Hugh Padgham, his albums were semi-automated (if never fully robotic) with QSound technology, digital pitch and synths. More to the point, Sting's songs dealt in the timeless virtues of catchy, singsong choruses, lovelorn lyrics and hazy salves. He might not have had the full cybernetic studio tricks or fuzzy guitars, but he still inhabited the same world as Radiohead, Pearl Jam and the rest. An album like *Soul Cages* owed as much to *Bleach* as to any number of early '60s Stax platters.

There was another, more personal point to Sting cannily prolonging his sell-by date: to balance the new tranquillity – and banality – of his home life. He was 'ecstatic . . . almost *too* happy' at Lake House. But he periodically felt the need to boot his image from the landed squire into something louder. A combination of restlessness, drive and the Wallsend work ethic kept him on the hoof at a time when Copeland and Summers, for two, had gone to stud. Unlike them, Sting would emerge live, at Madison Square Garden and in the Glastonbury mud, or on TV, plugging *Mercury Falling* and roasting James Taylor. In the rare moments he was neither on stage, hogging the airwaves or gracing the Style sections of the Sunday press, he was on the longest road-trip of all, the one that led to what Blake called the 'palace of wisdom'.

Ironically, it was Sting, who otherwise prided himself on the power of reason in the face of brute prejudice, who'd personalized his various campaigns in the 1980s and lashed out, casting his rivals as morally defective. If some of his shies were familiar, the flings were drop-dead. 'Open a vein' was his retort to one Tory MP rash enough to debate the Falklands with him in 1982. His concerts could be a rough ride, too, juddering to a crude yet seismic climax of froth and spit. Whether wading into the bouncers or inviting a heckler to meet him in the alley, Sting was a hard nut. All the toxic prick of the nickname was there in venomous gobs. He was a cradle thug with a paradoxical love of books and music. One of the Sumners had gone as far as to call his 'a psycho'.

By his mid-forties, Sting hadn't merely matured. He'd been reincarnated. He still defended the oppressed, the sick and the exploited, but that no longer meant laying siege to the Establishment. His credo had evolved from anarchy to arch-libertarianism. If he had a signature tune it was the old Cole Porter hit, 'Don't Fence Me In', rather than any ditty by the Sex Pistols.

Sting's life at Lake House was of parody-worthy serenity. During the summer he often came padding out to the garden, carrying a cup of tea, and sat in the boathouse or under the trees.

For all that he could look old and tired, he still insulted the ageing process. He was no Peter Pan-like freak, but he stubbornly ducked the pipe and slippers. In person, he was unexpectedly pink, brighter and bouncier than he had any right to look and feel. From his open shirt up to the reborn hair he had artfully pouffed each week at a London salon, Sting had the scrubbed rosy sheen of a man in peak shape. He worked out and did yoga. He meditated. He no longer kept a vampire's hours. When not reading or writing, he was apt to be out horse-riding or walking the dog. He watched football. He listened to the classics. He even sang in the shower. Just as Sting's musical tastes grew, so he acquired a new love of writers he'd slated as 'Nazis' or 'scum' – Ayn Rand, for example. Whether camping around on holiday with Styler or tearing up at Princess Diana's death, Sting was increasingly down to earth, fallible and, above all, human. He subsisted on his track record, not promises of future fullfilment. He was happy now.

Energy, will, brains: the words go round, like a comedian in a revolving door, from those who know Sting best. His mind is 'laser-sharp', says Adler. Miller compares it to a chess grand-master's – 'with a *great* endgame'. No barrier, it seemed, was too formidable, no boundary too sacred, to stymie the relentless forger of pop classics and closet fan of Ravel and Debussy. But coupled with his singular drive was an apparently boundless personal charm. Signing autographs, answering letters and backing causes, Sting appeared never to let up. Always there was work to do: the job of 'giving something back' to a public from whom money had teemed down for decades. One friend claims that Sting didn't need to exercise to control his weight: most times, he says, he 'slaved himself thin'. Time and again, fans harked at his flair for 'putting himself across'. One such talent was a gift for pithy and effective expression. Sting wasn't a good public orator. For years, he'd dreaded speeches like a curse. He'd called his 1989 address to the Altamira Indians 'a nightmare'. But from behind a song lyric – on stage at Carnegie Hall, perhaps, or duetting with Elton John – Sting's impact, when he chose to let go, was all too real. Lynn Vaughn would never forget the two men, standing by Princess Diana, singing at Versace's memorial service. It was, she says, 'a once-in-a-lifetime experience' – vivid, tragic, heartfelt, yet life-affirming and profound. Other fans round the world similarly speak of Sting's ability, like the Princess's own, to reach out and move them.

Who was this 46-year-old with the gammy knees and ears, soft-spoken, yet with the clout to hire and fire, casually buy a six-bedroom villa on Malibu beach and command fees of £300,000 for playing private concerts, like the one for Nomura Asset? Quite plainly, a smooth operator. Another quality that distinguished Sting was an almost legendary power of persuasion. He could tell the world, for example, via his publicist, that corporate entertainment didn't sully his image: 'Being a musician isn't a charity, it's a job like any other . . . if someone's willing to pay that sort of money for your services, I don't think there is any contradiction at all.'

The brazen yearning to cash in was manifest. Whether with private patrons like the Sultan, or across the boardroom table, Sting drove a hard deal. He was rudely aware of his own worth. But he also frankly admitted to a few intimates that he was slowing up. He told one musician, a tad surprisingly, he was physically and mentally 'knackered'. One day, of course, he'd give up. 'I'll say, "Put the corset away, I'm not going on stage tonight," and that'll be that,' he put it in *The Times*. Sting's cross-over into Broadway and Hollywood showed how much he worried about obsolescence, chiefly ways to stall it – and his cold-eyed view of the rock scene gave him no reason to think that his status would be elevated by cranking out more finger-popping, three-minute hits; just the opposite. Having said he was anticipating retirement, that didn't necessarily mean he wanted it. He was quite happy to deliver, and get paid millions for doing so, well into the next century. What Sting really craved, of course, was to bring his music more in line with middle-aged reality, thus avoiding the phantasmagoria of singing about being broke and lonely from the angle of a millionaire family-man.

As he kicked fifty, still popular and sought-after, Sting took more pleasure than ever in his power to consist of the inconsistent, to be a hive of contradictions, to make music out of opposites. Always hymenopteral (and so-named), he made a beeline for freedom of thought, art and speech. Whether in his lyrics or elsewhere, Sting flailed most of the prevailing norms of modern life. He led what amounted to a holy war for conservation, ecology and equal rights for the Third World. He personally favoured the broadest mix of ideals and cultures. He rued the drift away from a society of self-made men – as he proudly thought of himself – toward the welfare state that he considered the fruit of Old Labour. While he liked to call himself a socialist, the views he'd spewed for twenty years were more strictly Thatcherite, even Tory. He wanted to see the kind of world preserved that had spawned men like him.

He ran his crusades from the slant of a new, recycled personality. Sting's permanent shield of scorn, no longer needed, was stowed, and few of his fans had any inkling of all the hurts and humiliations wrought by the ugly years of neglect. A full revolution had brought him in a circle. 'I'm quite happy with the pattern of my life,' he said. 'I don't want any big upheavals . . . I just want to work with what I've got. I don't really have any more ambitions. That's a strange thing to say for an artist, but I don't. I'm not terribly ambitious; I don't need to succeed. I just need to stay healthy and sane and happy.' In most of his music, quotes and looks, the premium now was on comely style and sober values. Sting stood out, not stuck out. He disowned giantism, the need to be constantly king of the hill. He'd done that. Sting's answer to the collective mania of most rock shows was to puncture the frenzy with humour. Hence pranks like the green ten-gallon hat. Making and playing music on his own terms also had a personal spinoff. 'It's my therapy,' Sting told TROS-TV. 'I think without it I'd be completely insane, totally.'

In the years before, and particularly after Sting's confession, came reminders that music played a spiritual role, too. It was, as he said, 'what defines me'. Even his staunch Catholic parents might have appreciated the way in which their son substituted art for God. They may have understood, even better than he did, the complicated ties between his guilt-ridden youth and his consequent lust for glory. In his published accounts, Sting often called attention to the evident kinship between rock and religion. He was all too aware of the semi-divine airs of most pop stars. He drew perceptive parallels between the shows, full of smoke, noise and Shinto-like awe, and the sort of mass piety he knew at St Columba's. He told one reporter, with neat irony, 'I look at music as being a broad church.'

Nowhere was this truer than in his devotion to Hollywood. It was no Damascene conversion – Sting had been writing for films for years – but from the mid-1990s major studios were all over him, so much so that he wasn't sure whether he was a rocker or a musicologist who liked celluloid. Thus he covered 'A Day In The Life' for *Demolition Man*. He appeared on soundtracks or scores for *Sabrina*, *White Squall*, *Il Postino*, *Ace Ventura: When Nature Calls*, *Leaving Las Vegas*, *The Living Sea* and, aptly enough, *The Grotesque*. Significantly, between TV and radio spots and a mad east-coast tour schedule, he flew to Los Angeles to be at Elton John's Oscar party at the Mondrian hotel. Though unrewarded himself, Sting posed happily with Frances McDormand, winner of a gong for *Fargo*. While in California he took the time to meet Disney's head of animation, Peter Schneider. The result was a commission to write songs for *Kingdom of the Sun*, a remake of *The Prince and the Pauper* due in 2000.

When he was a boy, Audrey had taken him to the local cinema, where mother and son pored over sagas of heroes and heroines who overcame scrapes by feats that reflected courage, skill, cunning, wit, nobility, compassion and sheer grit. For years he'd be forced to endure setbacks and snubs before he could realize his childhood dream of scoring fame and fortune as a singer. Now that he had them, in spades, as one of rock's brightest lights, he made a conscious or unconscious bid to push the envelope of what it meant to be a star. By slaying Hollywood, Sting meant to make up for the ten years during which he'd been seen as no more than a dropout or clippie or file-clerk or, worst of all, 'a psycho'.

It would be stretching it to claim that Sting's soundtrack work made a nostalgic link for him to the lost world of the Wallsend Odeon. Even so, it was all part of a strategy that went back two decades. No sooner had Sting made it in 1978–79 than he'd begun to emerge from the shadow of being a mere rocker. He defined fame as a 'genre-busting, multi-media' thing. Minor names could afford to ply their puny one-track trades; real stars had globes to span. The scores he wrote were also scores he settled. Hollywood fame fostered the image of a Renaissance Man by exposing him to tens of millions of ordinary, rural folk who would never go near a gig. With *Sabrina* and the rest, Sting achieved his ambition of becoming not only a brand name, but a household word. He was reborn, a man of wealth and taste, one of the best-known entertainers in the world.

That kind of fame went both forwards and back. By 1999 Sting's celebrity left nothing to risk: the good deeds wooed the hard-core vote, while the border-crossing CDs and films could be relied on to raise interest among the marginals. Added to his latter-day pomp was the residual glory from the era of shellsuits and punk cockades. That meant The Police.

Starting with the trite coda of 1986's 'Don't Stand So Close To Me', A&M had gone to ever more rabid lengths to strip the group's assets. The box-set and live LP were followed by yet more dregs and lame remixes. By 1997, Sting had relaxed his own previous policy of non-cooperation on posthumous projects. He duetted with both Pato Banton and Ziggy Marley on *Message From Jamaica*, an auditory hall of mirrors best described as reggae's imitation of The Police imitating it. Puff Daddy reworked 'Every Breath' and 'Roxanne'. A slew of other projects followed for the sole benefit of completists and commercial entities. *Police Academy*, a set taken from the band's zany flirtation with Gong, was released on Pangaea that summer.

Most five-year wonders – names like Blondie come to mind – soon fade from view. One week they're playing to thousands, quoted breathily in *People* and on TV, surrounded by aides and toadies, courted and cosseted like a head of state, and the next they're auditioning for panto. It's as though they never existed. Some reappear from time to time, lurking on the edge of a revival or threatening a reunion. Sometimes they play again, ghostly vestiges of their once solid selves. The public ignores them or turns away embarrassed. A very select few are rehabilitated by circumstance or achievement. Although The Police were beneficiaries of some slick marketing, it wasn't mere hype that kept them ticking over, racking sales of two or three million CDs a year. That was true success, based largely on the deft fusion of their best work. Even the critics conceded that the band roamed where few pop stars had. If only as an intermediary between worlds, they were among the most influential bands of their time.

Perversely, probably the only person who wasn't thrilled about the group's longevity was Sting himself. Time and again, he harped on his deeply ambivalent view of the past. The Police had provided money, power and a launch-pad for his stratospheric solo career. They'd made him a star. But that sort of fame also took its toll. For five years it all went right and it all went wrong. As well as creative clashes and brawls in the dressing-room, Sting's first marriage had succumbed to what he called 'Success distort[ing] things, magnifying problems ... Even though we were in our late twenties and emotionally capable of handling it, we still fucked up.' Then there were drugs. From the safe haven of 1993, Sting would admit, 'We went through our coke stage, which was totally stupid. It exaggerated everything. Total paranoia.' Wild experimentation had taught Sting that cocaine's effect, on him, was of heightened aggression and megalomania. If anything, he needed less of that. What Sting wanted those days was a drug that induced greater timidity and an enhanced sense of insignificance. Finally, there was his self-portrayal as a 'very tomorrow kind of guy'. 'I most certainly won't listen to [*Message in a Box*],' he told *Q*. 'I'm not into nostalgia,' he informed VH-1. This dogged modernism reached its peak when, in a radio interview in October 1996, he seemed to forget Copeland's and Summers' names.

On the other hand, Sting's memory was jewel-sharp when it came to the due dates of fees and royalties. Making money had always charted high on his personal list of priorities. He not only netted millions from The Police's back roster. He reaped the harvest of his post-Virgin control of his own inventory. Thus the 1997 hit 'I'll Be Missing You'* by Puff Daddy – a cover of 'Every Breath' – brought him upwards of £400,000, even though he didn't play on it. Over the years, Sting had pulled some master strokes, both tactical and musical. But his best move, the shrewdest action of all, was the one he'd taken against Richard Branson. That single coup, executed at the cost of £150,000 and a few headlines, reunited him with a song catalogue worth tens of millions.

By the late 1990s, Sting had cooled his antagonism to his old band. After the trench warfare of the 1970s and the 1980s' fizzing rows, the ex-Police learned to co-exist. They were more conciliatory to each other and more vigilant of the group's legacy. Sting himself discovered new virtues in the music. There had, after all, been bottle in the message. 'We made some really good records,

*Sting himself covered the song as a tribute to Princess Diana.

a couple of duff ones,' he now said. 'A lot of it I'm very proud of.' Nor, in the light of his catchy, jazz-pop solo offerings, had The Police been a case of arrested development. 'We were a fucking great band,' Sting said. 'Stewart was a brilliant drummer. Andy was a brilliant technician and guitarist. I was a fucking brilliant songwriter and I sang and played bass. *At the same time!*'

Since their *de facto* split in 1983–84, The Police had never categorically ruled out a reunion. Fans continued to view them much like a carefully preserved vintage banger. There was a kind of permanence under the lumpy surface of their reissues. A plethora of gossip and souvenirs still did the rounds. But nobody could have anticipated the latest buzz about the rock equivalent of the unquiet dead. The rumoured revival of the band from behind their marble slab in 1997 nearly rivalled earlier, long-running speculation about the Beatles. Stories that The Police might go back on the beat reached a frenzy that late autumn. Comeback whispers grew in response to the latest anthology, (fleshed out by a hit remix), *The Best of The Police and Sting.* Even Copeland, whose personal equipment for the last studio dates had included a switchblade, was heard to murmur, 'I wouldn't rule it out.' Summers, now fifty-five, was uninterested. Typically, Sting was the swing-vote, exercising his gift for ambiguity and allusion with a sly 'Who knows?' before coming clean:

'Bullshit. I'd rather die.'

Of all pop's pretty faces which came and went in the early 1980s only Sting was still in the saddle as a rich, revered musician-cum-worthy fifteen years on. On a very simple level, the reason can be summed up in one word: excellence. He was the best at what he did, and one of the best ever. But his fame was built on more than a good voice and an ear for a tune. It didn't hurt that he was as svelte as a movie star and, like the big Hollywood names, liked by both sexes. More important, he was obviously intelligent about his craft. He could analyse music at any level, historically and technically (his deconstruction of classic rock songs was brilliant), in its broad patterns and types, as well as his own appeal. 'I have this little margin that's mine,' he'd said. Sting's market share was actually a significant slice of the £2.5-billion-p.a. British pie. He not only commanded fat private fees from the likes of Nomura and the Sultan of Brunei. He was the celebrity's celebrity, loved or lauded by Elizabeth Taylor, Pavarotti, Tom Cruise, Christian Slater, the late Princess, and, so he said, Frank Sinatra. Wherever music was heard, in the dry, empty hills of Africa or the green jungles of Brazil, Sting had his fans. In 1997 he filled a stadium in Pula, Croatia, only miles from the Bosnian front. While other stars had barely made the Pacific crossing, he was an idol in the Philippines, Malaysia and Vietnam. He stood above 1980s ephemera like Madonna. People who had never heard of her knew the face and, what's more, the name of Sting. That was on top of his core support, those who packed shows in Las Vegas or London, swapped chat on the Internet and dealt in merchandise and memorabillia. By 1998, Sting 'collectibles' outsold any other rocker's.

Why? That Sting was gifted helped. His versatility was at once cause for praise and scorn: troubling for those who prefer their gods to make a rule of consistency, yet testimony to Sting's panoramic view. At great personal cost, he'd made the arduous transition from pin-up to holy man, from saint to housewives' choice. He'd tumbled from his lonely summit of 1983 to the lesser level of entertainment, though he came to practise it in a more refined guise. Sting, in fact, provided the barometer for the whole greying of the pop market. Along with Elton, Clapton and Phil Collins, his albums and tours were both a touchstone and a gold-standard for the over-thirties. Even a relative dud like *Mercury Falling* did big business. Nominated for a Brit and two Grammys, it went platinum less than a year from release. While other brand names like U2 and R.E.M. saw their fan-base soften (and, in Prince's case, implode), Sting held his own as a family favourite.

Part was also due to the infrastructure that made other pop fiefdoms look criminally louche. As well as the Copeland dynasty and Kim Turner, a line-up of Christopher Burley, Danny Quatrochi, Billy Francis, Caroline Ryan and sundry staffers and gofers made Sting one of the best-managed men in rock. An army of salesmen, fan-club reps and mailshots (using a Freepost reply system) fairly flung Sting's wares on to the shelves. The IRS agency did the same thing in America. Steerpike and the rest banked the returns. With back-up like that, Sting's music, once whistled up the odd window-cleaner's ladder, was the preserve of a vast global audience. Not only did he shift the all-important 'units' – CDs and tapes; there were ancillary rights worth millions. You could hear 'It's Probably Me' in the pub or at the hairdresser. Miles licensed 'Fields Of Gold' to ad agencies and grocery chains. Tunes like 'When We Dance' quite literally went up in the world, piped into planes and elevators. Sting gave a boffo performance selling himself to film and TV. His kudos and assimilation into the mainstream took another giant leap in 1996, when the BBC needed title-music for its coverage of the Olympics. 'No problem,' said Miles. Twenty million viewers duly watched the credits roll over 'All This Time'.

In 1995 Sting made more than £9 million. Proving the value of touring, he boosted that by a third the next year. By 1997 the *Sunday Times* estimated his total wealth at £60 million, qualifying him to appear in their list of Britain's top 500 richest people. That summer he signed his £20 million agreement with EMI. This treaty (as Miles called it), exactly 10,000 times sweeter than Sting's Virgin contract, included his entire back catalogue and all current and future work worldwide. It came on top of a renegotiated deal with A&M. Within the space of a few short years, Sting had achieved a permanent place in the cultural super-league. The feat of brains and stamina that had, against the odds, led to this coup had begun on a back street in Wallsend.

In 1977, rock had gone through its cyclical fit with Abba, Pink Floyd and punk. Between the auto-havoc of the Sex Pistols and the on-with-the-show sneers of the megabands, creativity seemed to be taking a time-out. Then, after all the years of self-parody, up came something fresh, if not new. The songs were great, and The Police soon extended their palette to include vivid dabs of reggae and new wave. Suddenly they were turning out monsters. A legend loomed. After the band peaked in an orgy of mangled egos and malice, Sting's progress was essentially a straight line, with the novel detours of the rainforest and the other causes. What problems he had were largely artistic. Inside the public crowd-pleaser was a private avant-gardist. 'If rows of empty seats is it,' he half joked, 'that's what I'll do. Eventually, it'll come down to entertaining the dog.' Some of his best work seemed like the bastard offspring of 1920s modernism decked out with the poppy choruses and sly lyrics of a Sting hit. In The Police, he'd fought non-stop about direction and the 'vision thing'. As a solo star he did something similar, only with himself. Sting, though, was too wily to let his moments of self-doubt buck a career largely dependent on matching rhyming couplets with melodies. He'd summarized his own success in his brilliant, twelve-word précis – 'First you get lucky, and then to sustain that, you get smart.'

To pull that off, it helped to be someone on nodding terms with genius, with the self-restraining qualities of a rottweiler. Sting qualified on both fronts. His best music not only added to people's knowledge of their inner selves. It also took them out of themselves. It made them forget. Meanwhile, Sting's doggedness and drive weren't just high peaks but the whole Himalayas, the vast throughline of his life. The results spoke for themselves. If, from time to time, critics swarmed all over him, that, too, was a sure sign of his stature. Small fry have never made a big splash.

Sting, in short, was a creature who'd made a picture of himself and come to resemble it. Fans and foes alike were dealing with a survivor of epic proportions: from shunning the milkfloat to become a sacerdotal figure in pop culture; to carrying on, year after year, making tenacity part of the myth. Sting's wild ego had often verged on autism. But his quiet willpower was one of those heady mixes of genes, environment and pure, applied guts. He made himself, through sheer nerve, the king of the heap. Sting himself always stressed this aspect of his fame. 'I've earned every penny,' he said. 'I've sweated fucking hard for it. You have to. I don't believe human beings are set up psychologically to accept anything that's free.'

He'd turned from a moody mother's-boy into a charismatic, fêted living icon. A long distance for a single life. There were also, of course, the themes of Sting's energy, imagination and spirituality – in which Catholicism gave way to wary bouts of Calvinism – running from the cradle to, likely, the grave. The thing about his nickname wasn't just the hiving-off of waspish words (like 'pain' or 'buzz') but the suggestion of someone busy, smart, spiky, agile and all-too-capable of evasive action. That was him.

Appendix 1

Chronology

2 October 1951	Gordon Matthew Sumner born in Wallsend, Newcastle-upon-Tyne.
1958	Enters St Columba's Infants School and becomes an avid fan of *Ivanhoe* and *Treasure Island*. A year later, he graduates to the nearby junior school. He also sings in the local Catholic choir.
1959–60	Gordon discovers the guitar.
September 1963	Enrols at St Cuthbert's Grammar School. Though good at English, art and athletics, he hates it.
10 March 1967	Sees Jimi Hendrix play at the Club À Go Go in Newcastle. Gordon is transfixed.
1969	Makes his first, tentative stab at a musical career, playing in an acoustic duo with a friend named Elliot Dixon.
1970	Gordon leaves school with three A Levels, announcing his intention to be an R&B star. He takes a job in his father's dairy. When that proves insufficiently riveting, he works as a bus conductor. He will also dabble in building work, ditch-digging and the Inland Revenue.
1971	Under parental pressure, Gordon applies for

	a course at Northern Counties Teacher Training College.
1971–76	He passes through a succession of local semi-pro groups, including one, the Phoenix Jazzmen, where he's first called Sting. It sticks.
1975	He teaches at St Paul's First School, Cramlington, a few miles north of Newcastle. As well as continuing to play and write music, Sting meets a young actress named Frances Tomelty.
1 May 1976	They marry.
Winter 1976–77	Sting, part-financed by a songwriting deal with Virgin Music, moves to London with his wife and baby son. He falls in with an American drummer named Stewart Copeland and Copeland's exotic elder brother.
Spring 1977	Sting's family take a basement flat at 28A Leinster Square, Bayswater.
August 1977	Sting and Stewart Copeland recruit the guitarist Andy Summers into The Police. The name is a homage to Copeland's father's job in the CIA.
20 October 1977	Sting walks down a red-light street in Paris and writes the lyrics of 'Roxanne'.
Spring 1978	In a frenzy of activity, The Police begin recording their first album; Miles Copeland sells them to A&M; they dye their hair for a TV commercial; and hit the road as warm-up for the sci-fi-cum-hallucinogenic band Spirit.
3 May 1978	Sting joins the Performing Rights Society, majestically describing himself as an 'international recording artist and performer'. That summer, he beats Johnny Rotten to a star role in Franc Roddam's film *Quadrophenia*.
20 October 1978	The Police fly cut-rate to New York. Over the next four weeks they barnstorm north-eastern America. They come back broke but happy.
November 1978	The band's first album, *Outlandos d'Amour*, released.
13 February 1979	They reconvene in the studio.

21 February 1979	'Message In A Bottle' first played live. It proves to be a smash. Meanwhile, between April 1979 and February 1980 A&M conjure four failed singles into four re-released hits. A star is born.
Spring 1979	Second US tour.
24 July 1979	The Police headline at the Reading Festival. 'I felt like God,' says Sting, 'and I loved it.'
1 August 1979	Sting and his wife become co-directors of Steerpike Ltd, his holding company for the next twenty years. During 1979, The Police sell five million singles and two million albums. Mainly because he settles for low advances and high returns, Sting becomes rich, fast.
September 1979	'Message In A Bottle' released. The Police head back to America.
October 1979	The band's second album, *Reggatta de Blanc*, proves an astonishingly bold leap into superstardom. It makes the US Top 30 and number one in Britain.
18 December 1979	The Police play shows in two separate west London theatres. In scenes reminiscent of Beatlemania, they're transported between gigs by armoured truck.
20 January 1980	The band begin an unprecedented world tour, including virgin territory like India and Egypt, that winds down, eleven months later, in a tent on Tooting Common.
26 July 1980	The Police play in front of 40,000 fans at Milton Keynes. Onstage, all is joyous goodwill. Behind the scenes, Miles Copeland provokes a mini-riot by demanding that photographers each sign a contract waiving copyright of their pictures – only the latest example of his milking his star turn in a way that would have made Colonel Parker blush.
October 1980	*Zenyatta Mondatta* released. It, too, hits number one.
1 March 1981	Sting begins work on the BBC TV film *Artemis 81*.

15 June 1981	The Police, now tax exiles, start recording at George Martin's studio on Montserrat. It's a stunning realization of Sting's fantasy of life in the Caribbean. He also has new homes in Hampstead, north London, and Galway, Eire.
	Sting affects an ear-stud and has a nose job.
September 1981	The Police's single 'Invisible Sun', Sting's ambiguous dig at Northern Ireland, is promptly banned by the BBC.
October 1981	*Ghost in the Machine* released; yet another number one. Over the next three months, Sting and The Police scoop both Brits and Grammys.
July 1982	Sting sues Virgin Music. Meanwhile, his marriage falls apart and The Police, after five manic years, are at breaking-point. Sting finds solace with 28-year-old actress Trudie Styler.
September 1982	*Brimstone & Treacle*, starring Sting, released. His cover of 'Spread A Little Happiness' on the soundtrack gives him a first solo hit.
Winter 1982–83	Sting and Styler rent Ian Fleming's old home in Jamaica. Sitting at the author's bullet-wood desk, he writes the lyrics of 'Every Breath You Take'.
Spring 1983	Sting films *Dune* on location in Mexico.
	Back in London, he takes possession of a seventeenth-century manor house in The Grove, Highgate.
	The Police's fifth and, it turns out, last album, *Synchronicity*, is released. It busts the chart in Britain and America.
18 August 1983	Like the Beatles before them, The Police headline at Shea Stadium. The 70,000 fans go wild. Copeland and Summers both call it the thrill of their lives. That same night, Sting decides to quit.
1984	After the American tour, Sting makes back-to-back films – *The Bride* and the much-touted *Plenty*.

Spring 1985	Sting quietly recruits a jazz-funk group and records his first solo album, *The Dream of the Blue Turtles*. The Police never die a formal death, but soon succumb to the inevitable greatest-hits collections. Their past glories are endlessly recycled. An effort to reunite in the studio in 1986 ends in tears.
13 July 1985	Live Aid.
1985–86	Sting tours the world.
June 1986	Sting stars on Amnesty International's twenty-fifth anniversary tour. Copeland and Summers join him on selected dates. The trio aren't introduced as The Police, give no interviews, and leave afterwards in three separate cars. With that, Sting hopes, the band will 'snuff it'.
July 1987	Mike Figgis's film noir of Newcastle low-life, *Stormy Monday*, earns Sting rave notices.
October 1987	*Nothing Like the Sun*, Sting's second solo album, released.
December 1987	At the end of a year in which both his parents die and he suffers from writer's block, Sting is invited to visit the Brazilian rainforest. For the next five years, it becomes a burning fad. Sting takes critical flak but eventually succeeds in his goal of creating a national park for the Xingú Indians.
1988	Sting throws himself into a welter of acting jobs, charity work and galas that serve as the daily substitute for writing. In September, he begins a six-week tour for Amnesty. Sting appears on stage with the Indians' Chief Raoni. He stars opposite Kathleen Turner in *Julia and Julia*. After a year of non-stop globetrotting, Steerpike turns over £8,187,921, with more than £5 million in ticket sales.
February 1989	Sting revisits the rainforest. He co-authors a book, *Jungle Stories*.
November 1989	He opens in Brecht and Weill's *The Threepenny Opera* on Broadway. The show folds eight weeks into an eleven-month run.

January 1990	Another foray to Brazil; Sting meets with state president José Sarney.
Spring–summer 1990	After nearly three years, he begins writing and recording again.
October 1990	Sting becomes the latest rock star to record *Peter and the Wolf*.
January 1991	*The Soul Cages* released. In *Melody Maker*'s review, the album is 'the sound of Sting rummaging in the undergrowth for his "roots" ... quickly becomes morose, maudlin and whimpering ... the kind of pompous self-examination for which he deserves to be laughed at down the ages'. It hits number one.
2 October 1991	Sting turns forty. He celebrates along with 10,000 fans at the Hollywood Bowl. After a firework display, A&M present him with a speedboat.
January 1992	Sting puts down £2 million for his country seat, a sixty-acre estate called Lake House near Salisbury, Wiltshire.
April 1992	He collaborates with Eric Clapton on the song 'It's Probably Me'.
Spring 1992	Sting begins recording *Ten Summoner's Tales* in his home studio.
20 August 1992	Sting marries Trudie Styler at Camden Register Office. It's almost exactly a decade since they first got together. A church service follows two days later.
Summer 1992	Sting's old adviser-accountant, Keith Moore, is found to have stolen £6 million from him.
January 1993	Sting informs the world that he enjoys making love to his wife for five hours at a go.
March 1993	*Ten Summoner's Tales* released: yet another multi-platinum hit.
1993–94	Sting casually collaborates with, among others, Luciano Pavarotti, Julio Iglesias, Rod Stewart, Elton John and Tina Turner. He receives two honorary doctorates of music.
February 1995	He begins work on *The Grotesque*, an art-

	house film co-starring and produced by his wife.
Summer–autumn 1995	More recording at Lake House.
October 1995	Sting appears as the chief prosecution witness in Keith Moore's trial at Southwark Crown Court. His ex-employee gets six years.
March 1996	*Mercury Falling* released. Sting hits the road.
16 October 1996	In the latest of a series of exotic locales, he plays in Ho Chi Minh City.
July 1997	Sting treats himself to another home – this one, in Malibu, California, for $6 million. During the same month, he signs a deal with EMI Publishing worth £20 million.
22 July 1997	Sting sings at Gianni Versace's memorial service.
15 September 1997	Co-stars at a charity gala for the island of Montserrat.
December 1997	Sting donates 'I'll Be Missing You' to the Princess of Wales tribute album.
January 1998	Appears at *Twentieth Century Blues*, a Noël Coward tribute, in London.
February 1998	Sting plays host to the Chinese dissident Wei Jingsheng.
May 1998	Fundraises again for the rainforest, romping across stage with Madonna. Sting also cameos in the comedy thriller *Lock, Stock and Two Smoking Barrels*, part-produced by his wife.
June 1998	Sting takes part in CBS's *Late Show* spoof, roasting bandleader Paul Shaffer.
August 1998	The Sumners holiday in Florence. Even this makes copy when the *Mail on Sunday* reports that Sting pays to have two of his horses airlifted from Wiltshire to join them.
Autumn 1998	A&M, his record label of twenty years, shrinks to become 'a brand, not an organization'.
Winter 1998–99	Back in the studio.

Appendix 2

Bibliography

Anon, *The Concise Sting*, Wise Publications, 1993
——, *Newcastle At Work*, Newcastle City Libraries, 1987
——, *On the Beat*, Geneva Books, 1983
——, *The Police: A Visual Documentary*, Omnibus, 1985
——, *Police Confidential*, Macdonald, 1984
——, *The Police Released*, Big O Publishing, 1980
Bronson, Marsha, *Sting*, Exley Publications, 1993
Clarkson, Wensley, *Sting: The Secret Life of Gordon Sumner*, Blake
    Publishing, 1996
Milton, James, *The Police*, Kola, 1985
Sting and Jean-Pierre Dutilleux, *Jungle Stories: The Fight for the
    Amazon*, Barrie & Jenkins, 1989
Sullivan, Jim, *Sting and The Police*, Entertainment Today
    Publications, 1985
Underwood, Dana, *Outlando*, Carlton Press, 1986
Welch, Chris, *The Complete Guide to the Music of The Police and
    Sting*, Omnibus, 1995

Sources and
Chapter Notes

As usual, the author has his debts. The following notes show the principal sources used in writing each chapter. Formal interviews and on-the-record conversations are given by name. Typically, many requested that their comments remain anonymous, and thus no acknowledgement appears of the help, encouragement and kindness I got from a number of quarters, some of them surprising. Where Sting himself is quoted, the sources are his own published interviews, his comments to me of December 1996 or the memory of those who know him.

'Demolition Man' (Sting), © G. M. Sumner, Magnetic Publishing Limited

Chapter 1

A compelling account of, for one, Sting's wedding party was supplied by Reg Presley. Jack Bruce once made similar remarks to me about Eric Clapton's nuptials. The author is responsible for drawing the link between Cream and The Police, as well as for the rest of the chapter.

'Don't Stand So Close To Me' (Sting), © G. M. Sumner, Magnetic Publishing Limited
'Walking In Your Footsteps' (Sting), © G. M. Sumner, Magnetic Publishing Limited

Chapter 2

Invaluable help in retracing Sting's footsteps around Newcastle and the north came from: Alan Brown, Elliot Dixon, Hazel Dye, Alan English, Len Forin, Helen Hall, Steve Harvey, John Hedley, Den Hegarty, Cormac Loane, Edward Lovell, Sister Agnes Miller, Neil Rand, Tim Rice, John Spinks, Rik Walton, Dave Wood, John Wynn and W. Wynn. Richard Branson spoke to me about Sting's first contract.

I owe a special debt to the *Newcastle Chronicle*, St Columba's Presbytery and North Tyneside Council. Sting's and the Sumners' family trees were traced with help from the General Register Office and Wallsend Library. Other published sources included Marsha Bronson's *Sting* and Wensley Clarkson's *Sting: The Secret Life of Gordon Sumner*.

Help was also given by St Cuthbert's Grammar School, Northumbria Police and the archives of the Inland Revenue.

Chapter 3

Sources for this chapter included Richard Branson, John Guest, John Hedley, Andy Partridge and Reg Presley. Derek Green and Mike Noble, both formerly of A&M, spoke to me about Sting's and The Police's breakthrough. In this context, Dick Jordan, Miles Copeland's old business partner, was key on the days of 'Fall Out' and pogoing at the Roxy. Keith Moore, Sting's friend and accountant for fifteen years, corresponded with me from Wandsworth Jail.

My own travels took me to Leinster Square, Bayswater (still basically unchanged from Sting's day), as well as to Companies House and the Performing Rights Society. I visited Surrey Sound studios, scene of *Outlandos* and *Reggatta*; it's a treat to acknowledge this state-of-the-art facility. The previously named published sources, as well as *The Police: A Visual Documentary* were all used. Andy Hudson's quote about Frances Tomelty first appeared in *Sting: The Secret Life of Gordon Sumner. Melody Maker, New Musical Express* and *Sounds* were pored over at the British Newspaper Library.

Franc Roddam's *Quadrophenia* was re-released in 1997.

'Reggatta De Blanc' (Sting, Summers, Copeland), © G. M. Sumner, Andy Summers and Stewart Copeland, Magnetic Publishing Limited

Chapter 4

Comment on Sting's life among the rock glitterati was provided by the late William Burroughs, Derek Green, Jeff Griffin, Mike Noble, Andy Partridge and two friends, one of them involved with The Police, the other in the BBC, who prefer anonymity.

Rik Walton was particularly helpful in making the contrast between the old Sting and the new. Richard Branson was a major source for the account of the lawsuit that boiled over in July 1982. Keith Moore and the archives at Companies House again helped with details of Steerpike Ltd and Sting's other interests.

It's a pleasure to re-acknowledge Marsha Bronson's *Sting* and Wensley Clarkson's *Sting: The Secret Life of Gordon Sumner,* as well as James Milton's *The Police.* I should specially mention interviews with and profiles of Sting published in *Billboard, Creem, Interview, Melody Maker, New Musical Express, Rolling Stone* and *Sounds.*

The Burbidges' video *Police Around the World* gives a vital, if partial, account. I also watched *Outlandos to Synchronicities: A History of The Police Live!.*

'Walking On The Moon' (Sting), © G. M. Sumner, Magnetic Publishing Limited

'Driven To Tears' (Sting), © G. M. Sumner, Magnetic Publishing Limited

'Invisible Sun' (Sting), © G. M. Sumner, Magnetic Publishing Limited

'Every Little Thing She Does Is Magic' (Sting), © G. M. Sumner, Magnetic Publishing Limited

Chapter 5

Sting's reaction to the simultaneous crack-up of his marriage, his band and his mental health was vividly recalled by Len Forin, Derek Green, Keith Moore and others. The late Miles Davis also – trenchantly – once put his view of Sting at my disposal.

Documentary material was again obtained from Companies House, the General Register Office and Seattle Public Library. Among titles consulted were *Asahi Shimbun*, *Chicago Tribune*, the *Daily Express*, *Melody Maker*, *Le Monde*, *Musician*, the *New York Times*, *Rolling Stone* and the *Seattle Times*.

I visited the Château Marmont hotel, Hollywood, and The Grove, Highgate. Among the films and videos of this era, I should single out *The Synchronicity Concert* and *Bring on the Night*. I watched *Dune*.

'Darkness' (Copeland), © Stewart Copeland, Magnetic Publishing Limited

'Synchronicity II' (Sting), © G. M. Sumner, Magnetic Publishing Limited

'Wrapped Around Your Finger' (Sting), © G. M. Sumner, Magnetic Publishing Limited

'We Work The Black Seam' (Sting), © G. M. Sumner, Magnetic Publishing Limited

'Love Is The Seventh Wave' (Sting), © G. M. Sumner, Magnetic Publishing Limited

Chapter 6

Comment on Sting's successful bid for a solo career was provided by Len Forin, Derek Green, Jeff Griffin, Sister Agnes Miller, Mike Noble and Cat Sinclair.

I again visited Companies House, as well as Bugle House and the General Register Office, both in London. Secondary source material included the *Guardian*, the *Sun*, *The Times* and *Q*. The quote on Sting's writer's block was gleaned from *The Soul Cages* tour programme.

Details on Sting's crusade in the rainforest – the so-called 'bungle in the jungle' – were supplied by the Brazilian Embassy, Brazilian–American Cultural Institute and by *Jungle Stories: The Fight for the Amazon*. *Stormy Monday* is on video.

'If You Love Somebody Set Them Free' (Sting), © G. M. Sumner,
  Magnetic Publishing Limited

Chapter 7

Sources for the period 1988–92 included Jeff Griffin, Andy Partridge and an ex-colleague who prefers not to be named. Dave
Wood enlightened me about Sting's nostalgic return to Wallsend
in the winter of 1990–91. Keith Moore again supplied financial
details, as did the database at Companies House.

Further colour on Sting in Brazil came from sources at the
Daily Express and *World in Action*, as well as the Rainforest
Foundation. I again used Sting and Jean-Pierre Dutilleux's *Jungle
Stories*. Other published material included the previously named
books, most notably Wensley Clarkson's *Sting*, and articles in
Billboard, *Melody Maker*, *Rolling Stone*, the *Seattle Times* and the
Weekly. *Q* was also invaluable. I should acknowledge Helter
Skelter and the Music Exchange.

'Island Of Souls' (Sting), © G. M. Sumner, Magnetic Publishing
  Limited
'All This Time' (Sting), © G. M. Sumner, Magnetic Publishing
  Limited

Chapter 8

It was among the greatest pleasures of the book to interview
Larry Adler. I'm grateful to him for his dry insights into Sting,
Trudie Styler, the making of *Ten Summoner's Tales* and *The Gro-
tesque*.

Patrick Deuchar, Mike Noble and a spokesman for the Terence
Higgins Trust all put their views of Sting on record. I'm indebted
to Noel Chelberg, Peter Perchard and Amanda Ripley. George
Martin returned my call.

For descriptions of Lake House, *Architectural Digest*, the
memories of two visitors and my own trek to Wiltshire are all
responsible. Various accounts of Sting's wedding and the
revelries that followed have been published, chiefly in *Q*. I should
again thank Reg Presley, who was there. Sting's infamous double-
act with Bob Geldof also first appeared in *Q*.

I visited Estate House in London.

Chapter 9

Parting comment came from Larry Adler, Chuck Grice, Daniel Morgan and Mike Noble.

Of all the sources tapped for the events leading up to Keith Moore's trial, none was as astute as Moore himself, with whom I exchanged letters over the winter of 1996–97.

Newspapers and periodicals again included the *Daily Mirror*, *Q*, *Rolling Stone*, the *Sun* and the *Sunday Times*. My thanks to Ann Allsop, John Cottrell-Dormer, Karen Dowdall, Suzanne Duvel, Malcolm Galfe, Joan Lambert, Terry Lambert, Robin Parish and Jane Spalding for their help in running down press cuttings and videos.

Finally, I should mention Sting's fan club, Outlandos, an inexhaustible mine of data over the last year.

Index

Warner Books now offers an exciting range of quality titles by both established and new authors. All of the books in this series are available from:

Little, Brown and Company (UK),
P.O. Box 11,
Falmouth,
Cornwall TR10 9EN.

Fax No: 01326 317444.
Telephone No: 01326 372400
E-mail: books@barni.avel.co.uk

Payments can be made as follows: cheque, postal order (payable to Little, Brown and Company) or by credit cards, Visa/Access. Do not send cash or currency. UK customers and B.F.P.O. please allow £1.00 for postage and packing for the first book, plus 50p for the second book, plus 30p for each additional book up to a maximum charge of £3.00 (7 books plus).

Overseas customers including Ireland, please allow £2.00 for the first book plus £1.00 for the second book, plus 50p for each additional book.

NAME (Block Letters) ....

....

ADDRESS ....

....

....

☐ I enclose my remittance for ....

☐ I wish to pay by Access/Visa Card

Number ☐☐☐☐☐☐☐☐☐☐☐☐☐☐☐☐☐☐

Card Expiry Date ☐☐☐☐